Get a FREE eBook

To register this book, scan the code or go to
www.manning.com/freebook/mak2

By registering you get

- **FREE eBook copy**
  download in PDF and ePub

- **FREE online access**
  to Manning's liveBook platform

- **FREE audio**
  read and listen online in liveBook

- **FREE AI Assistant**
  it knows the book and what you are reading when it answers

- **FREE in-book testing**
  fun tests to lock in your knowledge

In Manning's liveBook platform you can share discussions and comments with other readers, add your own bookmarks and highlights, insert personal notes anywhere on the page, see color versions of all the book's graphics, download source code and other resources, and more!
To register, scan the code or go to www.manning.com/freebook/mak2

MANNING

Software Design
for Python Programmers

PRINCIPLES AND PATTERNS

RONALD MAK

MANNING
SHELTER ISLAND

For online information and ordering of this and other Manning books, please visit www.manning.com. The publisher offers discounts on this book when ordered in quantity.

For more information, please contact

    Special Sales Department
    Manning Publications Co.
    20 Baldwin Road
    PO Box 761
    Shelter Island, NY 11964
    Email: orders@manning.com

Manning Publications Co.
20 Baldwin Road
PO Box 761
Shelter Island, NY 11964

Development editor:	Marina Michaels
Technical editor:	Thomas Anthony Holdroyd
Review editor:	Dunja Nikitović
Production editor:	Andy Marinkovich
Copy editor:	Tiffany Taylor
Proofreader:	Jason Everett
Technical proofreader:	Steven Lott
Typesetter:	Tamara Švelić Sabljić
Cover designer:	Marija Tudor

ISBN 9781633439498

brief contents

contents

preface

I wrote this book to pass on what I've learned from decades of professional software development and teaching. I've studied, lived, worked, and taught in Silicon Valley my entire adult life. I've held senior engineering positions at established computer companies such as Sun Microsystems and Apple, and also at several startups. I've developed advanced software at IBM Research (data analytics regarding the causes of obesity), Lawrence Livermore National Laboratory (enterprise software for NIF, the National Ignition Facility fusion energy project), and NASA (data management code for the Mars rovers and the Orion spacecraft). I've taught software development at both the undergraduate and graduate levels at several universities, including San José State University, where I teach classes in the Computer Science, Computer Engineering, and Applied Data Science departments.

Working with students and other beginning programmers has taught me that it's important to practice good software design before bad habits set in. As students, we inadvertently learn "run and done": as soon as a program assignment runs successfully, it's done! After we turn it in, we may never have to see it again, so good design concepts such as maintainability are immaterial. We must unlearn that mentality to have a successful career as a professional software developer.

I am well aware of the pressures to get an application done on time and under budget. Therefore, I teach an iterative, incremental approach to software development. If we can't reach the last iteration and complete the product due to an upcoming deadline, we want the results of the next-to-last iteration (or the next-to-next-to-last iteration) to produce a minimum viable product (MVP). Well-designed applications can actually take less time to develop. Hopefully there will be the next release of the application to clean up design problems and add more features.

Experience is the best teacher

Besides studying the examples in this book, what is the key to becoming a top-tier programmer? It's practice, practice, practice! I hope the saying "Experience is the best teacher" applies both to you as a software developer and to me as the teacher and writer.

xiv   PREFACE

acknowledgments

This is a hard section to write! How can I acknowledge all my teachers from so many years ago who set me off on the right path, and all the people I've worked with who taught me so much about software development?

Therefore, I'll limit myself to thanking those who helped me write this book. First, my university students unknowingly showed me the best way to present and teach this material. My agent, Carole Jelen at Waterside Productions, Inc., got me started on this book. I greatly appreciate the careful, thoughtful feedback I received from my reviewers; several of them even tested my example programs. It took several rewrites, but I hope the final version of this book justifies their diligence. Two reviewers were colleagues at San José State University in Silicon Valley, so I especially want to thank Cay Horstmann and Robert Nicholson. Cay allowed me to borrow his date arithmetic and circular buffer examples from his earlier Java software design book. Tony Holdroyd and Steven Lott were excellent technical reviewers provided by the publisher, Manning. To all the reviewers: Akshay Phadké, Alex Martelli, Artur Baruchi, Brandon Darlington-Goddard, Christopher Fry, Dermot Doran, Gary Samuelson, Helio Loureiro, Himanshu Kandpal, Ivo van Hurne, João Dinis Ferreira, Joe Banks, Jon Rioux, Lana Crowell, Louis Luangkesorn, Natasha Kulkarni, Nicolantonio Vignola, Noah Flynn, Pat Viafore, Piti Champeethong, Rashan Smith, Rory Cawley, and Shantanu Kumar, your suggestions helped make this a better book.

I am extremely impressed by the dedication, care, and effort that Manning put into me and the writing of this book. Senior Development Editor (and fellow multi-cat parent) Marina Michaels and I spent many hours chatting online to improve my writing and to keep me encouraged through several revisions. I want Marina to be the editor for my next book and to continue exchanging cute pictures of cats with her. I also had several conversations with Associate Publisher Michael Stephens, who gave me some key tips.

What a career I'm having, working and teaching in Silicon Valley! I cannot give enough thanks for that.

about this book

This book is about writing well-designed software that's reliable, flexible, and maintainable. It covers requirements elicitation and analysis, design principles, and design patterns. There are many examples of poorly designed code and how applying the principles and incorporating the patterns improves the code. The goal of this book is simple: to make you a better programmer.

Who should read this book?

Python is now one of the most popular programming languages. Its programmers develop medium to large-scale applications in various domains, especially AI and data analytics. This book is for you if you want to become a top-tier Python programmer who can create well-designed applications that meet their requirements and that are more reliable, flexible, and maintainable. Well-designed applications are more bug-free, and they can cost less to produce and perform better at run time. We'll tackle the enemies of good software design: change and complexity. You'll be proud of the applications that you design and develop.

You will get the most out of this book if you are at least a beginning or intermediate Python programmer and understand the basics of object-oriented programming.

How this book is organized: A roadmap

The book has 16 chapters organized into five parts.

Part 1, "Introduction," introduces software design and a development methodology:

- Chapter 1 discusses what software design is and includes several design examples.
- Chapter 2 demonstrates iterative development to achieve good design.

xvi

Part 2, "Design the right application," discusses requirements and good class design:

- Chapter 3 is about how to analyze requirements and introduces UML diagrams.
- Chapter 4 is about good class design.

Part 3, "Design the application right," contains examples of good design principles such as encapsulation, loose coupling, coding to the interface, and hiding implementations:

- Chapter 5 explains why it's important to hide the implementations of classes.
- Chapter 6 explains why we shouldn't write code that surprises its users.
- Chapter 7 demonstrates how to design subclasses right.

Part 4, "Design patterns solve application architecture problems," shows how to apply industry-proven design patterns:

- Chapter 8 is about the Template Method and Strategy Design Patterns.
- Chapter 9 is about the Factory Method and Abstract Factory Design Patterns.
- Chapter 10 is about the Adapter and Façade Design Patterns.
- Chapter 11 is about the Iterator and Visitor Design Patterns.
- Chapter 12 is about the Observer Design Pattern.
- Chapter 13 is about the State Design Pattern.
- Chapter 14 is about the Singleton, Composite, and Decorator Design Patterns.

Part 5, "Additional design techniques," examines recursion, backtracking, and multithreading:

- Chapter 15 is about designing solutions with recursion and backtracking.
- Chapter 16 is about designing multithreaded programs.

I designed the book to be read in order, especially parts 1 through 4. In particular, chapters in part 4 refer to material covered by chapters in parts 2 and 3.

A few chapter sections are marked "optional." I included them for completeness and because their topics are interesting. Those sections are not required to understand the rest of the book.

About the code

Readers and students learn best with lots of examples. Therefore, I've included many examples of poorly designed programs with explanations of why they're bad and how to transform them into well-designed programs.

I tested the example programs in this book using Python 3.12, although you can run nearly all of them with earlier Python versions starting with 3.10. With the exception of chapter 3, each chapter has example programs. As much as possible, I used a limited set of Python features so that the design concepts are clear and to make it easier for you to apply the concepts to other object-oriented languages. I provide explanations whenever I stray from the basic language features.

This book contains source code both in numbered listings and in line with normal text. In both cases, source code is formatted in a `fixed-width font like this` to separate it from ordinary text. Sometimes code is also **in bold** to highlight important code pointed out in the text.

In many cases, the original source code has been reformatted: added line breaks and reworked indentation accommodate the available page space in the book. In rare cases, even this was not enough, and listings include line-continuation markers ( ). Additionally, comments in the source code have mostly been removed from the numbered listings. Instead, code annotations in the listings highlight important concepts.

You can get executable snippets of code from the liveBook (online) version of this book at https://livebook.manning.com/book/software-design-for-python-programmers. The complete code for the examples in the book is available for download from the Manning website at https://www.manning.com/books/software-design-for-python-programmers and from GitHub at https://github.com/RonMakBooks/SoftwareDesignPython.

liveBook discussion forum

Purchase of *Software Design for Python Programmers* includes free access to liveBook, Manning's online reading platform. Using liveBook's exclusive discussion features, you can attach comments to the book globally or to specific sections or paragraphs. It's a snap to make notes for yourself, ask and answer technical questions, and receive help from the author and other users. To access the forum, go to https://livebook.manning.com/book/software-design-for-python-programmers/discussion.

Manning's commitment to our readers is to provide a venue where a meaningful dialogue between individual readers and between readers and the author can take place. It is not a commitment to any specific amount of participation on the part of the author, whose contribution to the forum remains voluntary (and unpaid). We suggest you try asking the author some challenging questions lest his interest stray! The forum and the archives of previous discussions will be accessible from the publisher's website for as long as the book is in print.

about the author

RONALD MAK is a highly rated instructor of object-oriented analysis and design in C++, Java, and Python at San José State University in Silicon Valley. As a senior computer scientist at NASA and JPL, he developed software for major missions such as the Mars rovers and the Orion spacecraft. He was also a research staff member at IBM Research and an enterprise software strategist at the Lawrence Livermore National Laboratory. Earlier in his career, he was a senior software developer and engineering manager at various Silicon Valley companies such as Apple and Sun Microsystems. He has degrees in the mathematical sciences and in computer science from Stanford University. He is an inventor on seven software patents, and he has written books on compiler development, software engineering, and numerical computation that have been translated into several languages. Despite having done work on the relative motions of planets and performed calculations that involved Einstein's Theory of Relativity, Ron is still amazed that the sun comes up each morning and that bicycles don't tip over.

about the cover illustration

The figure on the cover of *Software Design for Python Programmers,* captioned "La Serva," or "The servant," is taken from a collection originally published in 1853 by Stabilimento Tipografico di G. Nobile, Napoli, and is provided by the George Peabody Library, Johns Hopkins University. Each illustration is finely drawn and colored by hand.

In those days, it was easy to identify where people lived and what their trade or station in life was just by their dress. Manning celebrates the inventiveness and initiative of the computer business with book covers based on the rich diversity of regional culture centuries ago, brought back to life by pictures from collections such as this one.

Part 1

Introduction

A well-designed, sustainable application should be the goal of every software development project. Passionate programmers want to use their object-oriented skills and apply good software design principles and industry-proven design patterns to build applications that are flexible, reliable, and maintainable. Well-designed software can be developed more quickly and pass tests sooner. We all want to be proud of the applications we've built. Developing production-quality software requires more diligence than turning in a weekly school programming assignment. Let's escape from the run-and-done mentality!

The development journey to a well-designed application is rarely straightforward. A proven way to achieve success is with a journey of design–code–test iterations. Along the way, we may have to backtrack due to erroneous design decision and redo some iterations. The journey becomes easier as we gain experience by encountering coding situations that good design principles can improve and recognizing software architecture problems that design patterns can solve.

The path to well-designed software

This chapter covers

- The basics of software design
- The benefits of good software design
- How to analyze an application's requirements to design the *right application*
- How to apply good design techniques to develop the *application right*

Well-designed programs do what they're supposed to do. They are more reliable, flexible, and maintainable than poorly designed programs. Furthermore, they are more easily tested and are often completed sooner. Well-designed programs are simply better in many ways.

To improve your software design skills, this book will teach you the principles and patterns that will enable you to develop well-designed, sustainable applications. A *sustainable* application is one that has a long life, so we want it to be reliable, flexible, and maintainable. Top-tier design skills are highly sought after by employers in today's competitive job market. Your career requires that you know and apply good software design techniques.

This book will improve your software design skills by teaching object-oriented *design principles* and *design patterns*. Design principles help to improve the design of a few lines of code: a function, an entire class, or a set of classes that work together. Design patterns provide models for solving common software architecture problems. These are built on design principles. This book focuses on Python, but you can use these skills in any modern object-oriented programming language.

Achieving well-designed software usually isn't a straightforward path. We first need to get the application's requirements, study them, and understand what the application is supposed to do. Multiple development iterations are often necessary to achieve good design, possibly with some backtracking to recover from bad design decisions. A well-designed application evolves from hard work.

To get the most out of this book, you should be at least a beginning to intermediate Python programmer. You should be familiar with basic data structures and their algorithms, and you should understand object-oriented programming (OOP). Furthermore, you should be able to program well enough to write simple applications and be able to edit, compile, debug, and run them. Because the techniques in this book for good design build on OOP concepts, we'll review those concepts briefly at the end of this chapter.

1.1   *What is software design?*

Design is a disciplined engineering approach to creating a solution to a problem. For software developers, the solution is a successful application that meets its requirements. We practice disciplined software engineering by applying the design techniques covered in this book to find the best solution path from the requirements to a well-designed, sustainable application. These techniques include design principles that improve our code and design patterns that help solve common software architecture problems.

Software design is an abstract concept! It won't be like learning how to create something concrete—a website, for example.

We learn by looking at examples of poorly and well-designed code.

Good design principles can help eliminate bad surprises where code doesn't behave as expected or has poor performance. The principles help make our code more flexible and able to handle changes such as new requirements. Design patterns operate at a higher level of design and are built from the design principles. The patterns are industry-proven models for creating custom solutions to common software architecture problems.

1.2 What you will learn from this book

This book is for beginner to intermediate software developers who want to learn good software design skills. It will also benefit more experienced developers who need a refresher on good design. By using many before-good-design and after-good-design program examples, this book will teach you how to

- Apply design principles to improve your code
- Employ design patterns that are industry-proven models for solving common software architecture problems
- Gather, validate, and analyze the requirements for an application to ensure that you write the right application and design it well
- Develop a well-designed application iteratively and backtrack to recover from bad design decisions

Learn by example

We learn best by example. It's not always very effective if someone simply tells us to use a certain design principle or design pattern. We want to see *how* and *why* the principle or pattern makes a program better. We'll try to justify each one with example applications. "Before" and "after" programs will highlight the design improvements.

This book's program examples are in Python, a very popular language for developing applications. So that we can concentrate on the design principles and design patterns, the program examples will use only basic features of the language.

NOTE The example programs in this book were tested with the 3.12 version of Python, although the programs should work with earlier versions starting with Python 3.10.

Will I be able to understand the program examples in this book?

The program examples use only basic Python features. The design techniques that this book teaches are language-independent, and you'll be able to port them to other object-oriented languages.

1.3 The benefits of good software design

A sustainable application has a lifespan during which it is deployed, successfully used by its customers, and continually maintained. New releases fix bugs and add new features as the application's requirements evolve. Good software design reliably creates sustainable applications. On the other hand, an unsustainable application can devolve into an unmanageable tangle of software "patches" to fix bugs and to add new features. At some point, no future programmer will want to touch it.

NOTE Although an application may require multiple individual programs working cooperatively, each example application in this book is relatively short and simple, making it easy to see the techniques that it exemplifies. Therefore, we'll often use the words *application* and *program* (referring to the program that implements the application) interchangeably.

We want to go beyond quick hacks and the just-get-it-done-on-time-no-matter-what style of programming. Of course, there is nothing wrong with doing a quick hack when it's appropriate. Sometimes you need your computer to do something, such as a short task to be done only once or not very often, and if a line or two of code or a short script will get it done, go for it!

No one can argue against finishing an application on time. By designing an application well, we can often complete it faster. A well-designed application evolves in a systematic manner. It attains the minimum viable product (MVP) status sooner, meaning it passes tests and meets the minimum set of requirements. If necessary, an MVP can be deployed as the application's first release. A well-designed application is easier to test, and it's more flexible when we need to add features or make other changes.

Our goal is to create well-designed applications that meet their requirements, are completed on time, and are maintainable. Well-designed software

- *Meets its requirements*—It does what it's supposed to do.
- *Is reliable*—It passes its tests and has fewer bugs.
- *Does what its users expect*—When we call a function or create an object, we should not be surprised by its result.
- *Is efficient*—It doesn't have hidden runtime performance problems.
- *Is flexible and scalable*—When requirements change, it is easy to add new features without increasing the complexity of the software.
- *Enables collaboration*—Developers can work together better and recover more quickly from bad design decisions.
- *Is maintainable*—Well-designed code is more understandable by future developers.
- *Uses good design techniques*—Good design techniques can improve the software by, for example, simplifying code and removing repeated code.
- *Employs appropriate design patterns*—Appropriate design patterns are industry-proven models for solving common software architecture problems.
- *Saves time and costs overall*—Good design results in fewer mistakes and major do-overs during development. Any extra time spent up front to do good design for a sustainable application will be compensated for by decreased maintenance time and costs after deployment and potentially a longer lifespan.
- *Is better code*—We can be proud to develop good code.

OK, I'm convinced that we should write well-designed programs. But how do I know that these are the right design principles and patterns that are worth learning?

The design principles and patterns that this book teaches have been used in industry by many programmers over many years. They are known to improve the design of applications.

1.4 A few design examples

Software design deals with many problems to improve our code. Here are a few illustrative examples; this book covers many others.

1.4.1 Leaking changes

The bane of all programmers is making changes to one part of a program that then require making changes to other parts. The changes may cascade to rewriting most, if not all, of the program. The following listing is an example Car class exhibiting this problem.

Listing 1.1 (Program 1.1 Changes): car.py (poorly designed)

```
class Car:
    def step_on_brake(self):
        print("Stepped on the brake.")

    def insert_key(self):
        print("Inserted the key.")

    def turn_key(self):
        print("Turned the key.")

    def step_on_accelerator(self):
        print("Stepped on the accelerator.")
```

In the next listing, class Driver uses class Car.

Listing 1.2 (Program 1.1 Changes): driver.py (poorly designed)

```
class Driver:
    def __init__(self, c):
        self._car = c

    def start_car(self):
        self._car.step_on_brake()
        self._car.insert_key()
        self._car.turn_key()
        self._car.step_on_accelerator()
```

If we aimed later for more modern cars, we might replace

```
def insert_key():
def turn_key():
```

with

```
def press_start_button():
```

in class `Car`. But then we would be forced to make changes to class `Driver`: the changes we make in class `Car` leak into class `Driver`. This problem becomes more acute in larger programs where we may not easily detect where leaks occurred. As we'll see in examples throughout this book, good software design helps to prevent such leaks by reducing dependencies among classes.

1.4.2   Code that's too complex

Class `Automobile` is complex because it tries to do too much. If something goes wrong, it will be harder to find the bug.

Listing 1.3   (Program 1.2 Changes): automobile.py (poorly designed)

```python
class Automobile:
    def __init__(self):
        self._brakes = []
        self._engine = None
        self._engine_oil = None
        self._heading = None
        self._headlights = []
        self._speed = None
        self._soap = None
        self._tires = []
        self._vacuum_cleaner = None

    def accelerate(self):
        print("Accelerating.")

    def adjust_headlights(self):
        print("Adjusting headlights.")

    def apply_brakes(self):
        print("Applying brakes.")

    def change_oil(self):
        print("Changing oil.")

    def change_tires(self):
        print("Changing tires.")

    def check_brakes(self):
        print("Checking brakes.")

    def check_tires(self):
        print("Checking tires.")
```

```
    def rotate_tires(self):
        print("Rotating tires.")

    def shut_off_engine(self):
        print("Shutting off engine.")

    def start_engine(self):
        print("Starting engine.")

    def tuneup_engine(self):
        print("Tuning up engine.")

    def turn_left(self):
        print("Turning left.")

    def turn_right(self):
        print("Turning right.")

    def vacuum_car(self):
        print("Vacuuming car.")

    def wash_car(self):
        print("Washing car.")

    def wax_car(self):
        print("Waxing car.")
```

The examples throughout this book show ways to avoid this very common problem by designing each class to have only one major responsibility.

Proliferation of classes is another way programs become too complex. Figure 1.1 illustrates how this can easily get out of hand.

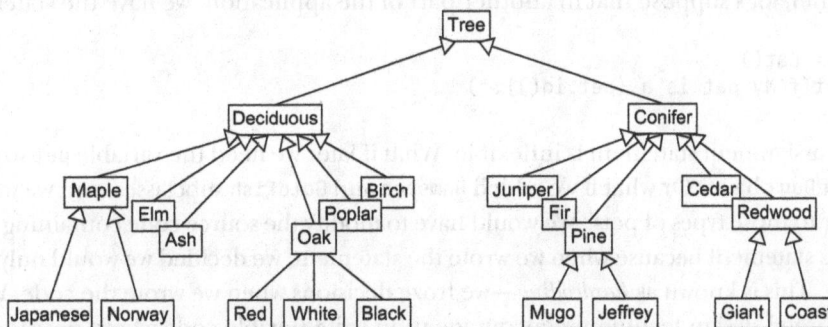

Figure 1.1 **A hierarchy of classes and subclasses. Does it have to be so complex? Good design techniques can simplify this data.**

Do we really need all those classes? Excessive subclasses can add extra dependencies and make the code harder to understand and debug. Good design can help to eliminate unnecessary classes from a program. However, sometimes applying good design techniques means adding classes to make a program more flexible. We'll see examples of both.

> Wait a minute! I thought object-oriented programming was all about classes, subclasses, and inheritance.

> Yes, but like all good things, you mustn't overdo it.

1.4.3   Inflexible code

Suppose we have an application with a class Pet and two subclasses, Cat and Dog.

Listing 1.4   (Program 1.3 Inflexible): pet.py

```python
class Pet:
    def id(self):
        return ''

class Cat(Pet):
    def id(self):
        return 'cat'

class Dog(Pet):
    def id(self):
        return 'dog'
```

Further, let's suppose that in another part of the application, we have the statements

```python
pet = Cat()
print(f'My pet is a {pet.id()}.')
```

The assignment statement is inflexible. What if later we need the variable pet to point to a pet Dog object? Or what if we added Hamster and Goldfish subclasses, and we wanted to refer to those types of pets? We would have to modify the source code containing the previous statement because when we wrote the statement, we decided we would only refer to a cat. This is known as *hardcoding*—we froze decisions when we wrote the code. We'll see how good design techniques encourage us to write flexible code where decisions (such as which type of Pet object to refer to) can be made dynamically during runtime.

1.4.4   Surprise!

If we write poorly designed code, that code may harbor nasty surprises for other programmers who use it, especially if the surprise is incorrect results. An example is the following Date class.

Listing 1.5   (Program 1.4 Surprise): date.py (poorly designed)

```
class Date:
    _MONTH_NAMES = [
        'JAN', 'FEB', 'MAR', 'APR', 'MAY', 'JUN',
        'JUL', 'AUG', 'SEP', 'OCT', 'NOV', 'DEC'
    ]

    def __init__(self, y, m, d):
        self._year = y
        self._month = m
        self._day = d

    def __str__(self):
        return f'{Date._MONTH_NAMES[self._month]} ' \
               f'{self._day}, {self._year}'
```

The main program creates and prints a date string in the following listing.

Listing 1.6   (Program 1.4 Surprise): main.py

```
from date import Date

if __name__ == '__main__':
    birthday = Date(2025, 9, 2)  # SEP 2, 2025
    print(birthday)
```

What date string does the program print?

That's an easy one! It's a straightforward class. The program prints SEP 2, 2025 just as the comment says.

You're going to get a nasty surprise! Instead, it prints OCT 2, 2025.

As many of our example programs demonstrate in this book, a well-designed program does what it's supposed to do and doesn't include surprises.

1.4.5   *Common architecture problems*

Programmers often encounter software architecture problems that are quite common. Design patterns provide models for developing custom solutions to many of these problems. For example, consider the situation where an application component, known as the publisher, produces data, and other application components, known as the subscribers, consume the data (figure 1.2). We'll see later in the book how the

Observer Design Pattern provides a model for us to develop a solution for this architecture problem.

1.5 *Make sure we're going to build the right application; then, build it right*

The critical start to designing an application is to acquire and analyze its requirements to ensure that we're developing the right application. An application, no matter how well designed, is not successful if it doesn't do what it's supposed to do. Getting good requirements is the primary topic in chapter 3. From the requirements, we can determine the initial set of classes. We then apply good design techniques to build the application right.

Figure 1.2   Publisher–subscriber is a common software architecture situation. One application component produces data that other application components consume. The Observer Design Pattern provides a model to solve this problem.

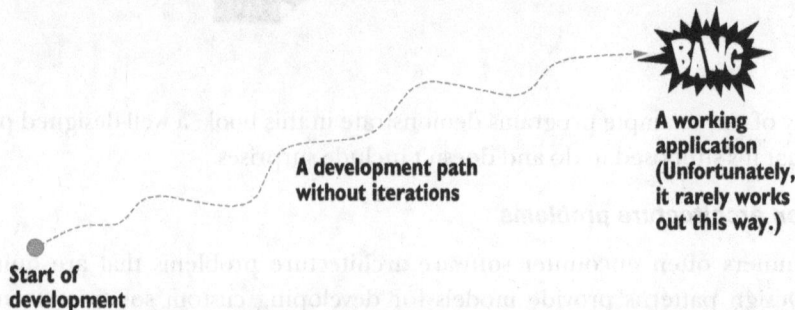

1.6 *Good design doesn't come easily*

It takes practice and experience to consistently develop well-designed software. Developing an application most often requires multiple design–code–test iterations. We must make design tradeoffs, and we may need to backtrack from poor design decisions. It's a rocky path to achieve good design. If instead of developing the software iteratively we tried to complete it in one prolonged coding marathon, we should not expect a successfully working application to simply appear by magic at the end. This Big Bang almost never occurs (figure 1.3).

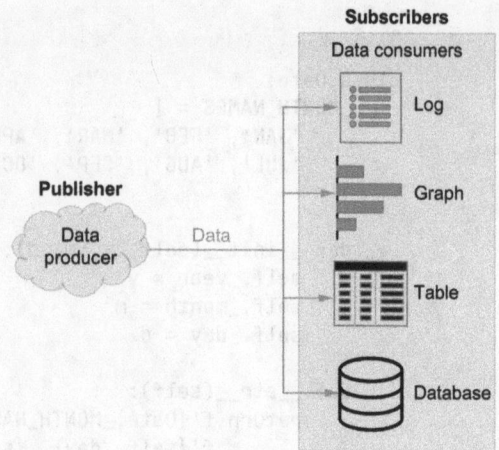

A development path without iterations

A working application (Unfortunately, it rarely works out this way.)

Start of development

Figure 1.3   The Big Bang theory of application development. If we write lots of code in a prolonged marathon instead of developing the software iteratively, we can only hope that the Big Bang at the end will magically produce a working application. Unfortunately, that magic rarely happens.

1.7 Change and complexity are the enemies of good design

Change and complexity are the primary challenges to good design, and they are the two themes that appear throughout this book. Change and complexity are inevitable facts of life for software developers. Any design that does not take change into consideration will soon run into trouble when the first change request comes in. Code can become messy and complex as a development project wears on, especially if there are multiple programmers on the project team. Design principles and design patterns are tools used to deal with change and complexity.

Change can occur during development. As we're writing the code, the application requirements may be altered. Or we might change our mind about the design and want to rewrite some of our code. After we've completed and deployed the application, we may get requests to add or modify features. Good design enables us to modify one part of our code without needing to modify other parts. Good design promotes the flexibility necessary to handle changes.

However, if we're not careful, trying to make an application flexible enough to handle many changes can increase its complexity. Our programs can become so complex that we won't be able to manage them. Good design also helps to keep our applications from getting out of hand. A good software designer must make tradeoffs often.

1.8 Design with object-oriented programming concepts

This book is about software design for the widely used OOP paradigm of application development. OOP concepts are the foundation of all the good design principles and design patterns covered in this book. Therefore, a quick review of the concepts will help ensure that we're all on the same page.

OOP is based on the following four main concepts:

- Encapsulation
- Abstraction
- Inheritance
- Polymorphism

A well-designed Python class *encapsulates* code by containing instance variables and methods. At run time, an application *instantiates* (creates) objects from a class. The instance variables constitute the *attributes* of the object.

During run time, an object undergoes state changes. Each state of the object is characterized by a unique set of values of its attributes. An object makes a transition from one state to another whenever one or more of its instance variables change values. The methods of an object can operate on the instance variables. These functions determine how an object *behaves* during run time.

A class's public attributes constitute its *interface* and can be accessed by any code, whereas its private attributes are accessible only by methods of that class. Protected members of a class are accessible only by methods of subclasses of that class.

In this book, we'll go beyond the strictly OOP meaning of encapsulation and use it to contain and isolate changes in an application. *Encapsulate What Varies* is a design principle we will use many times. Chapter 5 covers making members of a class private and protected to encapsulate changes to its implementation.

Are we talking about those leaking changes again?

Yes! Encapsulating parts of your code that can change is a primary way to prevent a change from forcing you to make changes in other parts.

Abstraction involves ignoring irrelevant details and paying attention only to what's important relative to the application we're developing. Properly using abstraction is an important way to reduce complexity.

Inheritance allows us to create subclasses (child classes) from a superclass (parent or base class). A parent class passes down state information (in the form of instance variables) and behavior (in the form of methods) to its subclasses. Each subclass can add its own additional state and behavior, or it can override (replace) any inherited state or behavior.

At run time, if we have a variable whose value is an object instantiated from one of the subclasses of a common superclass, *polymorphism* is a runtime mechanism that determines how the object behaves (i.e., which methods execute) based on which subclass instantiated the object. Polymorphism helps to simplify an application's design. Throughout this book, we will see that OOP concepts are the foundation for the design principles and design patterns that the book covers.

1.9   *What about AI-generated code?*

Programmers nowadays, especially beginning programmers, can use AI tools. If we give one of these tools a carefully worded prompt, it can generate reasonable code. At the very minimum, we must verify that the code runs and gives correct results.

But we must also check whether the generated code is well-designed and sustainable. Does it use good design principles? If the generated code is more than a class or two, does it have a good architecture? When appropriate, does the architecture incorporate industry-standard design patterns?

Design principles and design patterns are major topics of this book. After you've learned to write code on your own that employs the design principles and patterns, you will have acquired the skills to properly prompt the AI tools to generate well-designed code.

Summary

- Design is a disciplined engineering approach to creating a solution to a problem. In software engineering, the problem is to create working software, and the solution is a well-designed, sustainable application.

- Well-designed software is better in many ways, such as being more reliable, flexible, and maintainable. Good design helps ensure that applications are completed on time and do what their clients expect.

- It is possible to become a better programmer by using good software design techniques that include good design principles and design patterns.

- Good design principles help make our code more flexible and able to handle changes such as new requirements. Design patterns are industry-proven models for creating solutions to common software architecture problems.

- Software design starts by acquiring and analyzing an application's requirements to ensure that we're developing the right application. The application must do what it's supposed to do.

- Developing a well-designed, sustainable application nearly always requires multiple iterations with backtracking over bad design decisions. It's hard work. Don't rely on a magical Big Bang at the end of a marathon coding session.

- Good software design must deal with the major challenges of change and complexity.

- The design principles and design patterns in this book are based on the object-oriented programming concepts of abstraction, encapsulation, inheritance, and polymorphism.

- Encapsulation also means isolating the parts of a program that can change. Then, when changes do occur, they won't leak out and cause changes to other parts of the program.

Iterate to achieve good design

This chapter covers

- An iterative development strategy to achieve a well-designed application
- Backtracking to recover from bad design decisions
- Design principles to improve code

The development path to a well-designed application is almost never straight and narrow. As described in chapter 1, we should not have marathon coding sessions and then count on a magical Big Bang finish.

A much more rewarding development strategy takes an iterative approach. Each iteration builds on the accomplishments of the previous one. Such a strategy is more likely to result in a successful, well-designed application.

The example application in this chapter demonstrates the iterative development strategy, and it includes backtracking over a bad design decision. In addition, the chapter also deals with change and complexity, the major challenges to good design. It introduces several key design principles, which will appear repeatedly in subsequent chapters that introduce additional design principles.

16

2.1 Good application design requires an iterative process

By some accounts, Wolfgang Amadeus Mozart was such a musical genius that he could compose an entire symphony in his head and then write it down with few, if any, edits. Hardly any of us are programming Mozarts who can develop well-designed applications in our heads and then write the code perfectly all at once.

> **NOTE** I am not a programming Mozart. Even though the program examples in this book are all relatively short, each is the final version of several hidden iterations I made until I was satisfied.

Indeed, as represented by the informal design decision tree in figure 2.1, the road to a well-designed application is often bumpy, with wrong turns and dead ends that require backtracking and rewriting. Each branch of the tree is a development path that leads to either a successful application (the pot of gold) or a dead end (lumps of coal). If we took a dead-end branch, we must back up to the previous decision node and take another branch. After exhausting all possible branches at a node, we must back up again to the next-higher node. We hope eventually to find a path to a successfully completed application.

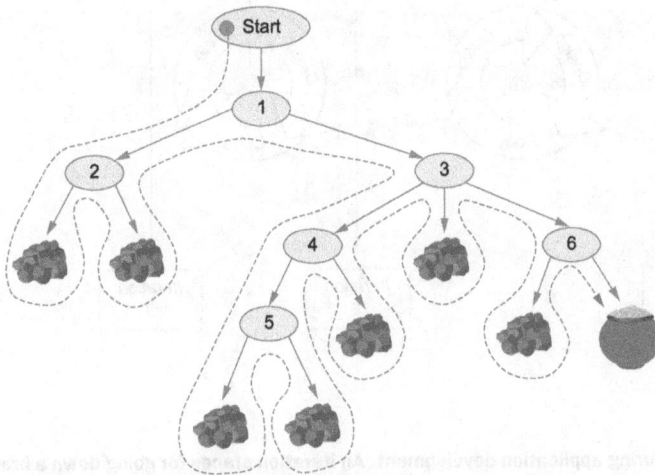

Figure 2.1   A design decision tree, with the application development path shown as the dotted line. Each tree node denotes a juncture during development when we must choose a path (i.e., branch) on which to continue. While designing and coding, if we head down a branch that leads to a dead end (the lumps of coal), we must backtrack to the previous decision node and try another branch. After trying all the branches at a node, we must backtrack to the next higher node and try the next branch from there. We hope to find the path to a successfully completed application (the pot of gold).

The design decision tree in the figure is somewhat misleading because it shows the entire tree with all the branches representing development paths. We rarely know in advance all the decisions we'll need to make while coding. Instead, we construct the decision tree node by node during program development. At each node, we decide the next path to take and create a branch. Of course, we should take the path that appears to be correct and that will result in a good design. However, if that branch turns out to be a decision and coding path leading to a dead end, either because some application requirements changed or because we simply made a bad design decision, we must go back to the node and create a new branch. Once we've run out of branches for a node, we must go back up to the parent node and create a new branch there. We hope to eventually find the path to a successfully completed application. In the worst case, we may have to backtrack to the topmost node and start over from there.

How does this work in practice? Modern agile software development practice advocates that development should progress in a series of iterations. An iteration can represent a trip down a branch of the decision tree. As shown in figure 2.2, each iteration consists of three phases: design, code, and test to incrementally improve or add more features to the application. Only after all of an iteration's tests have passed should we start the next iteration. An iteration can last anywhere from a few hours to around two weeks. If an iteration lasts longer than that, we're likely trying to do too much during the iteration.

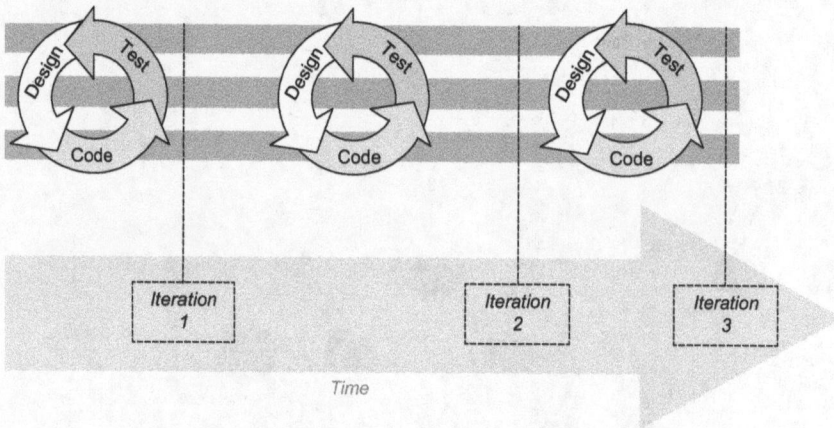

Figure 2.2   Iterations during application development. An iteration stands for going down a branch in the decision tree, including backing up and trying another branch. Each iteration includes designing, coding, and testing to incrementally improve or add more features to the application. The iterations can take different amounts of time: as little as a few hours or as long as two weeks.

Test-driven development

During each iteration, the intuitive order of activities is design–code–test. However, test-driven development (TDD) is a development process that uses the order test–design–code.

Using TDD, at the start of each iteration, we write the test programs for the features that we want to implement during the iteration. Of course, all the tests will initially fail because we haven't written the code yet that implements the features. The goal of each iteration is to design and write the code that will make all tests for that iteration pass.

As we saw with the decision tree, the series of iterations doesn't imply continuous forward progress. Some iterations are the result of backtracking and taking an alternate path. But don't despair! As you become a more experienced programmer, the decision tree becomes smaller, and you will need fewer iterations to complete your application. However, achieving good design remains a continuous-improvement process.

All those iterations and backtracking look too tedious! Is it really that much trouble to write well-designed software?

You'll need fewer iterations and less backtracking after you've gained more experience.

2.2 Don't let changes leak out

Woe to the programmer who discovers that making changes to one part of an application requires changes to other parts! In the worst-case scenario, major portions of the application, if not the entire application, will require rewriting.

Chapter 1 mentioned that one of the primary design challenges is accommodating change. If we write a significant application, we should anticipate what parts will change. There are numerous causes for code changes. Some of the common ones are the following:

- The requirements change. The requirements state what our application must do, or allow its users to do, and they may change both during development and after the application is finished.
- We change our minds about design during development.
- We add new features (or remove the ones that are not needed) from a completed application.

2.3 Iterate to achieve good design

For the example application in this section, we will eventually arrive at a good design that encapsulates changes and has other benefits, but only after several iterations of designing, coding, and testing. The example will also demonstrate how it's sometimes necessary to backtrack from a poor design decision that seemed right when we made it.

A note about the examples' coding style

To keep the example programs short and simple, we'll leave out descriptive and explanatory comments that applications normally should have in the source code. Instead, the printed examples will use code annotations.

In the example, we want to develop a book catalogue application that stores a list of books and allows a user to search for books that match the user's target attributes. Here are the application's initial requirements:

- A user must be able to add fiction books and their attributes to the catalogue.
- The attributes for each book shall be the book title and the author's last and first names.
- A user must be able to search for books that match the user's target attribute values.
- Searches for books shall depend on matching any number of target attributes.
- String matches of the book titles and authors' first and last names must be case-insensitive.
- A user must be able to specify any number of don't-care (wildcard) target attributes.
- Each don't-care attribute must by default match the corresponding attribute in all books in the catalogue. The remaining target attributes must match exactly.

The purpose of this example is to demonstrate development iterations. We want each iteration to improve the design of the application.

But beware! Possible bad design decisions ahead!
Even though the code after each iteration may look fine, we may discover that we made bad design decisions. Then, we must backtrack and rewrite code to make improvements.

Functions and methods

A *function* is defined outside of any classes and is therefore independent—it does not need to be called on an object. Many functions that we use are included with Python, such as len(), which returns the length of a string or list.

A *method* is a function that is defined as part of a class, and so it implements a behavior of an object instantiated from the class. A regular method must be called on an object of the class, such as shape.draw(). A static method (described for listing 2.2) must be called either on an object of the class or on the class itself.

Because a method is a function, functions and methods have many of the same design issues.

2.3.1   *Iteration 1: Initial cohesive classes*

Looking at the requirements, we can readily design two classes: Book and Catalogue. At run time, the catalogue will store Book objects. The private instance variables of Book are a book's private attributes: the book's _title and the author's _first and _last names. The constructor is passed the attribute values and initializes these instance variables.

Public, private, and protected instance variables and methods in Python

By convention, the names of a Python class's private instance variables and private methods begin with the underscore _ character, such as _x. Because the Python compiler doesn't enforce private names as in languages like Java and C++, using the underscore is only a safety measure to prevent unintentional access by code from outside the class. It is not meant to be a security measure. If a name is defined with a leading underscore in a class, we rely on programmers to treat it as private.

In a superclass, some programmers like to use the single underscore for the names of protected instance variables and methods and double underscores (such as __x) for private names. Protected members of a class in languages like Java and C++ are accessible from methods defined in the class itself and in its subclasses, but not from anywhere else.

Examples in this book will follow the suggestions under "Method Names and Instance Variables" in the PEP 8 Style Guide for Python Code (https://peps.python.org/pep-0008): "Use one leading underscore only for non-public methods and instance variables." Under "Designing for Inheritance," the style guide suggests, "If your class is intended to be subclassed, and you have attributes that you do not want subclasses to use, consider naming them with double leading underscores and no trailing underscores. This invokes Python's name mangling algorithm, where the name of the class is mangled into the attribute name. This helps avoid attribute name collisions should subclasses inadvertently contain attributes with the same name."

Therefore, in this program example, class Book initially has private instance variables _title, _last, and _first, and class Catalog has private instance variable _booklist and private method _is_match(). In iterations 3 and 4, when we'll define subclasses of Catalog, we'll rename its instance variable __booklist with two leading underscores to indicate that the subclasses shouldn't access that variable.

Python predefines the names of special methods, such as __init__() and __str__(), to have leading and trailing double underscores.

Listing 2.1   (Program 2.1 Books-1): book.py

```
class Book:
    def __init__(self, title, last, first):
        self._title = title            The Book class's instance
        self._last  = last             variables are private.
        self._first = first
```

```
@property
def title(self): return self._title

@property
def last(self): return self._last

@property
def first(self): return self._first

def __str__(self):
    return (f"{{TITLE: '{self._title}', LAST: '{self._last}', "
            f"FIRST: '{self._first}'}}")
```

> **The Book class's public read-only properties**

> **Returns a Book object's print string**

The __str()__ special method for a Book object returns a print string of a book's properties surrounded by braces, with a label for each attribute value. An example string would be

```
{TITLE: 'To Kill a Mockingbird', LAST: 'Lee', FIRST: 'Harper'}
```

The @property decorator

Python decorators are a form of *metaprogramming*—programming that modifies the code we're writing. Decorator actions occur each time we run our program, before Python executes the first line of code that we wrote.

Each @property decorator automatically creates a property object. A property object is named after the public method that follows the decorator, known as a *getter method*. Therefore, class Book in listing 2.1 has property objects named title, last, and first. A property object and its associated getter method are typically named after the private instance variable whose value the method gets, but without the leading underscore.

A property object provides a public but controlled way to access a private instance variable's value. It discourages access to a class's private instance variables from outside the class. We can access a property like an instance variable. If target is a Book object, we can write target.title, target.last, and target.first, and each access automatically calls the associated getter method.

Because a property is read-only, it is not possible to modify its value with an assignment statement. For example, the statement

```
target.last = "Smith"
```

is an error.

A property's name is not restricted to the name of a private instance variable. The property can be a value that's calculated at run time each time it's used. For example, in a Circle class, we can have public circumference and area properties and a private instance variable _radius:

```
from math import pi

class Circle:
    def __init__(self, radius):
        self._radius = radius

    @property
    def circumference(self): return 2*pi*self._radius

    @property
    def area(self): return pi*self._radius*self._radius
```

Chapter 5 will discuss how to use properties to modify the values of private instance variables.

In class `Catalogue` (listing 2.2), private instance variable `_booklist` is a list of `Book` objects stored in the catalogue. Public method `add()` creates a new `Book` object from a title and the author's last and first names and appends the object to the list. Public method `find()` searches the list for a matching book.

Private static method `_equal_ignore_case()` performs a case-insensitive comparison of two strings, `target_str` and `other_str`. An empty target string represents a don't-care attribute, in which case the comparison always returns true.

Listing 2.2   (Program 2.1 Books-1): catalogue.py

```
from book import Book

class Catalogue:

    @staticmethod
    def _equal_ignore_case(target_str, other_str):
        if len(target_str) == 0:                      ◀──── Always a true comparison if
            return True                                       the target string is empty
        else:
            return target_str.casefold() == other_str.casefold()   ◀────

    def __init__(self):                                    Compares the strings,
        self._booklist = []     ◀──── Private list of       ignoring case
                                      Book objects
    def add(self, title, last, first):
        book = Book(title, last, first)
        self._booklist.append(book)

    def _is_match(self, book, target):
        return (    Catalogue._equal_ignore_case(target.title,
                                                 book.title)
                and Catalogue._equal_ignore_case(target.last,
                                                 book.last)
                and Catalogue._equal_ignore_case(target.first,
                                                 book.first)
```

```
    )

def find(self, target):
    return [book for book in self._booklist
                if self._is_match(book, target)
           ]
```

Public method find() is passed a Book object named target that contains the target attributes. It uses list comprehension to create a list of books that match the target attributes. The list comprehension iterates over the books in _booklist and calls the private method _is_match(), passing each book in the list and the target book. Method _is_match() in turn calls the private static method _equal_ignore_case() to compare the target title, last name, and first name to the corresponding attributes of the book. The method returns the list of matching books or an empty list if no books matched.

Static methods

A @staticmethod decorator makes the method that follows it into a static method of the class. Such a method does not have a self parameter, and therefore it is not implicitly passed a reference to an object instantiated from the class. In listing 2.2, private static method _equal_ignore_case() returns a value based solely on argument values explicitly passed to it, not on the instance variables of an implicitly passed object.

To call a static method, precede the name of the method with the name of the class, as in Catalogue._equal_ignore_case. We can also call a static method on an object of the class, such as cat._equal_ignore_case if cat is a Catalogue object, but the static method will have no reference to the object.

We want to define classes that are *cohesive*, each with only a single primary responsibility. The Book class is responsible for storing a book's attributes. The Catalogue class is responsible for maintaining the list of Book objects, which includes adding new books to the list and finding book matches in the list.

The Single Responsibility Principle

The Single Responsibility Principle states that a well-designed class should be *cohesive*, meaning that it ought to have only a single primary responsibility. A poorly designed class has too many responsibilities. A cohesive class with a clear responsibility is easy to use—there should be no doubt what its purpose is. And a cohesive class is easy to maintain—all its methods and instance variables serve a single primary purpose.

In the test program main.py, function fill() loads the catalogue with some fiction books. The top-level main code performs test searches with some target books, and it calls function search() to do each search. Some of the target attributes are empty strings that represent don't-cares.

Listing 2.3   (Program 2.1 Books-1): main.py

```python
from book import Book
from catalogue import Catalogue

def fill(catalogue):                                    ◄── Fills the catalogue
    catalogue.add("Life of Pi", "Martel", "Yann")              with test Book objects
    catalogue.add("The Call of the Wild", "London", "Jack")

    catalogue.add("To Kill a Mockingbird", "Lee", "Harper")
    catalogue.add("Little Women", "Alcott", "Louisa")

    catalogue.add("The Adventures of Sherlock Holmes", "Doyle", "Arthur")
    catalogue.add("And Then There Were None", "Christie", "Agatha")

    catalogue.add("Carrie", "King", "Stephen")
    catalogue.add("It: A Novel", "King", "Stephen")
    catalogue.add("Frankenstein", "Shelley", "Mary")

    catalogue.add("2001: A Space Odyssey", "Clarke", "Arthur")
    catalogue.add("Ender's Game", "Card", "Orson")

def search(catalogue, target):                  ◄── Searches the catalogue
    print()                                          for a target book
    print("Find ", end="")
    print(target)

    matches = catalogue.find(target)

    if len(matches) == 0:
        print("No matches.")
    else:
        print("Matches:")

        for book in matches:
            print("  ", end="")
            print(book)

def test(catalogue):                            ◄── Test function
    target = Book("Life of Pi", "Martel", "Yann")
    search(catalogue, target)

    target = Book("", "King", "")
    search(catalogue, target)

    target = Book("1984", "Orwell", "George")
    search(catalogue, target)

    target = Book("", "", "")                   ◄── Target Book with don't-care
    search(catalogue, target)                        (wildcard) attributes
```

```
if __name__ == '__main__':
    catalogue = Catalogue()
    fill(catalogue)          │  Mainline code
    test(catalogue)
```

The output from the test run is

```
Find {TITLE: 'Life of Pi', LAST: 'Martel', FIRST: 'Yann'}
Matches:
  {TITLE: 'Life of Pi', LAST: 'Martel', FIRST: 'Yann'}

Find {TITLE: '', LAST: 'King', FIRST: ''}
Matches:
  {TITLE: 'Carrie', LAST: 'King', FIRST: 'Stephen'}
  {TITLE: 'It: A Novel', LAST: 'King', FIRST: 'Stephen'}

Find {TITLE: '1984', LAST: 'Orwell', FIRST: 'George'}
No matches.

Find {TITLE: '', LAST: '', FIRST: ''}
Matches:
  {TITLE: 'Life of Pi', LAST: 'Martel', FIRST: 'Yann'}
  {TITLE: 'The Call of the Wild', LAST: 'London', FIRST: 'Jack'}
  {TITLE: 'To Kill a Mockingbird', LAST: 'Lee', FIRST: 'Harper'}
  {TITLE: 'Little Women', LAST: 'Alcott', FIRST: 'Louisa'}
  {TITLE: 'The Adventures of Sherlock Holmes', LAST: 'Doyle',
  FIRST: 'Arthur'}
  {TITLE: 'And Then There Were None', LAST: 'Christie', FIRST: 'Agatha'}
  {TITLE: 'Carrie', LAST: 'King', FIRST: 'Stephen'}
  {TITLE: 'It: A Novel', LAST: 'King', FIRST: 'Stephen'}
  {TITLE: 'Frankenstein', LAST: 'Shelley', FIRST: 'Mary'}
  {TITLE: '2001: A Space Odyssey', LAST: 'Clarke', FIRST: 'Arthur'}
  {TITLE: 'Ender's Game', LAST: 'Card', FIRST: 'Orson'}
```

Running the example programs

All the example programs in this book use the 3.12 version of Python, although most of the examples should also work with earlier Python 3 versions starting with 3.10. You can run each program on the command line in a terminal window with the python command. For example, here's how to run source file main.py of a program, which contains the mainline code:

```
python main.py
```

You can also run the examples using any of the Python integrated development environments (IDEs) such as Spyder, Visual Studio Code, or Jupyter notebooks. An IDE generally includes a "smart" editor with syntax-checking and debugging features.

Apparently our application fulfills its requirements. Figure 2.3 depicts our progress thus far after one development iteration. We'll award ourselves a couple of gold coins.

2.3.2   *Iteration 2: Encapsulation, delegation, and loose coupling*

Now, suppose that we're given additional requirements to add two more book attributes—the publication year and the genre:

- The attributes for each fiction book shall include its publication year and its genre.
- The book genres shall be ADVENTURE, CLASSICS, DETECTIVE, FANTASY, HISTORIC, HORROR, ROMANCE, and SCIFI.

We need to make some code changes to accommodate the new requirements. Ostensibly, class Book needs two new instance variables for the year and the genre. Because the requirements give a specific list for the genres, we can define enumeration constants for them.

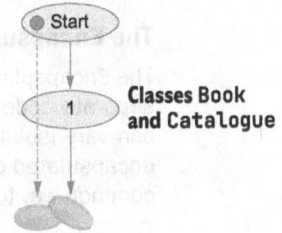

Figure 2.3   In our first development iteration, we created two classes: Book and Catalogue. The dotted line shows our development path. The application fulfills its current requirements.

Strings vs. enumeration types

Whenever there is a limited set of values, such as for the genre, using an enumeration type is preferable to using a string type. With strings, we must worry about case-sensitive versus case-insensitive comparisons. If we have a typo or a misspelling in a string, the resulting runtime logic error may be hard to detect. Comparisons of enumeration constant values during run time are very efficient, and Python will catch a misspelling of an enumeration constant before the application runs.

At this point, we can see that any attribute changes we make to class Book will require corresponding changes to class Catalogue (listing 2.2):

- Method add() has book attributes as parameters.
- The if statement in method find() references the book attributes.

Oops! Are the the changes we're making to class **Book** about to leak into class **Catalogue**?

Yes, and this unfortunate change leak will get worse if we add even more book attributes.

To plug the leak, we can encapsulate the code that will vary by putting the attributes into a separate class, Attributes (see listing 2.4).

The Encapsulate What Varies Principle

The Encapsulate What Varies Principle recommends that good software design should separate code that can vary from code that won't vary. Encapsulating the code that can vary isolates it from the rest of the program. Then, when changes occur to the encapsulated code, those changes won't leak out and cause other code to change. A common way to encapsulate code that can vary is to put it in a class by itself.

Because changing the book attributes necessitates changes to searching the attributes, we also need to encapsulate that behavior in class `Attributes`. Private method `is_match()` explicitly compares attributes and returns `True` or `False`, respectively, if they do or do not match. Special `Genre` value `UNSPECIFIED` and year value 0 will be don't-care search target values. To perform the case-insensitive string comparisons, we must move the private static method `_equal_ignore_case()` from class `Catalogue` to class `Attributes`.

Listing 2.4   (Program 2.2 Books-2): attributes.py

```
from enum import Enum

class Genre(Enum):          ◄─── Genre attribute
    UNSPECIFIED = 0
    ADVENTURE   = 1
    CLASSICS    = 2
    DETECTIVE   = 3
    FANTASY     = 4
    HISTORIC    = 5
    HORROR      = 6
    ROMANCE     = 7
    SCIFI       = 8

    def __str__(self): return self.name.lower()

class Attributes:

    @staticmethod
    def _equal_ignore_case(target_str, other_str):     ◄─── Class method, moved
        if len(target_str) == 0:                             from class Catalogue
            return True
        else:
            return target_str.casefold() == other_str.casefold()

    def __init__(self, title, last, first, year, genre):
        self._title = title
        self._last  = last
        self._first = first
        self._year  = year          │ Added year and
        self._genre = genre         │ genre attributes

    @property
```

```
    def title(self): return self._title

    @property
    def last(self): return self._last

    @property
    def first(self): return self._first

    @property
    def year(self):  return self._year

    @property
    def genre(self): return self._genre
```

Explicitly matches attributes, including year and genre

```
    def is_match(self, target_attrs):
        return (
                Attributes._equal_ignore_case(target_attrs.title,
                                              self._title)
            and Attributes._equal_ignore_case(target_attrs.last,
                                              self._last)
            and Attributes._equal_ignore_case(target_attrs.first,
                                              self._first)
            and (    (target_attrs.year  == 0)
                 or (target_attrs.year  == self._year))
            and (    (target_attrs.genre == Genre.UNSPECIFIED)
                 or (target_attrs.genre == self._genre))
        )

    def __str__(self):
        return (f"{{TITLE: '{self._title}', LAST: '{self._last}', "
                f"FIRST: '{self._first}', YEAR: {self._year}, "
                f"GENRE: {self._genre}}}")
```

The print string includes the year and genre attributes.

We replaced the `__str__()` special method for a Book object with one for an `Attributes` object that returns a print string for all the attributes, including the year and genre.

A Book object is now constructed from an `Attributes` object, as follows. Each Book object will point to its `Attributes` object.

Listing 2.5   (Program 2.2 Books-2): book.py

```
class Book:
    def __init__(self, attributes):
        self._attributes = attributes

    @property
    def attributes(self): return self._attributes
```

Each Book object will contain an Attributes object.

Class `Catalogue` needs changes to its `add()` and `find()` methods to handle the new `Attributes` class (listing 2.6). We pass the `Attributes` object `attrs` to method `add()`, which uses the object to construct a Book object to add to the booklist. We pass the target Attributes object target_attrs to method find().

```python
from attributes import Attributes
from book import Book

class Catalogue:
    def __init__(self):
        self._booklist = []

    def add(self, attrs):
        self._booklist.append(Book(attrs))

    def find(self, target_attrs):
        return [book for book in self._booklist
                    if book.attributes.is_match(target_attrs)
        ]
```

Constructs a Book object from the Attributes object

Delegates attribute matching to class Attributes

Method find() becomes much simpler. The method *delegates* attribute matching to class Attributes by calling the latter's is_match() method, and thus find() is no longer affected by any changes to book attributes.

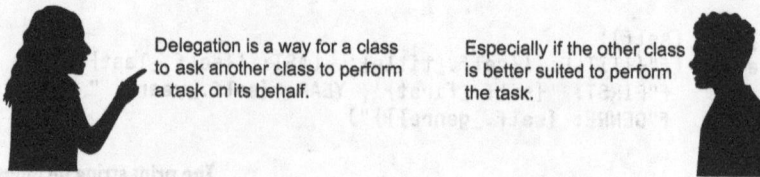

Delegation is a way for a class to ask another class to perform a task on its behalf.

Especially if the other class is better suited to perform the task.

Attribute matching fits better in a cohesive Attributes class.

The Delegation Principle

The Delegation Principle says to move functionality out of one class (the requester) and into another, more suitable class (the delegate) to make the two classes more cohesive. The requester class commonly has an instance variable that contains an object of the delegate class. A particular method in the delegate class implements the work to be done on behalf of the requester class. The requester class should not have any dependencies on how the delegate class does that work. At run time, an object of the requester class can request the work by calling that method on the object of the delegate class.

In our example, the requester is class Catalogue, and the delegate is class Attributes. Class Catalogue is now *loosely coupled* with class Attributes because we've minimized the dependencies of `Catalogue` on `Attributes`. Class `Catalogue` doesn't know the specific attributes that class `Attributes` maintains. Classes `Book` and `Attributes` are also loosely coupled with each other: class `Attributes` doesn't know that its objects are stored by `Book` objects, and class `Book` also doesn't need to know how class `Attributes` is implemented.

The Principle of Least Knowledge

Well-designed classes are *loosely coupled*, meaning that they ought to have few, if any, dependencies on each other. The less a class knows about how another class is implemented, the fewer dependencies it has on the other class. A class can hide its implementation by making its instance variables and methods private.

This is the Principle of Least Knowledge, which supports the Encapsulate What Varies Principle. If a class needs to change its implementation, the change can't affect any other code that doesn't depend on that implementation.

The test program main.py must change whenever the book attributes change. Example code to add a book to the catalogue is now

```
catalogue.add(Attributes("The Call of the Wild",
                          "London", "Jack",
                          1903, Genre.ADVENTURE))

catalogue.add(Attributes("To Kill a Mockingbird",
                          "Lee", "Harper",
                          1960, Genre.CLASSICS))
```

and example code to search for books is now

```
target_attrs = Attributes("Life of Pi", "Martel", "Yann",
                           2003, Genre.ADVENTURE)
search(catalogue, target_attrs)

target_attrs = Attributes("", "King", "", 0, Genre.HORROR)
search(catalogue, target_attrs)
```

However, we won't consider that an encapsulation failure because the testing code is not intrinsically a part of the application. We must assume that any means to load the catalogue from outside the application (such as from a file) must know about the current book attributes.

Some sample output is as follows:

```
Find {TITLE: '', LAST: 'King', FIRST: '', YEAR: 0, GENRE: horror}
Matches:
  {TITLE: 'Carrie', LAST: 'King', FIRST: 'Stephen', YEAR: 1974,
  GENRE: horror}
  {TITLE: 'It: A Novel', LAST: 'King', FIRST: 'Stephen', YEAR: 1986,
  GENRE: horror}
```

Figure 2.4 shows our progress after two iterations. We were able to handle a few more requirements, so let's award ourselves more gold coins.

2.3.3   *Iteration 3: More kinds of books and their attributes*

We've been concerned with changes to the Book attributes. But the kinds of books we store in the catalogue can also change. Here are more requirements:

- It must be possible to add cookbooks and their attributes to the catalogue.
- The attributes for a cookbook must include its region.
- The regions shall be CHINA, FRANCE, INDIA, ITALY, MEXICO, US, and UNSPECIFIED.

This may also be an opportunity to show off our object-oriented programming skills! Our application now must store both fiction and cookbooks in the catalogue. It's reasonable to make Book a superclass and design two new subclasses for it, Fiction and Cookbook. In the next listing, the constructor for subclass Fiction calls the constructor of its superclass and passes the initializing attributes: super().__init__(attrs).

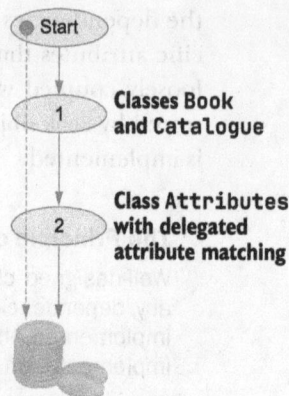

Classes Book and Catalogue

Class Attributes with delegated attribute matching

Figure 2.4   The second development iteration adds class Attributes, and class Catalogue delegates attribute matching to class Attributes.

Listing 2.7   (Program 2.3 Books-3): fiction.py

```
from book import Book

class Fiction(Book):
    def __init__(self, attrs):
        super().__init__(attrs)
```

Class Fiction is a subclass of class Book.

Calls the constructor of superclass Book

In the next listing, the constructor for subclass Cookbook also calls the superclass constructor.

Listing 2.8   (Program 2.3 Books-3): cookbook.py

```
from book import Book

class Cookbook(Book):
    def __init__(self, attrs):
        super().__init__(attrs)
```

Class Cookbook is a subclass of class Book.

Calls the constructor of superclass Book

We can also make Attributes a superclass (listing 2.9) and design two new subclasses for it, FictionAttrs and CookbookAttrs. Superclass Attributes maintains the instance variables __title, __last, and __first. The values of these attributes are shared by the subclasses, but their names should not be accessed by the subclasses. Therefore, we've renamed them with leading double underscores in accordance with the PEP 8 guidelines reproduced earlier. Method is_match() only compares the common attributes, and method __str()__ renders only them.

Listing 2.9 (Program 2.3 Books-3): attributes.py

```python
class Attributes:

    @staticmethod
    def _equal_ignore_case(target_str, other_str):
        if len(target_str) == 0:
            return True
        else:
            return target_str.casefold() == other_str.casefold()

    def __init__(self, title, last, first):
        self.__title = title
        self.__last  = last
        self.__first = first

    @property
    def title(self): return self.__title

    @property
    def last(self): return self.__last

    @property
    def first(self): return self.__first

    def is_match(self, target_attrs):
        return (
                Attributes._equal_ignore_case(target_attrs.title,
                                              self.__title)
            and Attributes._equal_ignore_case(target_attrs.last,
                                              self.__last)
            and Attributes._equal_ignore_case(target_attrs.first,
                                              self.__first)
        )

    def __str__(self):
        return (f"TITLE: '{self.__title}'"
                f", LAST: '{self.__last}'"
                f", FIRST: '{self.__first}'")
```

Private attributes renamed with leading double underscores

Compares only the private attributes

Renders only the private attributes

Subclass FictionAttrs contains the attributes unique to fiction books: genre and year (listing 2.10). Its constructor first calls the constructor of its superclass, Attributes, to initialize the inherited common instance variables title, last, and first. Then it initializes the year and genre instance variables of the subclass. We also moved the definitions of the Genre enumeration constants and their special method __str__() into class FictionAttrs.

Method `is_match()` first calls the superclass method `super().is_match()` to check the common title and the last and first name attributes. If that passes, then the subclass can check the fiction book's private `_year` and `_genre` attributes. The `__str__()` method renders the common attributes by calling `super().__str__()` before rendering the subclass's private attributes.

Listing 2.10   (Program 2.3 Books-3): fictionattrs.py

```python
from enum import Enum
from attributes import Attributes

class Genre(Enum): ...

class FictionAttrs(Attributes):
    def __init__(self, title, last, first, year, genre):
        super().__init__(title, last, first)
        self._year  = year
        self._genre = genre

    @property
    def year(self): return self._year

    @property
    def genre(self): return self._genre

    def is_match(self, target_attrs):
        if not super().is_match(target_attrs): return False

        return (
                (   (target_attrs.year  == 0)
                 or (target_attrs.year  == self._year))
             and
                (   (target_attrs.genre == Genre.UNSPECIFIED)
                 or (target_attrs.genre == self._genre))
        )

    def __str__(self):
        return ("{" + super().__str__() + \
                f", YEAR: {self._year} "
                f", GENRE: {self._genre.name.lower()}" + "}" )
```

First initializes the common attributes

Then initializes the year and genre for fiction books

Renders the common attributes before the subclass's private _year and _genre attributes

First matches the common attributes

Then matches the year and genre for fiction books

Renders the common attributes before the subclass's private _year and _genre attributes

---

Subclass `CookbookAttrs` contains the region attribute unique to cookbooks, as in the following listing. Its constructor, `is_match()`, and `__str__()` methods behave similarly to the ones in subclass `FictionAttrs`.

Listing 2.11   (Program 2.3 Books-3): cookbookattrs.py

```python
from enum import Enum
from attributes import Attributes
```

```
class Region(Enum):
    UNSPECIFIED = 0
    China      = 1
    France     = 2
    India      = 3
    Italy      = 4
    Mexico     = 5
    Persia     = 6
    US         = 7

    def __str__(self): return self.name

class CookbookAttrs(Attributes):
    def __init__(self, title, last, first, region):
        super().__init__(title, last, first)
        self._region = region

    @property
    def region(self): return self._region

    def is_match(self, target_attrs):
        if not super().is_match(target_attrs): return False

        return (   (target_attrs.region == Region.UNSPECIFIED)
                or (target_attrs.region == self._region))

    def __str__(self):
        return ("{" + super().__str__() + \
                f", REGION: {self._region}" + "}")
```

First initializes the common attributes

Then initializes the region for cookbooks

Renders the common attributes before the subclass's private _region attribute

First matches the common attributes

Then matches the region for cookbooks

Renders the common attributes before the subclass's private _region attribute

These are examples of the *Open-Closed Principle*. Once we've decided that class Attributes has captured the common instance variables and methods for all attributes, we *close* it for modification to provide code stability. We don't expect to make more changes to the class. But we *opened* the class for extensions in the form of subclasses such as FictionAttrs and CookbookAttrs to provide the flexibility to add more kinds of book attributes. Class Book and its subclasses are another example of this design principle.

The Open-Closed Principle

Closing a class to modification provides stability–programmers will always know what that code does and how to use it. But keeping it open for extensions in the form of subclasses allows adding functionality beyond what the closed superclass provides. That's the idea behind the Open-Closed Principle.

This principle supports loose coupling and encapsulation. For example, a Shape superclass can hide how it stores coordinates. It can have subclasses such as Rectangle and Circle that extend functionality by displaying the various shapes,

(continued)

but the subclasses are not dependent on how the coordinates are stored. If it ever becomes necessary to change the coordinates code in the superclass, the subclasses will inherit the changes but not require any code modifications.

Class Book has not changed (listing 2.5). As each Book object, whether Fiction or Cookbook, must contain its corresponding Attributes object, either FictionAttrs or CookbookAttrs, respectively, we'll put that instance variable in superclass Book. Therefore, Book contains the superclass Attributes, rather than specifically FictionAttrs or CookbookAttrs. This is an example of *coding to the interface*, because superclass Attributes serves as the interface of its subclasses.

The Code to the Interface Principle

If a class has several subclasses, our code should have the flexibility to work with any of the subclasses at run time. A Book object can contain either a FictionAttrs object or a CookbookAttrs object.

The Code to the interface Principle relies on polymorphism. Which is_match() method of class Catalogue is invoked at run time depends on the type of object (FictionAttrs or CookbookAttrs) that is assigned to instance variable book .attributes.

Class Catalogue now has an add() method that appends to _booklist either a Fiction book object created with a FictionAttrs object or a Cookbook object created with a CookbookAttrs object. It also needs find_fiction() and find_cookbook() methods, as in the following listing. Instance variable _booklist remains a list of Book objects, not specifically Fiction or Cookbook objects, another example of the Code to the Interface Principle.

Listing 2.12   (Program 2.3 Books-3): catalogue.py

```
from fiction import Fiction
from fictionattrs import FictionAttrs
from cookbook import Cookbook

class Catalogue:
    def __init__(self):
        self._booklist = []

    def add(self, attrs):                                    Adds a fiction book or a
        if isinstance(attrs, FictionAttrs): book = Fiction(attrs)   cookbook to the catalogue
        else:
                                            book = Cookbook(attrs)

        self._booklist.append(book)
```

```
def find_fiction(self, target_attrs):          ◄─── Finds matching fiction books
    return [book for book in self._booklist
                if (    isinstance(book, Fiction)      ◄──┐
                    and book.attributes.is_match(target_attrs))
           ]                                            Is this book a fiction book?

def find_cookbook(self, target_attrs):         ◄─── Finds matching cookbooks
    return [book for book in self._booklist
                if (    isinstance(book, Cookbook)      ◄──┐
                    and book.attributes.is_match(target_attrs))
           ]                                            Is this book a cookbook?
```

The add() method needs to determine whether the Attributes object that was passed to it is a FictionAttrs or a CookbookAttrs object. It calls the Boolean type-checking function isinstance(), which returns true if attrs is a FictionAttrs object.

Methods find_fiction() and find_cookbook() are similar. Each must verify that it searches the right kind of books, fiction or cookbook, by calling the isinstance() function. Both methods delegate attribute matching to the book.attributes object.

When the test program main.py loads books into the catalogue, it calls the Catalogue object's add() method with either a FictionAttrs object

```
catalogue.add(FictionAttrs("Little Women",
                           "Alcott", "Louisa",
                           1868, Genre.CLASSICS))
```

or a CookbookAttrs object:

```
catalogue.add(CookbookAttrs("The Woks of Life",
                            "Leung", "Bill",
                            Region.China))
```

I have a bad feeling about this code. Has it become more complex than it needs to be?

Yes, with all those runtime type checks and duplicated code, it can only get worse.

Indeed: what if the requirements change further, such that the catalogue must store and search for other kinds of books, and each kind has unique attributes? We made our application more complex by attempting to handle requirement changes: namely, new kinds of books and additional book attributes. Examples of the complexity include the following:

- Each kind of book requires a pair of Book and Attributes subclasses.
- Each kind of book requires a find() method in class Catalogue. These methods have similar code.

- Method add() in class Catalogue requires a call to the Boolean type-checking function isinstance() to determine whether the attributes are fiction or cookbook.
- Also in class Catalogue, each find() method requires a call to isinstance() to ensure that it will check the right kind of book. Otherwise, these methods have similar code.

If our application needs to manage more kinds of books, we will have an increase in subclasses, duplicate code, and runtime type checks.

The Don't Repeat Yourself Principle

Repeated code is often a sign of poor design, according to the Don't Repeat Yourself Principle, often abbreviated DRY. Not only does repeated code enlarge the size of a program, but it also makes the program harder to maintain. If we need to make a change to the code that's repeated, we'll need to make the same change to multiple copies of the code. We run the risk of missing a copy or inadvertently changing copies differently.

One way to eliminate repeated code is to share only one copy of it as a separate function or as a separate cohesive class.

Table 2.1 shows the current situation with fiction books and cookbooks, and what happens when we include how-to books.

Table 2.1　Our current design requires many classes to handle different kinds of books and their attributes

Kind of book	Classes	Attributes
All books	Book, Attributes	title, last, first
Fiction	Fiction, FictionAttrs	year, genre
Cookbook	Cookbook, CookbookAttrs	region
How-to	Howto, HowtoAttrs	subject

Figure 2.5 shows a diagram of our application architecture as we've designed it thus far.

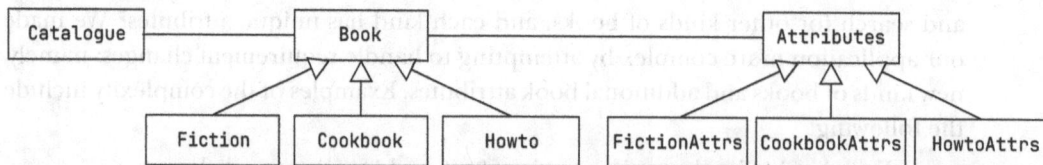

Figure 2.5　A diagram of our application architecture as we've designed it thus far, showing our classes and subclasses and their relationships

But isn't object-oriented programming all about classes and subclasses?

Yes, but we must be careful not to overdo it!

After the third iteration, we must admit that using subclasses to handle changes in the requirements for books and attributes was a poor design decision that won't scale well if there are more kinds of books. Figure 2.6 shows our progress after this iteration. We deserve those lumps of coal!

2.3.4 Iteration 4: A better design after backtracking

Let's take a deep breath, backtrack, and go down another decision branch. Recall the purposes of classes in object-oriented programming, as described in chapter 1. A class has instance variables to maintain an object's state at run time, and an object undergoes a state transition whenever the values of its instance variables change. A class also has methods to implement the object's behavior.

In our book catalogue application, as we've designed it thus far, subclasses `Fiction` and `Cookbook` have little to do with state or behavior. We don't need those subclasses. Class `Book` alone ought to be sufficient.

Start

1 — Classes Book and Catalogue

2 — Class Attributes with delegated attribute matching

3 — Add classes Fiction, Cookbook, FictionAttrs, and CookbookAttrs

Figure 2.6 The third development iteration added subclasses Fiction, Cookbook, FictionAttrs, and CookbookAttrs. This increase in the number of subclasses plus the added runtime type checking tell us that we took a wrong decision path.

Subclasses `FictionAttrs` and `CookbookAttrs` represent very similar behaviors, primarily performing attribute matching during book searches. However, they have different instance variables for their respective attributes. Is there a way to have the `Attributes` class alone handle all the different attributes and eliminate its subclasses? An `Attributes` object associated with any kind of `Book` object has to store both the name and the value of each attribute.

Whenever there are name–value pairs in a Python program, we should consider the dictionary data structure. A dictionary object contains *name–value* pairs, where the name serves as the key to retrieve the paired value. Therefore, the pairs in a dictionary are usually called *key–value* pairs. A Python dictionary's keys can be any immutable type, such as strings, numbers, and enumeration constants. The keys must be unique within

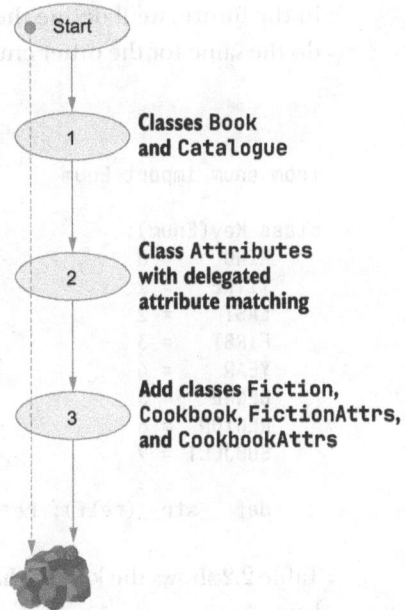

a dictionary. A dictionary's values can be any type, and the values do not need to be unique.

We can make each `Attributes` object a dictionary. For the dictionary's keys, we can define the enumeration class `Key` (listing 2.13). We need one `Key` enumeration constant per attribute across all kinds of books. For example, the dictionary value paired with key `KIND` will indicate the kind of book: `FICTION`, `COOKBOOK`, etc.; and the value paired with key `YEAR` will be an integer. To make it easier to change the list of enumeration constants in the future, we'll define the enumeration class `Key` in its own key.py source file. We'll do the same for the other enumeration classes.

Listing 2.13   (Program 2.4 Books-4): key.py

```
from enum import Enum

class Key(Enum):
    KIND    = 0
    TITLE   = 1
    LAST    = 2
    FIRST   = 3
    YEAR    = 4
    GENRE   = 5
    REGION  = 6
    SUBJECT = 7

    def __str__(self): return self.name
```

Table 2.2 shows the keys we have thus far and the datatype of the value paired with each key.

Table 2.2   Key–value pairs that represent book attributes. The datatype of the key is `class Key(Enum)`. The datatype of each paired value depends on the key.

Key constant	Datatype of paired value
KIND	class Kind(Enum)
TITLE	string
LAST	string
FIRST	string
YEAR	int
GENRE	class Genre(Enum)
REGION	class Region(Enum)
SUBJECT	class Subject(Enum)

It will be easy later to add new kinds of books, such as how-to books, to the `Kind` enumeration constants.

Listing 2.14   (Program 2.4 Books-4): kind.py

```
from enum import Enum

class Kind(Enum):
    FICTION  = 0
    COOKBOOK = 1
    HOWTO    = 2

    def __str__(self): return self.name.lower()
```

In the next listing, we define the Genre enumeration constants similarly.

Listing 2.15   (Program 2.4 Books-4): genre.py

```
from enum import Enum

class Genre(Enum):
    UNSPECIFIED = 0
    ADVENTURE   = 1
    CLASSICS    = 2
    DETECTIVE   = 3
    FANTASY     = 4
    HISTORIC    = 5
    HORROR      = 6
    ROMANCE     = 7
    SCIFI       = 8

    def __str__(self): return self.name.lower()
```

Likewise, in the following listing, we define the Region enumeration constants.

Listing 2.16   (Program 2.4 Books-4): region.py

```
from enum import Enum

class Region(Enum):
    UNSPECIFIED = 0
    China       = 1
    France      = 2
    India       = 3
    Italy       = 4
    Mexico      = 5
    Persia      = 6
    US          = 7

    def __str__(self): return self.name
```

And finally, we define the Subject enumeration constants.

```
from enum import Enum

class Subject(Enum):
    DRAWING  = 0
    PAINTING = 1
    WRITING  = 2

    def __str__(self): return self.name.lower()
```

We no longer need UNSPECIFIED constants. In our new design, if an attribute is missing in a search target, that attribute will be a don't-care.

We create and initialize an Attributes object by passing it a dictionary of key–value pairs. The __init__() constructor verifies that the value of each key–value pair in the dictionary has the correct datatype. This is an example of defensive programming—we don't ever want to create an invalid Attributes object.

```
from key import Key
from kind import Kind
from genre import Genre
from region import Region
from subject import Subject

class Attributes:

    @staticmethod
    def _equal_ignore_case(target_str, other_str): ...

    def __init__(self, dictionary):          ◄────── Attributes constructor
        for key, value in dictionary.items():    ◄──────
            if key == Key.YEAR:
                assert(isinstance(value, int))
            elif key in [Key.TITLE, Key.LAST, Key.FIRST]:
                assert(isinstance(value, str))
            elif key == Key.KIND:
                assert(isinstance(value, Kind))
            elif key == Key.GENRE:
                assert(isinstance(value, Genre))
            elif key == Key.REGION:
                assert(isinstance(value, Region))
            elif key == Key.SUBJECT:
                assert(isinstance(value, Subject))

        self._dictionary = dictionary
...
```

Iterates over the elements of the dictionary to verify that the value of each pair has the correct datatype

Private method _is_matching_key_value() checks the attributes dictionary for a matching target_key and target_value. If target_key is not in the dictionary, the method returns False. It returns True if target_key is in the dictionary and the dictionary's paired value is equal to target_value. However, if the values are strings, the method compares them by calling _equal_ignore_case().

Defensive programming

Well-designed applications practice defensive programming to guard against programming errors. Methods should create only proper objects from their parameter values.

Perform runtime value checks of function and method parameters to ensure that no invalid values are being passed in. However, to keep the example programs in this book short, their functions and methods generally do not have parameter checking.

Method is_match() iterates over the key–value pairs in dictionary target_attrs and checks each pair against the attributes dictionary by calling _is_matching_key_value(). It returns True only if all the pairs match. If a particular attribute (such as the year) isn't in target_attrs, then that attribute is a don't-care during matching.

Listing 2.19   (Program 2.4 Books-4): attributes.py (part 2 of 3)

Is the target key in the attributes dictionary?

```
...
def _is_matching_key_value(self, target_key, target_value):
    if target_key not in self._dictionary.keys(): return False
    if self._dictionary[target_key] == target_value: return True

    if isinstance(target_value, str):
        return Attributes._equal_ignore_case(
            self._dictionary[target_key], target_value)

    return False

def is_match(self, target_attrs):
    for target_key, target_value \
                in target_attrs._dictionary.items():
        if not self._is_matching_key_value(target_key,
                                           target_value):
            return False

    return True
...
```

Are the string values equal?

Are the values equal?

An example string that special method __str__() returns is

```
{KIND: fiction, TITLE: 'Carrie', LAST: 'King', FIRST: 'Stephen',
 YEAR: 1974, GENRE: horror}
```

Listing 2.20   (Program 2.4 Books-4): attributes.py (part 3 of 3)

```
...
    def __str__(self):
        last_key = list(self._dictionary.keys())[-1]
        ostr = '{'

        for key, value in self._dictionary.items():     ◄──── Iterates over the
            ostr += str(key.name) + ':                          key–value pairs of the
                                                               attributes dictionary
            if isinstance(value, str):
                ostr += "'" + value + "'"
            else:
                ostr += str(value)

            if key != last_key: ostr += ', '

        ostr += '}'
        return ostr
```

Class Book now has a special method __str__() that returns a print string of its attributes, but the rest of the class hasn't changed.

Listing 2.21   (Program 2.4 Books-4): book.py

```
class Book:
    def __init__(self, attributes):
        self._attributes = attributes

    @property
    def attributes(self): return self._attributes

    def __str__(self):
        return str(self._attributes)
```

Class Catalogue is much simpler, as shown in the following listing. We've eliminated the duplicate code and now follow the Don't Repeat Yourself Principle. There is only one find() method. We no longer need calls to isinstance() to do runtime type checks. A bonus of this design is that a book can have any attributes: it isn't limited to certain ones based on the kind of book.

Listing 2.22   (Program 2.4 Books-4): catalogue.py

```
from book import Book

class Catalogue:
    def __init__(self):
        self._booklist = []

    def add(self, attrs):
        book = Book(attrs)
```

```
            self._booklist.append(book)

        def find(self, target_attrs):
            return [book for book in self._booklist
                         if book.attributes.is_match(target_attrs)
                   ]
```

In the test program main.py, function `fill()` now enters a book into the catalogue with statements like this:

```
    attrs = {
        Key.KIND:  Kind.FICTION,
        Key.TITLE: "Life of Pi",
        Key.LAST:  "Martel",
        Key.FIRST: "Yann",
        Key.YEAR:  2003,
        Key.GENRE: Genre.ADVENTURE
    }
    catalogue.add(Attributes(attrs))
```

An example search is as follows:

```
    target_attrs = {
        Key.KIND:  Kind.FICTION,
        Key.LAST:  "KING",
        Key.GENRE: Genre.HORROR
    }
    search(catalogue, Attributes(target_attrs))
```

The string `"KING"` will match `"King"` in the catalogue. The output is

```
Find {KIND: fiction, LAST: 'KING', GENRE: horror}
Matches:
  {KIND: fiction, TITLE: 'Carrie', LAST: 'King', FIRST: 'Stephen',
 YEAR: 1974, GENRE: horror}
  {KIND: fiction, TITLE: 'It: A Novel', LAST: 'King', FIRST:
 'Stephen', YEAR: 1986, GENRE: horror}
```

Missing attributes are don't-cares, so this search will return all Chinese cookbooks:

```
    target_attrs = {
        Key.REGION: Region.China
    }
    search(catalogue, Attributes(target_attrs))
```

The output is

```
Find {REGION: China}
Matches:
  {KIND: cookbook, TITLE: 'The Wok of Life', LAST: 'Leung', FIRST:
```

```
'Bill', REGION: China}
 {KIND: cookbook, TITLE: 'Chinese Cooking for Dummies', LAST: 'Yan',
FIRST: 'Martin', REGION: China}
```

Figure 2.7 shows that after four iterations, we've arrived at an application design that successfully encapsulates changes to the kinds of books and their attributes. Only class `Attributes` will need modifications. Classes `Book` and `Catalogue` will not require modifications. We can award ourselves a pot of gold.

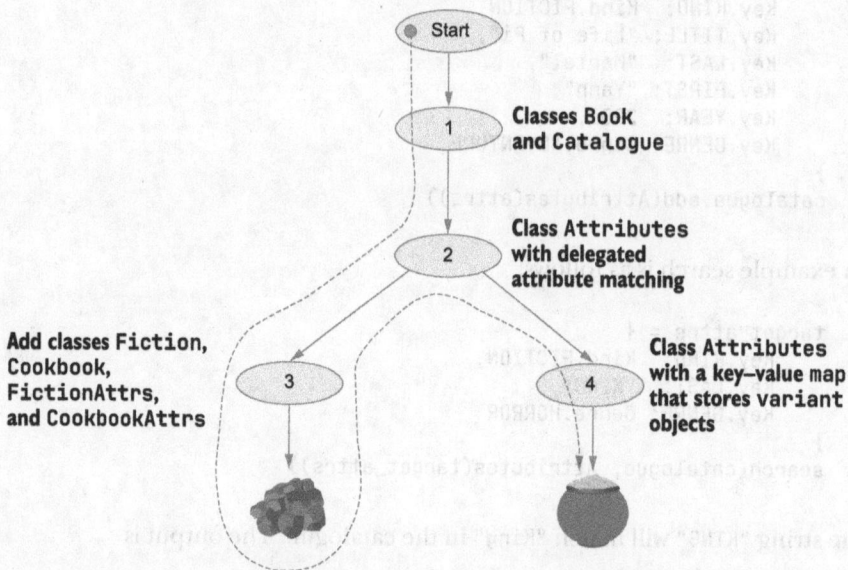

Figure 2.7 It took four iterations, including some backtracking, to find the development path to an application design that successfully encapsulates changes to the kinds of books and their attributes.

OK, so the final design got rid of all the **Book** and **Attribute** subclasses. But what if I discover that other parts of my application need to use those subclasses?

Then your design should keep the subclasses. Software design often requires making tradeoffs.

This chapter demonstrated developing the book application with four iterations. Virtually all significant applications will require multiple iterations, often many more than four. The following chapters will have shorter example programs, and we'll limit the number of iterations.

Summary

- It usually takes several development iterations to achieve a well-designed program. Be willing to backtrack from bad design decisions.
- The Single Responsibility Principle states that a class should be cohesive and have only one primary responsibility.
- The Encapsulate What Varies Principle states that code that can vary should be isolated to keep its changes from causing other code to change.
- The Delegation Principle states that one class can perform work on behalf of another class, where the work belongs to a more suitable cohesive class.
- The Principle of Least Knowledge states that classes should not know about each other's implementation. Thus the classes are loosely coupled, with few, if any, dependencies on each other.
- The Open-Closed Principle states that a class should be closed for modification but open for extension to provide both stability and flexibility.
- The Code to the Interface Principle states that for runtime flexibility, we should not write code that can work only with a specific subclass, but should instead use polymorphism and write code that can work with multiple subclasses.
- The Don't Repeat Yourself Principle states that well-designed code does not contain duplicate copies of code.
- OOP is important for good application design, but it's not a panacea for all design problems. Be smart about how to apply its concepts. For example, do not create too many subclasses unnecessarily and thereby make an application too complex.
- Using better data structures can simplify complex code.

Part 2

Design the right application

There are many benefits to having well-designed software. But an application, no matter how well designed, is a failure if it doesn't do what it is supposed to do. Before we can design an *application right*, we must determine what is the *right application*. Therefore, we must first gather and analyze the application's requirements. Those are not easy tasks, and we must do them carefully.

Once we have sufficient requirements, we're ready to analyze them and to start designing the classes of the application. We can meet the challenges of change and complexity by using good design principles to build cohesive and loosely coupled classes. We can document our design with Unified Modeling Language (UML) diagrams.

Get requirements to build the right application

3

Before we start worrying about building an *application right* (make it well-designed), we must ensure that we're going to build the *right application*. An application that doesn't do what the client wants is a failed, unsuccessful application, no matter how well-designed it may be. The *client* of an application can be a future end user (including yourself), your manager who requested you to write the application, the person who hired you as a software consultant or contractor, or any other stakeholder who wants a successful application.

51

In this chapter, we'll learn how to get good requirements for an application. Then we'll see how to analyze them to obtain the initial set of classes. Remember that requirements can change, and we must design accordingly and develop iteratively.

3.1   The overture to application design

Figure 3.1 shows a timeline of the major activities and milestones during the application development. The activities with the bold outlines, which are covered in this chapter, are the crucial overture to application design.

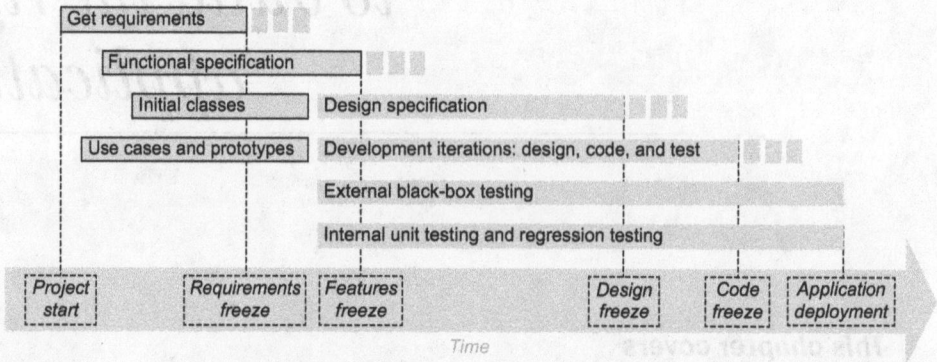

Figure 3.1   Timeline of the major activities when developing an application. The activities with bold outlines are the crucial prelude to application design. The dotted time spans following Get Requirements and Functional Specification suggest that their freeze dates must be flexible.

Suppose a client has asked us to develop a more advanced version of the book catalogue application from chapter 2. The client has some ideas about a "book catalogue server" that stores book data in some sort of database, and library customers searching for books are provided a form interface where they fill in and submit their desired book attributes. Moreover, a special type of end user with a librarian role is responsible for adding new books to the catalogue and updating or removing existing books (figure 3.2).

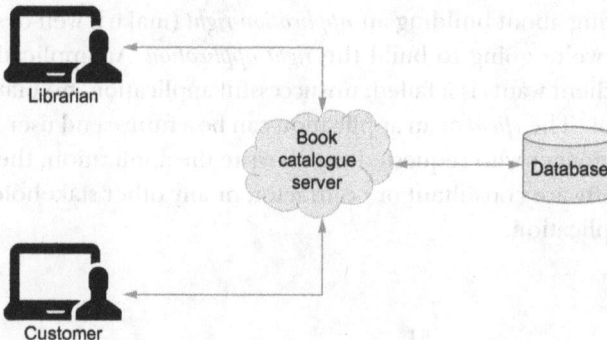

Figure 3.2   A more advanced version of the book catalogue application. A librarian interacts with the book catalogue server to enter new books into the catalogue, update existing books, and remove outdated ones. A customer interacts with the server to search for books. The books are stored in a backend database.

How can we convert these vague ideas into firm requirements to ensure that the application we eventually develop will fully satisfy the client? There are two kinds of requirements: functional and nonfunctional.

3.2   *Functional requirements: What must the application do?*

A *functional requirement* states a specific operation that the application must do, or a specific operation that the application must allow an end user to do, to be a successful application. In chapter 2, we saw functional requirements for our example book catalogue application. Based on those requirements, a list of operations that the application must do includes the following:

- Storing attributes for all books, including the book title and the author's first and last names
- Storing year and genre attributes for fiction books, a region attribute for cookbooks, and a subject attribute for how-to books
- Performing case-insensitive string matches
- Allowing don't-care target attributes for book searches

Based on the functional requirements, a list of operations that the application must allow its end users to do includes the following:

- Adding fiction books, cookbooks, and how-to books to the catalogue
- Searching the catalogue for books that match a given set of target attributes

We can rewrite these operations as requirements using strong auxiliary verbs such as *must* and *shall*:

- A user *must* be able to add fiction books, cookbooks, and how-to books and their attributes to the catalogue.
- The attributes for each book *shall* be the book title and the author's last and first names.
- The attributes of a fiction book *shall* include its publication year and genre: adventure, classics, detective, fantasy, historic, horror, romance, or science fiction.
- The attributes of a cookbook *shall* include its region: China, France, India, Italy, Mexico, Iran, or the United States.
- The attributes of a how-to book *shall* include its subject: drawing, painting, or writing.
- A user *must* be able to search the catalogue for books that match a given set of target attributes.
- String comparisons while matching attributes during book searches *shall* be case-insensitive.
- A user *must* be able to specify don't-care attributes for book searches.

When we listen to what clients tell us and then translate their desires into written requirements, we should not create statements using weaker auxiliary verbs such as *should* or *could*.

What's wrong with the auxiliary verbs *should* and *could*?

You want the requirements to be strong, definitive statements for the application we're currently developing. Leave the weaker verbs for a wish list for a future version of the application.

3.3   *Nonfunctional requirements: Constraints on the application*

A *nonfunctional requirement* imposes a specific restriction or constraint that the application must satisfy to be successful. These requirements involve issues such as performance, platforms, and maintainability.

We didn't list nonfunctional requirements in chapter 2 for our book catalogue application. Here's a list of nonfunctional requirements for the application:

- A book search must take under 2 seconds.
- The application must run on the Windows, macOS, and Linux platforms.
- The user interface shall be similar to the UI of the previous version.
- Displayed messages shall be customizable to be in English, Spanish, or Vietnamese.

Are the nonfunctional requirements less important than the functional requirements?

Absolutely not! The nonfunctional and functional requirements are equally important to build the right application.

Do not think that nonfunctional requirements are less important than functional requirements! A well-designed and fully functional application is a failure if its performance is unacceptable or if it doesn't run on the users' platforms.

> **Internationalization note**
>
> The last nonfunctional requirement listed for our example pertains to *internationalization*, sometimes abbreviated *I18N* (because, well, there are 18 letters between the initial *I* and the final *N* of the word). The process of adapting an application to a particular locale is called *localization (L10N)* and involves changing the natural language (English, Spanish, etc.) of text messages and making other text changes such as date, time, monetary formats, and character-encoding standards. If you're developing an internationalized application, encapsulate the affected parts of the application when the locales vary.

A requirement should not state how to design the application to meet the requirement. For example, the nonfunctional requirement about the user interface does not say to make forms from the old UI be included in the new UI. Requirements should not include design and implementation details.

What makes an ideal set of requirements? Ideal requirements for developing a well-designed application must themselves meet the following standards:

- *Clarity*—The requirements must be written clearly in nontechnical and jargon-free language to be understood by both the client and the software developers.
- *Consistency*—Requirements must not contradict each other. For example, we cannot have one requirement state that the application must run on Windows and macOS and another one state that the application must run only on Linux.
- *Correctness*—Each requirement must be correct. For example, a requirement for a medical application that states that the application must process pregnancy data from male patients is clearly wrong.
- *Completeness*—Any gaps in the requirements can lead to wrong guesses by the software developers and result in an application that doesn't do what the client wants.
- *Being realistic*—Do not include requirements that can't be satisfied, such as overly optimistic performance figures.
- *Being verifiable*—It must be possible to test the application to ensure that it satisfies every requirement.
- *Traceability*—Can we trace each requirement to a functionality or constraint of the application? We don't want the application to miss satisfying any requirements. Conversely, can we trace each functionality or constraint to a requirement? We don't want to load the application with unwanted features.

Will we always get ideal requirements?

Rarely! We must expect that the requirements will change as we engage more with the client.

3.4   *How to get requirements*

How do we get requirements for an application? Where do they come from? Because requirements dictate what will make the application successful, an obvious start is to ask the client about the application. This may involve an extended set of interviews—unless the application is trivial, more than a one-time interview will be needed. Ask questions and get clarifications. "Is this what you want? What do you mean by that? Do you want the application to do this or that?"

These requirements-gathering interviews require good interpersonal skills. We need to discover what our client wants and not introduce our own biases. We have a major bridge to cross: we assume that clients are experts in their domains (such as finance for a banking application), whereas we're the software development experts. Clients' expertise and vocabularies may not have much in common with ours.

But here's a major catch: *clients do not always know what they want!* Do not apply too much pressure to get requirements out of them, or they may start making things up. Your client may be thinking, "I'm paying these developers a lot, and they have a deadline. They won't get going unless I give them more requirements. I'd better give them *something* to make them start coding." This is a surefire way to get bad requirements, and bad requirements can only lead to bad applications.

Therefore, software developers must work hard to get requirements by other means. One way is to observe the ways people currently do their tasks and imagine how an application can improve their performance. Look at specific tasks being done manually or with legacy software, and devise requirements for the application to better automate those tasks.

In some software organizations, team members such as project managers, who may have better communication skills than the programmers, are responsible for interviewing the client to get the initial list of requirements. However, it's still important for the developers to have some hands-on contacts with the problems they are expected to solve.

Many meetings among the members of the development team may be necessary to decide on the lists of functional and nonfunctional requirements. In an ideal situation, an application's client is made a virtual member of the development team so they're always available to answer questions about requirements. Short of that situation, it is critical to maintain a communication channel between the developers and their client that is as open as possible. The feedback loop between the client and the development team must be tight and constantly active.

3.4.1   *A short requirements case study*

Figure 3.3 shows a simple scenario. Public libraries used to have card catalogues, which were physical banks of drawers that held index cards containing the attributes of the books in the library. The cards were alphabetized by book title, author's last name, and subject. Therefore, each book required at least three cards. Each drawer was labeled by the range of the alphabet of the cards it held.

A library customer looking for a book would consult the card catalogue to see if the library had the book, and if so, the cards indicated where to find it. Librarians maintained the card catalogue. It was a very manual process for both the librarians and the customers. Therefore, our client, the head librarian, hired us to automate the catalogue.

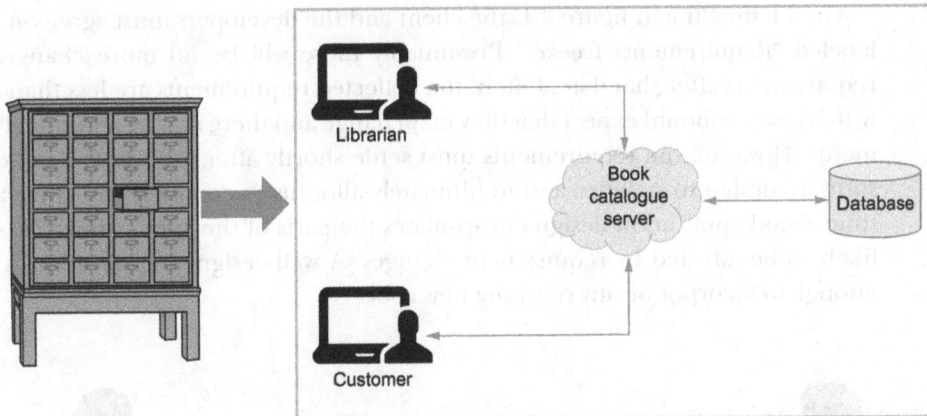

Figure 3.3 To automate a library's old-fashioned card catalogue with a software application, we must first get the requirements to develop the right application.

We must first get the requirements from the client to develop the right application. We interview the head librarian to learn how the librarians maintain the card catalogue and to ask what they think we can do to improve their work. We also interview the library's customers to understand how they search for books in the card catalogue and to ask what we can do to improve their searches. But perhaps the librarians can only suggest incremental improvements to their work, such as an online form to create and print cards for the drawers. Similarly, the library's customers may not have the imagination to come up with better searching methods. Therefore, we must observe the librarians working and the customers searching and apply our experience with computer-based applications to come up with more requirements. We can create and show prototypes of the new application to inspire better requirements. Getting requirements is another iterative process.

The librarians only suggested incremental improvements to their current processes.

We'll get much better requirements after closely observing how the librarians work and showing them some prototypes of the application.

3.4.2 *Stated and implied requirements*

The librarians and customers provide *stated* application requirements. By reading between the lines, we can conceive *implied* requirements. Yes, our interviewees said that requirements A and C are needed. But we know from our own experience (or common sense) that they will also need requirement B to properly automate their operations.

On the timeline in figure 3.1, the client and the developers must agree on the date labeled "Requirements freeze." Presumably there will be no more changes to the requirements after that date. Often, the collected requirements are less than ideal, in which case we should expect that they may change and there may be additional requirements. However, the requirements must settle shortly after the freeze date to enable software design to stabilize and to ultimately allow us to complete the application on time. Good application design encapsulates the parts of the application that are most likely to be affected by requirement changes. A well-designed application is flexible enough to incorporate any resulting new code.

Why have freeze dates if we're just going to ignore them?

We don't ignore them! They are important milestone dates for our project. If we miss a milestone by too much, that's a warning that our project might be late.

Software engineering

Requirements gathering and analysis is a major topic within the broader subject of software engineering. Software engineering covers project-level topics, including project management and schedules; development methodologies (such as extreme programming and test-driven development); enterprise application architectures; tools for task management, bug tracking, and software revision control; testing strategies; project documentation; product deployment and maintenance; and other topics. Software engineering in general, other than the topic of software design, is outside the scope of this book.

Entire books have been written about how to gather and analyze software requirements. This book can only give a brief outline of the process.

3.5   Unified Modeling Language diagrams for creating and documenting design

The Unified Modeling Language (UML) is an industry-standard family of diagrams to help software developers design an application and document the design. The following section covers UML use case diagrams that describe to both the application's client and its developers how an end user will interact with the application. Chapter 4 covers UML class, state, and sequence diagrams that further document the application's design.

UML diagramming is a useful skill in every software developer's repertoire. Not only are the diagrams important for documenting an application's design, but their visual nature makes them very helpful during software design and coding.

NOTE Most of the popular computer-based drawing tools provide palettes of the UML objects. During the development iterations, the diagrams are easy to create and manipulate to keep track of an application's evolving design.

3.6 *Use cases provide context for the requirements*

The lists of functional and nonfunctional requirements for an application are parts of the documentation that the development team writes to describe the application. Use cases provide context for the requirements and show how they determine the application's runtime behavior.

A use case describes how an end user of the application, often with a specified role (such as our book catalogue application's customer or librarian), will perform a sequence of actions to achieve a particular goal. Therefore, we write it from the point of view of that user. Because users can interact with the application in different ways to achieve various goals, we will need multiple use cases to cover the major goals.

Documentation of use cases typically consists of two parts. First, a UML *use case diagram* groups together several related use cases and shows which users interact with which use cases. The second part consists of a written *use case description* for each use case.

3.6.1 *UML use case diagram*

Figure 3.4 shows an example use case diagram for an advanced version of our book catalogue application. In this version, a backend database stores the books and their attributes.

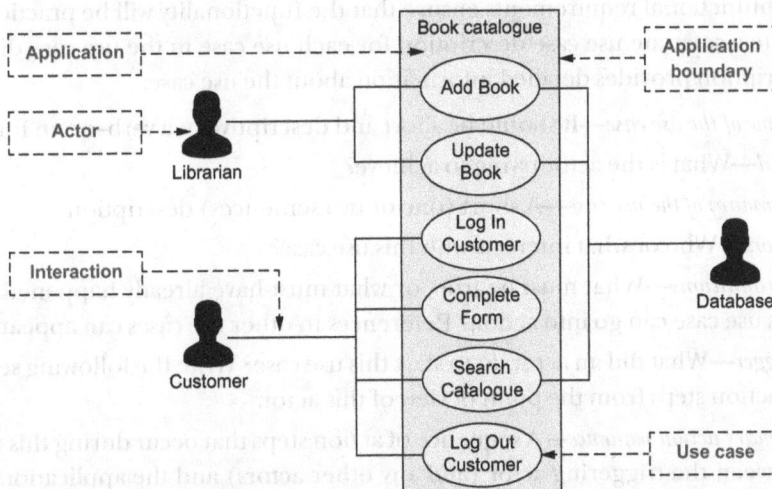

Figure 3.4   A UML use case diagram containing the names of six use cases for an advanced version of our book catalogue application. The labels in the dashed boxes and the dashed arrows indicate the various components of the diagram. When drawing a use case diagram, do not include these labels and arrows.

The diagram shows the names of several use cases and how various actors interact with them. The box that encloses the use cases represents the application and its boundary—it's important to know what's in the application and what's not. The name of each use case should be short and descriptive in a verb–noun form, such as "Add Book" and "Log In Customer." The figures represent actors who interact with the use cases. An *actor* is any agent external to the application that interacts with the application, and it can be a person (such as the librarian and the customer) or another application or system (such as the database system). The interaction lines indicate which use cases each actor can interact with.

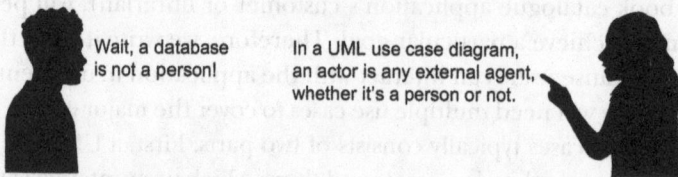

> Wait, a database is not a person!

> In a UML use case diagram, an actor is any external agent, whether it's a person or not.

A large application may have many use case diagrams, each containing a small number (at most about a half dozen) of use cases.

3.6.2 *Use case description*

Use cases provide context for the application's requirements. They show how the functional requirements determine the functionality of the application, and they also show which nonfunctional requirements ensure that the functionality will be practical.

We write a separate use case description for each use case in the use case diagrams. This description provides detailed information about the use case:

- *Name of the use case*—It should be short and descriptive in a verb–noun form.
- *Goal*—What is the actor trying to achieve?
- *Summary of the use case*—A short (one or two sentences) description.
- *Actors*—Who or what interacts with this use case?
- *Preconditions*—What must be true, or what must have already happened, before this use case can go into action? References to other use cases can appear here.
- *Trigger*—What did an actor do to start this use case? Write the following sequence of action steps from the point of view of this actor.
- *Primary action sequence*—A sequence of action steps that occur during this use case between the triggering actor (and any other actors) and the application. There should be no more than about 10 steps. If we need more steps, the use case may be too complex and should be broken up. The steps can refer to other use cases.
- *Alternate action sequences*—What action steps should occur if something goes wrong during the primary sequence?

- *Postconditions*—What will be the situation when this use case is finished?
- *Nonfunctional requirements*—Which nonfunctional requirements apply to this use case?
- *Glossary*—Define any terms in this use case that a reader may find confusing.

Write each use case from the point of view of the actor that triggers the use case.

Here is an example of a use case description for the advanced version of our book catalogue application. The customer fills out an online form that includes a Search button to specify the desired target book attributes for a book search:

- *Name of the use case*—Search Catalogue.
- *Goal*—Search the book catalogue for books that match the customer's target attributes.
- *Summary of the use case*—The customer searches the book catalogue using a set of target book attributes, and the catalogue returns a list of any books that match those attributes.
- *Actors*—The customer and the backend database.
- *Preconditions*—Books and their attributes are already loaded into the catalogue. See the use case Add Book. The customer has completed filling in the Attributes form with the target book attributes. See the use case Complete Form.
- *Trigger*—The customer clicks the Search button.
- *Primary action sequence:*

1. The application verifies that the Attributes form is correctly filled out.

2. The application formulates a database query from the book attributes in the form.

3. The application sends the query to the backend database server.

4. The database returns a list of matching books to the application.

5. The application formats the list of matching books for presentation.

6. The customer sees the list of matching books.

- *Alternate action sequence 1*—Incorrectly filled form. Replace primary sequence steps 2–6.

2. Highlight the incorrect form field.

3. Display an explanatory error message.

4. The customer corrects the erroneous form field.

5. Return to primary sequence step 1.

- *Alternate action sequence 2*—No matching books. Replace primary sequence steps 4–6.

4. The database returns an empty list.

5. The application displays "No books found."

- *Postconditions*—The customer sees either a list of matching books or the message "No books found." There were no changes to the book catalogue.
- *Nonfunctional requirements:*

Search results must return in under 2 seconds.

The customer shall be on a Windows, macOS, or Linux platform.

The application must be usable by a customer whose native language is English, Spanish, or Vietnamese.

- *Glossary:*
  - *Catalogue*—A searchable repository of books and their attributes
  - *Attribute*—A feature of a book that can be matched during a search, such as the book title or the author's name
  - *Customer*—A user who searches the book catalogue

Use case descriptions should be short, simple, and informal. Both the application's clients and its developers need to understand them. Therefore, we should not use overly technical language. There should be no implementation details. We must concentrate on what the application needs to do in response to an actor's triggering action, not how the application will do it.

Requirements come from a continuous engagement with the client of the application. Write down the requirements that are known so far, and create use cases. The use cases illustrate for the client how the application will behave under various scenarios. This can inspire more requirements. New requirements may, in turn, require new use cases. There may be several rounds of adding new requirements and creating new use cases. A substantial application with a rich set of actor interactions can have dozens of use cases.

A powerful way to elicit requirements is to show the client a prototype of the application. This can be some quick-and-dirty code that shows a few key use cases in action. Seeing a tangible piece of working code, however hacked together, will often inspire the client to point out what's missing or superfluous, or what doesn't work in a desired way. This prototype can be as simple as a deck of slides containing simulated screenshots of the application as it's being used. We then capture client comments and observations in new requirements or modify existing ones.

3.7   *The functional specification and software validation*

The development team writes a *functional specification* to document the application it's about to create. Its purpose is to inform both the application's client and the developers in nontechnical, jargon-free language.

> **NOTE** The format and contents of the functional specification are usually determined by the client's organization. Different organizations might give the document different names, such as External Reference Specification. It's external because this document views the application from the outside. It

should contain no internal implementation details. Implementation details belong in the *design specification* covered in chapter 4.

The functional specification should include the following content:

- *Application name*—For example, Book Catalogue.
- *Clear problem statement*—What is the problem that this application addresses? For example, the ability to store and search for books.
- *Objectives*—What is the application supposed to accomplish? For example, to create a means to enter books into a repository and then search for them using target book attributes.
- *Functional requirements*—A list of the functional requirements. The requirements should be stated strongly with the auxiliary verbs *must* and *shall*.
- *Nonfunctional requirements*—A list of the nonfunctional requirements. The requirements should be stated strongly with the auxiliary verbs *must* and *shall*.
- *Use cases*—UML use case diagrams and a use description for each use case.

A functional specification can also include an external test plan, a deployment plan, and a maintenance plan. These are often separate documents.

If it's included, the external test plan should describe black-box tests. These are tests that are doable without knowing the internals of the application code. For each test, the test plan describes what the input data or user action should be and the expected result. Black-box testing helps to verify that an application meets its functional and nonfunctional requirements. Such tests are often run by test engineers who were not part of the development team.

"Black box" sounds ominous.

It simply means we should treat the code we're testing as something we can't look inside to see how it's implemented.

How elaborate should the functional specification be? That often depends on the client's organization and the development methodology. Some organizations and methodologies place less emphasis on documentation and favor prototyping and tighter engagement with the client. Other organizations regard the functional specification as such an important document that they go to the extreme of considering it a contract between the client and the software developers. They may require multiple levels of management to sign off on a complete functional specification and then deem it frozen before allowing the developers to move on to designing the application.

But ideally, as suggested in figure 3.1 by the dotted time span, we should be allowed to modify the functional specification when we need to tweak requirements or discover new ones during application design and coding. It should be modifiable up to a certain point in time, often called the "features freeze," agreed to by the developers and the client. Even though it's initially movable, the functional specification serves as an important stake in the ground for both the developers and the client.

Regardless of whether it rises to the level of a contract, it is critical that the client of the application carefully read the functional specification, which should have no implementation details. By reading, understanding, and approving the functional specification, the client *validates* the application: that is, confirms that we are going to build the right application, one that meets the client's requirements.

Once the application is validated (remember that clients can still change their minds about the requirements), we can begin the design–code–test iterations. Testing is *verification* that we are building the software right—that we are implementing bug-free code to fulfill each and every requirement.

NOTE   Software verification and validation (software V&V) is a major topic in the fields of software engineering and software quality control.

3.8   *Where do classes come from?*

Once we have at least the first draft of the functional specification, we can start to think about the classes of the application. To create the initial set of classes, we analyze the application's functional requirements. Requirements analysis, the process of carefully examining an application's requirements during design, is a major software engineering topic. The rest of this chapter covers its most important points.

Here is an extended set of functional requirements for the more advanced version of our book catalogue application from chapter 2. Recall that functional requirements state what an application must do or allow a user to do:

- The book catalogue shall store different kinds of books and their attributes.
- A librarian must be able to add new books to the catalogue.
- A librarian must be able to update and delete existing books in the catalogue.
- The kinds of books shall include fiction, cookbooks, and how-to.
- All books must have title, author's last name, and author's first name attribute values.
- Fiction books must include the publication year and genre attributes.
- Genre must include adventure, classics, detective, fantasy, historic, horror, romance, and science fiction.
- Cookbooks must include the region attribute.
- How-to books must include the subject attribute.
- A customer must be able to search the catalogue by providing any number of desired target attribute values.
- A customer must complete a web browser-based form to specify target attribute values for book searches.

- A customer's input in the form must be verified for correct format and values.
- During searches, string attribute matches must be case-insensitive.
- A customer must be able to specify any number of don't-care (wildcard) target attributes.
- Each don't-care attribute must, by default, match the corresponding attribute in all books in the catalogue.
- A book in the catalogue shall match if it has all the attributes in the customer's target attributes and all the corresponding book and target attribute values are equal, or the target attribute is a don't-care.

3.8.1 *Textual analysis: Nouns can become classes*

Recall from section 1.8 that a class specifies the state and behavior of its objects at run time. To determine what classes our application should have, first find the nouns in the requirements: *book, catalogue, attribute, librarian, customer, kind, title, name, year, genre, region, subject, browser, form, input,* and *string*. The nouns represent potential classes, but as shown in table 3.1, it's a judgment call which nouns should become classes and which should become attributes in our application. This is the type of design decision that we may need to revisit during the development iterations.

Table 3.1 Decide whether each noun of the requirements should be a class

Noun	Class?
catalogue	Yes. The application implements a book catalogue.
book	Yes. The catalogue stores book objects.
attribute	Yes. Each book object has a set of attributes.
librarian	No. According to figure 3.4, a librarian is an agent outside of the application.
customer	No. According to figure 3.4, a customer is an agent outside of the application.
kind	No. It is an attribute value that is an enumeration constant.
title	No. It is an attribute value that is a string.
name	No. It is an attribute value that is a string.
year	No. It is an attribute value that is an integer.
genre	No. It is an attribute value that is an enumeration constant.
region	No. It is an attribute value that is an enumeration constant.
subject	No. It is an attribute value that is an enumeration constant.
browser	No. The application works with existing browsers.
form	Yes. The application manages a user input form.
input	No. It is an attribute value entered by a user into a form.
format	No. A format isn't a separate thing in the application.
value	No. An attribute value is an integer, string, or enumeration constant.
string	No. The application uses built-in Python strings.

We are left with these nouns that can become the initial classes in our application: *catalogue, book, attribute,* and *form*. For each class, we must determine its instance variables so that its objects can maintain state at run time. Table 3.2 may be the result after several design iterations like the ones described in chapter 2. Later iterations can discover more classes.

Table 3.2   The initial classes of the application

Class	State	Instance variables
Catalogue	List of books	`_booklist` (list of Book objects)
Book	Book attributes	`_attributes` (the book's attributes)
Attributes	Attribute values	`_dictionary` (dictionary of key–value pairs)
Form	Input values	Individual instance variables for the book attributes

3.8.2   *Textual analysis: Verbs can become methods*

Next, we must determine the runtime behavior of each class's objects from the verbs in the requirements: *store, add, update, delete, include, have, be, search, complete, verify, constitute, specify,* and *match*. We should consider only (transitive) verbs that perform some action on an object. Like table 3.2, table 3.3 may be the result after several design iterations.

Table 3.3   Determine the behavior of each class

Verb	Class	Method
add	Catalogue	`add()` a book to the booklist.
update	Catalogue	`update()` a book in the booklist.
delete	Catalogue	`delete()` a book from the booklist.
search	Catalogue	`find()` matching books in the booklist.
verify	Form	`verify()` user input in the form fields.
match	Attributes	`is_match()` check if attributes match.

Each class's methods work with that class's instance variables. For example, in class `Catalogue`, the `add()` method appends Book objects to the `_booklist` instance variable.

So, did the textual analysis give us all the classes that we'll need?

Absolutely not! These are just our initial classes. We'll come up with more classes during our development iterations.

Now that we have some initial classes, we need to make sure that we design them and any subsequent classes well. That's the topic of the next chapters.

Summary

- Functional requirements state what an application must do, or allow a user to do, for the application to be successful.

- Nonfunctional requirements impose restrictions or constraints that the application must meet to be successful. They are just as important as functional requirements. Examples are performance and platform requirements.

- State requirements using the strong verbs *must* and *shall*.

- Getting good requirements is crucial. Interview the application's clients or observe how people currently perform their tasks. Create prototypes of the application to show to the clients. Imagine ways an application can improve their productivity.

- Requirements come from a continuous engagement with clients, who may not always know what they want. Be prepared for the requirements to change during application design and even during coding.

- Good requirements are clear, consistent, correct, complete, realistic, verifiable, and traceable.

- Use cases provide context for the requirements and show how they determine the application's functionality. Document the use cases with UML use case diagrams and use case descriptions. Use cases can inspire new requirements.

- A functional specification written in nontechnical, jargon-free language informs both the clients and the software developers what the application will do. It can include an external test plan for black-box testing. Some organizations consider this document to be a contract between clients and developers. Ideally, it should be modifiable (up until the features-freeze milestone) to accommodate changes to the requirements.

- Clients validate that the software developers are going to build the right application by approving the functional specification. The developers verify that they are building the application right through testing. Software verification and validation is a major topic in the fields of software engineering and software quality control.

- Analyze the requirements to obtain the initial set of classes for the application. Determine which nouns become classes and which verbs become methods that implement behavior. Assign instance variables and methods to the classes.

- Don't fall victim to paralysis by analysis. Create and show prototypes, and then start the development iterations, and more classes will arise.

Good class design to build
the application right

This chapter covers

- The place of design in the application development process
- How to design classes well
- UML diagrams to aid class design
- The design specification

In chapter 3, we worked with our clients on the functional and nonfunctional requirements to ensure that we build the *right application*. Simple textual analysis produced our initial set of classes. In this chapter, we begin to design the classes well to ensure that we build the *application right*.

In chapter 1, we learned that design is a disciplined engineering approach to create a solution to a problem. For software development, that means applying good software design techniques to find the best development path to a well-designed application that meets its requirements. In chapter 2, we saw that the development path requires iterations and, most likely, backtracking.

This chapter discusses where application design fits within the overall development process. It covers some basic guidelines for good class design. Because most applications consist of multiple classes, we'll also examine how the classes can relate to each other. Chapter 3 introduced Unified Modeling Language (UML) use case diagrams. To document our class design, we'll use more of these industry-standard diagrams. Finally, a design specification pulls together all the design documentation for an application.

4.1 When do we do application design?

A major application is often created by several software developers working together as a team, with various activities overlapping over time. This chapter covers the design activities with the bold borders in figure 4.1.

Application design occurs during nearly the entire project. As we saw in chapter 3, we must first get the application's requirements. Creating use cases and prototypes helps to elicit requirements. The functional specification documents the requirements and use cases. We can choose the application's initial classes from its requirements. Some of the prototypes may result in more classes. Most of the application design subsequently occurs during the development iterations, where we expand and refine the initial set of classes. This chapter covers how to document our class design for our own benefit and for the design specification.

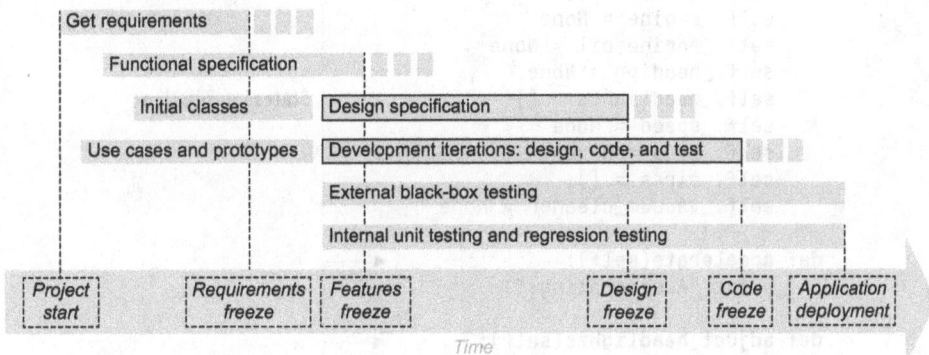

Figure 4.1 Creating an application involves many activities. This diagram shows when the activities start relative to each other and how they overlap in time. However, it does not show their relative durations. The major project milestones are presented at the bottom. Most of the application design occurs during the development iterations. The design specification documents our design. This diagram shows these activities with heavy borders. Their dotted timespans suggest that their freeze dates must be flexible.

Both external black-box testing (described in chapter 3) and internal testing (described later in this chapter) occur in parallel with the development iterations. The bottom of the diagram shows milestone dates, such as Project Start, Requirements Freeze, Features Freeze, and so forth, that a project schedule maintains. These are goals that the project team should meet to get an application deployed on time. However, many projects slip their freeze milestones. For example, the project manager may agree that new requirements are important enough to be included in the project past the Requirements Freeze milestone. If we allow a project to slip much past a milestone freeze date, we greatly increase the risk of not completing the project on time.

4.2 Two important goals for good class design

In chapter 3, we saw how performing a textual analysis of the requirements gives us a good start when determining our application's classes. But how can we be certain that we've put the instance variables and methods in the right classes? When we design classes, there are two important goals: cohesion and loose coupling.

4.2.1 Cohesion and the Single Responsibility Principle

A class is cohesive if it adheres to the Single Responsibility Principle (section 2.3.1). A well-designed class should have only one primary responsibility. Let's revisit the `Automobile` class from listing 1.3 in chapter 1.

Listing 4.1   (Program 4.1 Automobile-1): automobile.py (not cohesive)

```python
class Automobile:
    def __init__(self):
        self._brakes = []
        self._engine = None
        self._engine_oil = None
        self._heading = None
        self._headlights = []          States information
        self._speed = None
        self._soap = None
        self._tires = []
        self._vacuum_cleaner = None

    def accelerate(self):
        print("Accelerating.")

    def adjust_headlights(self):
        print("Adjusting headlights.")

    def apply_brakes(self):
        print("Applying brakes.")

    def change_oil(self):              Behaviors
        print("Changing oil.")

    def change_tires(self):
        print("Changing tires.")

    def check_brakes(self):
        print("Checking brakes.")

    def check_tires(self):
```

```
            print("Checking tires.")

    def rotate_tires(self):
        print("Rotating tires.")

    def shut_off_engine(self):
        print("Shutting off engine.")

    def start_engine(self):
        print("Starting engine.")

    def tuneup_engine(self):
        print("Tuning up engine.")

    def turn_left(self):                    ◄──── Behaviors
        print("Turning left.")

    def turn_right(self):
        print("Turning right.")

    def vacuum_car(self):
        print("Vacuuming car.")

    def wash_car(self):
        print("Washing car.")

    def wax_car(self):
        print("Waxing car.")
```

This class is not cohesive because it has too many state and behavior responsibilities:

- Automobile operation
  - *State*—_brakes, _engine, _heading, _speed
  - *Behavior*—accelerate(), apply_brakes(), shut_off_engine(), start_engine(), turn_left(), turn_right()
- Automobile maintenance
  - *State*—_engine_oil, _headlights, _tires
  - *Behavior*—adjust_headlights(), change_oil(), change_tires(), check_brakes(), check_tires(), rotate_tires(), tuneup_engine()
- Automobile cleaning
  - *State*—_soap, _vacuum_cleaner, _wax
  - *Behavior*—vacuum_car(), wash_car(), wax_car()

We need to break class Automobile into smaller classes, each of which has a single primary responsibility.

Listing 4.2 (Program 4.2 Automobile-2): automobile.py (cohesive)

```
class Automobile:                  ◄──── Responsible for
    def __init__(self):                   automobile operations
```

```
        self._brakes = []
        self._engine = None
        self._engine_oil = None
        self._heading = None
        self._headlights = []
        self._speed = None
        self._soap = None
        self._tires = []
        self._vacuum_cleaner = None

    def accelerate(self):
        print("Accelerating.")

    def apply_brakes(self):
        print("Applying brakes.")

    def shut_off_engine(self):
        print("Shutting off engine.")

    def start_engine(self):
        print("Starting engine.")

    def turn_left(self):
        print("Turning left.")

    def turn_right(self):
        print("Turning right.")

class Garage:                           ◀──── Responsible for
    def __init__(self, car):                   automobile maintenance
        self._car = car
        self._new_oil = None
        self._new_tires = []

    def adjust_headlights(self):
        print("Accelerating.")

    def change_oil(self):
        print("Changing oil.")

    def change_tires(self):
        print("Changing tires.")

    def check_brakes(self):
        print("Checking brakes.")

    def check_tires(self):
        print("Checking tires.")

    def rotate_tires(self):
        print("Rotating tires.")

    def tuneup_engine(self):
        print("Tuning up engine.")
```

```
class CarWash:                          ◄─────┐ Responsible for
    def __init__(self, car):                  │ automobile cleaning
        self._car = car
        self._vacuum_cleaner = None
        self._wax = None

    def vacuum_car(self):
        print("Vacuuming car.")

    def wash_car(self):
        print("Washing car.")

    def wax_car(self):
        print("Waxing car.")
```

Each of these classes is cohesive, with a single primary responsibility. Class `Automobile` is responsible for automobile operations. Class `Garage` is responsible for automobile maintenance. Class `CarWash` is responsible for automobile cleaning. The constructors of the latter two classes have a parameter `car`, the `Automobile` object, and perform their operations on that object. The Single Responsibility Principle is important for good class design. If changes are necessary, a cohesive class should have only one reason to change.

4.2.2 Loose coupling and the Principle of Least Knowledge

Loosely coupled classes have minimal dependencies on each other. Class A is dependent on class B if class A has references to class B. For example, class `Garage` depends on class `Automobile` because its instance variable `_car` is assigned an `Automobile` object.

Loosely coupled classes adhere to the Principle of Least Knowledge (section 2.3.2), which supports encapsulation. The less class A knows about the internal implementation details of class B, the less likely it is that changes to class B will affect class A.

We saw an example of the Principle of Least Knowledge in chapter 2. The dependency that class `Catalogue` (reproduced in listing 4.3) had on class `Attributes` was only through parameters `attrs` and `target_attrs`, which the class simply passed as arguments to other methods. The class required no knowledge of how class `Attributes` implemented the book attributes.

Listing 4.3 (Program 2.4 Books-4): catalogue.py

```
from book import Book

class Catalogue:
    def __init__(self):
        self._booklist = []

    def add(self, attrs):
        book = Book(attrs)
        self._booklist.append(book)

    def find(self, target_attrs):
```

```
return [book for book in self._booklist
            if book.attributes.is_match(target_attrs)
        ]
```

Class Attributes (reproduced in listing 4.4) had no dependencies at all on class Catalogue. It had no instance variables, parameters, or local variables that referred to Catalogue objects. Therefore, Attributes objects did not know that they were ultimately stored in a Catalogue object. Even though class Catalogue delegated attribute matching to class Attributes by calling the latter's Boolean is_match() method, class Attributes did not know what was calling that method.

Listing 4.4   (Program 2.4 Books-4): attributes.py

```
from key import Key
from kind import Kind
from genre import Genre
from region import Region
from subject import Subject

class Attributes:

    @staticmethod
    def _equal_ignore_case(target_str, other_str):
        if len(target_str) == 0:
            return True;
        else:
            return target_str.casefold() == other_str.casefold()

    def __init__(self, dictionary):
        self._dictionary = dictionary

        for key, value in dictionary.items():
            if key == Key.YEAR:
                assert(isinstance(value, int))
            elif key in [Key.TITLE, Key.LAST, Key.FIRST]:
                assert(isinstance(value, str))
            elif key == Key.KIND:
                assert(isinstance(value, Kind))
            elif key == Key.GENRE:
                assert(isinstance(value, Genre))
            elif key == Key.REGION:
                assert(isinstance(value, Region))
            elif key == Key.SUBJECT:
                assert(isinstance(value, Subject))

    def _is_matching_key_value(self, target_key, target_value):
        if target_key not in self._dictionary.keys(): return False
        if self._dictionary[target_key] == target_value: return True

        if isinstance(target_value, str):
            return Attributes._equal_ignore_case(
                self._dictionary[target_key], target_value)
```

```
    def is_match(self, target_attrs):
        for target_key, target_value \
                        in target_attrs._dictionary.items():
            if not self._is_matching_key_value(target_key,
                                            target_value):
                return False

        return True

    def __str__(self):
        last_key = list(self._dictionary.keys())[-1]
        ostr = '{'

        for key, value in self._dictionary.items():
            ostr += str(key.name) + ': '

            if isinstance(value, str):
                ostr += "'" + value + "'"
            else:
                ostr += str(value)

            if key != last_key: ostr += ', '

        ostr += '}'
        return ostr
```

Classes `Catalogue` and `Attributes` are loosely coupled. We saw how loose coupling encapsulates any changes in class `Attributes` from affecting class `Catalogue`. Loose coupling and the Principle of Least Knowledge are important for good class design.

4.3 UML class diagrams to document class design

We saw UML use case diagrams in chapter 3. UML class diagrams document class design. A class diagram consists of at least the name of the class. Optionally, it includes the names and datatypes of the class's instance variables and the *signatures* of its methods. A method's signature consists of the name of the method, the name and datatype of each parameter, and the datatype of the return value.

NOTE Google "UML drawing tools" for tools to draw these diagrams. Some of the tools are free.

Figure 4.2 shows four possible UML class diagrams for the class `Catalogue` (listing 4.3). The first diagram shows only the class name. The second diagram includes the instance variables but not the methods. The third diagram includes the methods in the bottom section but not the instance variables in the empty middle section. The fourth diagram includes the instance variables (middle section) and the methods (bottom section). The selection of a diagram depends on how much detail about the class we need to show. A diagram in a high-level description of the application could show less than a diagram in a low-level description.

Catalogue	Catalogue	Catalogue	Catalogue
-_booklist: list of Book	-_booklist: list of Book	+add(Attributes) +find(Attributes): list of Book	-_booklist: list of Book +add(Attributes) +find(Attributes): list of Book

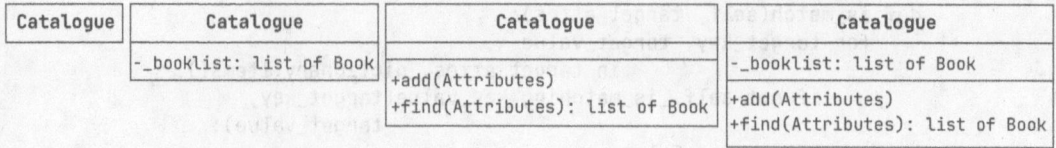

Figure 4.2   Possible UML class diagrams for class `Catalogue` that include different amounts of information. A plus sign (+) indicates what is intended to be public, and a minus sign (-) indicates what is intended to be private. How much information to include in a class diagram depends on whether the diagram is in high-level or low-level design documentation of the application.

Section 2.3 described how to indicate in Python classes that certain instance variables and members are meant to be private. A minus sign (-) in front of a name indicates that the member is private, and a plus sign (+) that the member is public. The datatype of an instance variable follows the name and a colon. The signature of each method does not need to include every detail about the parameters; we only show their datatypes. It's not necessary to include the constructors and the destructor of a class. If the method returns a value, put a colon after the parameters, followed by the return value's datatype. Unless it's important to show them, we can leave out getter and setter methods. Figure 4.3 is a possible UML class diagram for class `Attributes` (listing 4.4).

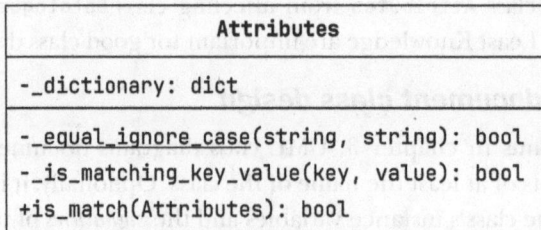

Attributes
-_dictionary: dict
-_equal_ignore_case(string, string): bool -_is_matching_key_value(key, value): bool +is_match(Attributes): bool

Figure 4.3   A UML class diagram for class `Attributes` that includes all three parts: its name, instance variables, and methods. Private method _equal_ignore_case() is underlined to indicate that it is a static method. This diagram is suitable for detailed design documentation.

Most applications consist of multiple classes, especially if they are well-designed, cohesive classes. The relationship between two classes determines how their objects can interact at run time. Therefore, it's important during class design to get the relationships right.

A class diagram that includes an application's classes should also indicate the relationships among them by connecting the diagrams with lines. Figure 2.5 in chapter 2, reproduced in figure 4.4, is such a diagram. Later in the chapter, we summarize the ways to specify the different relationships with class diagrams.

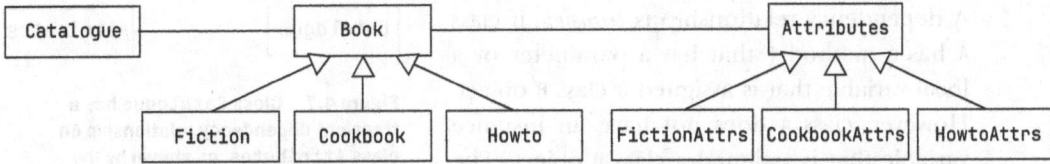

Figure 4.4 A UML class diagram that shows an application's multiple classes and their relationships. The relationship between two classes determines how their instantiated objects can interact at run time.

4.3.1 Dependency: The most basic relationship

A line connecting two classes, like the one between `Book` and `Attributes` in figure 4.4, represents a dependency relationship. Just as we can choose the amount of information to show for each class, we can also choose how much information to show about each relationship. A simple line between two classes indicates an unspecified dependency relationship. This gives the least amount of relationship information. An arrowhead clarifies

Figure 4.5 A UML diagram that shows (left to right) class `Catalogue`, a relationship, and class `Book`. The dependency relationship arrow going from class `Catalogue` to class `Book` indicates that class `Catalogue` depends on class `Book`. But class `Book` does not depend on class `Catalogue`.

what depends on what. In figure 4.5, class `Catalogue` depends on class `Book` (because a `Catalogue` object contains `Book` objects), but class `Book` does not depend on class `Catalogue`.

If we want to include more information about a relationship between two classes, we can label the dependency arrows (figure 4.6). For example, instance variable `_booklist` of class `Catalogue` is a list of `Book` objects (listing 4.3). When we label a relationship arrow with the instance variable name, we don't include the name in the middle section of the class diagram. Figure 4.6 also indicates multiplicity: a single (1) `_booklist` in a `Catalogue` object will contain zero or more (*) `Book` objects. A plus (+) means one or more. When it's appropriate, we can replace a * or a + with a specific number. At either end of the relationship arrow, we can even indicate a range of numbers like 2..5.

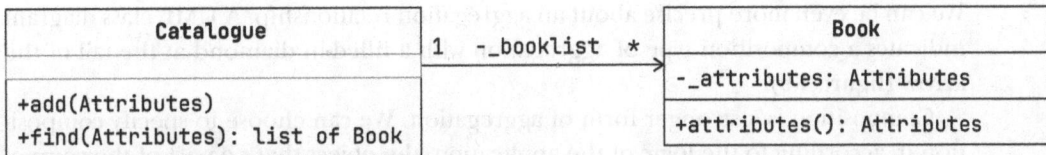

Figure 4.6 Diagrams that show more design detail. Class `Catalogue` depends on class `Book` via its private `booklist` instance variable. The multiplicity indicators show that a single (1) `Catalogue` object can contain zero or more (*) `Book` objects.

A dependency relationship is *transient* if class A has a method f that has a parameter or a local variable that is assigned a class B object. However, class A does not have an instance variable that is assigned a class B object. The relationship is transient because it exists only during a call to method f. In class Catalogue (listing 4.3), the add() and find() methods each receive an Attributes object (attrs and target_attrs, respectively). But class Catalogue does not have an instance variable that will be assigned an Attributes object. Therefore, the dependency on class Attributes exists only during a call to add() or to find(). Figure 4.7 shows this transient dependency relationship with the dashed arrow.

Figure 4.7   Class Catalogue **has a transient dependency relationship on class** Attributes**, as shown by the dashed dependency arrow. The** add() **method of class** Catalogue **receives a reference to an** Attributes **object, and the** find() **method is passed a reference to an** Attributes **object. The dependency exists only during calls to these methods.**

4.3.2   *Aggregation and composition: Objects that contain other objects*

UML class diagrams can be more precise in terms of the nature of a dependency. When a class aggregates (contains) another class, such as by having an instance variable that can hold an object of the other class, we can use the aggregation arrow that has an open diamond at the tail end next to the diagram for the container class (there is no arrowhead). Figure 4.8 explicitly shows that class Catalogue aggregates class Book. Each Catalogue object contains zero or more Book objects. In this example, we chose to include the information that _booklist is a list of Book objects.

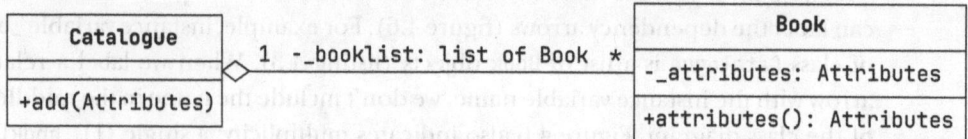

Figure 4.8   Class Catalogue **aggregates class** Book**. Each** Catalogue **object contains zero or more** Book **objects in a list instance variable named** booklist**. The open diamond at the tail of the dependency arrow is next to the diagram for the container class** Catalogue**.**

We can be even more precise about an aggregation relationship. A UML class diagram indicates a composition type of aggregation with a filled-in diamond at the tail of the arrow (figure 4.9).

Composition is a stronger form of aggregation. We can choose to specify composition if, according to the logic of the application, the object that's a part of the composition cannot exist outside of its container. In figure 4.9, an Attributes object cannot logically exist without its Book object. In contrast, with the Catalogue-Book aggregation, a Book object can logically exist outside of a Catalogue object.

Book
+attributes(): Attributes

-_attributes

1   1

Attributes
-_dictionary: dict
-_equal_ignore_case(string, string): bool -_is_matching_key_value(key, value): bool +is_match(Attributes): bool

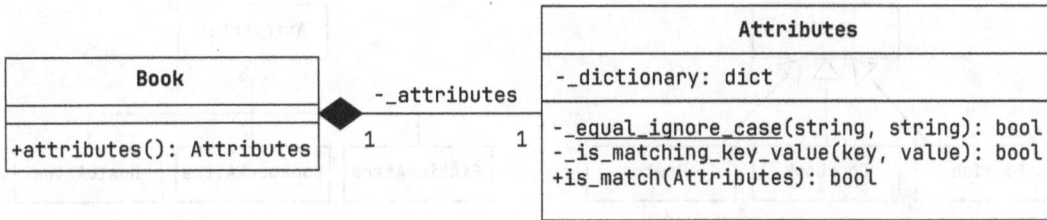

Figure 4.9   Class Book **is composed of class** Attributes. **Each** Book **object has one** Attributes **object. According to the logic of the application, an** Attributes **object cannot exist without being part of a** Book **object.**

Figure 4.10 shows both an aggregation relationship and a composition relationship to illustrate their difference. According to the logic of a hypothetical application, Book objects are contained by Bookshelf objects, but Book objects can exist outside of Bookshelf objects. A Bookcase object is composed of Bookshelf objects, but a Bookshelf object cannot exist without being a part of a Bookcase object.

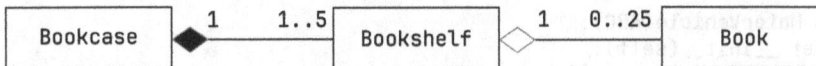

Bookcase	1 1..5	Bookshelf	1 0..25	Book

Figure 4.10   The difference between aggregation and composition. In this diagram, each Bookshelf **object can contain 0 through 25** Book **objects, and Book objects can exist outside of** Bookshelf **objects. Each** Bookcase **object is composed of 1 through 5** Bookshelf **objects, but a** Bookshelf **object cannot exist without being a part of a** Bookcase **object.**

4.3.3   *Generalization: Superclasses and their subclasses*

The generalization relationship involves superclasses, subclasses, and inheritance. The general class is the superclass.

After three development iterations of our book catalogue application in chapter 2, we had designed (poorly, as it turned out) a Book superclass and Fiction, Cookbook, and Howto subclasses. A UML diagram shows a superclass–subclass relationship with an arrow going from the subclass to the superclass, and the arrowhead is an open triangle against the superclass. Figure 4.11 also shows superclass Attributes and its subclasses FictionAttrs, CookbookAttrs, and HowtoAttrs with a different way of drawing the arrows. We can choose how to draw the arrows depending on which looks best for a diagram.

4.3.4   *Abstract classes and interfaces: What subclasses must implement*

A class is *abstract* if it is derived from the Python-supplied class ABC (for abstract base class). Listing 4.5 shows abstract class MotorVehicle with two abstract methods start_engine() and stop_engine(). We then must implement these two methods in subclasses

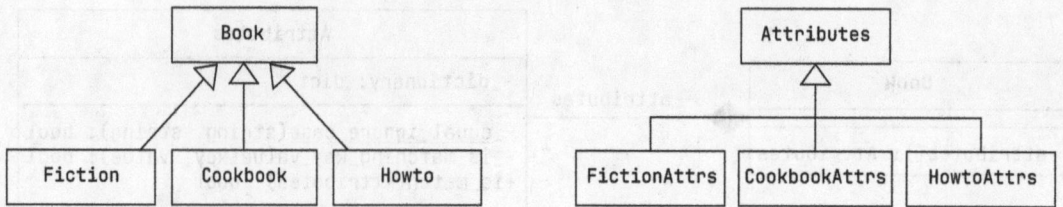

Figure 4.11   Superclass Book **has subclasses** Fiction, Cookbook, **and** Howto. **Also, superclass** Attributes **has subclasses** FictionAttrs, CookbookAttrs, **and** HowtoAttrs. **This figure shows two ways of drawing generalization diagrams.**

such as Car and Truck. Class MotorVehicle provides default implementations of methods accelerate(), turn_left(), turn_right(), apply_brakes(), and drive(), and the subclasses can choose whether to override them.

Listing 4.5   (Program 4.3 VehicleAbstract): motorvehicle.py

```
from abc import ABC, abstractmethod

class MotorVehicle(ABC):
    def __init__(self):
        self._brakes = []
        self._engine = None
        self._heading = None
        self._speed = 0

    @abstractmethod
    def start_engine(self):
        pass

    @abstractmethod
    def stop_engine(self):
        pass

    def accelerate(self):
        print('vehicle accelerates')

    def turn_left(self):
        print('vehicle turns left')

    def turn_right(self):
        print('vehicle turns right')

    def apply_brakes(self):
        print('vehicle applies brakes')

    def drive(self):
        self.start_engine();
        self.accelerate();
        self.turn_left();
        self.turn_right();
```

Instance variables to be inherited by the subclasses

Abstract methods to be implemented by the subclasses

```
        self.apply_brakes();
        self.stop_engine();
```

Abstract classes

An *abstract class* is a subclass of abc.ABC (for abstract base class). It contains one or more abstract methods created by the decorator @abstractmethod. An abstract method should not contain any code other than pass. An abstract class can contain instance variables and non-abstract methods.

Subclasses of the abstract class, known as its *concrete subclasses*, must implement (have code for) each of the abstract methods. Therefore, an abstract class forces each concrete subclass to implement its own behaviors. A subclass that doesn't implement all of the abstract methods is itself abstract.

It is an error to attempt to create an instance of an abstract class. We can only create instances of its concrete subclasses.

Subclass Car implements methods start_engine() and stop_engine(), and it inherits the remaining methods from its superclass, MotorVehicle.

Listing 4.6   (Program 4.3 VehicleAbstract): car.py

```
from motorvehicle import MotorVehicle

class Car(MotorVehicle):
    def start_engine(self):              ◄─────┐
        print('car starts engine')             ├── Implements abstract
                                                │   methods
    def stop_engine(self):               ◄─────┘
        print('car stops engine')
```

Subclass Truck implements methods start_engine() and stop_engine(). It also overrides the superclass implementations of methods turn_left() and turn_right().

Listing 4.7   (Program 4.3 VehicleAbstract): truck.py

```
from motorvehicle import MotorVehicle

class Truck(MotorVehicle):
    def start_engine(self):              ◄─────┐
        print('truck starts engine')           ├── Implements abstract
                                                │   methods
    def stop_engine(self):               ◄─────┘
        print('truck stops engine')

    def turn_left(self):                 ◄─────┐
        print('truck turns left')              ├── Overrides superclass
                                                │   methods
    def turn_right(self):                ◄─────┘
        print('truck turns right')
```

Figure 4.12 shows that in the UML class diagram for this example program, we indicate that a class is abstract by printing its name in italics or a slanted font. We also print the name of an abstract method in italics or a slanted font.

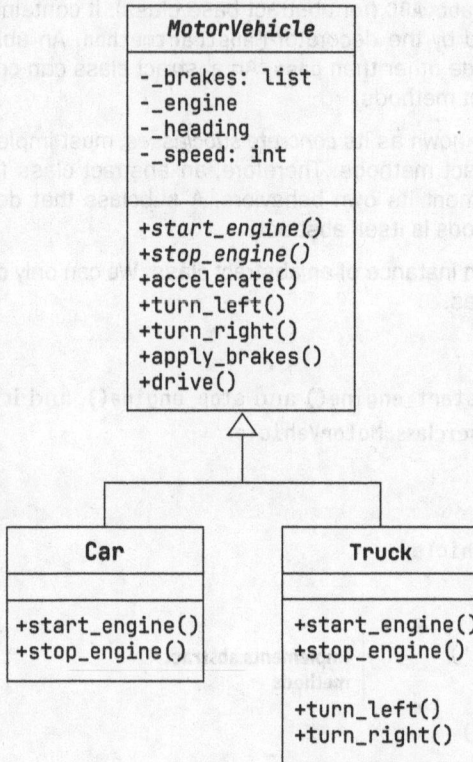

Figure 4.12   Class `MotorVehicle` is abstract, so its name is in a slanted font. Its methods `start_engine()` and `shut_off_engine()` are abstract, and so they are also in a slanted font. Subclasses `Car` and `Truck` must implement these abstract methods. The relationship arrow with the open triangle points to the superclass.

The test program main.py creates `Car` and `Truck` objects and calls the inherited `drive()` method on each.

Listing 4.8   (Program 4.3 VehicleAbstract): **main.py**

```
from car import Car
from truck import Truck

if __name__ == '__main__':
    car = Car()
    car.drive()

    print()

    truck = Truck()
    truck.drive()
```

The output from the program is as follows:

```
car starts engine
vehicle accelerates
vehicle turns left
vehicle turns right
vehicle applies brakes
car stops engine

truck starts engine
vehicle accelerates
truck turns left
truck turns right
vehicle applies brakes
truck stops engine
```

Interface classes

An *interface class* is an abstract class that contains only abstract methods and no instance variables. It serves as a model or blueprint for the concrete subclasses that implement the interface. An interface class defines all the behaviors that a subclass must have and forces the subclass to implement all of them.

Class `MotorVehicleInterface` is an interface class.

Listing 4.9   (Program 4.4 VehicleInterface): `motorvehicleinterface.py`

```python
from abc import ABC, abstractmethod

class MotorVehicleInterface(ABC):

    @abstractmethod
    def start_engine(self):
        pass

    @abstractmethod
    def stop_engine(self):
        pass

    @abstractmethod
    def accelerate(self):
        pass

    @abstractmethod
    def turn_left(self):
        pass

    @abstractmethod
    def turn_right(self):
        pass
```

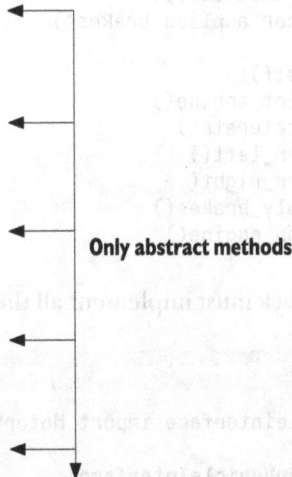

Only abstract methods

```
@abstractmethod
def apply_brakes(self):  ◄──┐
    pass                     │
                             ├─ Only abstract methods
@abstractmethod              │
def drive(self):  ◄──────────┘
    pass
```

In this version, class Car must implement all the abstract methods of the interface.

Listing 4.10   (Program 4.4 VehicleInterface): car.py

```python
from motorvehicleinterface import MotorVehicleInterface

class Car(MotorVehicleInterface):
    def __init__(self):
        self._brakes = []
        self._engine = None
        self._heading = None
        self._speed = 0

    def start_engine(self):
        print('car starts engine')

    def stop_engine(self):
        print('car stops engine')

    def accelerate(self):
        print('car accelerates')

    def turn_left(self):
        print('car turns left')

    def turn_right(self):
        print('car turns right')

    def apply_brakes(self):
        print('car applies brakes')

    def drive(self):
        self.start_engine()
        self.accelerate()
        self.turn_left()
        self.turn_right(
        self.apply_brakes()
        self.stop_engine()
```

Similarly, class Truck must implement all the methods.

Listing 4.11   (Program 4.4 VehicleInterface): truck.py

```python
from motorvehicleinterface import MotorVehicleInterface

class Truck(MotorVehicleInterface):
```

```
def __init__(self):
    self._brakes = []
    self._engine = None
    self._heading = None
    self._speed = 0

def start_engine(self):
    print('truck starts engine')

def stop_engine(self):
    print('truck stops engine')

def accelerate(self):
    print('truck accelerates')

def turn_left(self):
    print('truck turns left')

def turn_right(self):
    print('truck turns right')

def apply_brakes(self):
    print('truck applies brakes')

def drive(self):
    self.start_engine()
    self.accelerate()
    self.turn_left()
    self.turn_right()
    self.apply_brakes()
    self.stop_engine()
```

Figure 4.13 shows that in its UML class diagram, the label «interface» appears above the interface name MotorVehicleInterface. Dashed relationship arrows indicate that classes Car and Truck implement the interface. In a class diagram for an interface, italics or a slanted font is not necessary.

Using the same test program, the output becomes

```
car starts engine
car accelerates
car turns left
car turns right
car turns applies brakes
car stops engine

truck starts engine
truck accelerates
truck turns left
truck turns right
truck turns applies brakes
truck stops engine
```

Figure 4.14 summarizes the relationship lines and arrows in UML class diagrams.

```
          «interface»
      MotorVehicleInterface

    +start_engine()
    +stop_engine()
    +accelerate()
    +turn_left()
    +turn_right()
    +apply_brakes()
    +drive()
```

```
            Car

    -_brakes: list
    -_engine
    -_heading
    -_speed: int

    +start_engine()
    +stop_engine()
    +accelerate()
    +turn_left()
    +turn_right()
    +apply_brakes()
    +drive()
```

```
           Truck

    -_brakes: list
    -_engine
    -_heading
    -_speed: int

    +start_engine()
    +stop_engine()
    +accelerate()
    +turn_left()
    +turn_right()
    +apply_brakes()
    +drive()
```

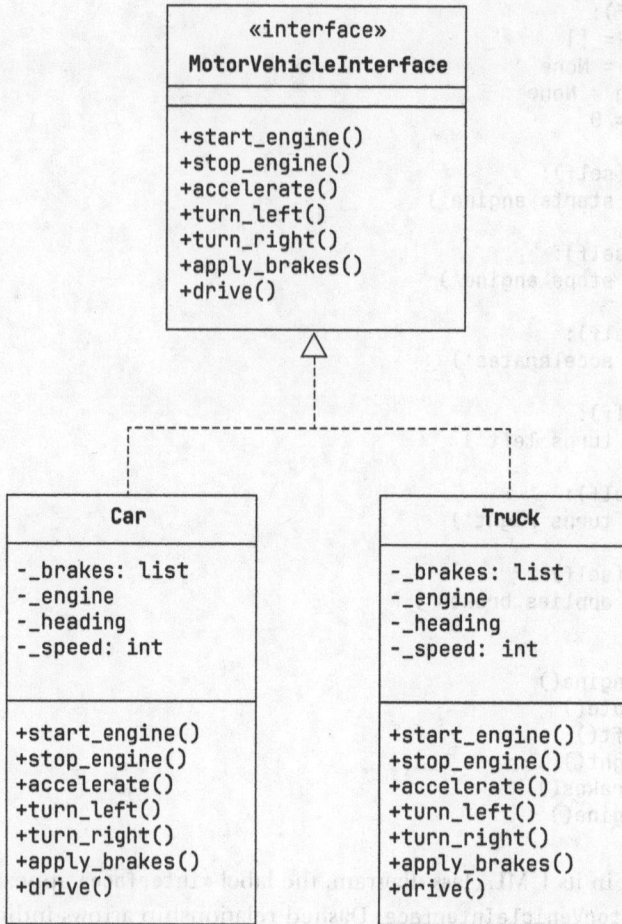

Figure 4.13 The label «interface» appears above the name of interface MotorVehicleInterface. All of its methods are abstract, and it contains no instance variables. The dashed relationship arrow with the open triangle indicates that subclasses Car and Truck implement the interface, and therefore, they must provide code for all the methods of the interface.

Diagram	Relationship
A —— B	An *unspecified dependency* between classes A and B.
A ——▶ B	Class A *depends* on class B.
A ----▶ B	Class A has a *transient dependency* on class B.
A ◇—— B	Class A *aggregates* (contains) class B.
A ◆—— B	Class A is *composed* of class B.
A —▷ B	Class A is a *subclass* of superclass B.
A ----▷ B	Class A *implements* interface class B.

Figure 4.14 Relationship lines and arrows in UML class diagrams

4.4   *UML state diagram: How an object changes state*

UML class diagrams document our classes and how we design them. However, those diagrams are static—they don't show how objects instantiated from the classes interact with each other at run time.

A UML state diagram provides dynamic runtime information. It focuses on a single object and how it changes state at run in response to events defined by its behaviors. Recall that an object's runtime state is determined by the unique values of its instance variables, and its behaviors are implemented by its methods. A state diagram allows us to visualize what happens to a particular object during run time and helps to ensure that we designed the class with the correct instance variables and methods.

Figure 4.15   A UML state diagram that shows the state changes of a `Car` **object during run time. Each box represents a state, and each arrow represents a transition from one state to another. Each transition is labeled with the behavior (event) that causes the transition. Such a diagram allows us to visualize what happens to a particular object during run time and helps to ensure that we designed the class with the correct instance variables and methods.**

Figure 4.15 is a UML state diagram for a `Car` object from figure 4.13. Each rounded box represents a state, and each arrow represents a transition from one state to another. Each arrow has a label that indicates the event that causes the transition. The object's behaviors define the kinds of events that can occur. In this example, the state of the `Car` object is characterized by the current values of the object's `speed` and `heading` instance variables. The filled-in circle is the starting point, and the filled-in circle with a circle around it is an ending point.

Each event in the diagram causes the `Car` object to change state. For example, starting the engine changes the object's initial state from parked to idling. Accelerating then changes the object's state to "heading north."

Figure 4.16 is a state diagram that will help to design a `Student` class in a hypothetical school simulation application. It includes more information about an object's runtime state transitions. The filled-in diamonds are the decision branch and merge points, and the decision conditions are the labels in square brackets. The heavy bars indicate where the transitions fork and join. The diagram shows the state changes of a student enrolling in a course.

4.5   *UML sequence diagram: How objects interact [optional]*

A UML sequence diagram also provides dynamic information. It shows at a high level the runtime interactions among the objects during a use case. It helps to ensure that

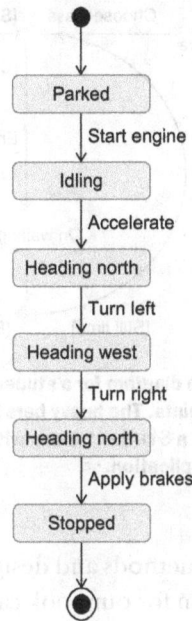

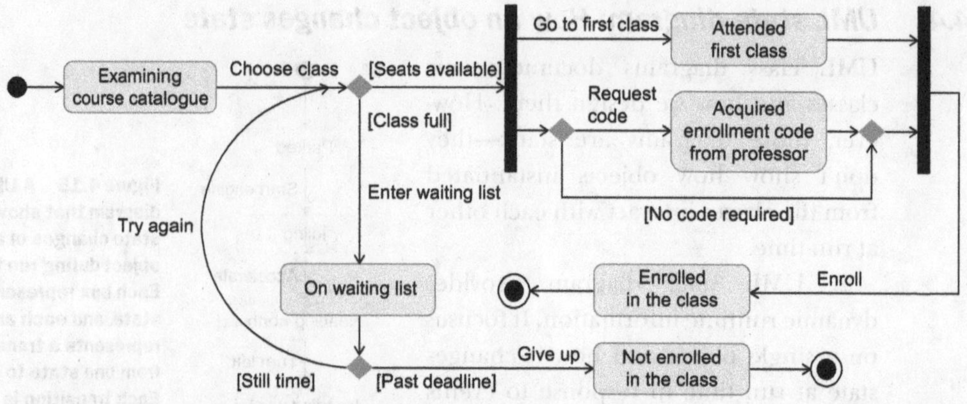

Figure 4.16   A state diagram for a student enrolling in a course. The filled-in diamonds are the decision branch and merge points. The heavy bars indicate where the transitions fork and join. Such a diagram would help to design a `Student` class with the correct instance variables and methods in a hypothetical school simulation application.

we assigned the methods and designed the class relationships correctly. Figure 4.17 is a sequence diagram for our book catalogue application in chapter 2.

The use case is a customer searching for books that match target book attributes. The figure at top left represents the customer. The boxes along the top of the diagram to the right of the stick figure represent objects instantiated from the classes. By convention, each class name is underlined to indicate that it's an object instantiated from the class. Time proceeds from top to bottom. The customer and each object have a lifeline represented by a dashed vertical line. Each vertical rectangle on a lifeline represents

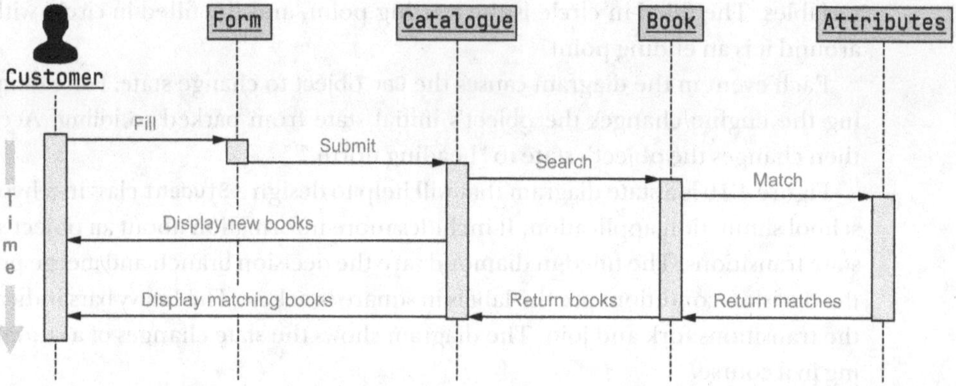

Figure 4.17   A UML sequence diagram for a customer searching for books that match target book attributes. At a high level, it shows the runtime interactions among objects involved in this use case as time goes from top to bottom. Such a diagram helps to ensure that we designed the class relationships correctly.

the time during which the customer or object is active in the use case. The labeled horizontal arrows represent the interactions among the objects. The objects' behaviors (i.e., their methods) determine the interactions. The objects implement these interactions with calls to methods.

In this scenario, a customer first interacts with a Form object to fill in the target book attributes and then clicks the Submit button. That notifies the Catalogue object to start a book search. In the meantime, the Catalogue object displays new books to the customer. The search interacts with Book objects, which in turn match against Attributes objects. The matching attributes cause a return of the corresponding Book objects. Finally, the Catalogue object displays these books to the customer.

Figure 4.18 is another example of a sequence diagram. This one is for a hypothetical bank ATM (automatic teller machine) application.

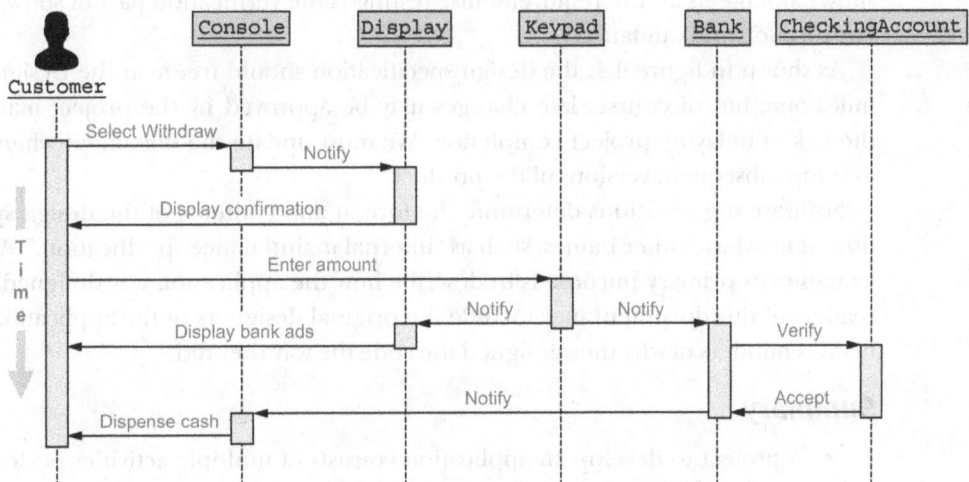

Figure 4.18 An example of a UML sequence diagram for the use case of a customer withdrawing cash from a bank ATM in a hypothetical banking application

The use case is a customer withdrawing cash. In this second scenario, an ATM customer first interacts with the Console object and selects the Withdraw option. That action notifies the Display object to display a confirmation message. Now the customer interacts with the Keypad object to enter the amount to withdraw. The Keypad object notifies the Bank object, and in the meantime, it also notifies the Display object to display bank ads. The Bank object asks the CheckingAccount object to verify the withdrawal amount. If the CheckingAccount object accepts the withdrawal, the Bank object notifies the Console object to initiate dispensing cash. As with the previous sequence diagram, this diagram helps to ensure that we assigned the methods and designed the class relationships correctly.

4.6   *The design specification and software verification*

The UML class, state, and sequence diagrams belong in the design specification. This is a technical document created by the development team that describes and justifies the design of the application. This document can contain implementation details, and it is meant to be read by the current and future developers of the application.

The design specification may include an internal test plan. Unlike the black-box tests in an external test plan described in chapter 3, an internal unit test can target and stress a particular piece of code. For example, a unit test can pass different parameter values to a method of a class and verify the return values. The developers should run unit tests. After a change to the code, and especially at the end of each development iteration, regression testing ensures that previously working code wasn't accidentally broken (i.e., the code hasn't regressed) by rerunning earlier unit tests. Internal testing verifies that we developed the application right—that it's bug-free (to the extent that the tests can show) and meets all the requirements. Testing is the verification part of software V&V (verification and validation).

As shown in figure 4.1, the design specification should freeze at the Design Freeze milestone; but of course, late changes may be approved by the project manager at the risk of delaying project completion. We must update the document whenever we develop subsequent versions of the product.

Software organizations determine the format and contents of the design specification. It may have other names, such as "internal maintenance specification." Whatever its name, its primary purpose is to describe how the application was designed. Future readers of this document may include the original designers of the application if they need reminders of why they designed the code the way they did.

Summary

- A project to develop an application consists of multiple activities performed in parallel by a team of developers. Design occurs throughout most of the project, particularly during the design–code–test development iterations.

- Well-designed classes are cohesive and follow the Single Responsibility Principle.

- Well-designed classes are loosely coupled and follow the Principle of Least Knowledge.

- An abstract class has at least one abstract method that its concrete subclasses must implement. It can also have instance variables and non-abstract methods.

- An interface class is an abstract class that has only abstract methods. It serves as a blueprint for all the behaviors that its concrete subclasses must implement.

- A UML class diagram provides information about an application's classes and their relationships. Each class diagram shows the class name and, optionally, its instance variables and methods. The amount of information to show depends on whether the diagram is part of a high-level or a low-level description of the application's design.

- Different types of arrows drawn between two class diagrams indicate the relationship between the classes: dependency, aggregation, composition, or generalization.

- A UML state diagram focuses on the state changes of a single object at run time. An event causes an object to make a transition from one state to another, and the events are defined by the object's behavior. Visualizing what happens to a particular object during run time helps to ensure that the object's class is well-designed with correct instance variables and methods.

- A UML sequence diagram shows the high-level interactions among objects at run time. How an object behaves during an interaction is determined by its methods. Visualizing these dynamic interactions helps to ensure that the classes are well-designed with correct methods and proper relationships.

- A design specification describes and justifies an application's design for its current and future developers. It contains the UML class, sequence, and state diagrams. Furthermore, it can include a test plan for internal testing.

- For the verification part of software V&V, software developers perform internal testing that includes unit and regression tests during the development iterations.

Part 3

Design the application right

Good design principles help us design the application right. These principles include minimizing dependencies among classes by hiding their implementations, leaving no surprises in our code, designing subclasses right, and choosing between "is-a" inheritance relationships and "has-a" aggregation relationships.

The design principles help us meet the challenges of change and complexity by creating cohesive and loosely coupled classes. We'll see in this part of the book that good design principles form the foundation of design patterns.

Hide class implementations

This chapter covers

- The importance of hiding the implementation of a class
- The Principle of Least Knowledge
- Lazy evaluation
- Getter and setter methods and immutable objects
- Rules of the Law of Demeter
- The Open-Closed Principle

Well-designed applications incorporate proven design principles. Chapter 4 discussed the importance of loose coupling in class design. Two loosely coupled classes have minimal dependencies on each other, which helps ensure that changes in one class don't cause changes in another class.

We can certainly be proud when other programmers admire and use the classes we wrote. But well-designed classes hide their implementations by making their instance variables and methods private. A class should expose by making public only those members that other programmers need to access.

This chapter covers design principles that support a strategy to minimize the dependencies among classes. Implementation hiding is an important part of encapsulation. If we hide the implementation of a class, other classes can't depend on what they can't access. Therefore, we can make changes to the implementation without forcing other classes to change in response.

The next chapter will cover more design principles. We'll see how the principles support each other and work together. Later chapters will cover design patterns that provide models we can use to develop custom solutions to common software architecture problems. The design principles are the foundation for the design patterns.

5.1   *The Principle of Least Knowledge and hidden implementations*

Recall that a class's instance variables represent state: each state of an object at run time is characterized by a unique set of values of its instance variables. A class's methods represent an object's runtime behavior. A class's *implementation* is the way we code instance variables and methods of the class.

For example, think again about the Book class from chapter 2 that represented a book in a catalogue. Its implementation may include components such as the book's title and author that represent inherent attributes of a book. No other class should be concerned about how we implement these attributes—they could be string values already assigned to the Book object or values dynamically looked up in a database when we ask for them. Certainly, a class from a customer application shouldn't be allowed to change a book's title or author. Therefore, these attributes should be private. However, the class should provide a public means for another class to access a book's title and author, but without needing to know their implementation.

The primary way to minimize the dependencies that class A has on class B is for class A to know as little as possible about the implementation of class B. This, of course, is the Principle of Least Knowledge (sections 2.3.2 and 4.2.2). This principle is also known as the *Law of Demeter*, named after the ancient Greek goddess of agriculture, with the allusion to growing software with loosely coupled classes. Class B should expose only as much of itself as necessary for other code to use the class, hiding the rest. By convention, hiding is accomplished in a Python class by starting the names of instance variables and methods with an underscore (_) to specify that they're private. Private methods, which should be called only by other methods of the class, are often called *helper methods*.

Hidden doesn't necessarily mean *invisible*. *Hidden* means *inaccessible*. *Hidden implementation code is effectively encapsulated.* We can make changes to the hidden implementation of a class without affecting any other code that uses the class. Because Python itself does not enforce privacy, we must trust all Python programmers to abide by the convention that an instance variable or method whose name starts with an underscore is intended to be a private and hidden implementation detail, and that whatever is hidden is subject to change.

Therefore, if we use a class that has an instance variable named _x or a method named _calculate_pay(), our code, which is outside the class, should not reference the variable or call the method, let alone depend on particular implementations.

If you change a member function in your class from public to private, then, for sure, someone will have written code in another class that depended on calling that function.

That's Murphy's Law for programmers!

Indeed, a good rule of thumb is the following: when designing a class, make every instance variable and method private (or protected) except those that must be public to enable other code to use the class. There's an old saying: "Once public, always public." If we make an instance variable or method public, we might not be able to change it to private later without forcing code rewrites.

5.2 Public getter and setter methods access hidden implementation selectively

In listing 5.1, the Item class hides how it implements state by making its instance variables _name, _weight, and _price private. Then the class uses public *getter* and *setter* methods, more formally known as *accessors* and *mutators*. Section 2.3 discussed the @property decorator, which creates a read-only property and associates a getter method with it. In class Item, the @price.setter decorator associates a public setter method with the price property.

Property setters

After we've used @property to create a property object, we can associate a setter method with it that sets a new value for a private instance variable, often with checks to ensure that the new value is valid. In class Item, the decorator @price.setter is associated with the setter method price(self, new_price). Then we can write an assignment to the property object:

```
item.price = 10.75
```

which automatically calls the setter method to verify and set the private instance variable _price to 10.75.

The @property decorator and property objects simplify and clarify our code and help to enforce hiding implementations.

Public properties of a class are meant to be used by any code instead of directly accessing and setting private instance variables. A getter method allows code to probe an Item object's current state without revealing how the state is implemented. A setter method allows code to modify an Item object's state, such as by providing a new value for private instance variable _price, without revealing how the state is implemented.

Listing 5.1   (Program 5.1 DemeterItem): item.py

```
class Item:
    def __init__(self, name, weight, price):
        self._name = name                          ← Hidden state
        self._weight = weight                         implementation
        self._price = price

    @property
    def name(self): return self._name        ←

    @property                                      Getter methods for
    def weight(self): return self._weight    ←    read-only properties

    @property
    def price(self): return self._price      ←

    @price.setter
    def price(self, new_price):              ←    Setter method
        assert new_price > 0
        self._price = new_price
```

As suggested in figure 5.1, the caller of the public getter method for the price does not
know how the class implements state. The method returns the current value of the private _price instance variable. In other versions of the application, the method could
obtain the price by other hidden means, such as a dynamic lookup in a price database.
Code that uses class Item should not depend on any particular implementation.

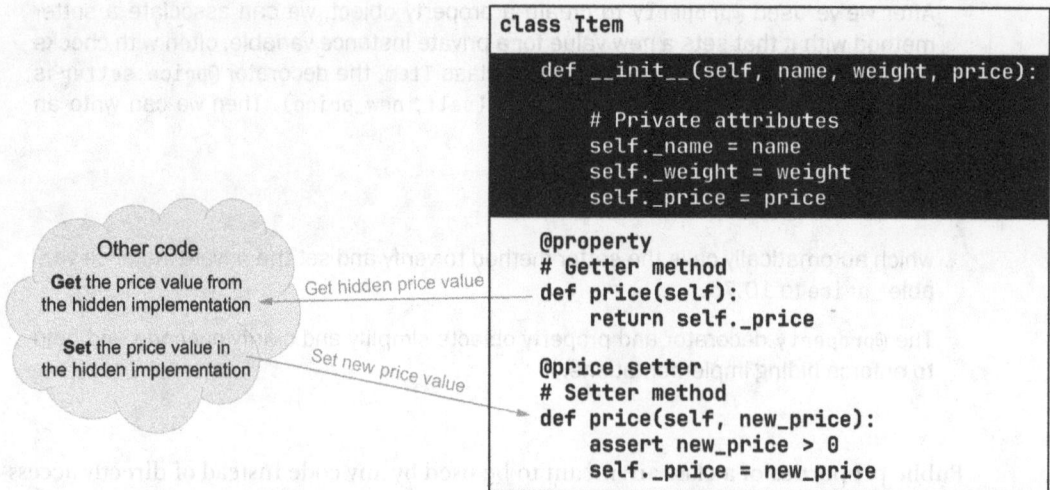

Figure 5.1   A getter method enables code to obtain the price value from an Item object's hidden state. A setter
method enables code to modify the price value in an Item object's hidden state. Neither method reveals how the
class implements state. For example, we might later decide to have getter method price() dynamically look up
the price from a database. We'll be able to make this change without affecting the method's caller.

By hiding how the class implements state and then providing public getter and setter methods, we can control how code can probe or modify an object's state at run time. For example, a runtime check can prevent a setter method from corrupting an object's state with an invalid value:

```
@price.setter
def price(self, new_price):
    assert new_price > 0
    self._price = new_price
```

A well-designed setter function won't allow an object to be put into an invalid state at run time.

That's just good defensive programming!

Of course, in a real application, we should handle a bad parameter value much more gracefully than by immediately aborting the program.

The test program main.py shows calling the getter and setter methods.

Listing 5.2   (Program 5.1 DemeterItem): main.py

```
from item import Item

if __name__ == '__main__':
    item = Item('whole chicken', 4.5, 10.31)

    print(f'  name: {item.name}')
    print(f'weight: {item.weight}')
    print(f' price: ${item.price}')
    print()

    item.price = 10.75
    print(f'new price: ${item.price}')
    print()

    item.price = -9.99
    print(f'new price: ${item.price}')
```

Implicit calls to the getter methods for the name, weight, and price

Implicit calls to the setter method for the price

The second call to the setter method attempts to set an erroneous price, causing the method to execute the assert statement to abort the program with a runtime error message. The program's output is

```
  name: whole chicken
weight: 4.5
 price: $10.31
```

```
new price: $10.75
----------------------------------------------------------------
AssertionError                    Traceback (most recent call last)
File ~/DemeterItem/main.py:15
     12 print(f'new price: ${item.price}')
     13 print()
---> 15 item.price = -9.99
     16 print(f'new price: ${item.price}')

File ~/DemeterItem/item.py:18, in Item.price(self, price)
     16 @price.setter
     17 def price(self, price):
---> 18     assert price > 0
     19     self._price = price
```

If we don't change the signatures of the public getter and setter methods (i.e., if we don't change how to call them), we'll be able to modify how the class implements state without forcing changes on code using the class. Section 5.4 discusses further the role of setter methods.

5.3   Class Date: A case study of implementation hiding

The development iterations of the following example application demonstrate the importance of hiding a class implementation and the problems we can run into if we don't hide the implementation. Let's suppose the application maintains the dates of scheduled appointments by using a Date class. A calendar date consists of a year, a month, and a day of the month. Therefore, class Date can hide its implementation by making its instance variables _year, _month, and _day private.

Day and date

Dates are important for many applications. Unfortunately, everyday terminology can be confusing. A *day* is any 24-hour period, which is midnight to midnight by convention. In the Gregorian calendar in use today throughout much of the world, a specific day is identified by a *date* consisting of three integer values: a *year*, a *month*, and a *day of the month*. An example date (written in the U.S. format) is 9/2/2025 for September 2, 2025.

In common use, the meanings of the words *day* and *date* often overlap. We refer to special days using only a month and a day of the month (e.g., to*day* is July 20, my birth*day* is September 2, New Year's *Day* is January 1). However, Don's birth*date* was January 10, 1938. To add to the confusion, the day of the month is itself called a *date* (e.g., today's *date* is the 12th). It should be clear from context which *day* is meant: for instance, Christmas *Day* is December 25, and there are 12 *days* of Christmas.

In our examples, class Date comprises three private instance variables—_year, _month, and _day—where _day is short for day of the month.

> If we were to design a Day class, it would have a one-to-one aggregation with the Date class: each Day object would have an instance variable that references a Date object representing its identifying date.

Next, suppose that the application must perform date arithmetic with the Date objects:

- What is the date n days from this date, where n can be positive (for a date after this date) or negative (for a date before this date)?
- How many days are there from this date to another date?

Unfortunately, date arithmetic with the Gregorian calendar is notoriously difficult because of its rules:

- April, June, September, and November each have 30 days.
- February has 28 days, except for leap years when it has 29 days.
- All other months have 31 days.
- Years that are divisible by four are leap years, except that after 1582, years divisible by 100 but not 400 are not leap years.
- There is no year 0. Year 1 CE is preceded by year 1 BCE (year –1).
- During the switchover to the Gregorian calendar, 10 days were dropped. The next date after October 4, 1582, was October 15, 1582.

5.3.1 Iteration 1: Date arithmetic with loops

Listing 5.3 shows the beginning of class Date. The private class constants are needed to perform date arithmetic according to the Gregorian calendar rules. The private state consists of _year, _month, and _day, which the constructor __init__() initializes. In an actual application, the constructor should check the values of the parameters. The three getter methods allow access to a Date object's state.

Special method __repr__() returns the string representation of a Date object in the U.S. format: that is, month/day/year. For example, 9/2/2025 is September 2, 2025. It calls the getter methods self.year, self.month, and self.day.

Listing 5.3 (Program 5.2 DateArithmetic-1): date.py (1 of 4; *very inefficient!*)

```
class Date:
    _JANUARY  = 1
    _FEBRUARY = 2
    _DECEMBER = 12

    _GREGORIAN_START_YEAR = 1582          Private constants for the
    _GREGORIAN_START_MONTH = 10           Gregorian calendar rules
    _GREGORIAN_START_DATE = 15
    _JULIAN_END_DATE = 4

    _DAYS_IN_MONTH = ( 31, 28, 31, 30, 31, 30,
                       31, 31, 30, 31, 30, 31 )
```

```
    def __init__(self, year, month, day):
        self._year = year
        self._month = month                    Private state
        self._day = day                        implementation

    @property
    def year(self): return self._year        ◄────────┐

    @property
    def month(self): return self._month      ◄───  Public getter methods

    @property
    def day(self): return self._day          ◄────────┘

    def __repr__(self):
        date_string = f'{self.month}/{self.day}/'
        if self.year > 0: date_string += str(self.year)
        else:             date_string += str(-self.year) + ' BCE'

        return date_string
```

In listing 5.4, the two private static methods return the number of days in a month and whether a year is a leap year, respectively. The private method _compare_to() compares the self date to the other date. If the former comes before the latter in time, the method returns –1. If the former comes after the latter in time, the method returns 1. If both dates are the same date, the method returns 0. What's important is whether the return value is negative, zero, or positive.

Listing 5.4   (Program 5.2 DateArithmetic-1): date.py (2 of 4; *very inefficient!*)

```
@staticmethod
def _days_in_month(year, month):
    if (month == Date._FEBRUARY) and Date._is_leap_year(year):
        return 29
    else:
        return Date._DAYS_IN_MONTH[month - 1]

@staticmethod
def _is_leap_year(year):
    if year%4 != 0: return False
    if year < Date._GREGORIAN_START_YEAR: return True

    return (year%100 != 0) or (year%400 == 0)

def _compare_to(self, other):        ◄───────  Returns a positive value if the
    if self._year > other.year: return 1       self date comes after the other
    if self._year < other.year: return -1      date; returns a negative value if
                                               the self date comes before the
    if self._month > other.month: return 1     other date; and returns 0 if
    if self._month < other.month: return -1    both dates are the same

    return self._day - other.day
```

Methods _next_date() and _previous_date() in the following listing each apply the Gregorian calendar rules to calculate the date that follows the self date and the date that precedes the self date, respectively. Each method returns a new Date object.

Listing 5.5 (Program 5.2 DateArithmetic-1): date.py (3 of 4; *very inefficient!*)

```
def _next_date(self):          ◄──┐  Applies Gregorian calendar
    y = self._year                 │  rules to return the next date
    m = self._month
    d = self._day

    if (    (y == Date._GREGORIAN_START_YEAR)
        and (m == Date._GREGORIAN_START_MONTH)
        and (d == Date._JULIAN_END_DATE)
    ): d = Date._GREGORIAN_START_DATE
    elif d < Date._days_in_month(y, m): d += 1
    else:
        d = 1
        m += 1

        if m > Date._DECEMBER:
            m = Date._JANUARY
            y += 1

            if y == 0: y += 1

    return Date(y, m, d)

def _previous_date(self):      ◄──┐  Applies Gregorian calendar rules
    y = self._year                 │  to return the previous date
    m = self._month
    d = self._day

    if (    (y == Date._GREGORIAN_START_YEAR)
        and (m == Date._GREGORIAN_START_MONTH)
        and (d == Date._GREGORIAN_START_DATE)
    ): d = Date._JULIAN_END_DATE
    elif d > 1: d -= 1
    else:
        m -= 1

        if m < Date._JANUARY:
            m = Date._DECEMBER
            y -= 1

            if y == 0: y -= 1

        d = Date._days_in_month(y, m)

    return Date(y, m, d)
```

Method add_days() in listing 5.6 starts with the self date and iterates day by day n days into the future if the value of argument n is positive, or n days into the past if the value of n is negative. Method days_from() starts with the self date and iterates day by day to count days either into the past or into the future, depending on whether this date falls after or before the Date argument, respectively. Both methods call private methods _previous_date() and _next_date() in their loops. The loops of method days_from() also calls private method _compare_to().

Listing 5.6   (Program 5.2 DateArithmetic-1): date.py (4 of 4; *very inefficient!*)

```
def add_days(self, n):
    date = self                    ◀────  Starts with a
                                          copy of this date
    while n > 0:
        date = date._next_date()   ┐  Loops n days
        n -= 1                     ┘  into the future

    while n < 0:
        date = date._previous_date()  ┐  Loops n days
        n += 1                         ┘  into the past

    return date

def days_from(self, other):
    date = self                    ◀────  Starts with a
                                          copy of this date
    n = 0

    while date._compare_to(other) > 0:
        date = date._previous_date()   ┐  Loops to count
        n += 1                          ┘  days in the past

    while date._compare_to(other) < 0:
        date = date._next_date()       ┐  Loops to count
        n -= 1                          ┘  days in the future

    return n
```

If the dates are far apart, the program will do a lot of looping!

Also, the calls to the member functions _previous_date() and _next_date() are expensive due to the Gregorian calendar rules.

It's even worse than that. Each iteration of methods add_days() and days_from() gets a new Date object when it calls _previous_date() or _next_date(). Each call to methods add_days() and days_from() returns only the Date object created by the last iteration, so the prior iterations fill memory with unused Date objects.

The next listing is a simple test program.

Listing 5.7 (Program 5.2 DateArithmetic-1): main.py *(very inefficient!)*

```
from date import Date

if __name__ == '__main__':
    date1 = Date(2025, 9, 2)
    date2 = Date(2027, 4, 3)

    print(f'{date1 = }')
    print(f'{date2 = }')

    print()

    count = date2.days_from(date1)
    print(f'{count = }')

    print(f'{date1.add_days(count) = }')
    print(f'        should be {date2 = }')

    print()

    count = date1.days_from(date2)
    print(f'{count = }')

    print(f'{date2.add_days(count) = }')
    print(f'        should be {date1 = }')
```

The output is as follows:

```
date1 = 9/2/2025
date2 = 4/3/2027

count = 578
date1.add_days(count) = 4/3/2027
        should be date2 = 4/3/2027

count = -578
date2.add_days(count) = 9/2/2025
        should be date1 = 9/2/2025
```

The application is functional and appears to perform the date arithmetic correctly. However, it is terribly inefficient. Method `add_days()` must loop as many times as the value of argument n. Method `days_from()` must loop as many times as there are days from the `self` date to the `Date` argument `other` and call method `_compare_to()` at the beginning of each loop. Calls to methods `_next_date()` and `_previous_date()` inside the loops are expensive because of the Gregorian calendar rules. Each call creates and returns a new `Date` object. This is clearly a poor design (figure 5.2). We need to backtrack and come up with a better design.

Start

1

Date arithmetic by looping day by day with Gregorian calendar rules

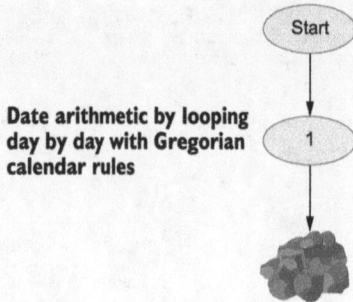

Figure 5.2   The version of class Date from iteration 1 performs date arithmetic correctly, but it does it poorly because of expensive looping day by day with the Gregorian calendar rules. This version deserves a lump of coal.

5.3.2   *Iteration 2: Julian day numbers simplify date arithmetic*

A much more efficient way to perform date arithmetic is to use a *Julian day number* to identify each day instead of the Gregorian year, month, and day of the month. The Julian day number of a particular day is the number of days since noon on January 1, 4713 BCE, of the Gregorian calendar. We'll use a Julian day number only at noon so that the number is always a whole number. Date arithmetic is trivial with Julian day numbers.

Julian day number

Do not be puzzled by the various calendar uses of the name "Julian." Astronomers use *Julian day numbers* to identify days rather than using the year, month, and day of the month.

Julian day numbers are not related to the Julian *calendar* introduced by the Roman emperor Julius Caesar in 45 BCE. The 16th-century historian Josephus Justus Scaliger invented the concept and named it after his father, Julius.

A Julian day number counts the *number of days* since noon on January 1, 4713 BCE, of the Gregorian calendar, so that day at noon has Julian day number 0. Because it takes hours of the day into account, a Julian day number can have a fractional part, but it's whole at noon.

There are complicated algorithms for converting between a day's Julian day number and its corresponding Gregorian year, month, and day of the month. The algorithms in the following application are from *Numerical Recipes, the Art of Scientific Computing*, 3rd edition, by William H. Press et al. (Cambridge University Press, 2007).

A useful milepost to check code that converts between Julian day numbers and Gregorian dates is Julian day number 2,440,000, which corresponds to the Gregorian date May 23, 1968.

The second design iteration of class Date uses Julian day numbers. As in the previous version of the class, we want to hide how we implement the state of its objects, so instance variable julian is private. We no longer need private instance variables _year, _month, and _day. But we'll need to be able to convert from year, month, and day values to a Julian number and vice versa. As seen in the next listing, this version needs two new class constants, _MAX_DAYS_IN_MONTH and _MONTHS_PER_YEAR.

Listing 5.8 (Program 5.3 DateArithmetic-2): date.py (1 of 2; could be better!)

```python
import math

class Date:
    _JANUARY  = 1
    _FEBRUARY = 2
    _DECEMBER = 12

    _GREGORIAN_START_YEAR = 1582
    _GREGORIAN_START_MONTH = 10
    _GREGORIAN_START_DATE = 15
    _JULIAN_END_DATE = 4

    _MAX_DAYS_IN_MONTH = 31
    _MONTHS_PER_YEAR   = 12

    _DAYS_IN_MONTH = ( 31, 28, 31, 30, 31, 30,
                       31, 31, 30, 31, 30, 31 )
```

Private static method _to_julian() converts a year, month, and day of the month to a Julian day number using an established algorithm. Given year, month, and day values, it returns the calculated Julian day number.

Listing 5.9 (Program 5.3 DateArithmetic-2): Date.Py (2 of 4; could be better!)

```python
    @staticmethod
    def _to_julian(year, month, day):      ◀─── Private static method to convert
                                                 year, month, and day of the
        y = year                                 month to a Julian day number
        if year < 0: y += 1

        m = month
        if month > Date._FEBRUARY: m += 1
        else:
            y -= 1
            m += 13

        j = (math.floor(math.floor(365.25*y) + math.floor(30.6001*m))
                + day + 1720995)

        term = (Date._MAX_DAYS_IN_MONTH
                   *(month + Date._MONTHS_PER_YEAR*year))
        GREGORIAN_CUTOFF = (
            Date._GREGORIAN_START_DATE +
            Date._MAX_DAYS_IN_MONTH
               *(Date._GREGORIAN_START_MONTH +
```

```
                          Date._MONTHS_PER_YEAR*Date._GREGORIAN_START_YEAR)
             )

        if day + term >= GREGORIAN_CUTOFF:
            x = math.floor(0.01*y)
            j += 2 - x + math.floor(0.25*x)

        return j          ◀━━━  Returns the calculated
                                Julian day number
```

Private static method _to_ymd() converts a Julian number to year, month, and day of the month values, which it returns as a tuple.

Listing 5.10   (Program 5.3 DateArithmetic-2): date.py (3 of 4: could be better!)

```
    @staticmethod
    def _to_ymd(julian):
        GREGORIAN_CUTOFF = 2299161      ◀━━  Private static method to convert
                                             a Julian day number to year,
        ja = julian                          month, and day of the month

        if julian >= GREGORIAN_CUTOFF:
            jalpha = math.floor(
                (float(julian - 1867216) - 0.25)/36524.25)
            ja += 1 + jalpha - math.floor(0.25*jalpha)

        jb = ja + 1524
        jc = math.floor(
                6680.0 + (float(jb - 2439870) - 122.1)/365.25)
        jd = math.floor(365*jc + (0.25*jc))
        je = math.floor((jb - jd)/30.6001)

        day = jb - jd - math.floor(30.6001*je)

        month = je - 1
        if month > Date._DECEMBER: month -= 12

        year = jc - 4715
        if month > Date._FEBRUARY: year -= 1
        if year <= 0: year -= 1

        return (year, month, day)   ◀━━━┘  Returns a tuple
```

Listing 5.11 shows that the __init__() constructor receives its argument values in list parms to handle two cases. It can be called with a single argument, a Julian day number, in which case the constructor sets the value of _julian directly. Or the constructor can be called with three arguments—year, month, and day of the month values—in which case it must calculate the value of _julian by calling method _to_julian() with the three argument values. The public getter methods for the year, month, and day properties must first convert the Julian day number by calling _to_ymd() and then return the appropriate value from the tuple.

Using Julian day numbers makes date arithmetic much more efficient. Method add_days() simply adds the value of argument n to the self date's Julian day number to create and return a new Date object. Method days_from() subtracts the Julian day number of the other date from the self date's Julian day number and returns the number of days.

Because we hid the implementation of class Date, we were able to change the implementation radically without causing code that uses the class to change. We can call the Date constructor to create a Date object as before and call the public getter methods _year(), _month(), and _day() without change to get the date's year, month, and day of the month. Furthermore, we can call the public methods add_days() and days_from() the same way as before and get the same expected results.

Listing 5.11   (Program 5.3 DateArithmetic-2): date.py (4 of 4; could be better!)

```
def __init__(self, *parms):
    if len(parms) == 1:
        self._julian = parms[0]          ◄──  Julian number passed
    else:                                     as a single argument
        self._julian = Date._to_julian(*parms)   ◄──  Year, month, and day passed
                                                       as three arguments
@property
def year(self):
    year, _, _ = Date._to_ymd(self._julian)   ◄──┐
    return year                                    │
                                                   │
@property                                          │
def month(self):                                   First converts the
    _, month, _ = Date._to_ymd(self._julian)  ◄──  Julian day number to
    return month                                   year, month, day
                                                   │
@property                                          │
def day(self):                                     │
    _, _, day = Date._to_ymd(self._julian)    ◄──┘
    return day

def add_days(self, n):                        ┌─ Returns a new Date object after an
    return Date(self._julian + n)        ◄──  │  addition to the Julian day number

def days_from(self, other):                   │ Returns the result of a
    return self._julian - other._julian  ◄──  │ subtraction of Julian day numbers
```

The same test program (listing 5.7) produces the same output.

Although it may do date arithmetic very efficiently, the second iteration of class Date introduced a different inefficiency. Private method _to_julian() computes the Julian day number corresponding to a Gregorian year, month, and day of the month. Conversely, private method _to_ymd() converts the year, month, and day of the month to a corresponding Julian day number. Both are complicated due to the Gregorian calendar rules.

Each of the public getter methods year(), month(), and day() must first call _to_ymd() before it can return the year, month, or day of the month, respectively. Special method __repr__() also relies on _to_ymd().

We made some
operations faster
but others slower!

If you squeeze one part of
a balloon, you might make
another part bigger!

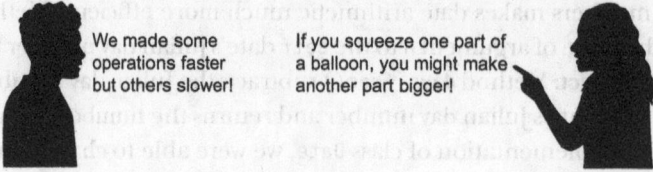

We still don't have a good design (figure 5.3). But we can improve the efficiency of
class Date with a third iteration.

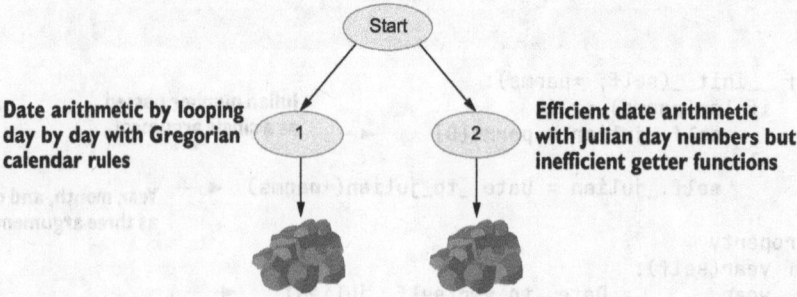

Start

Date arithmetic by looping
day by day with Gregorian
calendar rules

1

2

Efficient date arithmetic
with Julian day numbers but
inefficient getter functions

Figure 5.3   The version of class Date from iteration 2 performs data arithmetic very efficiently using
Julian day numbers, but getter methods for the year, month, or day of the month must each call an
expensive conversion algorithm. We get yet another lump of coal.

5.3.3   *Iteration 3: A hybrid approach with lazy evaluation*

How can we have fast access to the year, month, and day of the month along with efficient date arithmetic? This third iteration of class Date takes a hybrid approach. As
shown in the following listing, this version has all four private instance variables: _year,
_month, _day, and _julian.

Listing 5.12   (Program 5.4 DateArithmetic-3): date.py (1 of 2: efficient hybrid)

```
class Date:
    ...
    def __init__(self, *parms):
        if len(parms) == 1:
            self._julian = parms[0]
            self._ymd_valid = False
            self._julian_valid = True
        else:
            self._year, self._month, self._day = parms
            self._ymd_valid = True
            self._julian_valid = False
```

The values of _year, _month, and _day
are valid after the Date object is
created, but the value of _julian is not.

The value of _julian is valid after the Date object is created,
but the values of _year, _month, and _day are not.

```
                                                          ┌─ Validates the values of
    def _validate_ymd(self):              ◄──────┘   _year, _month, and _day
        if not self._ymd_valid:
            self._year, self._month, self._day = \
                                       Date._to_ymd(self._julian)
            self._ymd_valid = True

    def _validate_julian(self):     ◄──┐ Validates the value of _julian
        if not self._julian_valid:
            self._julian = \
                Date._to_julian(self._year, self._month, self._day)
            self._julian_valid = True
```

Boolean instance variables _ymd_valid and _julian_valid help to ensure that, whenever necessary, the value of _julian and the values of the trio _year, _month, and _day are synchronized. Private method _validate_ymd() synchronizes the values of the trio with the current value of _julian. Private method _validate_julian() synchronizes the value of _julian with the current values of the trio.

This code is more efficient because instance variables _ymd_valid and _julian_valid prevent unnecessary calls to the expensive conversion methods _to_ymd() and _to_julian() when the values of _year, _month, and _day are already synchronized with the value of _julian.

In the following listing, public getter methods year(), month(), and day() each must first call method _validate_ymd() to ensure that the value it returns is synchronized with the current value of _julian. Public methods add_days() and days_from(), both of which perform date arithmetic with Julian day numbers, must each call method _validate_julian() to ensure that the value of _julian is synchronized with the current values of _year, _month, and _day.

Listing 5.13   (Program 5.4 DateArithmetic-3): date.py (2 of 2: efficient hybrid)

```
    @property
    def year(self):
        self._validate_ymd()      ◄──────┐
        return self._year

    @property
    def month(self):
        self._validate_ymd()      ◄──────  Validates the values of _year, _month, and
        return self._month                 _day before returning their values

    @property
    def day(self):
        self._validate_ymd()      ◄──────┘
        return self._day

    def add_days(self, n):
        self._validate_julian()   ◄──────┐ Validates the Julian numbers
        return Date(self._julian + n)     ▼ before doing date arithmetic
```

```
def days_from(self, other):
    self._validate_julian()          ◄──┐   Validates the Julian numbers
    other._validate_julian()         ◄──┘   before doing date arithmetic
    return self._julian - other._julian
```

We call method _to_ymd() only when we're about to access the values of _year, _month, and _day. We call method _to_julian() only when we're about to perform date arithmetic using the value of _julian. This is an example of the *Lazy Evaluation Principle*, where we delay performing a calculation until we need the result, which makes our code more efficient by preventing unnecessary calculations.

> **The Lazy Evaluation Principle**
>
> If at run time we don't need the result of a calculation immediately, we should be lazy and postpone the calculation until we need the result. The Lazy Evaluation Principle is especially useful to improve performance if the calculation is expensive or time-consuming.

A **Date** object in effect caches the values of **_year**, **_month**, and **_day** and the value of **_julian**. It recomputes them only when necessary.

So it pays to be lazy and wait until the last possible moment to do an expensive calculation!

Because we hid the implementation of class Date with private instance variables and provided public getter methods, we were again able to refactor the code to further improve its efficiency. We encapsulated the implementation changes. Code that uses class Date only needs to know that a Date object's state is characterized by its year, month, and day of the month, and that Date objects can perform date arithmetic efficiently. We've hidden the use of Julian day numbers to support date arithmetic (figure 5.4).

5.4 *Public setter methods carefully modify hidden implementation*

A public getter method allows code to probe an object's state without revealing how the state is implemented. On the other hand, a public setter method allows code to modify an object's state, also without revealing how the state is implemented.

None of the three versions of class Date in this chapter so far have provided any public setter methods. Therefore, once we've constructed a Date object at run time with year, month, and day of the month values, the object is *immutable*—there is no way to change its state. Immutable objects are often justified by an application's logic. We'll learn more about immutable objects in section 5.7.

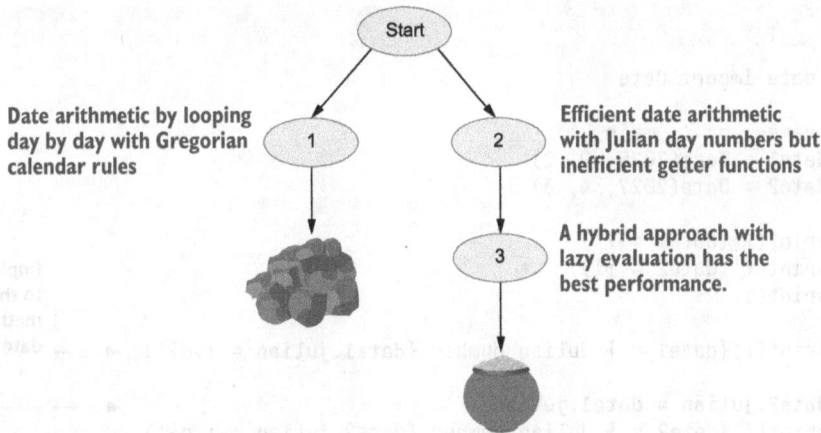

Figure 5.4 The version of class `Date` from iteration 3 is a hybrid that uses lazy evaluation. It has the best performance of the three versions. This version deserves the pot of gold.

Listing 5.14 shows another version of class `Date`. This version selectively allows access to another part of its implementation: its Julian day number. Public method `julian()` is now both a getter method and a setter method. As a setter method, it changes the state of a `Date` object, and it does it defensively in a safe manner. Therefore, in this version, `Date` objects are mutable.

Listing 5.14 (Program 5.5 DateArithmetic-4): date.py (mutable)

```
class Date:
    ...
    @property
    def julian(self):                        Getter method for
        self._validate_julian()              the Julian day number
        return self._julian

    @julian.setter
    def julian(self, j):                     Setter method for the
        assert(j >= 0)                       Julian day number

        self._julian = j
        self._julian_valid = True
        self._ymd_valid = False
    ...
}
```

Method `julian()` behaves as both a getter and a setter. As a setter, it checks the value of its argument before using it and aborts the program if the value is negative. A real application should handle this error more gracefully than immediately aborting.

The new test program exercises accessing and setting a `Date` object's Julian day number.

Listing 5.15   (Program 5.5 DateArithmetic-4): main.py (mutable)

```python
from date import Date

if __name__ == '__main__':
    date1 = Date(2025, 9, 2)
    date2 = Date(2027, 4, 3)

    print(f'{date1 = }')
    print(f'{date2 = }')
    print()

    print(f'{date1 = } Julian number {date1.julian = :,d}')

    date2.julian = date1.julian
    print(f'{date2 = } Julian number {date2.julian = :,d}')
    print()

    for j in [0, 2440000, 3000000]:
        date1.julian = j
        print(f'set Julian number {j = :9,d} ==> {date1 = }')
```

> Implicit call to the getter method date1.julian

> Implicit calls to the setter method date2.julian and the getter method date1.julian

The printed results are as follows:

```
date1 = 9/2/2025
date2 = 4/3/2027

date1 = 9/2/2025 Julian number date1.julian = 2,460,921
date2 = 9/2/2025 Julian number date2.julian = 2,460,921

set Julian number j =         0 ==> date1 = 1/1/4713 BCE
set Julian number j = 2,440,000 ==> date1 = 5/23/1968
set Julian number j = 3,000,000 ==> date1 = 8/15/3501
```

5.5   *Beware of dangerous setter methods*

Should we always favor providing setter methods? What about the values of the trio year, month, and day of the month in the hidden implementation? Let's see what can happen if we provide additional setter methods.

Listing 5.16   (Program 5.6 DateArithmetic-5): date.py (dangerous setters)

```python
class Date:
    ...
    @year.setter
    def year(self, y):
        assert(y != 0)

        self._validate_ymd()
        self._year = y
        self._julian_valid = False
```

```
@month.setter
def month(self, m):
    assert(Date._JANUARY <= m <= Date._DECEMBER)

    self._validate_ymd()
    self._month = m
    self._julian_valid = False


@day.setter
def day(self, d):
    assert(1 <= d <= 31)

    self._validate_ymd()
    self._day = d
    self._julian_valid = False
    ...
}
```

In an actual application, setter method set_day() will need a much more comprehensive validation of its parameter value that takes into consideration the current month and year. The following listing is a test program for this poorly designed version of class Date.

Listing 5.17   **(Program 5.6 DateArithmetic-5): main.py (dangerous setters)**

```
from date import Date

if __name__ == '__main__':
    date = Date(2030, 1, 31)
    print(f'starting: {date = } {date.julian = }')

    date.month = 2                              ◄────  Problematic setting
    print(f'modified: {date = } {date.julian = }')       of the month

    j = date.julian
    date.julian = j
    print(f'surprise: {date = } {date.julian = }')
```

The output is

```
starting: date = 1/31/2030 date.julian = 2462533
modified: date = 2/31/2030 date.julian = 2462564
surprise: date = 3/3/2030 date.julian = 2462564
```

By providing setter methods to set a Date object's private _year, _month, and _day instance variables individually, we were able to put the object into an invalid state: the nonexistent date February 31, 2030. Then, by resetting the Julian day number of that nonexistent date, we ended up with March 3, 2030—a nasty surprise. We must never allow a setter method to put an object into an invalid state. The next chapter will discuss code surprises.

Poorly designed setter functions can get us into a lot of trouble!

We must practice defensive programming with setter functions. Also, not every private member variable should have a public setter function.

If we want to allow setting the year, month, and day of the month of an existing Date object, a much safer alternative is to provide a setter method that modifies all three at once. Then it will be much easier in an actual application for the setter method to check the arguments to ensure that the combination of all three values results in a valid Date object. Of course, the Date constructor that takes year, month, and day of the month values should also check those values.

5.6   Rules from the Law of Demeter support the Principle of Least Knowledge

The Law of Demeter prescribes several rules that help us design proper loosely coupled classes and thereby support the Principle of Least Knowledge. By following these rules, we avoid designing a class that has certain problematic dependencies on another class. Specifically, they tell whether a method a() of class A can call a method b() of another class B:

1   Method a() can call method b() on a class B object if class A aggregates the object (i.e., class A has an instance variable whose value is a reference to a class B object).

2   Method a() can call method b() on a class B object if the object was passed as an argument to a().

3   Method a() can call method b() on a class B object if a() instantiated the class B object.

4   Method a() should not call method b() on a class B object that was returned by a call to method c() on a class C object.

The Law of Demeter basically says that a class should only call methods of objects that are close to it. In rule 4, methods a() and b() are not considered to be close, because the class B object comes from class C. We want to minimize the dependencies of class A on class C.

Classes DemeterAuto, Engine, and Sparkplug provide examples that obey and disobey the law's rules.

Listing 5.18   (Program 5.7 DemeterAuto): auto.py

```
class Sparkplug:
    def __init__(self, name):
        self._name = name

    def replace(self):
```

```
        print(f'Replaced sparkplug {self._name}')

class Engine:
    def __init__(self, sparkplug):
        self._sparkplug = sparkplug

    @property
    def sparkplug(self): return self._sparkplug

    def replace_sparkplug(self):
        self._sparkplug.replace()
```

Obeys: _splarkplug is an instance variable of class Engine (rule 1).

```
class DemeterAuto:
    def __init__(self, engine):
        self._engine = engine

    def service_sparkplug(self, plug):
        plug.replace()
```

Obeys: plug is a parameter of method service_sparkplug() (rule 2).

```
    def maintain_auto(self):
        self._engine.replace_sparkplug()
```

Obeys: _engine is an instance variable of class DemeterAuto (rule 1).

```
        plug1 = self._engine.sparkplug
        plug1.replace()
```

Disobeys: the value of plug1 is an object returned by object _engine (rule 4).

```
        plug2 = Sparkplug('plug2')
        plug2.replace()
```

Obeys: the value of plug2 is instantiated by method maintain_auto() (rule 3).

5.7   But is the implementation really hidden?

To write an application that stores employee records, we could have a class `Employee` that records an employee's birthdate via a reference to a `Date` object. We want an `Employee` object to be immutable by a regular user of the application: after we've created an object, the employee's ID, name, and birthdate should not be changeable by such a user. All three private instance variables (`_employee_id`, `_name`, and `_birthdate`) are in the hidden state implementation, and the class itself has no setter methods.

Let's assume that a different class of the application, say `EmployeeForAdmin`, also aggregates class `Date` but needs to allow an administrative user to correct an error in an employee's birthdate. Therefore, we can use our mutable version of class `Date` with its public `julian()` setter method. However, a regular user should not be able to modify an employee's birthdate. Is making `_birthdate` private sufficient?

Listing 5.19   (Program 5.8 HiddenDate-1): employee.py (faulty design)

```
class Employee:
    def __init__(self, employee_id, name, birthdate):
        self._employee_id = employee_id
        self._name = name
        self._birthdate = birthdate

    @property
```

```
    def employee_id(self): return self._employee_id

    @property
    def name(self): return self._name

    @property
    def birthdate(self):  return self._birthdate

    def __str__(self):
        return (
            f'Employee #{self._employee_id}\n'
            f'   Name: {self._name}\n'
            f'   Birthdate: {self._birthdate}\n'
        )
```

Because class `Employee` has no setter methods, is an `Employee` object truly immutable? The following listing is a test program.

Listing 5.20   (Program 5.8 HiddenDate-1): main.py (faulty design)

```
from date import Date
from employee import Employee

if __name__ == '__main__':
    marys_birthdate = Date(2000, 1, 10)                         Is this Employee
    mary = Employee(1234567890, 'Mary', marys_birthdate)       object immutable?
    print(mary)

    marys_birthdate.julian += 366     ◄───  Changes the birthdate
    print(mary)                              year to 2001

    date = mary.birthdate            Changes the birthdate
    date.julian += 365               year to 2002
    print(mary)
```

Here's the output:

```
Employee #1234567890
  Name: Mary
  Birthdate: 1/10/2000

Employee #1234567890
  Name: Mary
  Birthdate: 1/10/2001

Employee #1234567890
  Name: Mary
  Birthdate: 1/10/2002
```

Obviously, the `Employee` object is not immutable. There were several design failures:

- We first dynamically created a new `Birthday` object and assigned it to variable `marys_birthdate`. We used `marys_birthdate` to create the `Employee` object.

- Because we had a reference to the `Birthday` object that is now embedded in the `Employee` object, we were able to use that reference, `marys_birthdate`, to change the employee's birth year.

- Using the `birthdate` property, we set variable `date` to the `Employee` object's embedded `Birthday` object. We used the variable to change the employee's birth year again.

The **birthdate** property exposed my "hidden" implementation.

This is a subtle design fault that is often overlooked.

This surely is a subtle design fault. If a class instantiates objects that are supposed to be immutable, but it has improperly designed getter methods, we can inadvertently modify an object's state at run time.

There are remedies to ensure that the `Employee` objects are immutable, as shown in the following listing. The class constructor should store a *copy* of the `Date` object that is passed to it. The property should return a *copy* of the embedded `Date` object. Then it will not be possible to change the birthdate embedded in the `Employee` object.

Listing 5.21 (Program 5.9 HiddenDate-2): employee.py (corrected design)

```python
from copy import copy

class Employee:
    def __init__(self, employee_id, name, birthdate):
        self._employee_id = employee_id
        self._name = name
        self._birthdate = copy(birthdate)          ◄──── Stores a copy of the Date
                                                         object that is passed in
    @property
    def employee_id(self): return self._employee_id

    @property
    def name(self): return self._name

    @property
    def birthdate(self): return copy(self._birthdate)   ◄──── Returns a copy of the
                                                               stored Date object
    def __str__(self):
        return (
            f'Employee #{self._employee_id}\n'
            f'  Name: {self._name}\n'
            f'  Birthdate: {self._birthdate}\n'
        )
```

With the same test program, the output shows that the employee's birthdate did not change:

```
Employee #1234567890
  Name: Mary
  Birthdate: 1/10/2000

Employee #1234567890
  Name: Mary
  Birthdate: 1/10/2000

Employee #1234567890
  Name: Mary
  Birthdate: 1/10/2000
```

5.8   *The Open-Closed Principle supports code stability*

In chapter 2, during the third development iteration of the book catalogue application, we created several subclasses for the superclass Attributes. Figure 5.5 shows that ill-fated design.

Although we ultimately determined that having many subclasses was a poor design for the application, figure 5.5 is a good example of the Open-Closed Principle, according to which we should close a class against modification but open it for subclassing (section 2.3.3). It assumes we are confident that a class has captured all the common attributes and behaviors of a set of objects and therefore the design of that class should not change. That supports code stability. However, we allow extending the class for

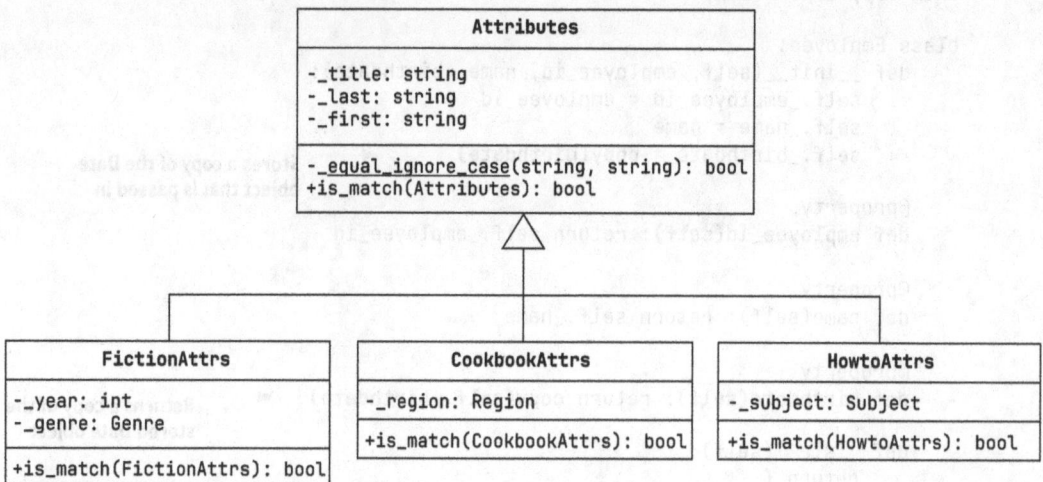

Figure 5.5   A design of the book catalogue application with superclass Attributes and its subclasses. In the class diagram for Attributes, the name of private method _equal_ignore_case() is underlined to indicate that it is static.

objects that have attributes and behaviors beyond the common ones. In other words, the closed class is the superclass, and the extensions are its subclasses.

The Open-Closed Principle is another way to design classes with hidden implementations. By denoting the instance variables and methods of the superclass to be private, we can hide how we implement the common parts of the state and behavior inherited by its subclasses. In class `Attributes`, instance variables `_title`, `_last`, and `_first` are meant to be private. `FictionAttrs` extends `Attributes`, so a `FictionAttrs` object hides how it implements the `_title`, `_last`, and `_first` parts of its state. The subclass extends the hidden state implementation with the addition of private `_year` and `_genre` instance variables.

The following listing is another example of the Open-Closed Principle. Suppose that class `Mammal` has all the common attributes and behaviors of mammals that a particular application needs. Therefore, we can close this class.

Listing 5.22   (Program 5.10 Mammals): mammal.py

```python
from abc import abstractmethod

class Mammal:
    def __init__(self, weight, height):
        self.__weight = weight          # Hidden state implementation
        self.__height = height          # of this superclass

    @property
    def weight(self): return self.__weight      # Common public getters

    @property
    def height(self): return self.__height

    def _snore(self):                   # Private behavior implemented
        print('Zzzz')                   # by the subclasses

    @abstractmethod
    def eat(self):
        pass
                                        # Common public behaviors to be
                                        # implemented by the subclasses
    @abstractmethod
    def perform(self):
        pass

    def sleep(self):                    # Common public behavior
        print('close eyes')            # implemented by this superclass
        self._snore()
```

We close class `Mammal`, but we can keep it open for extension. In the following two listings, subclasses `Human` and `Cat` each extend `Mammal` by adding their instance variables and methods. Each subclass must define abstract methods `eat()` and `perform()`.

Listing 5.23   (Program 5.10 Mammals): human.py

```
from mammal import Mammal

class Human(Mammal):
    def __init__(self, weight, height, needs_glasses):    ← Initializes the
        super().__init__(weight, height)                     superclass object
        self._needs_glasses = needs_glasses    ← Hidden extended state
                                                  implementation for humans
    def _read_book(self):    ←
        if self._needs_glasses:       Hidden extended behavior
            print('squint')           implementation for humans
        print('turn pages')

    def eat(self)
        print('eat with knife and fork')    ← Subclass implementation
                                               of abstract methods
    def perform(self):    ←
        self._read_book()
        self.sleep()
```

Subclass Human keeps the implementation of its part of the state (instance variable _needs_glasses) and behavior (method _read_book()) hidden.

Listing 5.24   (Program 5.10 Mammals): cat.py

```
from mammal import Mammal

class Cat(Mammal):
    def __init__(self, weight, height, fur_factor):    ← Initializes the
        super().__init__(weight, height)                  superclass object
        self._fur_factor = fur_factor    ← Hidden extended state
                                            implementation for cats
    def _shed(self):    ←
        if self._fur_factor > 1.0:       Hidden extended behavior
            print('shed a lot')          implementation for cats
        else:
            print('shed a little')

    def eat(self):    ←
        print('eat from a bowl')    Subclass implementation
                                    of abstract methods
    def perform(self):    ←
        self._shed()
```

Subclass Cat keeps the implementation of its part of the state (instance variable _fur_factor) and behavior (method _shed()) hidden.

Because they are declared to be abstract in superclass Mammal, both subclasses must implement the public methods eat() and perform(). The implementation of the common parts of the state (height and weight) and behavior (snoring) of each subclass is hidden by their superclass Mammal. The following listing is a test program.

Listing 5.25   (Program 5.10 Mammals): main.py

```python
from human import Human
from cat import Cat

if __name__ == '__main__':
    ron = Human(77.11, 1.85, True)
    print('Human Ron')
    print(f'{ron.weight = } kg, {ron.height = } m')
    ron.eat()
    ron.perform()

    print()

    buddy = Cat(5.55, 0.30, 1.25)
    print('Cat Buddy')
    print(f'{buddy.weight = } kg, {buddy.height = } m')
    buddy.eat()
    buddy.perform()
```

The output is as follows:

```
Human Ron
ron.weight = 77.11 kg, ron.height = 1.85 m
eat with knife and fork
squint
turn pages
close eyes
Zzzz

Cat Buddy
buddy.weight = 5.55 kg, buddy.height = 0.3 m
eat from a bowl
shed a lot
```

We implement a common core implementation in a superclass and lock it from further changes to support code stability, but we can extend the implementation in subclasses. We can hide the common and extended implementations.

Summary

- Python programmers must respect the convention that names of instance variables and methods that begin with an underscore are denoted to be private and therefore have hidden implementations.

- Minimize dependencies on a class by hiding how the class implements state to support encapsulation. Hide instance variables and methods by denoting them to be private. When the hidden implementation of a class is encapsulated, we can refactor the implementation to improve it without causing changes to any code using the class.

- Properties allow controlled access to hidden object state. A property can return values from an object's state without revealing how the state is implemented. A property setter can modify an object's state without revealing how the state is implemented.

- A property should never allow an object to be put into an invalid state. We must be careful what property setters to provide.

- An immutable class creates objects that cannot be modified after we've constructed them. Such a class should not provide property setters that modify an object's state.

- A class whose objects are supposed to be immutable must not provide references to hidden state implementation because that would allow other code to use the references to modify an object's state at run time.

- According to the Lazy Evaluation Principle, runtime performance should be improved by delaying an expensive calculation until its results are needed.

- The Law of Demeter prescribes rules to guide designing classes that have no problematic dependencies on other classes. Method a() of class A can call method b() on a class B object if class A aggregates class B, or if the class B object was passed as an argument to method a(), or if method a() instantiated the class B object. Method a() should not call method b() if the class B object was returned by another object's method.

- The Open-Closed Principle says to close a superclass for modification but open it for extensions by subclasses. The superclass can hide and encapsulate the implementation of the common parts of the state and behavior inherited by its subclasses. This principle supports code stability.

*Don't surprise
your users*

6

This chapter covers

- The Principle of Least Astonishment and how to avoid surprising your users
- Preventing unexpectedly poor runtime performance
- Careful coding with Python lists, tuples, and arrays
- Refactoring code to improve performance
- Applying programming by contract to a class and its methods

We all love surprise parties, but being surprised by the results of a function call is a definite sign of poor design. Well-designed software should not contain any surprises that can cause runtime logic errors or poor performance.

Ideally, when we design a class, its objects will behave and perform just the way its users expect. A user can be another programmer who uses the class or an end user who interacts with the application. Unexpected behavior can lead to runtime logic errors or applications that don't perform well.

This chapter covers some common unwanted code surprises and ways to eliminate them. Some bad surprises are simply how Python works. However, other surprises are a result of preventable coding faults, such as the common off-by-one error. A well-named function or method won't mislead another programmer into believing that it does something other than what its name suggests.

We can avoid the surprise of poor performance with more efficient programming or a better choice of data structures. Even a built-in data structure such as a list can be inefficient if we don't take advantage of its features. The concept of programming by contract can eliminate many surprises by making explicit what another programmer can expect from a class we wrote.

6.1   No surprises and the Principle of Least Astonishment

There are many ways in which poor design can cause surprises. The *Principle of Least Astonishment* states that there should be few, if any, surprises in our code.

The Principle of Least Astonishment

There should be few, if any, surprises for programmers (including ourselves later) who use our code. Surprises can cause logic and runtime errors and make code difficult to maintain.

This section covers two sources of surprises: off-by-one errors and misnamed functions. The common off-by-one error can cause hard-to-find logic errors in a program, but it is easily preventable as long as we are careful about such matters as how many times a loop executes. A function or method that we wrote and misnamed may cause another programmer to experience perplexing logic errors by assuming the function does something other than what its name suggests. Section 6.2 is devoted to another insidious source of surprises: poor performance.

6.1.1   Off-by-one errors

It's easy, even for an experienced programmer, to make an off-by-one error, where a computed value is one more or one less than expected, or an operation occurs one more or one fewer time than expected. These deceptive errors are hard to find, and they can cause surprising runtime logic errors. A classic off-by-one error is a loop that goes around one too few or one too many times.

Listing 6.1   (Program 6.1 SurpriseLoop): main.py

```
if __name__ == '__main__':
    count = 0
    i = 5
    while i <= 10:          ◄───┐  Potential off-by-one error: the loop executes not
        count += 1               10 − 5 = 5 times, but 10 − 5 + 1 = 6 times.
```

```
        print(f'{count = }, {i = }')
        i += 1
```

Indeed, this loop executes six times:

```
count = 1, i = 5
count = 2, i = 6
count = 3, i = 7
count = 4, i = 8
count = 5, i = 9
count = 6, i = 10
```

> Of course, if the loop termination is instead **i < 10**, the loop will indeed iterate five times. But then **i** will not reach the value 10.

> I can see how off-by-one errors are common with loops.

Here's a sneakier example. Suppose we have an application that maintains the dates of scheduled appointments. Listing 6.2 shows a Date class that the application can use. Its private instance variables year, month, and day record a date's year, month, and day of the month, respectively, and we pass integer values to the constructor to initialize those variables. Therefore, if we pass the values 2025, 2, and 4, we expect to create a Date object that represents the date February 4, 2025. To keep this example short, we'll leave off checking the constructor's parameter values.

Listing 6.2   (Program 6.2 SurpriseDate-1): date .py (off-by-one error!)

```
class Date:
    _MONTH_NAMES = (
        'JAN', 'FEB', 'MAR', 'APR', 'MAY', 'JUN',
        'JUL', 'AUG', 'SEP', 'OCT', 'NOV', 'DEC'
    )

    def __init__(self, year, month, day):
        self._year = year
        self._month = month
        self._day = day

    def __str__(self):
        return (f'{Date._MONTH_NAMES[self._month]} '
                f'{self._day}, {self._year}')
```

Private class tuple of array of month names

Private class variable _MONTH_NAMES is a private static constant string array of month names. The special method __str__() returns a Date object in the form "month day, year," where the month is a capitalized three-letter abbreviation, such as

FEB 4, 2025

The following listing is a short test program.

Listing 6.3   (Program 6.2 SurpriseDate-1): main.py (off-by-one error!)

```python
from date import Date

if __name__ == '__main__':
    date = Date(2025, 2, 4)  # February 4, 2025
    print(date)
```

The output from this program is

```
MAR 4, 2025
```

A nasty surprise! We expected FEB, not MAR.

This is only one example of the ubiquitous off-by-one error caused by list and tuple index values beginning with 0 and not 1. This surprise is compounded by the Date class having a major inconsistency: year and day of the month values are exact, but a month value apparently must be one less. This is not obvious to the programmer who uses class Date, and hence the runtime logic error.

A well-designed class needs to remove the surprise. The following listing shows one way to do so. Special method __str__() silently subtracts 1 from self._month when indexing into the MONTH_NAMES string array.

Listing 6.4   (Program 6.3 SurpriseDate-2): date.py

```python
class Date:
    ...

    def __str__(self):
        return (f'{Date._MONTH_NAMES[self._month - 1]} '   ◀─── Subtracts 1 from
                f'{self._day}, {self._year}')                    the month value
```

This simple fix removes the surprise, and the output is correct:

```
FEB 4, 2025
```

Subtracting 1 from month has a tiny runtime cost. But if the cost is a concern, then there is another solution.

Listing 6.5   (Program 6.4 SurpriseDate-3): date.py

```python
class Date:
    _MONTH_NAMES = (
        '',                                          ◀─── Dummy first element
        'JAN', 'FEB', 'MAR', 'APR', 'MAY', 'JUN',
        'JUL', 'AUG', 'SEP', 'OCT', 'NOV', 'DEC'
    )
```

```
    def __init__(self, year, month, day):
        self._year = year
        self._month = month
        self._day = day

    def __str__(self):
        return (f'{Date._MONTH_NAMES[self._month]} '  ◀──┤ No longer needs
                f'{self._day}, {self._year}')                  to subtract 1
```

Now there is a dummy first element (an empty string) in _MONTH_NAMES[0], and special method __str_() no longer needs to subtract 1 from self._month. We've eliminated this runtime cost at the expense of one unused array element. Again, class Date behaves as expected, and the test program produces the correct output. However, we must be careful that this latter solution doesn't create a surprise elsewhere. For example, the tuple _MONTH_NAMES contains 13 values rather than 12, as may be expected.

6.1.2 *Misnamed functions can mislead their callers*

A frequent source of unwanted surprises for a programmer using another programmer's code is a poorly named function that does something unexpected when called. Often, we know what we intend a function to do as we write it, and therefore, we may not realize that the name we chose is ambiguous or misleading. Or the name may have been appropriate when we wrote the function, but we subsequently modified the function without changing its name.

Here's an example of how a poorly named function called by an unwary user can lead to a runtime logic error. Class SortedList consists of the public static method merge that has two list parameters, list1 and list2.

Listing 6.6   (Program 6.5 SurpriseMerge-1): sortedlist.py (misnamed function)

```
class SortedList:

    @staticmethod
    def merge(list1, list2):
        len1 = len(list1)
        len2 = len(list2)

        merged = []
        i1 = i2 = 0

        while (i1 < len1) and (i2 < len2):
            if list1[i1] <= list2[i2]:
                merged.append(list1[i1])
                i1 += 1                           Merges list1 and list2
            else:
                merged.append(list2[i2])
                i2 += 1

        if i1 < len1:
            merged += list1[i1:]        ◀──┤ Appends the remainder of list1
```

```
        elif i2 < len2:
            merged += list2[i2:]      ◀──┘  Appends the remainder of list2

        i = 0
        while i < len(merged):
            j = i + 1

            while j < len(merged):
                if merged[i] == merged[j]:       Removes
                    merged.pop(j)                duplicate values
                else:
                    j += 1

            i += 1

        return merged
```

In listing 6.7, our test program initializes two sorted lists, list1 and list2, and passes them to the static method SortedList.merge(). (In an actual application, we should check that the values in the two lists are indeed sorted.) Based on the method name, we expect the method to return a list that contains all the merged values from list1 and list2. The program then prints the frequencies of the values in the merged list.

Listing 6.7 (Program 6.5 SurpriseMerge-1): main.py (misnamed function)

```
from sortedlist import SortedList
from collections import Counter

if __name__ == '__main__':
    list1 = [ 2, 5, 5, 5, 7, 11, 11, 11, 13, 13 ]
    list2 = [ 0, 1, 2, 2, 2, 2, 4, 4, 5, 6, 7, 7, 9, 11 ]

    print(f'    {list1 = }')
    print(f'    {list2 = }')

    merged_list = SortedList.merge(list1, list2)    ◀──  Merges the two lists
    print(f'{merged_list = }')

    print()
    print('Frequency table')
                                                         Prints the frequencies of the
    for i, count in Counter(merged_list).items():   ◀──  values in the merged list
        print(f'{i:7d}: {count}')
```

The output is as follows:

```
       list1 = [2, 5, 5, 5, 7, 11, 11, 11, 13, 13]
       list2 = [0, 1, 2, 2, 2, 2, 4, 4, 5, 6, 7, 7, 9, 11]
merged_list = [0, 1, 2, 4, 5, 6, 7, 9, 11, 13]

Frequency table
```

```
 0: 1
 1: 1
 2: 1
 4: 1
 5: 1
 6: 1
 7: 1
 9: 1
11: 1
13: 1
```

Surprise! We have a serious logic error. Because the function unexpectedly removed all the duplicate values, each frequency is at most 1. A better name for the function that won't mislead a programmer might be `merge_and_deduplicate`.

6.2 Poor performance is an unwelcome surprise

Poor runtime performance is another bad surprise, caused by often hidden, inefficient programming. Poor performance can even come from using a built-in data structure such as a list, if we don't fully use its features.

Poor performance can cause longer running time or using too much memory or other resources. An application that does what it's supposed to do (i.e., it meets its functional requirements) but performs poorly (i.e., it fails to meet a nonfunctional performance requirement) is an unwelcome surprise. Poor performance can result from careless use of a data structure.

6.2.1 Bad design can cause unexpected performance problems

Choosing the right algorithms is an important part of good design. A function that implements a poorly chosen algorithm can lead to unexpected performance problems, such as long running time for the unwary caller of the function.

Consider the static method `SortedList.merge()` in listing 6.6. As the lengths of the two vectors grow linearly, the running time of the function grows exponentially.

The growing running times are due to the way the method removes the duplicate values from the merged list. The second `while` loop contains a nested third `while` loop, but a much better design would not require nested loops. We create a set from the merged list and then create a list from the set elements. Because a set does not allow duplicate values, we can replace the two `while` loops and the `return merged` statement with this return statement

```
return list(set(merged))
```

and the code will run faster.

However, an even better solution is to prevent duplicate values from entering the merged list, as in the next listing. By taking advantage of the sorted lists, we simply don't append a value to `merged_list` if it equals the last appended value.

Listing 6.8   (Program 6.6 SurpriseMerge-2): sortedList.py (runs faster)

```
class SortedList:

    @staticmethod
    def merge_and_deduplicate(list1, list2):
        len1 = len(list1)
        len2 = len(list2)

        merged = []
        i1 = i2 = 0

        while (i1 < len1) or (i2 < len2):

            if (    (i1 < len1)
                and ((i2 == len2) or (list1[i1] <= list2[i2]))):

                if (len(merged) == 0) or (list1[i1] != merged[-1]):
                    merged.append(list1[i1])
                i1 += 1
            else:
                if (len(merged) == 0) or (list2[i2] != merged[-1]):
                    merged.append(list2[i2])
                i2 += 1

        return merged
```

Doesn't append a duplicate value (a value equal to the last appended value)

This improved version of the merge function scales well. As the lengths of the two SortedList objects increase linearly, the function's run time increases approximately linearly in proportion.

> **Refactoring**
>
> We *refactor* code by redesigning it to improve it in some way, such as making it perform more efficiently, but without changing its functionality or how to use it. Refactoring is a common operation during development iterations.

6.2.2   *Performance surprises of lists, tuples, and arrays*

Most Python applications use the ubiquitous built-in list data structure to store an ordered sequence of values. A list greatly simplifies programming with high-level operations such as slicing and concatenation, and we can change, insert, append, and delete elements from a list. A list's size can change dynamically, but we don't have to deal with allocating or deallocating elements. However, we must know how to take advantage of the capabilities of lists and similar data structures to get good runtime performance.

For example, the following listing shows that we can get much better performance by using list comprehension to fill a list rather than using a for loop. Many programming languages have for loops, and we may be tempted to use one here. But Python's list comprehension runs faster because it is optimized for creating and filling a list. The `for` loop code is generic and requires a call to function `append()` for each element.

Listing 6.9   (Program 6.7 ListPerformance-1): main.py

```python
from time import perf_counter

SIZE = 10_000_000

if __name__ == '__main__':
    lst = []

    start_time = perf_counter()
    for i in range(SIZE):              # Fills the list with a for loop and
        lst.append(10*i)               # calls to the append() function
    elapsed_time_for_loop = perf_counter() - start_time

    print('     for loop elapsed time = '
          f'{elapsed_time_for_loop:6.4f} seconds')

    start_time = perf_counter()        # Creates the list and fills it
    lst = [10*i for i in range(SIZE)]  # with a list comprehension
    elapsed_time_comprehension = perf_counter() - start_time

    print('comprehension elapsed time = '
          f'{elapsed_time_comprehension:6.4f} seconds')

    print()

    improvement = (
        (elapsed_time_for_loop - elapsed_time_comprehension)
            /elapsed_time_for_loop
    )
    print(f'{improvement = :4.1%}')
```

Here's some example output from this program:

```
     for loop elapsed time = 0.7970 seconds
comprehension elapsed time = 0.5777 seconds

improvement = 27.5%
```

That last bit of refactoring made a huge difference!

List comprehension is optimized for creating and filling lists.

The next example is another demonstration of how taking advantage of a list object's built-in functionalities can improve performance. It also shows that replacing a list with a tuple or an array can further improve performance.

The example involves a list of 10,000,000 random values from 1 to 5, inclusive, that can represent the results of a scientific experiment. We want to compare averages of different samples of the values. The program first calculates the average of all the values, then the average of a sample of every 50th value, the average of every 100th value, the average of every 1,000th value, and finally the average of every 10,000th value. Therefore, the stride (step) values are 1, 50, 100, 1,000, and 10,000.

Class `SampleAverages` in listing 6.10 has three static methods. Method `use_for_loop()` uses a for loop over every stride[th] element of the `values` to compute the average. Method `use_stride()` instead uses the list slice operator `[::stride]` to select the values to average. We will call it first with a list argument and then with a tuple argument. Method `use_numpy()` also uses the slice operator, but with a `numpy` array and the `numpy` function `mean()`.

Listing 6.10   (Program 6.8 ListPerformance-2): averages.py (1 of 2)

```python
import numpy as np
from time import perf_counter

class SampleAverages:

    @staticmethod
    def use_for_loop(values, stride):
        count = 0
        total = 0

        for i in range(int(len(values)/stride)):        ◄———┐ Uses a for loop
            count += 1
            total += values[i*stride]

        return total/count

    @staticmethod
    def use_stride(values, stride):
        selection = values[::stride]        ◄——┐
        count = len(selection)                  │
                                                │ Uses the stride operator
        return sum(selection)/count

    @staticmethod
    def use_numpy(values, stride):
        selection = values[::stride]        ◄——┘

        return np.mean(selection)        ◄——  Calls the numpy
                                              mean() function
    @staticmethod
    def do_calculations ...
```

Listing 6.11 shows static method `do_calculations()`. It calls one of the averaging methods shown in the previous listing to calculate all the sample averages, one per stride value, for one `sequence` of values. It returns the elapsed time to compute all the sample averages. The `sequence` can be a list, a tuple, or a numpy array. The method also calculates the percentage of improvement over another timing. The method's `avgs_function` parameter is passed one of the averaging methods `use_for_loop()`, `use_stride()`, or `use_numpy()`.

Listing 6.11   (Program 6.8 ListPerformance-2): averages.py (2 of 2)

```
@staticmethod
def do_calculations(sequence, strides, avgs_function, label,
                    other_label=None, other_et=None):
    avgs = []

    start_time = perf_counter()
    for stride in strides:
        avgs.append(avgs_function(sequence, stride))

    et = perf_counter() - start_time

    print(f'{label} elapsed time = {et:6.4f} seconds')
    print(f'{avgs = }')
    print()

    if other_et is not None:
        improvement = (other_et - et)/other_et
        print(f'Improvement of {label} over {other_label}: '
            f'{improvement:4.1%}')
        print()

    return et
```

Annotations:
- **Calculates the average for all the strides**
- **Calls use_for_loop(), use_stride(), or use_numpy()**
- **Total elapsed time over all the strides**
- **Calculates the improvement over another timing**

The test code in main.py creates the list of random values and calls method `use_for_loop()` and method `use_stride()` with the list. Then it converts the list to a tuple and calls method `use_stride()` with the tuple. Finally, it converts the list to a numpy array and calls method `use_numpy()` with the array.

Listing 6.12   (Program 6.8 ListPerformance-2): main.py

```
import random
import numpy as np
from averages import SampleAverages

SIZE = 10_000_000
STRIDES = (1, 50, 100, 1000, 10_000)

if __name__ == '__main__':
    random.seed(0)
    lst = [random.randint(1, 5) for _ in range(SIZE)]
```

```
for_loop_label      = 'for loop'
list_stride_label   = 'list stride'
tuple_stride_label  = 'tuple stride'
array_stride_label  = 'ndarray stride'

elapsed_time_for_loop = \
    SampleAverages.do_calculations(
        lst, STRIDES,
        SampleAverages.use_for_loop,
        for_loop_label)

elapsed_time_list_stride = \
    SampleAverages.do_calculations(
        lst, STRIDES,
        SampleAverages.use_stride,
        list_stride_label,
        other_label=for_loop_label,
        other_et=elapsed_time_for_loop)

tpl = tuple(lst)

elapsed_time_tuple_stride = \
    SampleAverages.do_calculations(
        tpl, STRIDES,
        SampleAverages.use_stride,
        tuple_stride_label,
        other_label=list_stride_label,
        other_et=elapsed_time_list_stride)

arr = np.array(lst)

elapsed_time_array_stride = \
    SampleAverages.do_calculations(
        arr, STRIDES,
        SampleAverages.use_numpy,
        array_stride_label,
        other_label=tuple_stride_label,
        other_et=elapsed_time_tuple_stride)

overall = ( (elapsed_time_for_loop - elapsed_time_array_stride)
            /elapsed_time_for_loop
          )
print(f'Overall improvement: {overall:4.1%}')
```

The following output clearly shows that using a list and a `for` loop to compute the sample averages has the worst performance. Performance improves by replacing the `for` loop with the slice operator containing the stride. Using a tuple instead of a list further improves the performance. The best performance uses a `numpy` array and the `mean()` function:

```
for loop elapsed time = 0.9100 seconds
avgs = [2.99985, 2.999335, 3.00003, 2.9792, 2.984]

list stride elapsed time = 0.1496 seconds
```

```
avgs = [2.99985, 2.999335, 3.00003, 2.9792, 2.984]

Improvement of list stride over for loop: 83.6%

tuple stride elapsed time = 0.0830 seconds
avgs = [2.99985, 2.999335, 3.00003, 2.9792, 2.984]

Improvement of tuple stride over list stride: 44.5%

ndarray stride elapsed time = 0.0114 seconds
avgs = [2.99985, 2.999335, 3.00003, 2.9792, 2.984]

Improvement of ndarray stride over tuple stride: 86.3%

Overall improvement: 98.8%
```

Python lists are so easy to use! They're powerful, too. I can append, insert, and delete elements and not have to maintain a dynamic array.

Yes, they're powerful. They do a lot for you automatically at run time. But if you're not careful, lists can have surprising performance problems.

6.3 *Programming by contract helps eliminate surprises [optional]*

The bottom line: Never leave surprises in your code! One way to eliminate surprises in a class that we write is to include a contract for programmers who use the class. The contract for a method states explicitly what *preconditions* must be true when a caller calls the function and what *postconditions* the caller can expect to be true when the function returns. The contract also states the *class invariant*. During run time, the class invariant must be true for each object after the object is created, and it must remain true for each object before and after every call to a method that mutates the object's state. (It may be violated temporarily by an object undergoing mutation.) The invariant ensures that there are never any objects left in an invalid state.

NOTE In this book, sections marked "optional" describe less commonly used design techniques and can be skipped on first reading without loss of continuity.

By defining the preconditions and postconditions of methods of a class and the class invariant, both the programmers and the users of a class can be confident that objects of the class will behave correctly as expected at run time and therefore not have surprises.

Programming by contract

The concept of *programming by contract* was first proposed by the object-oriented programming pioneer Bertrand Meyer. His Eiffel programming language had constructs that allowed a programmer to define preconditions, postconditions, and invariants,

> *(continued)*
>
> and the language checked at run time that they were true. This was especially helpful while debugging a program. The checks could be turned off when the application was deployed so they didn't hurt performance.

The Python language doesn't have native support for programming by contract. However, we can still implement its concepts using existing features of the language. Although it's probably overkill to use contracts on every class of an application, it may be wise to use them on the most critical classes.

This section shows how we can program a circular buffer class by contract. We'll add preconditions and postconditions to its methods and devise a class invariant. We'll also see how the contract helps ensure that the class is correctly designed.

6.3.1   *Programming a circular buffer by contract*

The following example demonstrates programming by contract on a class that implements a circular buffer. Private instance variable `_buffer` is a buffer implemented as a list with a `_capacity`, the maximum number of elements we allow the buffer to contain. Public method `add()` inserts an element at the tail of the buffer, and public method `remove()` removes an element from the head of the buffer and returns the element's value. Private instance variables `_head` and `_tail` are the indexes of the head and tail elements, respectively. Private instance variable `_count` keeps track of how many elements are currently in the buffer.

Public method `add()` increments instance variable `_tail` after adding a new value to the buffer. The value of `_tail` wraps around to the other end of the buffer when it exceeds the buffer capacity. Public method `remove()` increments instance variable `_head` after removing a value from the buffer. Its value also wraps around to the other end of the buffer when it exceeds the buffer capacity.

Private method `_class_invariant()` computes the class invariant and returns `True` if the invariant holds or `False` otherwise. Public methods `add_precondition()` and `add_postcondition()` implement the pre- and postconditions of method `add()`, respectively. Public methods `remove_precondition()` and `remove_postcondition()` implement the pre- and postconditions of method `remove()`, respectively.

Listing 6.13   (Program 6.9 CircularBuffer-1): buffer.py

```
class CircularBuffer:

    def _class_invariant(self):                          ◄——  Private method to test
        return (    (0 <= self._head < self._capacity)         the class invariant
                and (0 <= self._tail < self._capacity)
                )

    def __init__(self, capacity):
```

```
        self._capacity = capacity
        self._head = 0
        self._tail = 0
        self._count = 0
        self._buffer = [0]*capacity

        assert self._class_invariant(), \
                'class invariant is false'
```

Checks the class invariant after
constructing a circular buffer

```
    @property
    def count(self): return self._count

    def add_precondition(self):
        return self._count < self._capacity
```

Precondition for adding:
the buffer is not full

```
    def add_postcondition(self):
        return self._count > 0
```

Postcondition for adding:
the buffer is not empty

```
    def add(self, value):
        assert self.add_precondition(), \
                'add_precondition is false'
```

Checks the precondition
before adding

```
        self._buffer[self._tail] = value
        self._tail = (self._tail + 1)%self._capacity
        self._count += 1
```

Checks the postcondition
before returning

```
        assert self.add_postcondition(), \
                'add_postcondition is false'
        assert self._class_invariant(), \
                'class_invariant is false'
```

Checks the class invariant
before returning

```
    def remove_precondition(self):
        return self._count > 0
```

Precondition for removing:
the buffer is not empty

```
    def remove_postcondition(self):
        return self._count < self._capacity
```

Postcondition for removing:
the buffer is not full

```
    def remove(self):
        assert self.remove_precondition(), \
                'remove_precondition is false'
```

Checks the precondition
before removing

```
        value = self._buffer[self._head]
        self._head = (self._head + 1)%self._capacity
        self._count -= 1
```

Checks the postcondition
before returning

```
        assert self.remove_postcondition(), \
                'remove_postcondition is false'
        assert self._class_invariant(), \
                'class_invariant is false'
```

Checks the class invariant
before returning

```
        return value
```

The test program in main.py exercises the circular buffer.

Listing 6.14   (Program 6.10 CircularBuffer-1): main.py

```
from buffer import CircularBuffer

SIZE = 5

if __name__ == '__main__':
    buffer = CircularBuffer(SIZE)

    for value in range(10, 101, 10):
        if buffer.add_precondition():          Checks the add precondition
            buffer.add(value)                   before calling buffer.add()
            print(f'added {value}')

    for _ in range(10):
        if buffer.remove_precondition():        Checks the remove precondition
            value = buffer.remove()             before calling buffer.remove()
            print(f'removed {value}')

    buffer.remove()    ◀──────  Calls buffer.remove() without
                                first checking its precondition
```

The output of the test program is as follows:

```
added 10
added 20
added 30
added 40
added 50
removed 10
removed 20
removed 30
removed 40
removed 50
------------------------------------------------------------------
AssertionError                      Traceback (most recent call last)
File ~/SoftwareDesign/programs/Python6.9-CircularBuffer-1/main.py:18
    15          value = buffer.remove()
    16          print(f'removed {value}')
---> 18 buffer.remove()

File ~/SoftwareDesign/programs/Python6.9-CircularBuffer-1/buffer.py:47,
 in CircularBuffer.remove(self)
    46 def remove(self):
---> 47     assert self.remove_precondition(), \
    48             'remove_precondition is false'
    50     value = self._buffer[self._head]
    51     self._head = (self._head + 1)%self._capacity

AssertionError: remove_precondition is false
```

The following sections explain the preconditions, postconditions, class invariant, and
output of this program.

6.3.2   *Precondition: What must be true before calling a method or function*

The precondition of a method or function must be true when a method or function is called. *It is the caller's responsibility to check the precondition before making the call.*

> **The Precondition Principle**
>
> The *precondition* of a method or function is a condition (a Boolean expression) that must be true when we call the function. According to programming by contract, if the precondition of a function is true, and we call the function, the function must guarantee that it will behave properly. It is the responsibility of the caller to check the precondition before making the call. If the precondition is false, but we call the function anyway, the function is not required to behave in a manner suitable or convenient for the caller.
>
> If the precondition is for a method of a class, then the class must provide some public means for the caller to check the validity of the precondition. Because it's the caller's responsibility to do so, the function has no obligation to check whether the precondition is met.
>
> If you design a method or function with a precondition, be sure to document that the caller needs to check the precondition before making a call.

In class `CircularBuffer` (listing 6.13), the precondition to calling method `add()` is that the buffer is not full: `self._count < self._capacity`. Therefore, the test program (listing 6.14) first checks that precondition. It doesn't try to add if the buffer is full. The precondition to calling method `remove()` is that the buffer is not empty: `self._count > 0`. It doesn't try to remove an element if the buffer is empty.

If the precondition of a function is true, and we call the function, the function must guarantee that it will behave properly. For function `add()`, that means it must properly add the value to the tail of the buffer and advance instance variable `_tail`. Function `remove()` must properly remove a value from the head of the buffer, advance instance variable `_head`, and return the removed value.

Because it's the caller's responsibility to check the precondition of a function, the function is relieved of the obligation to check it. What happens if the precondition of a function is not met, but we call the function anyway? The function is not required to behave in a manner suitable to the caller. For example, if we call method `add()`, and the buffer is already full, ways that the function can behave include the following:

- Assumes the caller checked the precondition and proceeds to add the new value to the buffer, thereby overwriting an existing value. This also causes the value of instance variable `_tail` to cross the value of instance variable `_head` and the value of instance variable `_count` to exceed the capacity of the buffer.
- Checks the precondition and, if it's not met, does not add the new value but instead does nothing or prints an error message.
- Checks the precondition and, if it's not met, aborts the program.

If we don't check the precondition of method remove() and call it when the buffer is empty, ways that the function can behave include the following:

- Assumes the caller checked the precondition and proceeds to remove a value from the buffer, thereby potentially returning a value that had previously been returned. This also causes the value of instance variable _head to cross the value of instance variable _tail and the value of instance variable _cent to go negative.
- Checks the precondition and, if it's not met, does not remove a value but instead does nothing, prints an error message, or returns a dummy value.
- Checks the precondition and, if it's not met, aborts the program.

In class CircularBuffer, we chose the abort option for both methods. In each function, the assert checks the value of the function's precondition and immediately aborts the program if the precondition is not met. Programming by contract allows a function's programmer to code a behavior that may not necessarily be convenient for the caller. Another option, especially in an actual application, is to raise an exception that the caller must handle.

The test program (listing 6.14) made its last call to remove() without first checking the function's precondition. The buffer was empty, so the function aborted the program with an assertion failure.

That's too brutal! If you call a function despite its precondition not being met, you're at the mercy of its programmer as to what happens.

Good software design puts responsibilities on the caller of the function, too.

If the precondition of a method or function includes the fact that the function will raise an exception for bad argument values, we consider the exception to be part of the contract with the caller. Then the caller is no longer obligated to check the argument values before calling the function.

6.3.3   *Postcondition: What must be true after returning from a function*

However, if a function was called when its precondition was met, then *it is the responsibility of the function to meet its postcondition* before returning.

The Postcondition Principle

The *postcondition* of a function is a condition (a Boolean expression) that must be true when the function returns. According to programming by contract, if a function is called when its precondition is met, *it is the responsibility of the function to meet its postcondition before returning.*

We can assume that if we call a function and it returns, it behaved properly, and the postcondition is true. This relieves us from the obligation to do an error check after the call. (Of course, we still can check.)

In class `CircularBuffer` (listing 6.13), if we call method `add()` after confirming that its precondition is met, the function must successfully add the new value to the buffer, and thereafter, the buffer cannot be empty. Before the function returns, it checks its postcondition: `self._count > 0`. For this example, the function aborts the program if the postcondition isn't met.

If we call method `remove()` after confirming that its precondition is met, the function must successfully remove a value from the buffer and return it, and thereafter, the buffer cannot be full. Before the function returns, it checks its postcondition: `self._count < self._capacity`. In this example, the function aborts the program if the postcondition isn't met.

In an actual application, a function would somehow try a different way to meet its postcondition rather than simply abort the program. A possible remedy is to raise an exception if a problem occurs. Doing so changes the function's contract. The postcondition will then be that the function either succeeds or raises an exception.

So, if a function has a postcondition returned, does that mean I don't need to write code to check any part of the postcondition after returning?

No, you don't. But if you want to practice defensive programming, you might still want to write code to perform some runtime checking.

6.3.4   *Class invariant: What must remain true of object states*

A class invariant ensures that no invalid objects are created at run time and that each of its objects never enters an invalid state.

The Class Invariant Principle

The *class invariant* is a condition (a Boolean expression) involving the class's state implementation that must be true after each object is created at run time (i.e., after each constructor call). It must remain true each time after an object is mutated by a setter function or any other function that changes the object's state. The class invariant ensures that no invalid objects are created and that no object ever enters an invalid state. Typically, the class invariant is a relationship among the class's instance variables.

In class `CircularBuffer` (listing 6.13), the class invariant says that the values of instance variables `head` and `tail` are both always greater than or equal to 0 and less than the buffer capacity:

```
(     (0 <= self._head < self._capacity)
  and (0 <= self._tail < self._capacity)
)
```

The private Boolean method `_class_invariant()` performs this test, and we must call it before the constructor returns and before each of the methods `add()` and `remove()` returns. The constructor sets an object's initial state, and the two methods modify the object's state. Just as with the function preconditions and postconditions in this example class, the program aborts if the class invariant is ever false. An actual application might raise an exception instead.

Is this a valid class invariant? When an object is first created, instance variables `_head` and `_tail` are each set to 0, which satisfies the `0 <=` parts of the invariant. Methods `add()` and `remove()` each increment `tail` and `head` by 1 and then perform the modulo operation with instance variable `capacity` on the sum:

```
(self._tail + 1)%self._capacity
```

and

```
(self._head + 1)%self._capacity
```

The result of a modulo operation is always a value from 0 up to but not including the value of the divisor (`self._capacity` in this case), so the values of `_head` and `_tail` remain `0 <=` and `< self._capacity`. Therefore, we have a valid invariant.

The class invariant can be violated while an object's state is changing. For example, in function `add()`, had we written

```
self._tail = self._tail + 1;
self._tail = self._tail% self._capacity
```

the value of `_tail` could briefly equal the value of `_capacity` before the modulo operation occurred. However, the class invariant must be true again before the function returns.

Finding an appropriate invariant for a class can be challenging. The class invariant we chose for class `CircularBuffer` is not sufficient on its own to ensure that the buffer will operate correctly. For example, it does not guarantee that the values of instance variables `_head` and `_tail` do not cross each other. The class invariant works together with the preconditions and postconditions of the methods to guarantee that the buffer will operate correctly.

Proving a program to be correct

Theoretically, if we can specify the proper class invariants and the preconditions and postconditions for each method in every class of a program, we can prove that the program is correct. However, this is very difficult in practice for all but the simplest programs.

Famous computer scientist Don Knuth once said about a program he had written, "Beware of bugs in the above code; I have only proved it correct, not tried it" (https://www-cs-faculty.stanford.edu/~knuth/faq.html).

Summary

- Code should behave as expected by its users.
- The Principle of Least Astonishment states that there should be few, if any, surprises in well-designed software. Some surprises are due to the way Python operates. We can also inadvertently put surprises in our code.
- Off-by-one errors are common, and they can lead to insidious runtime logic errors that are hard to find.
- A poorly named function can mislead a caller of the function to believe that it does something other than what its name suggests.
- Poorly designed code can have unexpected bad runtime performance, which includes longer-than-expected running times or excessive use of memory and other resources.
- A Python list is easy to use and very powerful. However, we should use built-in features such as list comprehension and slicing to ensure good performance. Using tuples or numpy arrays instead of lists can improve performance.
- Programming by contract ensures that users of a class we wrote won't be surprised by how its objects behave at run time.
- The Precondition Principle states that the caller of a function must ensure that the function's precondition is true before making the call. If the precondition is not true but the function is called anyway, the function can behave in a manner that might not be convenient for the caller. A typical behavior in an application is for the function to raise an exception. On the other hand, if the precondition is true, the function must guarantee that it will perform correctly.
- The Postcondition Principle states that the function must ensure that its postcondition is true before returning.
- The Class Invariant Principle involves a condition that must remain true at run time. It ensures that none of the class's objects are left in an invalid state. In an application, the class can raise an exception if any object violates its invariant.

Design subclasses right

This chapter covers

- When to override and when to overload methods
- Type hints and method overriding
- The Liskov Substitution Principle
- Designing classes and subclasses properly with is-a and has-a relationships
- The Favor Composition over Inheritance Principle
- Factory classes
- Using programming by contract correctly when designing subclasses

As described in section 1.8, inheritance is one of the main concepts of object-oriented programming. When we create an application with class hierarchies of superclasses and subclasses, we must design the subclasses right to achieve a well-designed application.

In this chapter, we will examine several important design issues. We should know when to override methods and when to overload methods, and whether to use type hints. The Liskov Substitution Principle states that we should be able to replace a superclass object with one of its subclass objects, and it provides additional rules to help ensure that we designed the subclasses correctly. The Favor Composition over Inheritance Principle involves making design tradeoffs between is-a relationships and has-a relationships among classes to avoid hardcoding object behaviors in the source code and instead provide the flexibility to make behavior decisions at run time. We can increase the flexibility of our code further by using factory classes. If we use Programming by Contract (introduced in section 6.3) with subclasses, we must be extra careful when testing the preconditions and postconditions of any overriding methods.

7.1 When to override and when to overload methods

This section describes method overriding and overloading, used by the example programs in this and the previous chapters. Good class design can use both concepts, so we should know how to use them properly when designing classes.

7.1.1 Override superclass methods to get subclass behavior

Method overriding involves superclasses and their subclasses. A method of a subclass overrides a method of the superclass if the two methods have the same signature. The *signature* of a method consists of its method name, the number and order of its parameters, and the datatype of its return value. The names of the parameters do not matter in the signature.

In statically typed languages like Java and C++, where we must explicitly specify the datatype of each parameter, method signatures include the order of the parameters, such as int, float vs. float, int. But Python is dynamically typed, and we don't specify the datatypes of the parameters or return values. Therefore, Python methods with the same name can have different signatures based only on having different numbers of parameters. (We'll discuss Python's type hints feature shortly.)

We should use method overriding when we want a subclass object to have similar but not exactly the same behavior as a superclass object. The subclass's overriding method implements the desired subclass behavior. At run time, polymorphism can determine whether to call the superclass method or the overriding method from one of the subclasses. We'll use the Code to the Interface Principle (section 2.3.3).

Figure 7.1 shows an example of method overriding. Methods _cost() and print_cost() in subclass Organic-Item override the methods with the same signatures in superclass Item,

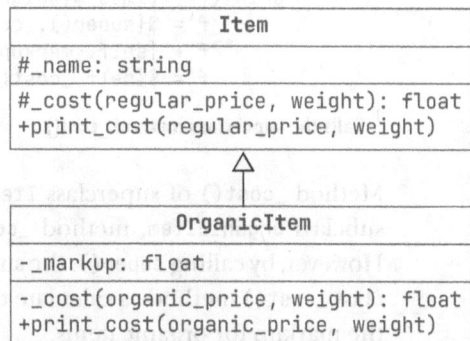

```
┌─────────────────────────────────────┐
│               Item                   │
├─────────────────────────────────────┤
│ #_name: string                       │
├─────────────────────────────────────┤
│ #_cost(regular_price, weight): float │
│ +print_cost(regular_price, weight)   │
└─────────────────────────────────────┘
                  △
                  │
┌─────────────────────────────────────┐
│            OrganicItem               │
├─────────────────────────────────────┤
│ -_markup: float                      │
├─────────────────────────────────────┤
│ -_cost(organic_price, weight): float │
│ +print_cost(organic_price, weight)   │
└─────────────────────────────────────┘
```

Figure 7.1 Methods _cost() **and** print_cost() **in the subclass** OrganicItem **override the corresponding methods in superclass** Item **with the same signature.**

despite the differences in their parameter names, regular_price and organic_price. The UML diagram indicates that instance variable _name and method _cost() in the superclass Item are protected—they should be accessible only by the Item objects or OrganicItem subclass objects. Subclass OrganicItem also has a private instance variable _markup, which is the percentage price markup for an organic item.

The following listing shows superclass Item and its subclass.

Listing 7.1   (Program 7.1 Item): item.py

```python
class Item:
    def __init__(self, name):
        self._name = name
    w
    def _cost(self, regular_price, weight):            ◄────
        return regular_price*weight
                                                    Methods to be
                                                    overridden
    def print_cost(self, regular_price, weight):       ◄────
        print(f'The total cost of {self._name} '
            f'is ${regular_price:.2f}/lb')
        print(f'  times ${weight:.1f} lbs '
            f'= ${self._cost(regular_price, weight):.2f}')

class OrganicItem(Item):
    def __init__(self, name, markup):
        super().__init__(name)
        self._markup = markup

    def _cost(self, organic_price, weight):            ◄────
        markup_factor = 1 + self._markup/100;
        return super()._cost(organic_price, weight)*markup_factor
                                                    Overriding
                                                    methods in the
                                                    subclasses
    def print_cost(self, organic_price, weight):       ◄────
        print(f'The total cost of organic {self._name} '
            f'is ${organic_price:.2f}/lb')
        print(f'  times ${weight:.1f} lbs '
            f'= ${super()._cost(organic_price, weight):.2f} '
            f'+ {self._markup}% extra '
            f'= ${self._cost(organic_price, weight):.2f}')
```

Calls the superclass method _cost()

Method _cost() of superclass Item returns the regular cost of price times weight. In subclass OrganicItem, method _cost() overrides method _cost() of the superclass. However, by calling super(), the subclass _cost() method can call the overridden superclass _cost() method to calculate the regular price, and then the subclass method adds the markup for organic items.

A call to method print_cost() on a superclass Item object in turn calls the superclass _cost() method. Calling method print_cost()on a subclass OrganicItem object invokes the overriding method of the subclass, which in turn calls the subclass _cost() method. Polymorphism determines which methods to call.

In listing 7.2, the test program in main.py demonstrates the results of the method overriding. Variable peach is first assigned an Item object, and therefore, the print_cost() method of class Item is called. Next, the same variable is assigned an OrganicItem object, and then the print_cost() method of subclass OrganicItem is called.

Listing 7.2 (Program 7.1 Item): main.py

```python
from item import Item, OrganicItem

if __name__ == '__main__':
    peach = Item('peaches')
    peach.print_cost(2.99, 2)

    print()

    peach = OrganicItem('peaches', 25)
    peach.print_cost(2.99, 2)
```

The output is as follows:

```
The total cost of peaches is $2.99/lb
  times $2.0 lbs = $5.98

The total cost of organic peaches is $2.99/lb
  times $2.0 lbs = $5.98 + 25% extra = $7.48
```

7.1.2 *Type hints and method overriding*

Although Python is fundamentally a dynamically typed language, we can use type hints in a Python program. Type hints help to document the programmer's intent and prevent programming errors. Before running a program, we can run a type checker, which uses type hints to help ensure that the variables and parameters are used as intended. Some Python packages also take advantage of type hints. But type hints are ignored at run time, and therefore the language remains dynamically typed.

The following is an example of how a method can be overridden despite the use of type hints, which may not be what the programmer intended. (Such bad design can be flagged by type-checking tools.)

Listing 7.3 (Program 7.2 BadOverride): superclass.py (bad design!)

```python
class Superclass:
    def operate(self, x: str, y: str):
        return x + y

class Subclass(Superclass):
    def operate(self, x: int, y: int):   ◄── Overrides despite type hints
        return x*y

supe = Superclass()
```

```
sub = Subclass()

print(f"{supe.operate('Hi, ', 'Ron') = }")
print(f"{sub.operate(2, 3) = }")
print(f"{sub.operate('Hi, ', 'Ron') = }")
```

The main shows how a runtime error can result from unexpected overriding.

Listing 7.4   (Program 7.2 BadOverride): main.py (bad design!)

```
from superclass import Superclass, Subclass

if __name__ == '__main__':
    supe = Superclass()
    sub  = Subclass()

    print(f"{supe.operate('Hi, ', 'Ron') = }")
    print(f"{sub.operate(2, 3) = }")
    print(f"{sub.operate('Hi, ', 'Ron') = }")    ◀──────┘ Wrong method called
```

Because `Subclass.operate()` overrides `Superclass.operate()` despite the type hints, the second call to `sub.operate()` calls the subclass method rather than the superclass method, as was probably intended. The unfortunate output is

```
supe.operate('Hi, ', 'Ron') = 'Hi, Ron'
sub.operate(2, 3) = 6
Traceback (most recent call last):
  File "/Users/rmak/SoftwareDesign/programs/Python7.2x-BadOverride/
superclass.py", line 12, in <module>
    print(f"{sub.operate('Hi, ', 'Ron') = }")
             ^^^^^^^^^^^^^^^^^^^^^^^^^^^^
  File "/Users/rmak/SoftwareDesign/programs/Python7.2x-BadOverride/
superclass.py", line 5, in operate
    def operate(self, x: int, y: int): return x*y
                                               ~^~
TypeError: can't multiply sequence by non-int of type 'str'
```

7.1.3   *Overload methods that have similar or equivalent behaviors*

Method overloading occurs when two or more methods of a class have the same name but different signatures. We should overload a set of methods when they are so strongly related that it doesn't make sense to invent a different name for each method.

Method overloading is very common

Function overloading is very common in Python programs. For example, if we consider the + operator a method (it maps to the special `__add__()` method of a class), we have operator overloading. If its two arguments are integer or real values, the operator returns their sum by performing arithmetic addition. However, if the two arguments are string values, the operator performs string concatenation and returns a string value equal to the value of the second string added to the end of the value of the first string. The built-in `len()` function (which uses the special `__len__()` method) can return the length of a string, list, tuple, or any other sequence.

We can use function overloading for well-designed applications in the following situations:

- The functions perform conceptually similar operations. For example,

```
def write_text(some_text):...        ◀──┐ Writes to the terminal
def write_text(some_text, text_file): ...  ◀──┐
                                            └ Writes to a file
```

- The functions perform the same operation and produce identical results. For example,

```
def draw_circle(x, y, radius): ...
def draw_circle(point, radius): ...
```

In these two examples, if class Point has public x and y instance variables, the second function can call the first:

```
def draw_circle(point, radius):
    draw_circle(point.x, point.y, radius)
```

- The functions perform equivalent operations. For example,

```
def search(genre, year, title): ...
def search(region, title): ...
```

If a Python class has multiple methods with the same name, even if they have different signatures, only the last method in the class definition is used. Therefore, we must use runtime parameter checking to achieve method overloading. The following is a simple example.

Listing 7.5 (Program 7.3 Shape) shape.py

```
import math

class Shape:
    def area(self, arg1, arg2=None):
        return (math.pi*arg1*arg1 if arg2 is None
                    else arg1*arg2
               )
```

Method area() checks its arg1 and arg2 parameters at run time to determine whether to calculate the area of a rectangle or the area of a circle. The following main shows that, in effect, the method is overloaded.

Listing 7.6   (Program 7.3 Shape) main.py

```
from shape import Shape

if __name__ == '__main__':
    rectangle = Shape()
    print(f'{rectangle.area(2, 3) = }')

    circle = Shape()
    print(f'{circle.area(1.0) = :6.4f}')
```

The output is

```
rectangle.area(2, 3) = 6
circle.area(1.0) = 3.1416
```

Here's another example. Class Line has an overloaded length() method that accepts the endpoint coordinates of a line in various ways, including floats, lists, dictionaries, or Point objects. A Point object stores its *x* and *y* coordinates as properties.

Listing 7.7   (Program 7.4 Line) point.py

```
class Point:
    def __init__(self, x, y):
        self._x = x
        self._y = y

    @property
    def x(self): return self._x

    @property
    def y(self): return self._y

    def __repr__(self):
        return f'Point({self._x}, {self._y})'
```

Method length() of the Line class is overloaded by checking its parameters at run time. It checks both the number of parameters and their datatypes.

Listing 7.8   (Program 7.4 Line) line.py

```
import math
from point import Point

class Line:
    def length(self, *args):
```

```
        argslen = len(args)

        if argslen == 1:
            x1, y1, x2, y2 = args[0]

        elif argslen == 2:
            arg2, arg2 = args

            if type(arg2) is dict:
                x1 = arg2['x']
                y1 = arg2['y']
            elif type(arg2) is Point:
                x1 = arg2.x
                y1 = arg2.y
            else:  # arg1 is list or tuple
                x1, y1 = arg2

            if type(arg2) is dict:
                x2 = arg2['x']
                y2 = arg2['y']
            elif type(arg2) is Point:
                x2 = arg2.x
                y2 = arg2.y
            else:  # arg2 is list or tuple
                x2, y2 = arg2

        elif argslen == 4:
            x1, y1, x2, y2 = args

        else:
            raise Exception(f'Unsupported arguments: {args}')

        d1 = x1 - x2
        d2 = y1 - y2

        return math.hypot(d1, d2)
```

The following main makes several overloaded calls to method `length()` with different numbers and datatypes of arguments.

Listing 7.9   (Program 7.4 Line) main.py

```
from line import Line
from point import Point

def line_lengths():
    line_tuples = Line()
    p1 = (1, 1)
    p2 = (4, 5)
    print(f'  {p1 = }')
    print(f'  {p2 = }')
    print(f'{line_tuples.length(p1, p2) = }')
    print()
```

```
        line_dicts = Line()
        p1 = {'x': 1, 'y': 1}
        p2 = {'x': 4, 'y': 5}
        print(f'  {p1 = }')
        print(f'  {p2 = }')
        print(f'{line_dicts.length(p1, p2) = }')
        print()

        line_points = Line()
        p1 = Point(1, 1)
        p2 = Point(4, 5)
        print(f'  {p1 = }')
        print(f'  {p2 = }')
        print(f'{line_points.length(p1, p2) = }')
        print()

        line_ints = Line()
        print(f'{line_ints.length(1, 1, 4, 5) = }')

        line_floats = Line()
        print(f'{line_floats.length(1.0, 1.0, 4.0, 5.0) = }')

        line_list = Line()
        print(f'{line_list.length([1, 1, 4, 5]) = }')

        line_error = Line()
        print(f'{line_error.length(1, 1, 4) = }')

if __name__ == '__main__':
    try:
        line_lengths()
    except Exception as error:
        print()
        print(f'*** ERROR: {error}')
```

The output is as follows:

```
  p1 = (1, 1)
  p2 = (4, 5)
line_tuples.length(p1, p2) = 5.0

  p1 = {'x': 1, 'y': 1}
  p2 = {'x': 4, 'y': 5}
line_dicts.length(p1, p2) = 5.0

  p1 = Point(1, 1)
  p2 = Point(4, 5)
line_points.length(p1, p2) = 5.0

line_ints.length(1, 1, 4, 5) = 5.0
line_floats.length(1.0, 1.0, 4.0, 5.0) = 5.0
line_list.length([1, 1, 4, 5]) = 5.0

*** ERROR: Unsupported arguments: (1, 1, 4)
```

7.1.4 *Overloading with multimethod and type hints*

Method length() in listing 7.8 showed that writing explicit runtime checks to achieve an overloaded method can result in code that is complex and prone to error. The @multimethod decorator together with type hints allow a class to have multiple methods with the same name but different signatures differentiated by datatypes. This reduces complexity and increases readability by splitting the code of method length() among its overloaded counterparts. Python is still dynamically typed, but before our code executes, @multimethod generates the appropriate runtime code so that the correct overloaded method will be called based on the call's arguments. This offers Python the same overloading capabilities as languages such as Java and C++.

Install the multimethod module with the following command in a terminal or command window:

```
python -m pip install multimethod
```

The following version of class Line demonstrates the use of the @multimethod decorator. This example purposely has no overloaded length() method for integer parameters. Class Point is unchanged from listing 7.7.

Listing 7.10 (Program 7.5 MultimethodLine) line.py

```python
import math
from multimethod import multimethod
from point import Point

class Line:
    @staticmethod
    def _pythagoras(x1: float, y1: float,
                    x2: float, y2: float) -> float:
        d1 = x1 - x2
        d2 = y1 - y2
        return math.hypot(d1, d2)

    @multimethod
    def length(self, x1: float, y1: float,
               x2: float, y2: float) -> float:
        return Line._pythagoras(x1, y1, x2, y2)

    @multimethod
    def length(self, coordinates: list) -> float:
        x1, y1, x2, y2 = coordinates
        return Line._pythagoras(x1, y1, x2, y2)

    @multimethod
    def length(self, point1: dict, point2: dict) -> float:
        x1 = point1['x']
        y1 = point1['y']
        x2 = point2['x']
        y2 = point2['y']
```

```
        return Line._pythagoras(x1, y1, x2, y2)

    @multimethod
    def length(self, point1: Point, point2: Point) -> float:
        x1 = point1.x
        y1 = point1.y
        x2 = point2.x
        y2 = point2.y
        return Line._pythagoras(x1, y1, x2, y2)

    @multimethod
    def length(self, point1: tuple, point2: tuple) -> float:
        x1, y1 = point1
        x2, y2 = point2
        return Line._pythagoras(x1, y1, x2, y2)
```

As in the previous example, the following main makes several overloaded calls to method `length()` with different numbers and datatypes of arguments.

Listing 7.11   (Program 7.5 MultimethodLine) main.py

```
from line import Line
from point import Point

def line_lengths():
    line_tuples = Line()
    p1 = (1, 1)
    p2 = (4, 5)
    print(f'  {p1 = }')
    print(f'  {p2 = }')
    print(f'{line_tuples.length(p1, p2) = }')
    print()

    line_dicts = Line()
    p1 = {'x': 1, 'y': 1}
    p2 = {'x': 4, 'y': 5}
    print(f'  {p1 = }')
    print(f'  {p2 = }')
    print(f'{line_dicts.length(p1, p2) = }')
    print()

    line_points = Line()
    p1 = Point(1, 1)
    p2 = Point(4, 5)
    print(f'  {p1 = }')
    print(f'  {p2 = }')
    print(f'{line_points.length(p1, p2) = }')
    print()

    line_list = Line()
    print(f'{line_list.length([1, 1, 4, 5]) = }')

    line_floats = Line()
    print(f'{line_floats.length(1.0, 1.0, 4.0, 5.0) = }')
```

```
        line_ints = Line()
        print(f'{line_ints.length(1, 1, 4, 5) = }')

if __name__ == '__main__':
    try:
        line_lengths()
    except Exception as error:
        print()
        print(f'*** ERROR: {error}')
```

Here is the output:

```
   p1 = (1, 1)
   p2 = (4, 5)
line_tuples.length(p1, p2) = 5.0

   p1 = {'x': 1, 'y': 1}
   p2 = {'x': 4, 'y': 5}
line_dicts.length(p1, p2) = 5.0

   p1 = Point(1, 1)
   p2 = Point(4, 5)
line_points.length(p1, p2) = 5.0

line_list.length([1, 1, 4, 5]) = 5.0
line_floats.length(1.0, 1.0, 4.0, 5.0) = 5.0

*** ERROR: ('length: 0 methods found',
  (<class 'line.Line'>, <class 'int'>, <class 'int'>, <class 'int'>,
  <class 'int'>), set())
```

7.2   *The Liskov Substitution Principle and proper subclasses*

Inheritance is one of the main concepts of object-oriented programming (section 1.8). When we create applications with a class hierarchy of superclasses and their subclasses, we must design the subclasses right to achieve a well-designed application. The Liskov Substitution Principle helps to ensure that we designed proper subclasses for a superclass.

The Liskov Substitution Principle

Wherever there is a superclass object in a program, we should be able to substitute an object from one of its subclasses. In other words, we should be able to replace each occurrence of a superclass object in the source code with an object from one of its subclasses. This substitution should be possible because an object that is an instance of a subclass object is also an instance of the superclass.

The Liskov Substitution Principle states that if we designed the subclasses properly, after we make such a substitution, the program should run without logic or runtime

---

(continued)

errors, although it may produce different but meaningful results. Subclasses that violate this design principle were designed improperly.

This principle was named after object-oriented programming pioneer and professor Barbara Liskov of the Massachusetts Institute of Technology (MIT).

The following example shows how a program can fail if we disregard the principle. In this version of the CircularBuffer class (from section 6.3), we implement the buffer as a list—a very bad idea, as we'll soon see, but we'll do it to demonstrate a point—and so CircularBuffer is a subclass of list.

Listing 7.12   (Program 7.6 CircularBuffer-2): buffer.py (poorly designed)

```
class CircularBuffer(list):
    def __init__(self, buffer_size):          ◄──   Implements a circular buffer
        self._buffer_size = buffer_size               as a list (bad design!)
        self._head = 0
        self._tail = 0
        self._values_count = 0

        for _ in range(buffer_size):
            self.append(None)          ◄──

    @property
    def values_count(self): return self._values_count

    def add(self, value):
        self[self._tail] = value          ◄──
        self._tail = (self._tail + 1)%self._buffer_size
        self._values_count += 1

    def remove(self):
        value = self[self._head]
        self._head = (self._head + 1)%self._buffer_size     Uses list indexing
        self._values_count -= 1                             operations

        return value

    def __str__(self):          ◄──   Prints the buffer
        i = self._head                 contents in order
        c = self._values_count         from head to tail

        result = 'Contents:'

        while c > 0:
            result += f' {self[i]}'          ◄──
            i = (i + 1)%self._buffer_size
            c -= 1

        return result
```

How convenient! We can use inheritance and say that our circular buffer is a list.

That's a very object-oriented thing to do. But violating the Liskov Substitution Principle often leads to serious logic errors.

As in our previous version of class `CircularBuffer`, method `add()` adds a new value to the buffer at its tail. Method `remove()` removes a value from the buffer at its head. To keep this version of the class short, we'll leave out the pre- and postconditions and the class invariant. Because the buffer is a list, we can use list indexing operations: `self[head]`, `self[tail]`, and `self[i]`. The special method `__str__()` prints the contents of the buffer in order from head to tail.

The following listing is test code in main.py. It performs two invalid operations because we violated the Liskov Substitution Principle.

Listing 7.13 (Program 7.6 CircularBuffer-2): main.py (poorly designed)

```python
from buffer import CircularBuffer

BUFFER_SIZE = 5

if __name__ == '__main__':
    buffer = CircularBuffer(BUFFER_SIZE)

    for value in range(10, 51, 10):
        buffer.add(value)

    print(buffer)

    buffer[1] = 99          ◀—— Invalid modification of
    print(buffer)               a value in the buffer

    print(f'{buffer.remove() = }')
    print(f'{buffer.remove() = }')
    print(buffer)

    buffer.pop(1)           ◀—— Invalid removal of a
    print(buffer)               value from the buffer
```

The output from the program is as follows:

```
Contents: 10 20 30 40 50
Contents: 10 99 30 40 50
buffer.remove() = 10
buffer.remove() = 99
Contents: 30 40 50
------------------------------------------------------------
IndexError                              Traceback (most recent call last)
```

```
File ~/CircularBuffer-2/main.py:21
     18 print(buffer)
     20 buffer.pop(1)
---> 21 print(buffer)

File ~/CircularBuffer-2/buffer.py:33, in CircularBuffer.__str__(self)
     30 result = 'Contents:'
     32 while c > 0:
---> 33      result += f' {self[i]}'
     34      i = (i + 1)%self._buffer_size
     35      c -= 1
```

IndexError: list index out of range

A circular buffer is logically not a list. We should not attempt to treat the `CircularBuffer` object (the subclass) as a list object (the superclass) and take advantage of a list's indexing to modify a value in the buffer, nor should we remove a value using the list `pop()` method. These operations will corrupt the circular buffer and result in runtime logic errors, causing the program to crash. The program failed because subclass `CircularBuffer` violated the Liskov Substitution Principle: we cannot substitute a `CircularBuffer` object for a list object in our code because we can't use list operations on a circular buffer.

We can fix the program by not making `CircularBuffer` a subclass of `list`; instead, the `CircularBuffer` class can contain an instance variable that is a list. In other words, class `CircularBuffer` aggregates a list. This is the difference between the is-a (inheritance) relationship and the has-a (aggregation) relationship. The Liskov Substitution Principle can help us decide which one to use. We can rewrite `CircularBuffer` as a standalone class that has a private instance variable `buffer` that is a list.

Listing 7.14   (Program 7.7 CircularBuffer-3): buffer.py

```
class CircularBuffer:
    def __init__(self, buffer_size):          ◄─── Not a subclass of list
        self._buffer_size = buffer_size
        self._head = 0
        self._tail = 0
        self._values_count = 0
        self._buffer = [None]*buffer_size       ◄─── Aggregated list

    @property
    def values_count(self): return self._values_count

    def add(self, value):
        self._buffer[self._tail] = value        ◄┐
        self._tail = (self._tail + 1)%self._buffer_size
        self._values_count += 1
                                                 │  Indexing operations
                                                 │  on the aggregated list
    def remove(self):
        value = self._buffer[self._head]        ◄┘
        self._head = (self._head + 1)%self._buffer_size
        self._values_count -= 1
```

```
        return value

    def __str__(self):
        i = self._head
        c = self._values_count

        result = 'Contents:'

        while c > 0:
            result += f' {self._buffer[i]}'
            i = (i + 1)%self._buffer_size
            c -= 1

        return result
```

Indexing operations
on the aggregated list

Class `CircularBuffer` hides its aggregated list. The public methods `add()` and `remove()` control access to the list and use list indexing operations, but the class does not enable invalid operations.

The following test code in main.py only performs valid `add()` and `remove()` operations on a circular buffer.

Listing 7.15 (Program 7.7 CircularBuffer-3): main.py

```
from buffer import CircularBuffer

BUFFER_SIZE = 5

if __name__ == '__main__':
    buffer = CircularBuffer(BUFFER_SIZE)

    for value in range(10, 51, 10):
        buffer.add(value)

    print(buffer)

    print(f'{buffer.remove() = }')
    print(f'{buffer.remove() = }')
    print(buffer)
```

The program no longer crashes, and it runs properly. Its output is

```
Contents: 10 20 30 40 50
buffer.remove() = 10
buffer.remove() = 20
Contents: 30 40 50
```

7.3 *Choosing the is-a and has-a relationships*

An object-oriented application often contains multiple superclasses and their subclasses, and classes with instance variables that reference other classes. Therefore, designing such an application well requires choosing between is-a (inheritance) and has-a (aggregation) relationships, or using a good combination of the two.

Consider an application involving children's toys. This application includes several different toys: toy car, model airplane, and train set. For each toy, we want to model its play action behavior (roll it on the floor or fly it in the air) and its sound behavior (engine noises or the choo-choo sound).

7.3.1   Using is-a

Our first version of the application architecture involves primarily is-a relationships between the abstract superclass Toy and its subclasses (figure 7.2). The Toy subclasses can have different behaviors, but each must implement the what(), play(), and sound() methods. As the figure clearly shows, this version of the application uses is-a relationships. ToyCar, ModelAirplane, and TrainSet are subclasses of Toy.

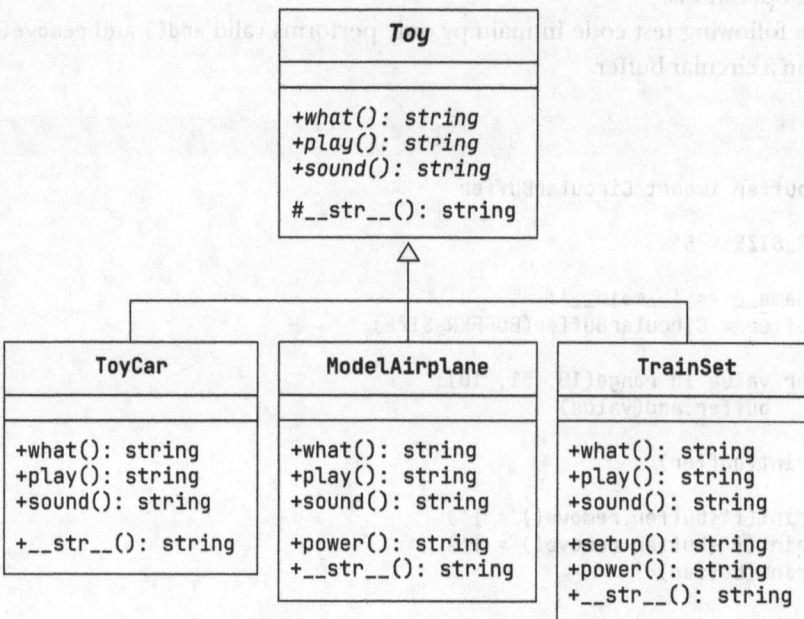

Figure 7.2   **This version of the application uses is-a relationships between the Toy subclasses and their superclass. Two design faults are the duplicated code, which violates the Don't Repeat Yourself Principle, and the hardcoded play action and sound behavior of each toy.**

We can imagine that in a real application, each toy could have more behaviors, and each behavior would involve more than simply returning a string, as shown in the following listing.

Listing 7.16   (Program 7.8 Toys-1): toy.py (poorly designed)

```python
from abc import ABC, abstractmethod

class Toy(ABC):

    @abstractmethod
    def what(self): pass

    @abstractmethod
    def play(self): pass

    @abstractmethod
    def sound(self): pass

    def __str__(self):
        return (f'{self.what()}\n'
                f'   play: {self.play()}\n'
                f'  sound: {self.sound()}\n'
                )

class ToyCar(Toy):
    def what(self):  return 'TOY CAR'
    def play(self):  return 'roll it'
    def sound(self): return 'RRrr RRrr'

class ModelAirplane(Toy):
    def what(self):  return 'MODEL AIRPLANE'
    def play(self):  return 'fly it'
    def sound(self): return 'RRrr RRrr'

    def power(self): return 'wind up'

    def __str__(self):
        return (   super().__str__()
                + f'  power: {self.power()}\n'
                )

class TrainSet(Toy):
    def what(self):  return 'TRAIN SET'
    def play(self):  return 'roll it'
    def sound(self): return 'choo choo'

    def setup(self): return 'lay down track'
    def power(self): return 'insert batteries'

    def __str__(self):
        return (   super().__str__()
                + f'  setup: {self.setup()}\n'
                + f'  power: {self.power()}\n'
                )
```

Common behaviors to be
implemented by each subclass

A serious fault of this design is the duplicated code among the subclasses, which violates the Don't Repeat Yourself Principle (section 2.3.3). For example, both `ToyCar` and

TrainSet have the same code that implements their play() methods, and both ToyCar and ModelAirplane have the same code for their sound() methods. This will be a more serious problem if the code that implements each method does more or if we add more subclasses and behaviors.

Another fault is that each toy's play action and sound behavior are hardcoded in the source code for each Toy subclass. For example, the source code that implements class TrainSet hardcodes that a train set is played with by rolling it and that it makes the choo-choo sound. The following test code in main.py exercises the behaviors.

Listing 7.17   (Program 7.8 Toys-1): main.py (poorly designed)

```
from toy import ToyCar, ModelAirplane, TrainSet

if __name__ == '__main__':
    car = ToyCar()
    print(car)

    plane = ModelAirplane()
    print(plane)

    train = TrainSet()
    print(train)
```

The output is as follows:

```
TOY CAR
    play: roll it
    sound: RRrr RRrr

MODEL AIRPLANE
    play: fly it
    sound: RRrr RRrr
    power: wind up

TRAIN SET
    play: roll it
    sound: choo choo
    setup: lay down track
    power: insert batteries
```

7.3.2   *Using is-a with multiple inheritance*

One way to avoid duplicating code among the methods of the Toy subclasses is to make each unique play action and sound behavior an individual class. Then we can share those behavior classes by having the Toy subclasses inherit them (figure 7.3). The figure shows that each of the Toy methods is intended to be protected, although that feature is not supported directly by Python.

Both the ToyCar and TrainSet subclasses inherit and share the RollPlay class, and both the ToyCar and ModelAirplane subclasses inherit and share the EngineSound class. ModelAirplane also inherits the FlyPlay class, and TrainSet also inherits the ChooChooSound class.

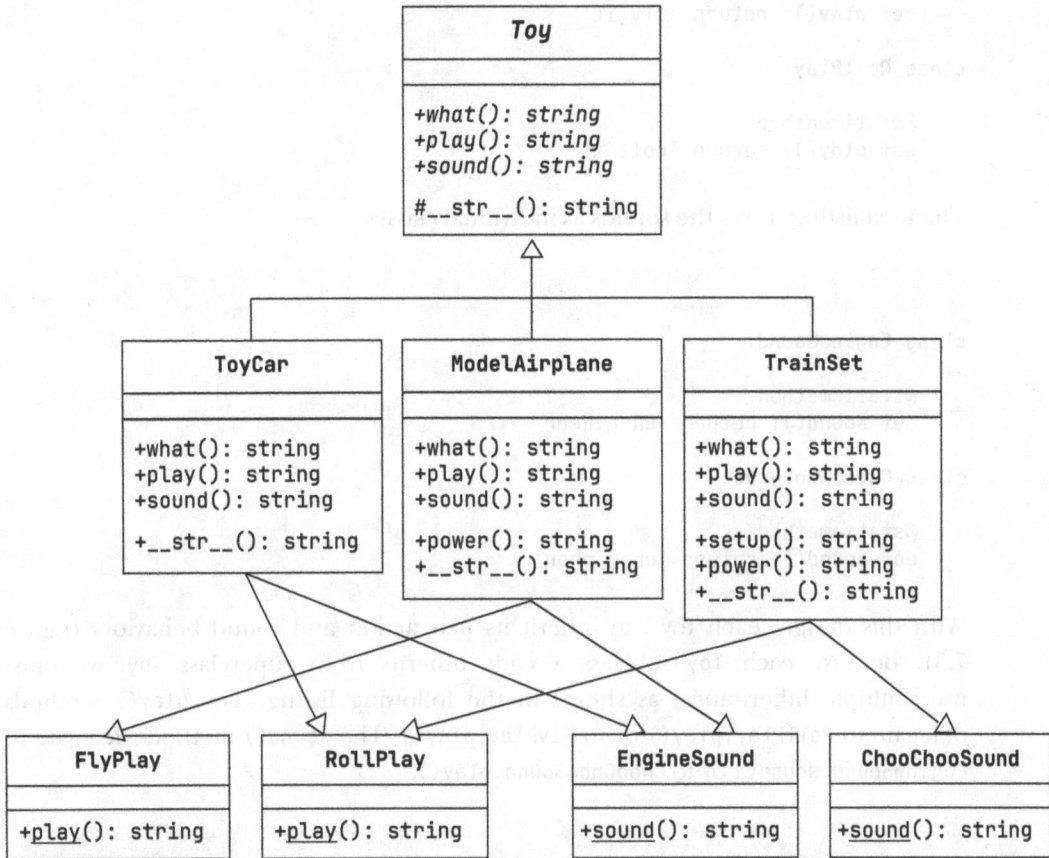

Figure 7.3 Each play action and sound behavior is a separate class. Each Toy subclass has an is-a relationship with the Toy superclass and an is-a relationship with the play action and sound classes. By sharing these classes, we've eliminated some code duplication, but each toy still has hardcoded behaviors.

That last class diagram has way too many tangled relationships!

Unfortunately, it's easy to make a mess with multiple inheritance.

The following listing shows the play actions as individual classes.

Listing 7.18   (Program 7.9 Toys-2): playaction.py (multiple inheritance)

```python
class FlyPlay:

    @staticmethod
```

```
    def play(): return 'fly it'

class RollPlay:

    @staticmethod
    def play(): return 'roll it'
```

The next listing shows the sounds as individual classes.

Listing 7.19   (Program 7.9 Toys-2): sound.py (multiple inheritance)

```
class EngineSound:

    @staticmethod
    def sound(): return 'RRrr RRrr'

class ChooChooSound:

    @staticmethod
    def sound(): return 'choo choo'
```

With this design, each toy can inherit its play action and sound behaviors (figure
7.3). Because each Toy subclass already inherits from superclass Toy, we must
use multiple inheritance, as shown in the following listing. The play() methods
delegate to RollPlay.play() or to FlyPlay.play(). The sound() methods delegate to
EngineSound.sound() or to ChooChooSound.play().

Listing 7.20   (Program 7.9 Toys-2): toy.py (multiple inheritance)

```
from abc import ABC, abstractmethod
from playaction import RollPlay, FlyPlay
from sound import EngineSound, ChooChooSound

class Toy(ABC): ...

class ToyCar(Toy, RollPlay, EngineSound):          ◄──────┐
    def what(self):  return 'TOY CAR'                      │
    def play(self):  return RollPlay.play()                │
    def sound(self): return EngineSound.sound()            │
                                                           │
                                                           │
class ModelAirplane(Toy, FlyPlay, EngineSound):    ◄────┐  │
    def what(self):  return 'MODEL AIRPLANE'             │  │
    def play(self):  return FlyPlay.play()               │  │
    def sound(self): return EngineSound.sound()          │  │ Multiple inheritance

    def power(self): return 'wind up'

    def __str__(self):
        return (   super().__str__()
                 + f'  power: {self.power()}\n'
               )
```

```
class TrainSet(Toy, RollPlay, ChooChooSound):        ◄──── Multiple inheritance
    def what(self):  return 'TRAIN SET'
    def play(self):  return RollPlay.play()
    def sound(self): return ChooChooSound.sound()

    def setup(self): return 'lay down track'
    def power(self): return 'insert batteries'

    def __str__(self): ...
```

The same test program (listing 7.17) generates the same output as before.

For each subclass of Toy, our second version of the application adds is-a relationships with the classes for the play action and sound behaviors, in addition to its previous is-a relationship with the Toy superclass. For example, a ModelAirplane is a Toy, and it is also a FlyPlay and an EngineSound. This version solved the code duplication problem because there is only one sharable copy of each play action and each sound. However, the source code for each toy's subclass still hardcodes the toy's behaviors, but this time using multiple inheritance.

7.3.3 *Using has-a*

To have more flexibility in how the toys behave, we want to avoid hardcoding each toy's play and sound behaviors in the source code of its subclass and instead be able to determine the toy's behaviors at run time. To accomplish this, our final version of the toy application replaces the is-a relationships between the toys and their behaviors with has-a relationships. Figure 7.4 diagrams both the is-a and has-a relationships of this final version of the application.

First we make each play action implement interface PlayAction. Each PlayAction class must implement method play() in a way appropriate for the subclass.

Listing 7.21   (Program 7.10 Toys-3): playaction.py (has-a relationships)

```
from abc import ABC, abstractmethod

class PlayAction(ABC):

    @staticmethod
    @abstractmethod
    def play(self): pass

class RollPlay(PlayAction):

    @staticmethod
    def play(): return 'roll it'

class FlyPlay(PlayAction):

    @staticmethod
    def play(): return 'fly it'
```

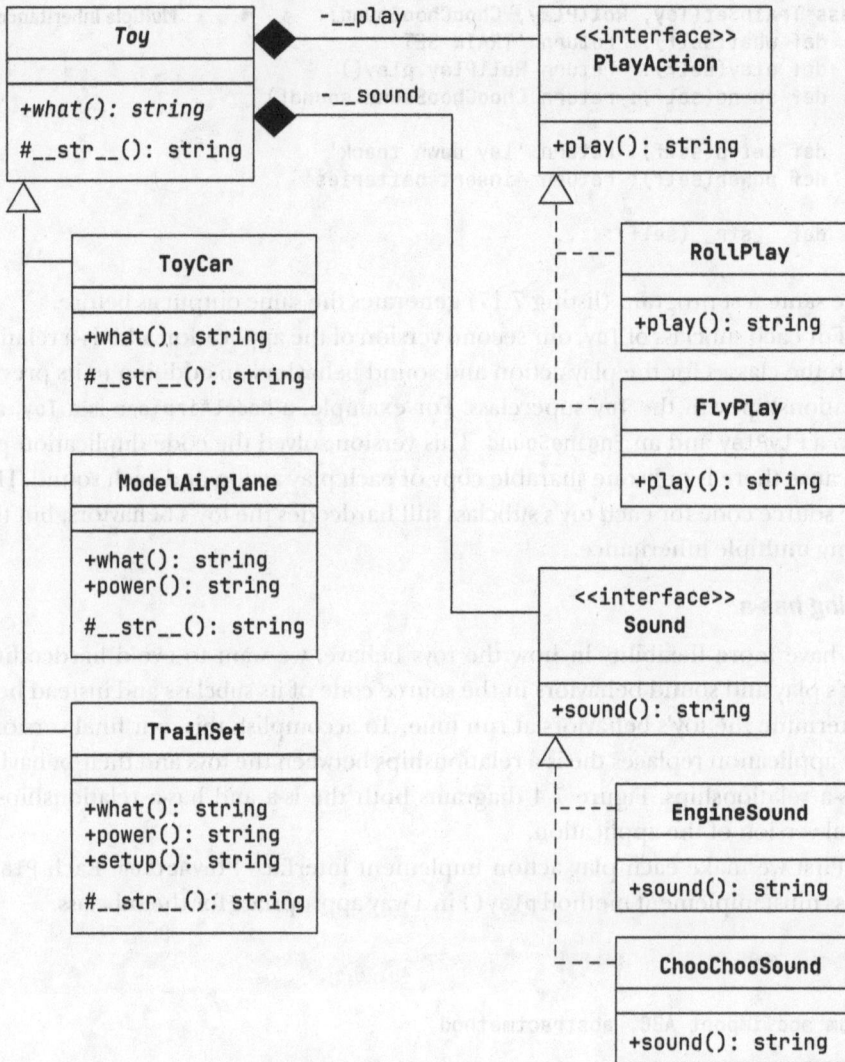

Figure 7.4   Each Toy subclass uses an is-a relationship to the Toy superclass. The Toy superclass uses has-a relationships to the PlayAction and Sound classes, which allows the Toy subclasses to access and share play action and sound behaviors. This design is more flexible and has loose coupling between the toys and their play action and sound behaviors. The toy behaviors are no longer hardcoded in the source code but can be specified whenever a toy object is created at run time. A toy's behaviors can also be modified at run time by calling the sound and play setter methods.

Similarly, we make each sound implement interface Sound. Each Sound class must implement method sound() in a way appropriate for the subclass.

Listing 7.22 (Program 7.10 Toys-3): sound.py (has-a relationships)

```python
from abc import ABC, abstractmethod

class Sound(ABC):

    @staticmethod
    @abstractmethod
    def sound(): pass

class EngineSound(Sound):

    @staticmethod
    def sound(): return 'RRrr RRrr'

class ChooChooSound(Sound):

    @staticmethod
    def sound(): return 'choo choo'
```

We've applied the Open-Closed Principle (sections 2.3.3 and 5.8) to both interfaces PlayAction and Sound. We can add new play action and sound behaviors without changing their interfaces.

Class Toy maintains has-a relationships with the play action and sound behaviors via its private __play and __sound instance variables. Subclasses ToyCar, ModelAirplane, and Trainset maintain is-a relationships with their superclass Toy.

Listing 7.23 (Program 7.10 Toys-3): toy.py (has-a relationships)

```python
class Toy(ABC):
    def __init__(self, play, sound):
        self.__play = play                    ◀── Has-a relationship
        self.__sound = sound                  ◀──     to play behavior
                                                      Has-a relationship to
    @abstractmethod                                   sound behavior
    def what(self): pass

    @property                                 Delegates the play behavior to
    def play(self):                           a PlayAction subclass object
        return self.__play.play()      ◀──    determined at run time

    @property
    def sound(self):
        return self.__sound.sound()    ◀──    Delegates the sound behavior to
                                              a PlayAction subclass object
    @play.setter                              determined at run time
    def play(self, play):
        self.__play = play

    @sound.setter
    def sound(self, sound):
        self.__sound = sound
```

```python
    def __str__(self):
        return (f'{self.what()}\n'
                f'    play: {self.__play.play()}\n'
                f'    sound: {self.__sound.sound()}\n'
                )

class ToyCar(Toy):
    def __init__(self, play, sound):
        super().__init__(play, sound)

    def what(self):  return 'TOY CAR'

class ModelAirplane(Toy):
    def __init__(self, play, sound):
        super().__init__(play, sound)

    def what(self):  return 'MODEL AIRPLANE'
    def power(self): return 'wind up'

    def __str__(self):
        return (   super().__str__()
                + f'    power: {self.power()}\n'
                )

class TrainSet(Toy):
    def __init__(self, play, sound):
        super().__init__(play, sound)

    def what(self):  return 'TRAIN SET'
    def setup(self): return 'lay down track'
    def power(self): return 'insert batteries'

    def __str__(self):
        return (   super().__str__()
                + f'    setup: {self.setup()}\n'
                + f'    power: {self.power()}\n'
                )
```

In this version of the application, class Toy follows the Delegation Principle (section 2.3.2) and delegates the play action and sound behaviors to the PlayAction and Sound classes. None of the Toy subclasses has hardcoded these behaviors. Instead, PlayAction and Sound objects representing these behaviors are passed to each Toy subclass's constructor when a Toy object is created at run time.

Object-oriented programming is about classes and subclasses, but we must be very careful how we design them and determine their relationships.

Good class design is critical if we want our code to be flexible and maintainable.

The test code main.py in the following listing creates each `Toy` object and creates and passes the appropriate `PlayAction` and `Sound` objects to the constructors. It also demonstrates changing the sound behavior of the `TrainSet` object at run time.

Listing 7.24   (Program 7.10 Toys-3): main.py (has-a relationships)

```
from toy import ToyCar, ModelAirplane, TrainSet
from playaction import RollPlay, FlyPlay
from sound import EngineSound, ChooChooSound

if __name__ == '__main__':
    car = ToyCar(RollPlay(), EngineSound())          ◀──────┐
    print(car)                                               │
                                                             │  Determines each toy's
    plane = ModelAirplane(FlyPlay(), EngineSound())  ◀───────┤  behaviors when
    print(plane)                                             │  constructing a toy object
                                                             │
    train = TrainSet(RollPlay(), ChooChooSound())    ◀──────┘
    print(train)

    train.sound = EngineSound()    ◀──┐  Modifes a train set's
    print(train)                       └  sound behavior
```

The output from this final version of the application is as follows:

```
TOY CAR
    play: roll it
    sound: RRrr RRrr

MODEL AIRPLANE
    play: fly it
    sound: RRrr RRrr
    power: wind up

TRAIN SET
    play: roll it
    sound: choo choo
    setup: lay down track
    power: insert batteries

TRAIN SET
    play: roll it
    sound: RRrr RRrr
    setup: lay down track
    power: insert batteries
```

Using the has-a relationship instead of the is-a relationship between the toys and their play action and sound behaviors is an example of the Favor Composition over Inheritance Principle.

The Favor Composition over Inheritance Principle

A design that uses composition (has-a relationships where classes aggregate other classes) is often better than inheritance (is-a relationships of subclasses to super-classes). Inheritance is determined by the source code, and therefore, it hardcodes behavior. Composing behaviors at run time is much more flexible. Composition also makes it easier to share code and reduce duplication.

Because has-a relationships often involve delegation, the principle is also known as the Favor Delegation over Inheritance Principle.

Using this design principle gives us several benefits:

- *Flexibility*—The behaviors are not hardcoded in the source code and can be assigned and modified at run time.
- *Code sharing*—The behaviors are shared, thereby reducing code duplication.
- *Delegation*—The behaviors are delegated to the PlayAction and Sound subclasses.
- *Loose coupling*—Class Toy and its subclasses have no knowledge of the implementation of the PlayAction and Sound subclasses. The PlayAction and Sound subclasses have no dependencies on the Toy subclasses.
- *Encapsulation*—We can add and modify toy behaviors in the future without the need to change the Toy superclass or any of its subclasses.
- *Reduced complexity*—The class hierarchies are simplified. No multiple inheritance is needed.

7.4   *Use a factory function with the Code to the Interface Principle*

Code such as

```
toy = TrainSet(RollPlay(), ChooChooSound())
```

is inherently inflexible because variable toy is hardcoded to only point to a TrainSet object. What if, during a different run of the application, we need to initialize variable toy to a different Toy object? To obtain even more flexibility, where we hardcode less and allow more to be determined at run time, we can use a *factory function* or *factory method* that encapsulates creating a Toy object. The purpose of a factory function or method is to encapsulate creating and returning objects from different subclasses of a superclass. A parameter value determines which subclass object to create and return. The factory methods are often static members of a factory class. Our ToyFactory class encapsulates creating and returning Toy objects in the static factory method make().

Listing 7.25   (Program 7.11 Toys-4) toyfactory.py

```
from toy import ToyCar, ModelAirplane, TrainSet

class ToyFactory:
```

```
toy_classes = [ToyCar, ModelAirplane, TrainSet]    ◄──┐  Toy classes to instantiate

@staticmethod
def make(toy_type, play, sound):    ◄──┐  Factory method that makes
    return toy_type(play, sound)        │  a toy depending on the type
```

The Factory Principle

If a program creates different objects at run time, we can encapsulate the creation of the objects in a factory function or method. The value of a parameter passed to the factory determines which object to create and return. The objects that a factory can create are usually from subclasses of a common supertype. Using a factory function or method gives us the flexibility to determine at run time what type of object to create.

We can implement a factory method as a static method of a separate factory class, or the factory method can be a static method of the supertype itself.

The test program in the following listing shows that now we have the flexibility to determine at run time which Toy object to create depending on the value of variable toy_class.

Listing 7.26   (Program 7.11 Toys-4): main.py

```
from toyfactory import ToyType, ToyFactory
from playaction import RollPlay, FlyPlay
from sound import EngineSound, ChooChooSound

if __name__ == '__main__':
    roll_play = RollPlay()
    fly_play  = FlyPlay()

    engine_sound    = EngineSound()
    choo_choo_sound = ChooChooSound()

    #           ToyCar        ModelAirplane   TrainSet
    plays  = [roll_play,     fly_play,       roll_play]
    sounds = [engine_sound,  engine_sound,   choo_choo_sound]

    for toy_class, play, sound \                                 ─┐  Calls the
            in zip(ToyFactory.toy_classes, plays, sounds):       │  factory method
        toy = ToyFactory.make(toy_class, play, sound)    ◄───────┘  to make a toy
        print(toy)
```

Here is this program's output:

```
TOY CAR
  play: roll it
  sound: RRrr RRrr
```

```
MODEL AIRPLANE
    play: fly it
    sound: RRrr RRrr
    power: wind up

TRAIN SET
    play: roll it
    sound: choo choo
    setup: lay down track
    power: insert batteries
```

Hardcoding behaviors is inherently inflexible. We won't be able to make changes later without rewriting the source code.

For greater flexibility, write code that allows choosing and changing behaviors at run time.

7.5   *Programming by contract with subclasses [optional]*

We need to be extra careful with subclasses if we use programming by contract (section 6.3), especially when adhering to the Code to the Interface Principle (section 7.4). We can have problems if a subclass overrides methods of its superclass and the overridden superclass methods have pre- and postconditions.

Consider class Shipment and its subclasses Expedited and International. In listing 7.27, the cost for all Shipment objects (which represent shipping packages by regular mail) has the precondition that _cost must be equal to 1 or more, as specified by class variable _min_cost. In an actual application, public method calculate_days() would calculate the number of days for a particular shipment. In this example, we'll simply hardcode the instance variable _calculated_days to 5. This meets the postcondition that the number of days must be between 1 and 14, inclusively, as specified by the class variables _min_days and _max_days.

> Listing 7.27   (Program 7.12 ContractShipment): shipment.py (poorly designed)

```python
from enum import Enum
from exceptions import CostException, DaysException

class ShipmentKind(Enum):
    REGULAR      = 1
    EXPEDITED    = 2
    INTERNATIONAL = 3

    def __str__(self): return self.name

class Shipment:
    _min_cost = 1
```

```
    _min_days = 1
    _max_days = 14

    def __init__(self):
        self._cost = 0
        self._days = 0
        self._calculated_days = 5

    @property
    def kind(self): return ShipmentKind.REGULAR

    @property
    def cost(self): return self._cost

    @property
    def days(self): return self._calculated_days

    @cost.setter
    def cost(self, cost):
        # precondition
        if cost >= self._min_cost:          ◄───── Defensively checks that the
            self._cost = cost                        cost precondition is true
        else:
            raise CostException(cost, self._min_cost)

    def calculate_days(self):
        self._days = self._calculated_days
        print(f'  calculated days = {self._days}')

        # postcondition
        if not (self._min_days <= self._days          │ Verifies that the days
                              <= self._max_days):      │ postcondition is true
            raise DaysException(self._days, self._min_days,
                                           self._max_days)
```

Although it's the caller's responsibility to check, setter method cost() defensively
checks the precondition for the cost, and it raises a CostException if the precondition
is false. Method calculate_days() is responsible for verifying the postcondition for the
calculated number of days before returning, and it raises a DaysException if the postcondition is false. We define these two exceptions in the following listing.

Listing 7.28   (Program 7.12 ContractShipment): exceptions.py

```
class CostException(Exception):
    def __init__(self, cost, min_cost):
        self._cost = cost
        self._min_cost = min_cost

    @property
    def cost(self): return self._cost

    @property
    def min_cost(self): return self._min_cost
```

```
class DaysException(Exception):
    def __init__(self, days, min_days, max_days):
        self._days = days
        self._min_days = min_days
        self._max_days = max_days

    @property
    def days(self): return self._days

    @property
    def min_days(self): return self._min_days

    @property
    def max_days(self): return self._max_days
```

Subclass Expedited in the following listing has the precondition that the cost must be equal to 5 or more. We'll hardcode _calculated_days to 2, which meets the postcondition that the number must be between 1 and 3, inclusively.

Listing 7.29   (Program 7.12 ContractShipment): expedited.py (poorly designed)

```
from shipment import ShipmentKind, Shipment

class Expedited(Shipment):
    _min_cost = 5
    _min_days = 1
    _max_days = 3

    def __init__(self):
        self._cost = 0
        self._calculated_days = 2

    @property
    def kind(self): return ShipmentKind.EXPEDITED
```

Subclass International in the following listing has the precondition that the cost must be equal to 10 or more. We'll hardcode _calculated_days to 20, which meets the postcondition that the number must be between 7 and 21, inclusive.

Listing 7.30   (Program 7.12 ContractShipment): international.py (poorly designed)

```
from shipment import ShipmentKind, Shipment

class International(Shipment):
    _min_cost = 10
    _min_days = 7
    _max_days = 21

    def __init__(self):
        self._cost = 0
        self._calculated_days = 20
```

```
@property
def kind(self): return ShipmentKind.INTERNATIONAL
```

Table 7.1 summarizes the pre- and postconditions.

Table 7.1 Cost preconditions and day postconditions

Class	Kind	Cost precondition	Days postcondition
Shipment	REGULAR	cost >= 1	1 <= days <= 14
Expedited	EXPEDITED	cost >= 5	1 <= days <= 3
International	INTERNATIONAL	cost >= 10	7 <= days <= 21

The test code in main.py calls function ship() three times, passing it in turn a Shipment object, an Expedited object, and an International object. Each call also passes a cost. Function ship() sets shipment.cost only if the cost precondition is true. The function defensively checks that the days postcondition is true after calling method shipment .calculate_days() even though it's the responsibility of the method to ensure that the postcondition is met.

Listing 7.31   (Program 7.12 ContractShipment): main.py (poorly designed)

```
from shipment import Shipment
from expedited import Expedited
from international import International
from exceptions import CostException, DaysException

def ship(shipment, *, cost):
    try:
        print(f'Shipping {shipment.kind}')
        print(f'  setting {cost = }')

        if cost >= 1:                          ◀──── Checks the cost
            shipment.cost = cost                      precondition

        shipment.calculate_days()
        days = shipment.days
                                               ◀──── Defensively checks the
        if not (1 <= days <= 14):                     days postcondition
            raise DaysException(days, 1, 14)

    except CostException as ex:
        print(f'*** Cost {ex.cost} violates cost precondition: '
              f'cost >= {ex.min_cost}')
    except DaysException as ex:
        print(f'*** Days {ex.days} violates days postcondition: '
              f'{ex.min_days} <= days <= {ex.max_days}')
    else:
        print('Shipped OK!')
```

```
        print()

if __name__ == '__main__':
    ship(Shipment(),     cost=1)
    ship(Expedited(),    cost=4)
    ship(International(), cost=112)
```

The output is as follows:

```
Shipping REGULAR
  setting cost = 2
  calculated days = 5
Shipped OK!

Shipping EXPEDITED
  setting cost = 4
*** Cost 4 violates cost precondition: cost >= 5

Shipping INTERNATIONAL
  setting cost = 11
  calculated days = 20
*** Days 20 violates days postcondition: 1 <= days <= 14
```

The first shipment went OK, and there were no raised exceptions. However, the second call to ship(), with the Expedited object, raised a CostException. Although its cost value of 4 met the Shipment object's cost precondition of cost >= 1, the value failed the Expedited object's cost precondition of cost >= 5.

The third call to ship(), with the International object, raised a DaysException. Although the hardcoded day value of 20 met the International object's days postcondition of 7 <= days <= 21, the value failed the Shipment object's days precondition of 1 <= days <= 14.

Why were exceptions raised? The problem is that function ship() tested the cost and days values against the pre- and postconditions, respectively, of superclass Shipment. That was OK when the value of the shipment parameter was indeed a Shipment object. But figure 7.5 shows why the CostException was raised when the value of the shipment parameter was an Expedited object with a cost value of 4. Figure 7.6 shows why the DaysException was raised when an International object calculated a days value of 20.

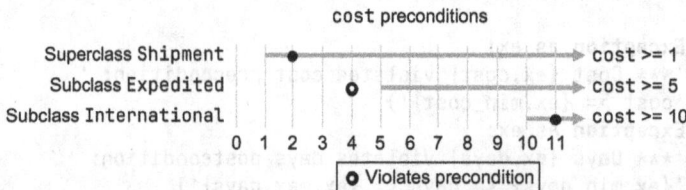

Figure 7.5   **Cost 4 satisfies the superclass's precondition but violates the subclass's precondition.**

days postconditions

Superclass Shipment		1 <= days <= 14
Subclass Expedited		1 <= days <= 3
Subclass International	0 1 2 3 4 5 6 7 8 9 10 11 12 13 14 15 16 17 18 19 20 21	7 <= days <= 21

○ Violates postcondition

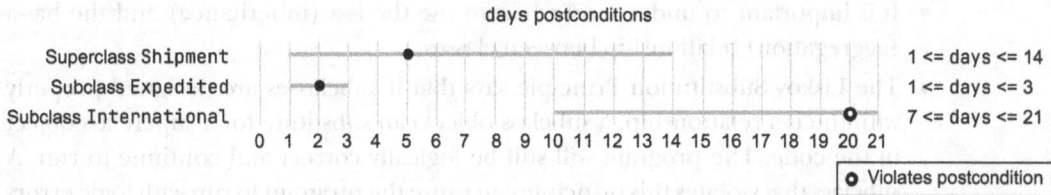

Figure 7.6 A days value of 20 satisfies the subclass's postcondition but violates the superclass's postcondition.

One solution is to ensure that the values that satisfy the precondition of a subclass method are a subset of the values that satisfy the precondition of the overridden superclass method. Conversely, the values that satisfy the postcondition of a subclass method should be a superset of the values that satisfy the postconditions of the overridden superclass method. In other words, the precondition of a subclass method cannot be more restrictive than the preconditions of the overridden superclass method, and the postconditions of a superclass method cannot be more restrictive than the postconditions of the overriding subclass method.

Another solution is for the superclass and each subclass to publicly expose their pre- and postconditions as Boolean methods. Then callers of their methods can use polymorphism to verify the pre- and postconditions that are specific to the object types.

Programming by contract is messy with overriding member functions.

Like all contracts, they must be very carefully written.

Summary

- A well-designed application should contain only well-designed subclasses that support good design principles.
- The signature of a function consists of its name and the number, datatypes, and order of its parameters. It does not include the names of its parameters.
- A method of a subclass overrides a method with the same signature in its superclass. At run time, we want to call the overriding function if the object was instantiated from the subclass.
- Overloaded functions have the same name but otherwise different signatures. In a well-designed application, a set of overloaded functions has operations that are conceptually similar, the same, or equivalent.

- It is important to understand when to use the is-a (inheritance) and the has-a (aggregation) relationship between classes.

- The Liskov Substitution Principle says that if subclasses are designed properly with the is-a relationship, a subclass object can substitute for a superclass object in the code. The program will still be logically correct and continue to run. A subclass that violates this principle can cause the program to run with logic errors or crash.

- The Favor Composition over Inheritance Principle says that there are software design situations where using the has-a relationship instead of the is-a relationship results in classes and subclasses that are more flexible, better encapsulated against changes, less complex, and more loosely coupled.

- The has-a relationship can prevent hardcoding behaviors in the source code of classes. It provides the flexibility to set object behaviors when creating the objects at run time and to later modify the behaviors.

- A factory function encapsulates object creation. It prevents hardcoding by giving us the flexibility to determine at run time what objects to create.

- The pre- and postconditions of the methods of a superclass and its subclasses must be carefully designed so the conditions aren't violated when those methods are called on the superclass and subclass objects.

Part 4

Design patterns solve application architecture problems

Design patterns take our object-oriented software design skills up to the next level. They represent models from which we can create well-designed solutions to many common software architecture problems. Software architecture refers to how we structure the code of our application—the classes and subclasses we design and how they relate to one another and interact at run time. Developers over many years and across different industries have proven that these patterns model reliable and flexible solutions that adhere to good design principles.

Some example architecture problems that design patterns can help solve are the following:

- An application uses a family of algorithms. Can we encapsulate each algorithm and make them interchangeable?
- An application needs to create different sets of objects. These objects can be organized into several categories or families. Can it be flexible about object creation but not mix up objects from different families?
- An application manages several different sequences of objects. Can the application process the objects one at a time from a sequence without needing to know how any of the sequences are implemented?
- One object of the application produces a stream of data at run time that other objects of the application consume. Can we design the application so

that the producer doesn't need to know who the consumers are or what each consumer does with the data, and be able to add or remove consumers at run time?

The design patterns covered in these chapters are based on the object-oriented concepts and design principles covered in the previous chapters. Common goals among the patterns include encapsulating what varies and designing classes that are cohesive and loosely coupled. Design patterns can reduce hardcoding options so that applications can flexibly make choices at run time.

Design patterns are not copy-and-paste source code, nor are they code we import from libraries. We adapt a pattern by using it as a model to write custom code designed to solve a particular architecture problem in our application. These models involve cooperating classes and are not about creating elementary data structures such as vectors, maps, trees, or linked lists.

Design patterns were not invented; instead, they were discovered. Over many years, experienced developers encountered common software architecture problems in many software projects. From the best solutions to these problems, they saw patterns in the design of the classes, the relationships among the classes, and the runtime interactions of their objects.

An experienced programmer can recognize an architecture problem that can be solved with an appropriate design pattern and then decide whether to use the pattern as the model to create a solution to the problem. The four computer scientists who first conceived the idea of software design patterns wrote a book that described 23 original patterns. The chapters in this part of the book will cover 13 of them.

Design patterns and the Gang of Four

The concept of design patterns was first popularized by the book *A Pattern Language: Towns, Building, Construction* by Christopher Alexander et al. (Oxford University Press, 1977). This book contained patterns for solving common architectural problems of physical buildings (where to put doors and windows, how many stories, etc.) and how to design neighborhoods.

Four computer scientists—Erich Gamma, Richard Helm, Ralph Johnson, and John Vlissides—adapted the concept to solve common architectural problems of object-oriented software. They wrote *Design Patterns: Elements of Reusable Object-Oriented Software* (Addison-Wesley, 1995). This book is often called the *Gang of Four* (GoF) book. It contains 23 software design patterns organized into 3 categories: creational, structural, and behavioral patterns. Chapters 8–14 describe 13 of the most common patterns. In sidebars, I've quoted the intent of each pattern directly from the GoF book, and these quotes are attributed with the notation (GoF *nnn*), where *nnn* is the page number of the book.

Numerous authors have since discovered and written about other software design patterns. These new patterns are often used in specialized software fields, such as networking and web, database, and GUI programming. Programming paradigms other than object-oriented, such as functional programming, have their own design patterns.

The benefits of design patterns

Whenever we encounter a software architecture problem while developing an application, we should not assume that the problem is unique. If we can use a design pattern, we won't have to reinvent the wheel.

Design meetings will be much more productive if all the application developers are well-versed in design patterns. For example, during a meeting, one developer might say, "We should use the Strategy Design Pattern to solve this problem." Every other developer in the meeting will know what that means and how the code should be written. Design patterns are a design vocabulary that keeps meetings at a high level and not bogged down by the coding details of how to implement a solution. A pattern prescribes the relationships among the solution's classes and the runtime interactions of their objects. A well-designed application can be modeled from multiple design patterns.

Explaining the design patterns

The following chapters explain each design pattern according to this outline:

1. Before using the design pattern
   a. A description of the software architecture problem the design pattern solves
   b. A description of a short application that has the architecture problem
   c. A UML diagram and "before" application code that demonstrates the problem
   d. A list of faults with that solution before using the design pattern
2. After using the design pattern
   a. A UML diagram and "after" application code modeled from the design pattern
   b. A list of benefits of that second solution
3. The design pattern's generic model
   a. A UML diagram of the design pattern's generic model
   b. A table that relates the components of the pattern's generic model with components of our second solution of the application

A common question is, "How do I know when to use a design pattern?" It takes some experience and practice to recognize when to use a pattern and to know which one.

A design pattern is not a thing but an abstract model from which we can create a custom solution to a software architecture problem. Therefore, to explain the patterns, the chapters in this part of the book contain many before and after UML diagrams and code examples. *It's important to study the examples carefully and understand the faults of the before solution and the benefits of the after solution modeled from each pattern.*

The sports examples

The application examples for the design patterns involve a school athletics department; the sports of baseball, volleyball, and (American) football; and generating reports about the games. For readers unfamiliar with baseball and volleyball, here are highly simplified explanations of how the games are played and scored. Some of the examples also involve football but don't use the scoring rules of that game.

Baseball

Baseball is played by two teams, each with nine players. The teams take turns batting (offense) and fielding (defense). The game is played on a field containing a baseball diamond, which consists of home plate at one corner and, moving counterclockwise, first, second, and third bases at the other corners. The sides of the diamond are 90 feet long (approximately 27 meters). The playing field extends beyond the diamond.

The batting team sends its players one at a time, in a preassigned order, to be the *batter* and stand by home plate with a baseball bat. That player is *at bat*. One player on the fielding team, designated the *pitcher*, stands at the center of the diamond and throws the baseball over home plate, and the batter attempts to hit the baseball with the bat.

A batter who manages to hit the ball attempts to run counterclockwise around the bases. Depending on how well the other team fields the ball and how well the batter runs, the batter can safely reach first base (*hits a single*), second base (*hits a double*), or third base (*hits a triple*) or run all the way around (*hits a homer*). Any players currently on the bases also attempt to advance. Each player who crosses home plate scores a run (a point) for the team.

If, after several attempts, the batter fails to hit the ball thrown by the pitcher, the batter is *out*. A batter who hits the ball but fails to successfully reach one of the bases is also out. After every three outs by the batting team's players, the teams switch roles. Each team taking a turn batting and fielding constitutes an *inning* of play, and after nine innings, the game is over. Therefore, in this greatly simplified version of the game, the game is over after each team has made 27 outs.

Volleyball

Volleyball is played by two teams, each with six players, on a rectangular court separated by a net that is approximately 2.5 meters tall. A round of play starts when a player on one team *serves* the ball by hitting it over the net with their hands. Thereafter, the teams hit the ball back and forth over the net until one team fails to do so, thereby giving the other team a point and ending the round.

The examples simplify the game by having the teams alternate serving after each round. The game ends when a team wins by attaining 15 points.

The Template Method
and Strategy Design
Patterns

This chapter covers

- The Template Method Design Pattern
- The Strategy Design Pattern

Each design pattern is an industry-proven model from which we can create a well-designed solution to a common software architecture problem. A design pattern is only a model because it is rarely a solution we can use directly—we use it as the basis to create a custom solution to an architecture problem in our application. This chapter covers two design patterns: the Template Method Design Pattern and the Strategy Design Pattern.

Application development, and programming in general, involve algorithms and data. To use a cooking metaphor, the data is the ingredients, and the algorithms are the steps of the recipe. The two design patterns in this chapter are models for a software architecture that must manage multiple algorithms.

Our example application for the Template Method Design Pattern generates sports reports. The basic outline of the reports is the same, but parts of the report differ. The example application for the Strategy Design Pattern shows how to deploy strategies to recruit players and reserve venues for different sports. The strategies are interchangeable, and at run time, the application can determine which one to deploy, depending on the sport.

For each of the two patterns, we'll have example code that doesn't use the pattern, followed by example code modeled by the pattern. Then we'll see the improvement the pattern makes.

NOTE Be sure to read the introduction to part 4 of the book for important information about design patterns in general and to learn how this and subsequent chapters teach each pattern. In addition, in case you're unfamiliar with the games of baseball and volleyball, which are used in some of the examples, the introduction includes the basics of how the games are scored.

8.1   The Template Method Design Pattern defines the steps of an algorithm

We often use templates in real life that define the algorithms we perform daily. For example, consider the steps to back out of a parking space in a parking lot:

1 Step on the brake.
2 Start the car.
3 Shift into reverse.
4 Step on the accelerator to back out slowly.
5 Turn the steering wheel.
6 Step on the brake.
7 Shift into drive.
8 Step on the accelerator to move forward.

No matter what make or model of car you're driving, these are the steps and the order in which you must follow them. Steps 1, 4, 5, 6, and 8 are likely the same for all cars. But steps 2, 3, and 7 might be different, depending on the car. Starting the car may involve turning a key in the ignition or pressing a start button. The gear shift lever might be located behind the steering wheel or by your side, or shifting gears might entail a set of push buttons.

Similarly, an application might use an algorithm that has several steps in a fixed order. Some of the steps may be common, but other steps may vary. The first several code examples in this section will demonstrate how the Template Method Design Pattern can help solve a software architecture problem that defines an algorithm with steps in a prescribed order, where some of the steps are common and implemented by a superclass, but others are implemented by subclasses.

Suppose a school's athletics department wants an application that prints a short report after each baseball and volleyball game. The baseball report about the performance of one team during the game consists of a text section with some statistics displayed in a table and a graphics section with a simple bar chart. An example of such a report is

```
BASEBALL GAME REPORT

   Hit type
22 singles
13 doubles
 2 triples
 2 homers

End of report
```

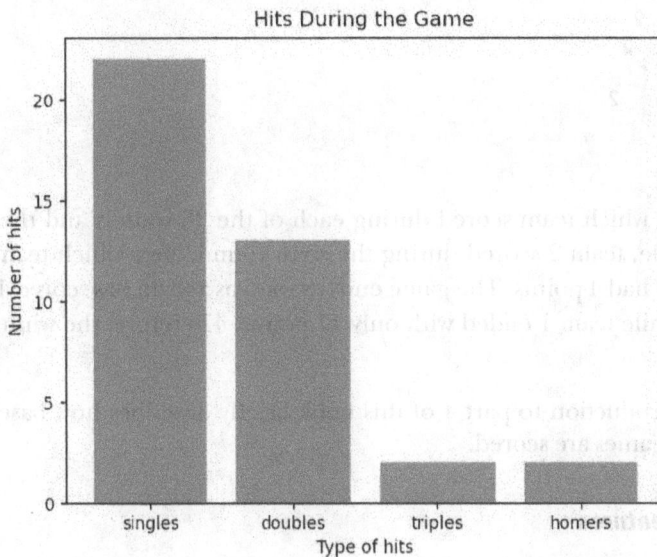

The volleyball report includes the winner, the winning score, and how each team scored its points during the rounds of the game. An example of such a report is

```
VOLLEYBALL GAME REPORT

Winner was Team 2
The winning score was 15 to 11

    ....5...10...15
 1: 2
 2:  2
 3:    2
 4: 1
 5: 1
 6:    2
```

```
 7:    1
 8:      2
 9:    1
10:      1
11:        2
12:      1
13:        2
14:      1
15:          2
16:          2
17:      1
18:          2
19:        1
20:            2
21:        1
22:              2
23:              2
24:              2
25:        1
26:              2
```

End of report

The report shows which team scored during each of the 26 rounds and the running score. For example, team 2 scored during the sixth round, after which team 1 had 2 points and team 2 had 4 points. The game ends as soon as a team has scored 15 points, so team 2 won, while team 1 ended with only 11 points. Therefore, the winning score was 15 to 11.

NOTE The introduction to part 4 of this book briefly describes how baseball and volleyball games are scored.

8.1.1 Desired design features

An application that produces the baseball and volleyball reports should have the following features:

- *DF 1*—The report generation steps are in a fixed order.
- *DF 2*—Corresponding steps between the two reports that are executed the same way should be coded the same.
- *DF 3*—Corresponding steps between the two reports that are executed differently will have custom code for those steps in each report.
- *DF 4* —There is little or no duplicated code.

8.1.2 Before using the Template Method Design Pattern

Generating a game report consists of the following steps:

1 Print the report header.
2 Acquire data from the game.

3 Analyze the data.

4 Print the report.

5 Print the report footer.

Class `BaseballReport` has private methods that implement these steps (figure 8.1). It depends on class `BaseballData`, which uses a random number generator to generate test data for the report. (Review chapter 4 for UML diagramming standards.)

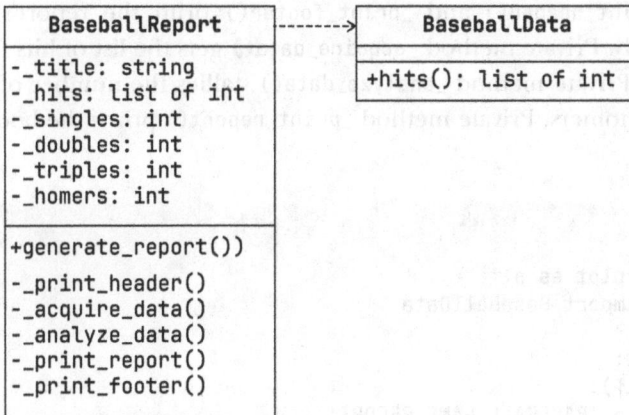

Figure 8.1 The public method `generate_report()` of class BaseballReport calls its private methods that perform the steps to generate a baseball game report. It depends on class BaseballData to generate random test data for the report.

A random number generator in class `BaseballData` creates realistic data for the baseball report, as shown in the following listing. The constructor uses the function `random.gauss()` to generate normally distributed integer values that represent hits (singles, doubles, triples, homers) and outs for the team's players during the game. It appends each hit to the private list `_hits` and stops after 27 outs.

Listing 8.1 (Program 8.1 Reports): baseball_data.py (poor design before DP)

```python
import random
from time import time_ns

class BaseballData:
    def __init__(self):
        random.seed(time_ns())
        self._hits = []           ◄── List of randomly generated hits

        outs = 0

        while outs < 27:
            hit = int(abs(random.gauss(0.0, 1.75)))    ◄── Randomly generates a hit

            if hit > 4:
                hit = 4
```

```
            if hit != 0:
                self._hits.append(hit)
            else:
                outs += 1


    @property
    def hits(self): return self._hits
```

Listing 8.2 shows that public method generate_report() of class BaseballReport calls its private methods to execute the steps in the correct order to generate a game report. Private methods _print_header() and _print_footer() print the report's header and footer, respectively. Private method _acquire_data() gets the list of hits from the BaseballData object. Private method _analyze_data() tallies the number of singles, doubles, triples, and homers. Private method _print_report() prints the body of the game report.

Listing 8.2   (Program 8.1 Reports): baseball_report.py (poor design before DP)

```
import matplotlib.pyplot as plt
from baseball_data import BaseballData

class BaseballReport:
    def __init__(self):
        self._title = 'BASEBALL GAME REPORT'
        self._hits = None

        self._singles = 0
        self._doubles = 0
        self._triples = 0
        self._homers  = 0

    def _print_header(self):
        print(self._title)
        print()

    def _acquire_data(self):
        data = BaseballData()
        self._hits = data.hits

    def _analyze_data(self):
        for hit in self._hits:
            if hit == 1:
                self._singles += 1
            elif hit == 2:
                self._doubles += 1
            elif hit == 3:
                self._triples += 1
            elif hit == 4:
                self._homers += 1

    def _print_report(self):
```

```
        print('  Hit type')
        print(f'{self._singles:2d} singles')
        print(f'{self._doubles:2d} doubles')
        print(f'{self._triples:2d} triples')
        print(f'{self._homers:2d} homers')

        plt.bar(['singles', 'doubles', 'triples', 'homers'],
                [self._singles, self._doubles,
                 self._triples, self._homers])
        plt.title('Hits During the Game')
        plt.xlabel('Type of hits')
        plt.ylabel('Number of hits')
        plt.show()


    def _print_footer(self):
        print()
        print('End of report')

    def generate_report(self):
        self._print_header()
        self._acquire_data()
        self._analyze_data()
        self._print_report()
        self._print_footer()
```

Annotations on the code:
- **Table section of the report** (points to the first group of print statements)
- **Bar chart section of the report** (points to the plt statements)
- **Steps to generate the report** (points to the generate_report body)

Class `VolleyballReport` follows the same outline of steps to print a volleyball game report (figure 8.2). It depends on class `VolleyballData`, which uses a random number generator to generate test data for the report.

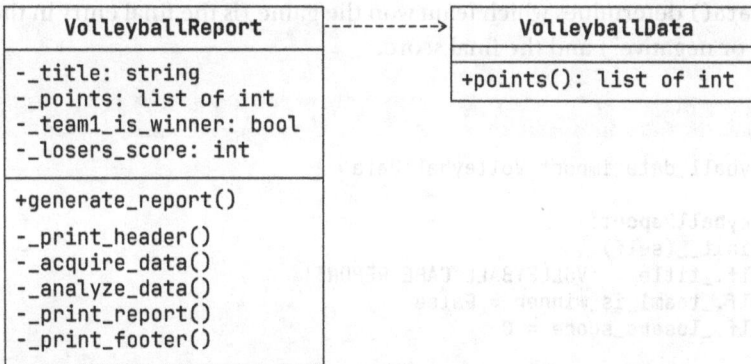

VolleyballReport
-_title: string
-_points: list of int
-_team1_is_winner: bool
-_losers_score: int
+generate_report()
-_print_header()
-_acquire_data()
-_analyze_data()
-_print_report()
-_print_footer()

VolleyballData
+points(): list of int

Figure 8.2 The public method `generate_report()` of class `VolleyballReport` calls its private methods, which perform the steps to generate a volleyball game report. It depends on class `VolleyballData` to generate random test data for the report.

Like class `BaseballData`, class `VolleyballData` uses a random number generator function `random.randint()` to generate the private list `_points` that the teams had accumulated by the end of each round during a simulated game. To distinguish the two teams' points (local variables `score1` and `score2`), the points of the second team are made negative. The simulated game ends when one team attains 15 points.

Listing 8.3   (Program 8.1 Reports): volleyball_data.py (poor design before DP)

```python
import random
from time import time_ns

class VolleyballData:
    def __init__(self):
        random.seed(time_ns())
        self._points = []           # Accumulated randomly
                                    # generated points

        score1 = score2 = 0

        while (score1 < 15) and (score2 < 15):
            if random.randint(1, 2) == 1:       # Randomly adds the point
                score1 += 1                      # for team 1 or team 2
                self._points.append(score1)
            else:
                score2 += 1
                self._points.append(-score2)

    @property
    def points(self): return self._points
```

Now we can implement class `VolleyballReport`. In the following listing, public method `generate_report()` calls its private methods to execute the same steps in the same order as method `generate_report()` does in class `BaseballReport`. Private method `_analyze_data()` determines which team won the game (is the final entry in the points list positive or negative?) and the final score.

Listing 8.4   (Program 8.1 Reports): volleyball_report.py (poor design before DP)

```python
from volleyball_data import VolleyballData

class VolleyballReport:
    def __init__(self):
        self._title = 'VOLLEYBALL GAME REPORT'
        self._team1_is_winner = False
        self._losers_score = 0

    def _print_header(self):
        print(self._title)
        print()

    def _acquire_data(self):
        data = VolleyballData()
        self._points = data.points

    def _analyze_data(self):
```

```
            self._team1_is_winner = self._points[-1] > 0        ◄───  Determines
                                                                      which team
            for i in range(len(self._points) - 1, 0, -1):             won
                if (   (     self._team1_is_winner
                        and (self._points[i] < 0))
                    or (    not self._team1_is_winner              Finds the losing score
                        and (self._points[i] > 0))                 in the _points list
                ):
                    self._losers_score = abs(self._points[i])
                    break

    def _print_report(self):
        winner = 1 if self._team1_is_winner else 2
        print(f'Winner was Team {winner}')
        print(f'The winning score was 15 to {self._losers_score}')
        print()
        print('        ....5...10...15')

        for index, score in enumerate(self._points):
            print(f'{index + 1:3d}:', end='')
            winner = 1 if score > 0 else 2
            print(f"{' '*abs(score)}{winner:1d}")

    def _print_footer(self):
        print()
        print('End of report')

    def generate_report(self):
        self._print_header()
        self._acquire_data()            Steps to generate
        self._analyze_data()            the report
        self._print_report()
        self._print_footer()
```

The test program in main.py can generate either a volleyball game report or a baseball game report, depending on whether we started the program on the command line with the -b or -v option, respectively.

Listing 8.5   (Program 8.1 Reports): main.py (poor design before DP)

```
import sys
from baseball_report import BaseballReport
from volleyball_report import VolleyballReport


if __name__ == '__main__':
    if len(sys.argv) < 2:
        print('Usage: report -b | -v')

    elif sys.argv[1] == '-b':
        baseball_report = BaseballReport()
        baseball_report.generate_report()       Generates a baseball report

    else:
```

```
volleyball_report = VolleyballReport()
volleyball_report.generate_report()
```
| **Generates a volleyball report**

If we wanted to produce a football game report later, we would create classes Football-Data and FootballReport, and the latter would then follow the same steps.

It's pretty obvious what the problem is with this design. There's too much duplicated code! That violates DF 4.

This is the architecture problem that we'll be able to solve with the model that the Template Method Design Pattern gives us.

Indeed, the main fault with this solution is as follows:

- *Duplicated code*—In classes BaseballReport and VolleyballReport, we've duplicated the code for methods _print_header() and _print_footer() that represents common report generation operations. Report generation follows the same steps for each sport, so we've also duplicated the code for method generate_report() in each class.

8.1.3   *After using the Template Method Design Pattern*

In response to this architecture problem, the Template Method Design Pattern comes to the rescue to reduce code duplication. A superclass outlines the steps of an algorithm (to produce a game report, in our example application), and it can implement shared common steps. Subclasses manage the different ways to implement the remaining steps. A method in the superclass, known as the *template method*, calls the methods that perform the steps in the proper order (figure 8.3).

> ### The Template Method Design Pattern
>
> "Define the skeleton of an algorithm in an operation, deferring some steps to subclasses. Template Method lets subclasses redefine certain steps of an algorithm without changing the algorithm's structure." (GoF p. 325)

Using the Template Method Design Pattern to model our architecture gives us some major benefits:

- *Algorithm outline*—The GameReport superclass sets the standard for game report generation by declaring methods that implement the steps of the algorithm. The template method generate_report() calls the step methods in the proper order.

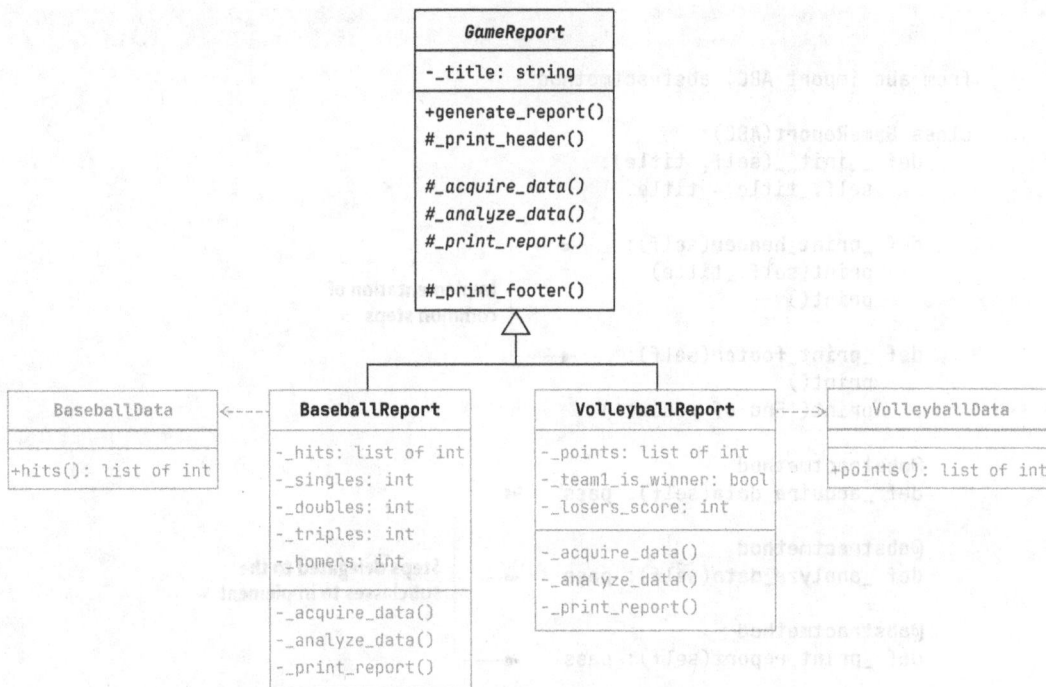

Figure 8.3 This version of the application is modeled from the Template Method Design Pattern. The abstract superclass `GameReport` outlines the steps in the proper order for the algorithm to generate a report. It implements the common steps `_print_header()` and `_print_footer()` and delegates the remaining steps `_acquire_data()`, `_analyze_data()`, and `_print_report()` to the `BaseballReport` and `VolleyballReport` subclasses. The public template method `generate_report()` in the superclass calls the step methods in the proper order. The grayed-out portions of the diagram haven't changed logically from figures 8.1 and 8.2.

- *Reduced code duplication*—Method `generate_report()` and the step methods `_print_header()` and `_print_footer()` in the superclass implement common behavior, which eliminates code duplication. This supports the Don't Repeat Yourself Principle (section 2.3.3). The subclasses implement the remaining step methods.

- *Open-Closed Principle*—Superclass `GameReport` follows the Open-Closed Principle (section 2.3.3). We won't modify it, but we can extend it with the report subclasses.

- *Encapsulated steps*—The report subclasses follow the Encapsulate What Varies Principle (section 2.3.2) to encapsulate the varying steps to generate game reports.

- *Cohesive and decoupled classes*—Each report subclass is cohesive and decoupled from the other report subclasses.

In the abstract superclass `GameReport`, method `generate_report()` is the template method that outlines the steps of the report generation algorithm.

Listing 8.6   (Program 8.2 Reports-TemplateDP): game_report.py

```python
from abc import ABC, abstractmethod

class GameReport(ABC):
    def __init__(self, title):
        self._title = title

    def _print_header(self):        ◄──┐
        print(self._title)             │   Implementation of
        print()                        │   common steps

    def _print_footer(self):        ◄──┘
        print()
        print('End of report')

    @abstractmethod
    def _acquire_data(self): pass   ◄──┐

    @abstractmethod                    │   Steps delegated to the
    def _analyze_data(self): pass   ◄──┤   subclasses to implement

    @abstractmethod                    │
    def _print_report(self): pass   ◄──┘

    def generate_report(self):      ◄──  The template method outlines
        self._print_header()             the steps to print a report.
        self._acquire_data()
        self._analyze_data()
        self._print_report()
        self._print_footer()
```

Class `BaseballReport` is now a subclass of `GameReport`. It only needs to implement methods `_acquire_data()`, `_analyze_data()`, and `_print_report()`, which are specific to baseball game reports. The implementations of these methods are unchanged from listing 8.2.

Listing 8.7   (Program 8.2 Reports-TemplateDP): baseball_report.py

```python
import pandas as pd
import matplotlib.pyplot as plt
from game_report import GameReport
from baseball_data import BaseballData

class BaseballReport(GameReport):
    def __init__(self):
        super().__init__('BASEBALL GAME REPORT')

        self._singles = 0
        self._doubles = 0
        self._triples = 0
        self._homers = 0
```

```
def _acquire_data(self): ...       ◄─┐
                                     ├── Steps specific to baseball
def _analyze_data(self): ...       ◄─┤   game reports
                                     │
def _print_report(self): ...       ◄─┘
```

The same is true for class `VolleyballReport`. The implementations of methods `acquire_data()`, `analyze_data()`, and `print_report()` are unchanged from listing 8.3.

Listing 8.8   (Program 8.2 Reports-TemplateDP): volleyball_report.py

```python
from game_report import GameReport
from volleyball_data import VolleyballData

class VolleyballReport(GameReport):
    def __init__(self):
        super().__init__('VOLLEYBALL GAME REPORT')

        self._team1_is_winner = False
        self._losers_score = 0

    def _acquire_data(self): ...       ◄─┐
                                         │
    def _analyze_data(self): ...       ◄─┼── Steps specific to
                                         │   volleyball game reports
    def _print_report(self): ...       ◄─┘
```

Classes `VolleyballData` and `BaseballData` are unchanged. The same test program (listing 8.5) prints the same types of reports as in the previous version.

8.1.4   *Template Method's generic model*

Figure 8.4 shows the generic model of the Template Method Design Pattern. From a design pattern's generic model, we can create a custom solution to an architecture problem. Table 8.1 shows how the example application applies the pattern.

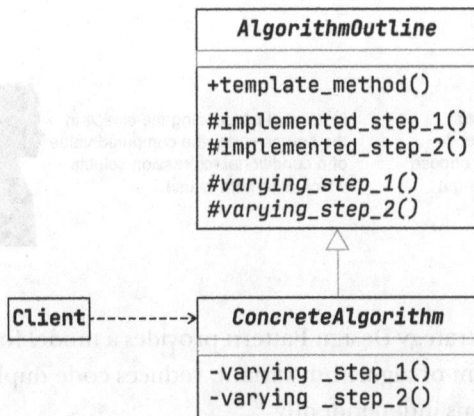

Figure 8.4   The generic model of the Template Method Design Pattern. We can compare it with figure 8.3. The methods of the abstract superclass `AlgorithmOutline` outline the steps of the algorithm. Method `template_method()` calls the methods representing the steps in the correct order. The superclass implements the common steps and delegates implementing the varying steps to its concrete subclasses.

Design pattern generic model

It is from a design pattern's generic model that we can create a custom solution to an architecture problem. Remember that a design pattern is not copy-and-paste code or code included from a library. Once we've identified a problem for which an appropriate design pattern can model a solution, we must tailor the solution to solve the specific problem in our application.

Experience teaches us to recognize whether an architecture problem can be solved by a design pattern and whether its benefits make its use worthwhile.

Table 8.1   The Template Method Design Pattern as applied by the example application

Design pattern	Applied by the example application
Client class	Main
Superclass AlgorithmOutline	Superclass GameReport
Subclass ConcreteAlgorithm	Subclasses BaseballReport and VolleyballReport
template_method()	generate_report()
Common steps	_print_header() and _print_footer()
Varying steps	_acquire_data(), _analyze_data(), and _print_report()

8.2   *The Strategy Design Pattern encapsulates algorithms*

With the next design pattern, we continue the theme of an application that must manage multiple algorithms, but we'll do it in a somewhat different way. The Strategy Design Pattern provides a model for a software architecture problem that involves a family of algorithms, or several variants of an algorithm, that need to be interchangeable at run time.

Interchangeable means we design the application so that, without code modifications, at run time it can choose one of the algorithms from among a family of algorithms.

Instead of hardcoding the choice in the source code, the computed value of a conditional expression selects which algorithm to use.

For this architecture problem, the Strategy Design Pattern provides a model for a solution that encapsulates each algorithm or algorithm variant, reduces code duplication, and allows us to modify the algorithms independently.

Hardcoding vs. runtime flexibility

Hardcoding refers to the code we've written in the source file. When we hardcode, we make decisions when we write the code about how the program will behave at run time. Once we've hardcoded, we can't make changes to the program's behavior without modifying the code. This may also require extensive retesting and rewriting documentation.

Many design patterns provide models for software architectures that have runtime flexibility so the application can make behavior decisions when running. For example, the Strategy Design Pattern enables an application to choose which algorithm to use based on a logical decision. Our testing and documentation should cover all the algorithms before we deploy the application. A well-designed architecture can also minimize code changes if we later add new algorithms or modify existing ones.

To demonstrate the Strategy Design Pattern with a concrete example, we'll start with an application that involves three sports: baseball, football, and volleyball. For each sport, we need to execute an algorithm to recruit players and an algorithm to reserve a venue.

8.2.1 Desired design features

An application that has different algorithms for recruiting players and reserving venues for the three sports should have the following features:

- *DF 1*—Each sport should implement code for both algorithms.
- *DF 2*—It should be straightforward to add or delete sports.
- *DF 3*—It should be straightforward to add, delete, or modify algorithms for the sports.
- *DF 4*—It should be possible to make algorithm choices at run time.
- *DF 5*—It should be possible for sports to share algorithms, such as one for reserving a particular venue.

8.2.2 Before using the Strategy Design Pattern

The first version of the application is simple and straightforward (figure 8.5). Superclass `Sport` has abstract methods `recruit_players()` and `reserve_venue()` that invoke the two algorithms. Subclasses `Baseball`, `Football`, and `Volleyball` each must implement these methods.

> **Listing 8.9   (Program 8.3 Sports): sport.py (poor design before DP)**

```
from abc import ABC, abstractmethod

class Sport(ABC):
    _SPORT_TYPE = ''

    @property
```

```
def SPORT_TYPE(self): return self._SPORT_TYPE

@abstractmethod
def recruit_players(self): pass   ◄──

@abstractmethod
def reserve_venue(self): pass     ◄──
```

To be implemented by subclasses

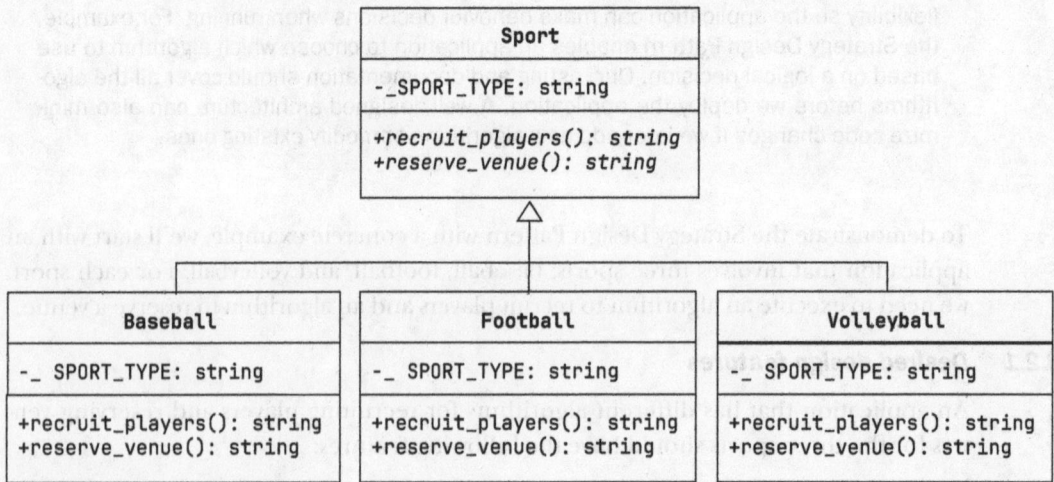

Figure 8.5   The first version of our sports application. Superclass class `Sport` **has abstract methods representing algorithms that each of the subclasses** `Baseball`, `Football`**, and** `Volleyball` **must implement to recruit players and reserve a venue.**

To keep this example application simple, each algorithm simply returns a descriptive string, as shown in the following listing. In an actual application, the algorithms of a family can have more complex behaviors.

Listing 8.10   (Program 8.3 Sports): sports.py (poor design before DP)

```python
from sport import Sport

class Baseball(Sport):
    _SPORT_TYPE = 'BASEBALL'

    def recruit_players(self):
        return 'baseball players'

    def reserve_venue(self):
        return 'stadium'

class Football(Sport):
    _SPORT_TYPE = 'FOOTBALL'
```

```
    def recruit_players(self):
        return 'football players'

    def reserve_venue(self):
        return 'stadium'

class Volleyball(Sport):
    _SPORT_TYPE = 'VOLLEYBALL'

    def recruit_players(self):
        return 'volleyball players'

    def reserve_venue(self):
        return 'open field'
```

Our test code in main.py generates a report for each sport.

Listing 8.11   (Program 8.3 Sports) main.py (poor design before DP)

```
from sports import Baseball, Football, Volleyball

def generate_report(sport):
    print(sport.SPORT_TYPE)
    print(f'  players: {sport.recruit_players()}')
    print(f'    venue: {sport.reserve_venue()}')
    print()

if __name__ == '__main__':
    for sport in [Baseball(), Football(), Volleyball()]:
        generate_report(sport)
```

The output is
```
baseball
  players: baseball players
    venue: stadium

football
  players: football players
    venue: stadium

volleyball
  players: volleyball players
    venue: open field
```

This solution relies on inheritance: Baseball, Football, and Volleyball each is-a Sport. We can spot some serious shortcomings in this architecture design:

- *Duplicated code*—For example, the statement return 'stadium' representing a venue algorithm is repeated several times. This will be a major problem with more sports or if the algorithms have more complex behaviors.

- *Lack of encapsulation*—If, for example, the stadium is unavailable and the sports that use it must have a different venue, we'll need to change the code in multiple places.

- *Hard-to-reuse code that ought to be shared*—If another sport needs the stadium venue, we can't easily reuse that code without duplicating it.
- *Hardcoded players and venues*—We will have to rewrite code to change them.

8.2.3   *After using the Strategy Design Pattern*

The Strategy Design Pattern provides a model that we can use to solve this architecture problem (figure 8.6). This solution relies on composition—has-a relationships—for the two families of algorithms. The algorithms are organized as superclasses and subclasses. Class Sport uses aggregation and the Code to the Interface Principle (section 2.3.3) with the PlayerStrategy and VenueStrategy interfaces. Class Sport has-a player algorithm family referenced by instance variable player_strategy, and it has-a venue algorithm family referenced by instance variable venue_strategy. The Strategy Design Pattern calls each algorithm a strategy, so these names are appropriate. Each of the Sport subclasses Baseball, Football, and Volleyball is now much simpler.

The Strategy Design Pattern

"Define a family of algorithms, encapsulate each one, and make them interchangeable. Strategy lets the algorithm vary independently from clients that use it." (GoF p. 315)

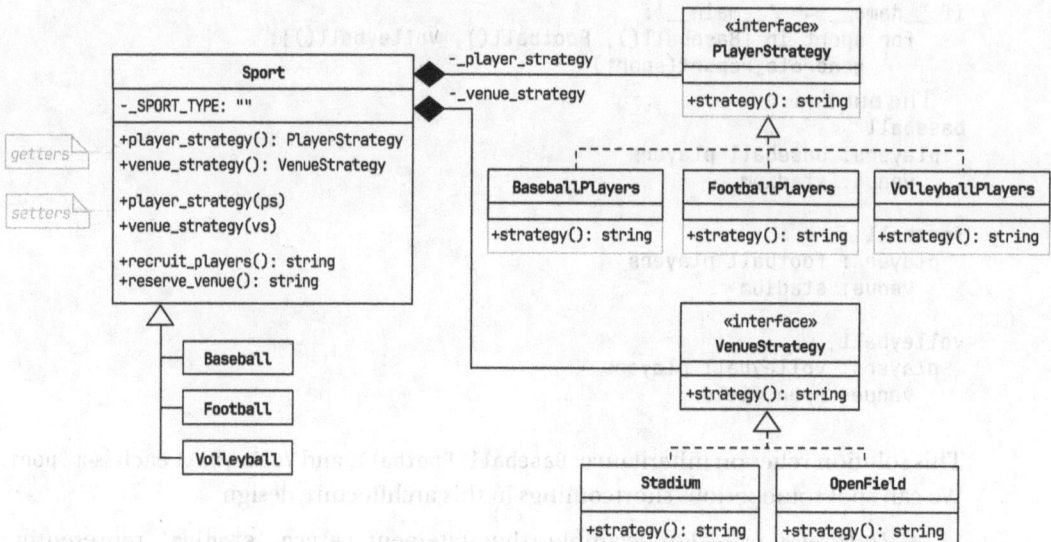

Figure 8.6   This version of the application is modeled from the Strategy Design Pattern for the sport teams and venues. The player family of algorithms implement the PlayerStrategy interface, and the venue family of algorithms implement the VenueStrategy interface. Class Sport uses has-a relationships to aggregate the algorithms. Each player and venue algorithm has a strategy() method. The Baseball, Football, and Volleyball subclasses are now much simpler, and each one sets the _SPORT_TYPE, _player_strategy, and _venue_strategy instance variables of the Sport superclass.

Advantages of applying the Strategy Design Pattern include the following:

- *Reusable shared code*—For example, subclass `Stadium` follows the Don't Repeat Yourself Principle (section 2.2.3). Both the baseball and football teams play in the stadium.

- *Encapsulated algorithms*—It will be possible to make changes to the interchangeable algorithms in the classes that implement `PlayerStrategy` and `VenueStrategy` interfaces without modifying the other classes. This is the Encapsulates What Varies Principle (section 2.3.2).

- *The Open-Closed Principle*—Superclass `Sport` is closed to changes, but we can extend it with subclasses. We can add and remove sports without affecting the superclass.

- *Favor has-a over is-a*—Class `Sport` aggregates the strategy classes, such as `Baseball-Players` and `Stadium`, rather than relying on its subclasses to implement the strategies (section 7.3). Class `Sport` uses the Code to the Interface Principle (section 2.3.3) because its instance variables `player_strategy` and `venue_strategy` reference the strategy interfaces `PlayerStrategy` and `VenueStrategy`, respectively.

- *Runtime flexibility*—The application can supply strategies for the sports during run time rather than hardcoding them. For example, a `Volleyball` object's venue strategy can change from `OpenField` to `Stadium`.

"Has-a" aggregation allows our code to make strategy decisions at run time. But using the Strategy Design Pattern in this version required more classes than in the previous version. It seems more complicated!

Design often requires making tradeoffs and compromises. Use a design pattern if you want its benefits. It may not be worth the effort for a trivial application or an application that's used only once.

Because our example application is so small to begin with, using the Strategy Design Principle can make it more complicated by adding classes. Each strategy simply returns a descriptive string. A more realistic application might have more strategies, and the strategies might have more behaviors. Then the benefits of the Strategy Design Pattern can really shine. Each strategy might include multiple methods. We'll see in the following listings that the creators of `Sport` objects determine the superclass's initial strategies, and they can change the strategies later during run time.

> **Listing 8.12 (Program 8.4 Sports-StrategyDP): sport.py**

```
class Sport:
    _SPORT_TYPE = ''

    def __init__(self, player_strategy, venue_strategy):
        self._player_strategy = player_strategy
        self._venue_strategy  = venue_strategy
```

Aggregates the initial player and venue strategies

```
        @property
        def SPORT_TYPE(self): return self._SPORT_TYPE

        @property
        def player_strategy(self): return self._player_strategy    ◄──┐

        @property                                                      │ Returns the
        def venue_strategy(self): return self._venue_strategy    ◄─────┘ strategies

        @player_strategy.setter
        def player_strategy(self, ps):    ◄──┐
            self._player_strategy = ps        │
                                              │ Dynamically sets
        @venue_strategy.setter                │ the strategies
        def venue_strategy(self, vs):    ◄────┘
            self._venue_strategy = vs

        def recruit_players(self):
            return self._player_strategy.strategy()

        def reserve_venue(self):
            return self._venue_strategy.strategy()
```

As figure 8.6 shows, each strategy to recruit players implements interface Player-Strategy, and each must implement the strategy() method to allow superclass Sport to execute the algorithm to recruit players. Because its subclasses set its instance variable player_strategy, class Sport follows the Delegation Principle (section 2.3.2) by delegating to its subclasses the choice of which player recruitment algorithm to execute.

Listing 8.13   (Program 8.4 Sports-StrategyDP): player_strategy.py

```
from abc import ABC, abstractmethod

class PlayerStrategy(ABC):
    @abstractmethod                           Strategy method to be
    def strategy(self): pass    ◄──────────── implemented by the subclasses

class BaseballPlayers(PlayerStrategy):
    def strategy(self):
        return 'baseball players'

class FootballPlayers(PlayerStrategy):
    def strategy(self):
        return 'football players'

class VolleyballPlayers(PlayerStrategy):
    def strategy(self):
        return 'volleyball players'
```

Similarly, each strategy to reserve a venue implements interface VenueStrategy, and each must implement the strategy() method that allows the superclass Sport to execute the strategy to reserve a venue. As with the player strategy, class Sport delegates to its subclasses the choice of which algorithm to execute when they set instance variable `venue_strategy`.

Listing 8.14   (Program 8.4 Sports-StrategyDP): venue_strategy.py

```python
from abc import ABC, abstractmethod

class VenueStrategy(ABC):
    @abstractmethod
    def strategy(self): pass          ◀──── Strategy method to be
                                             implemented by the subclasses
class Stadium(VenueStrategy):
    def strategy(self):
        return 'stadium'

class OpenField(VenueStrategy):
    def strategy(self):
        return 'open field'
```

In this example application, each player and venue strategy consists of only a method that returns a descriptive string.

Each Sport subclass sets the initial strategies appropriately. For example, when we instantiate a Baseball object, its constructor calls the constructor of superclass Sport to set _player_strategy to BaseballPlayers and _venue_strategy to Stadium.

Listing 8.15   (Program 8.4 Sports-StrategyDP): sports.py

```python
from sport import Sport
from player_strategy import BaseballPlayers, FootballPlayers, \
                            VolleyballPlayers
from venue_strategy import Stadium, OpenField

class Baseball(Sport):
    _SPORT_TYPE = 'BASEBALL'

    def __init__(self):
        super().__init__(BaseballPlayers(),
                         Stadium())              Initial baseball strategies

class Football(Sport):
    _SPORT_TYPE = 'FOOTBALL'

    def __init__(self):
        super().__init__(FootballPlayers(),
                         Stadium())              Initial football strategies

class Volleyball(Sport):
    _SPORT_TYPE = 'VOLLEYBALL'

    def __init__(self):
        super().__init__(VolleyballPlayers(),
                         OpenField())            Initial volleyball strategies
```

Class Sport will not need to change if we add new Sport subclasses. We can use the Open-Closed Principle (section 2.3.3) and close superclass Sport for modification. Each Sport subclass initializes the strategies, but now we have the flexibility to change a strategy at run time by calling a setter function.

Listing 8.16   (Program 8.4 Sports-StrategyDP): main.py

```python
from sports import Baseball, Football, Volleyball
from venue_strategy import Stadium

def generate_report(sport):
    print(sport.SPORT_TYPE)
    print(f'  players: {sport.recruit_players()}')
    print(f'    venue: {sport.reserve_venue()}')
    print()

if __name__ == '__main__':
    for sport in [Baseball(), Football(), Volleyball()]:
        generate_report(sport)

    volleyball = Volleyball()
    volleyball.venue_strategy = Stadium()
    generate_report(volleyball)
```

> Dynamically changes volleyball's venue strategy

The output shows that now it is possible to change a strategy at run time:

```
BASEBALL
  players: baseball players
    venue: stadium

FOOTBALL
  players: football players
    venue: stadium

VOLLEYBALL
  players: volleyball players
    venue: open field

VOLLEYBALL
  players: volleyball players
    venue: stadium
```

I love how the Strategy Design Pattern is built on top of good design principles.

It does neatly package the principles for us.

Indeed, design patterns help ensure that we use good design principles. The patterns simplify the software design process and facilitate design meetings among the developers.

8.2.4 Strategy's generic model

Figure 8.7 shows the generic model of the Strategy Design Pattern. As we said earlier, from a design pattern's generic model, we can create a custom solution to an architecture problem. Table 8.2 shows how the example application applies the pattern.

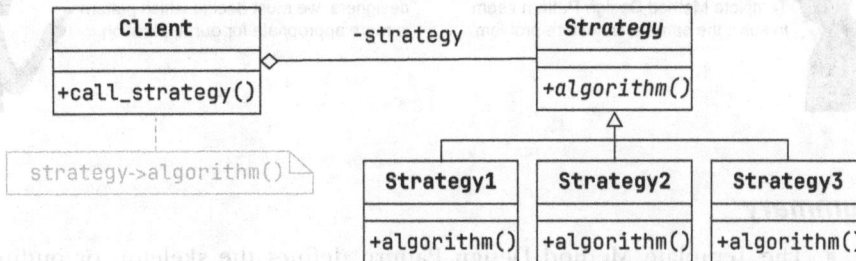

Figure 8.7   The generic model of the Strategy Design Pattern. Compare to figure 8.6.

Table 8.2   The Strategy Design Pattern as applied by the example application

Design pattern	Applied by the example application
Class `Client`	Superclass `Sport`
Superclass `Strategy`	Interfaces `PlayerStrategy` and `VenueStrategy`
Subclasses `Strategy1`, `Strategy2`, etc.	Classes `BaseballPlayers`, `FootballPlayers`, `VolleyballPlayers`, `Stadium`, and `OpenField`
`algorithm()`	`strategy()` methods
`strategy->algorithm()`	`_player_strategy.strategy()`, `_venue_strategy.strategy()`

8.3   Choosing between Template Method and Strategy

The Template Method Design Pattern and the Strategy Design Pattern have a similar goal: to encapsulate algorithms. Their main differences are the following:

- Template Method relies on inheritance: the is-a relationship. The outline of the algorithm is in the superclass, and the encapsulated parts of the algorithm are in subclasses. Template Method allows the superclass to implement common steps of the algorithm.

- Strategy aggregates whole algorithms and makes them interchangeable. It uses composition: the has-a relationship. The Strategy subclasses (the PlayerStrategy and VenueStrategy) are composed by the Client class (superclass Sport).

- In the Strategy model, the Client class is loosely coupled to the Strategy subclasses. We can add, remove, or update the subclasses later.

We must decide which design pattern to use depending on the application's needs and architecture.

The Strategy Design Pattern and the Template Method Design Pattern seem to solve the same architecture problem.

Yes, they are similar. As software designers, we must decide which pattern is more appropriate for our application.

Summary

- The Template Method Design Pattern defines the skeleton or outline of an algorithm and defers the implementation of some of the steps to subclasses. It lets subclasses redefine certain steps of an algorithm without changing the algorithm's structure.

- The Template Method Design Pattern relies on inheritance: the is-a relationship.

- The Strategy Design Pattern encapsulates each algorithm in a family of algorithms and makes them interchangeable. At run time, an application can choose which algorithm to use.

- The Strategy Design Pattern uses composition: the has-a relationship. The client class is loosely coupled to the strategy subclasses.

The Factory Method
and Abstract Factory
Design Patterns

This chapter covers

- The Factory Method Design Pattern
- The Abstract Factory Design Pattern

Chapter 8 mentioned that application development is about algorithms and data. The two design patterns in this chapter model ways applications can become more flexible by deploying software factories to create objects during run time.

The Factory Method Design Pattern provides a model for creating a group of related objects. Our example application shows how the design pattern allows a school athletic department to delegate responsibilities to the varsity sports and intramural sports organizations. The Abstract Factory Design Pattern goes further and provides a model for creating families of objects and prevents mixing objects from different families. We'll expand the example application to ensure that the varsity sports and intramural sports organizations keep their responsibilities apart from each other.

In this chapter, we'll again develop the example application incrementally. We'll adapt the appropriate patterns one at a time to model solutions to the architecture design problems as we encounter them.

NOTE   Be sure to read the introduction to part 4 of the book for important information about design patterns in general and to learn how this and subsequent chapters teach each pattern.

9.1   The Factory Method Design Pattern lets subclasses create objects

A common software architecture problem involves a group of related objects. For example, suppose we're developing an application for a manufacturer of automobile engines for Ford and GM cars. The manufacturer works on engines for only one type of car at a time. But it doesn't always know ahead of time which type it will work on. Then there's the possibility that another car manufacturer may later ask it to make engines. Should we have an EngineManufacturer class that manages the engines for all types of cars and decides which ones to make? Should it have subclasses? How easy would it be to add another type of car and its engines? The Factory Method Design Pattern provides a model for encapsulating object creation by delegating their creation to subclasses.

For a concrete example, let's expand our example sports application to include an AthleticsDept class that manages two categories of sports: varsity and intramural. The class will also be responsible for generating the recruiting and venues report like the one in chapter 8.

9.1.1   Desired design features

The application should have the following features:

- *DF 1*—Similar to our Strategy Design Pattern example in chapter 8, each sport will be responsible for recruiting players and acquiring a venue.
- *DF 2*—The AthleticsDept class manages the sports teams without the danger of accidentally mixing up its responsibilities for the varsity and intramural teams.
- *DF 3*—It should be easy to add categories and sports, such as club sports.

9.1.2   Before using Factory Method

Figure 9.1 shows our first design for the application. Classes PlayerStrategy and VenueStrategy don't change from the Strategy Design Pattern example (program 8.4, figure 8.6). But now we have varsity and intramural categories with varsity and intramural players.

Interface PlayerStrategy hasn't changed, but it has new varsity and intramural player classes that implement it, as shown in listing 9.1. Each must implement method strategy(). There are no changes to interface VenueStrategy and the classes that implement it.

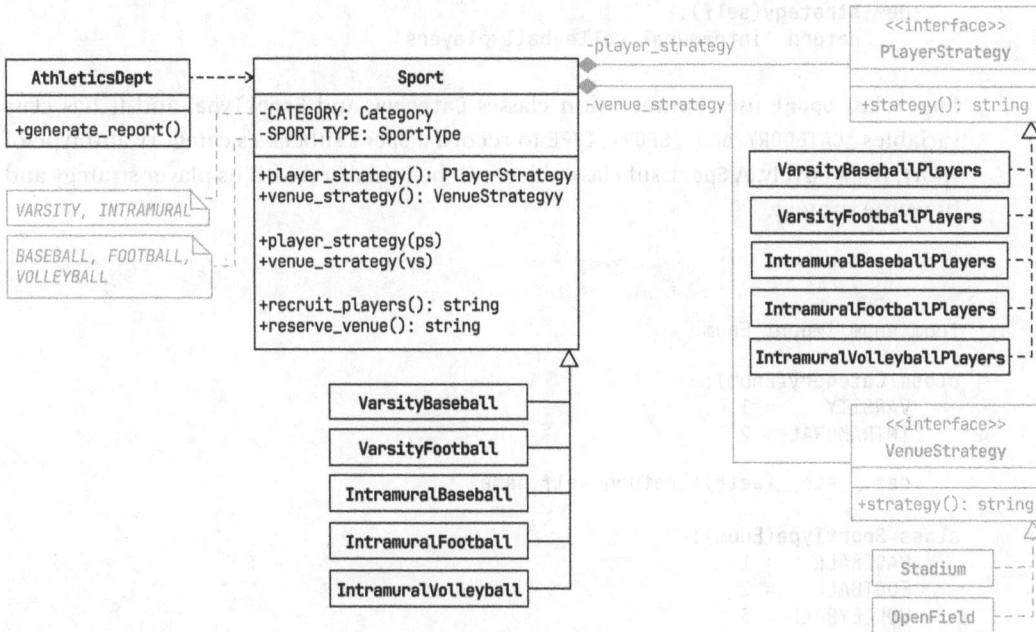

Figure 9.1   Class AthleticsDept generates the report for varsity and intramural sports. The grayed-out portions of the diagram haven't changed logically from figure 8.6.

Listing 9.1   (Program 9.1 Provisions) player_strategy.py (poor design before DP)

```python
from abc import ABC, abstractmethod

class PlayerStrategy(ABC):
    @abstractmethod
    def strategy(self):
        pass

class VarsityBaseballPlayers(PlayerStrategy):
    def strategy(self):
        return 'varsity baseball players'

class VarsityFootballPlayers(PlayerStrategy):
    def strategy(self):
        return 'varsity football players'

class IntramuralBaseballPlayers(PlayerStrategy):
    def strategy(self):
        return 'intramural baseball players'

class IntramuralFootballPlayers(PlayerStrategy):
    def strategy(self):
        return 'intramural football players'

class IntramuralVolleyballPlayers(PlayerStrategy):
```

```
    def strategy(self):
        return 'intramural volleyball players'
```

Superclass Sport uses enumeration classes Category and SportType, and it has class variables _CATEGORY and _SPORT_TYPE to record a Sport subclass's category and type of sport, respectively. A Sport subclass object will be initialized with its player strategy and its venue strategy.

Listing 9.2   (Program 9.1 Provisions) sport.py (poor design before DP)

```
from enum import Enum

class Category(Enum):
    VARSITY    = 1
    INTRAMURAL = 2

    def __str__(self): return self.name

class SportType(Enum):
    BASEBALL   = 1
    FOOTBALL   = 2
    VOLLEYBALL = 3

    def __str__(self): return self.name

class Sport:
    _CATEGORY = None
    _SPORT_TYPE = None

    def __init__(self, player_strategy, venue_strategy):
        self._player_strategy = player_strategy
        self._venue_strategy  = venue_strategy

    @property
    def CATEGORY(self): return self._CATEGORY

    @property
    def SPORT_TYPE(self): return self._SPORT_TYPE

    @property
    def player_strategy(self): return self._player_strategy

    @property
    def venue_strategy(self): return self._venue_strategy

    @player_strategy.setter
    def player_strategy(self, ps):
        self._player_strategy = ps

    @venue_strategy.setter
    def venue_strategy(self, vs):
        self._venue_strategy = vs

    def recruit_players(self):
```

```
            return self._player_strategy.strategy()

        def reserve_venue(self):
            return self._venue_strategy.strategy()
```

Class Sport has new subclasses, one for each varsity and intramural sport, as shown in
the next listing. The varsity teams play in the stadium, but unfortunately, the intramural teams are relegated to the open field.

Listing 9.3   (Program 9.1 Provisions) sports.py (poor design before DP)

```python
from sport import Category, SportType, Sport
from player_strategy import VarsityBaseballPlayers, \
                            VarsityFootballPlayers, \
                            IntramuralBaseballPlayers, \
                            IntramuralFootballPlayers, \
                            IntramuralVolleyballPlayers
from venue_strategy import Stadium, OpenField

class VarsityBaseball(Sport):
    _CATEGORY = Category.VARSITY
    _SPORT_TYPE = SportType.BASEBALL

    def __init__(self):
        super().__init__(VarsityBaseballPlayers(),
                        Stadium())

class VarsityFootball(Sport):
    _CATEGORY = Category.VARSITY
    _SPORT_TYPE = SportType.FOOTBALL

    def __init__(self):
        super().__init__(VarsityFootballPlayers(),
                        Stadium())

class IntramuralBaseball(Sport):
    _CATEGORY = Category.INTRAMURAL
    _SPORT_TYPE = SportType.BASEBALL

    def __init__(self):
        super().__init__(IntramuralBaseballPlayers(),
                        OpenField())

class IntramuralFootball(Sport):
    _CATEGORY = Category.INTRAMURAL
    _SPORT_TYPE = SportType.FOOTBALL

    def __init__(self):
        super().__init__(IntramuralFootballPlayers(),
                        OpenField())

class IntramuralVolleyball(Sport):
    _CATEGORY = Category.INTRAMURAL
    _SPORT_TYPE = SportType.VOLLEYBALL
```

```
    def __init__(self):
        super().__init__(IntramuralVolleyballPlayers(),
                         OpenField())
```

Class `AthleticsDept` is responsible for generating the sports report.

Listing 9.4   (Program 9.1 Provisions) athletics_dept.py (poor design before DP)

```
from sport import Category, SportType
from sports import VarsityBaseball, VarsityFootball, \
                    IntramuralBaseball, IntramuralFootball, \
                    IntramuralVolleyball

class AthleticsDept:
    def generate_report(self, which):
        sport = None

        match which:
            case [Category.VARSITY, SportType.BASEBALL]:
                sport = VarsityBaseball()
            case [Category.VARSITY, SportType.FOOTBALL]:
                sport = VarsityFootball()

            case [Category.INTRAMURAL, SportType.BASEBALL]:
                sport = IntramuralBaseball()
            case [Category.INTRAMURAL, SportType.FOOTBALL]:
                sport = IntramuralFootball()
            case [Category.INTRAMURAL, SportType.VOLLEYBALL]:
                sport = IntramuralVolleyball()

        print(f'{sport.CATEGORY} {sport.SPORT_TYPE}')
        print(f'  players: {sport.recruit_players()}')
        print(f'    venue: {sport.reserve_venue()}')
        print()
```

To set its local variable `sport`, method `generate_report()` uses a `match` statement on parameter `which`, whose value will be a tuple such as `[Category.VARSITY, SportType`
`.BASEBALL]` containing a category and a sport type.

> All those cases! Smells like trouble to me. This could violate DF 2 if we're not careful.

> I would hate to add more categories and sports to this code. That violates DF 3.

A long sequence of `case` patterns in a `match` statement can result in code that's error-prone. We must do pattern matching carefully. If the patterns from different `case` clauses overlap in what they match, the `case` with the first match executes.

The following is the test program for this version of the application.

Listing 9.5   (Program 9.1 Provisions) main.py (poor design before DP)

```
from sport import Category, SportType
from athletics_dept import AthleticsDept

if __name__ == '__main__':
    dept = AthleticsDept()

    dept.generate_report([Category.VARSITY, SportType.BASEBALL])
    dept.generate_report([Category.VARSITY, SportType.FOOTBALL])

    dept.generate_report([Category.INTRAMURAL, SportType.BASEBALL])
    dept.generate_report([Category.INTRAMURAL, SportType.FOOTBALL])
    dept.generate_report([Category.INTRAMURAL, SportType.VOLLEYBALL])
```

The output is as follows:

```
VARSITY BASEBALL
  players: varsity baseball players
    venue: stadium

VARSITY FOOTBALL
  players: varsity football players
    venue: stadium

INTRAMURAL BASEBALL
  players: intramural baseball players
    venue: open field

INTRAMURAL FOOTBALL
  players: intramural football players
    venue: open field

INTRAMURAL VOLLEYBALL
  players: intramural volleyball players
    venue: open field
```

We can readily recognize some notable shortcomings of this architecture:

- *Many patterns* in a match statement can be awkward and error-prone.
- *Not encapsulating the potentially changing code* means we will have to modify the AthleticsDept class's generate_report() method if we add or remove sports or add a new sports category, such as club sports.
- *Multiple responsibilities* for class AthleticsDept. Besides generating the report, it must also create the Sport objects.

9.1.3   *After using Factory Method*

The Factory Method Design Pattern helps to alleviate these and other shortcomings. It uses the Factory Principle (section 7.4) in a specific architectural pattern. We want to encapsulate creating the Sport objects and remove that responsibility from class AthleticsDept.

Following the pattern, we make AthleticsDept abstract, with two subclasses, VarsityDept and IntramuralDept (figure 9.2). It has an abstract static method create_sport(). Each of the two subclasses serves as a factory class. Subclass VarsityDept implements create_sport(), which creates and returns a varsity Sport object. Subclass IntramuralDept implements create_sport(), which creates and returns an intramural Sport object. Therefore, each create_sport() is a factory method.

The Factory Method Design Pattern

"Define an interface for creating an object, but let subclasses decide which class to instantiate. Factory Method lets a class defer instantiation to subclasses." (GoF p. 107)

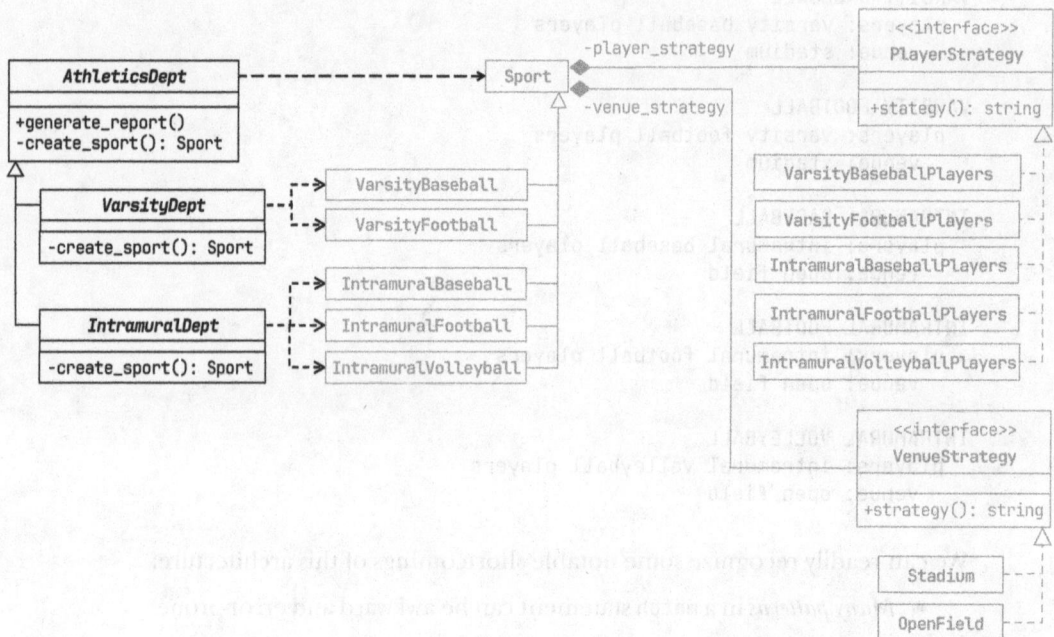

Figure 9.2   This version of the application is modeled from the Factory Method Design Pattern. Superclass AthleticsDept **delegates creating** Sport **objects to its subclasses. Subclasses** VarsityDept **and** IntramuralDept **are factory classes. Each implements the factory function** create_sport()**, which creates and returns an appropriate varsity or intramural** Sport **object. The grayed-out portions of the diagram have not changed logically from figure 9.1.**

Figure 9.2 shows some of the advantages of this revised architecture:

- *Encapsulated changes* make it easier to add new categories, such as club sports. This is the Encapsulate What Varies design principle (section 2.3.2).

- *The Open-Closed Principle* allows class `AthleticsDept` to remain stable (section 2.3.3) for generating reports with its `generate_report()` method. We can extend the class by adding more subclasses, such as `ClubDept`, but the class is closed to further modification.

- *Use of factory classes* in the form of the two subclasses `VarsityDept` and `Intramural-Dept`, which handle the varsity and intramural sports categories, respectively. Class `AthleticsDept` follows the Delegation Principle (section 2.3.2) by delegating the creation of `Sport` objects to these subclasses. It will be easier to vary the sports of the two categories.

- *Cohesive classes.* Each of the `AthleticsDept` subclasses follows the Single Responsibility Principle (section 2.3) and is responsible only for creating its `Sport` objects. The match statements can be shorter and thereby less prone to error.

- *Loosely coupled classes.* The `AthleticsDept` subclasses are no longer dependent on the implementation of the `Sport` subclasses. This is the Principle of Least Knowledge (section 2.3.2).

Subclasses **VarsityDept** and **IntramuralDept** are the factory classes, and **AthleticsDept** delegates creating the **Sport** objects to its subclasses.

We used the Factory Method Design Pattern to model a custom solution to our architecture problem.

Abstract class `AthleticsDept` has two concrete subclasses, `VarsityDept` and `Intramural-Dept`, which are factory classes. Each subclass implements the virtual method `create_sport()`, the factory method, to create and return a varsity or an intramural `Sport` object, respectively.

Listing 9.6 (Program 9.2 Provisions-FactoryDP) athletics_dept.py

```
from abc import ABC, abstractmethod
from sport import  SportType
from sports import VarsityBaseball, VarsityFootball, \
                   IntramuralBaseball, IntramuralFootball, \
                   IntramuralVolleyball

class AthleticsDept(ABC):
    @abstractmethod
    def create_sport(self, sport_type):        ◄────┐  Abstract factory method
        pass

    def generate_report(self, sport_type):
        sport = self.create_sport(sport_type)

        print(f'{sport.CATEGORY} {sport.SPORT_TYPE}')
```

```
            print(f'  players: {sport.recruit_players()}')
            print(f'    venue: {sport.reserve_venue()}')
            print()

class VarsityDept(AthleticsDept):
    def create_sport(self, sport_type):    ◀──── Factory method for
        match sport_type:                          varsity sports
            case SportType.BASEBALL:
                return VarsityBaseball()
            case SportType.FOOTBALL:
                return VarsityFootball()
            case _:
                return None;

class IntramuralDept(AthleticsDept):
    def create_sport(self, sport_type):    ◀──── Factory method for
        match sport_type:                          intramural sports
            case SportType.BASEBALL:
                return IntramuralBaseball()
            case SportType.FOOTBALL:
                return IntramuralFootball()
            case SportType.VOLLEYBALL:
                return IntramuralVolleyball()
            case _:
                return None;
```

Before we used the Factory Method Design Pattern, class `AthleticsDept` was responsible for creating all the `Sport` objects using a long `match` statement (listing 9.4). The design pattern refactors the architecture with two factory subclasses: `VarsityDept` and `IntramuralDept`.

Each factory subclass creates and returns an appropriate `Sport` object. Therefore, superclass `AthleticsDept` delegates the creation of a `Sport` object to its subclasses. When its method `generate_report()` calls the factory method `create_sport()` at run time, which `Sport` object is created depends on whether `generate_report()` was called on a `VarsityDept` object or an `IntramuralDept` object. The `match` statements in the `create_sport()` factory methods are shorter and simpler.

Our application uses delegation and factory classes.

Factory classes and the Delegation Principle together constitute the Factory Method Design Pattern.

The test program (listing 9.7) for this version of the application calls method `generate_report()` either on a `VarsityDept` object or on an `IntramuralDept` object. If it's a `VarsityDept` object, `generate_report()` calls the factory method `create_sport()`,

The Factory Method Design Pattern lets subclasses create objects 219

which uses polymorphism to create a varsity `Sport` object. But if it's an `IntramuralDept` object, the factory method uses polymorphism to create an intramural `Sport` object.

Listing 9.7 (Program 9.2 Provisions-FactoryDP) main.py

```python
from sport import SportType
from athletics_dept import VarsityDept, IntramuralDept

if __name__ == '__main__':
    varsity = VarsityDept()

    varsity.generate_report(SportType.BASEBALL)
    varsity.generate_report(SportType.FOOTBALL)

    intramural = IntramuralDept()

    intramural.generate_report(SportType.BASEBALL)
    intramural.generate_report(SportType.FOOTBALL)
    intramural.generate_report(SportType.VOLLEYBALL)
```

The output is unchanged from the previous version of the application.

9.1.4 Factory Method's generic model

Figure 9.3 shows the generic model of the Factory Method Design Pattern. From a design pattern's generic model, we can create a custom solution to an architecture problem. Table 9.1 shows how the example application applies the pattern.

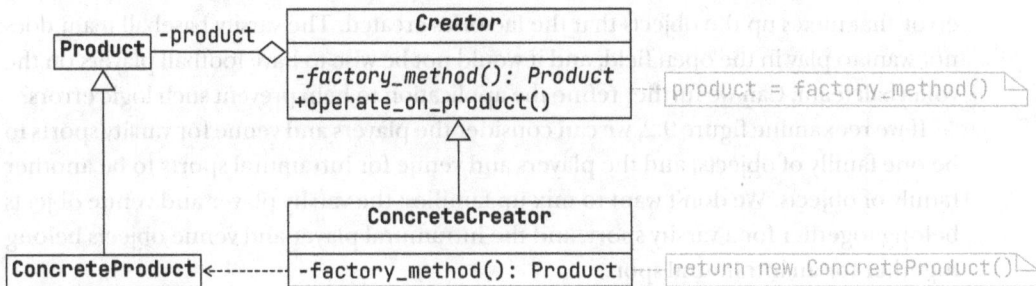

Figure 9.3 The generic model of the Factory Method Design Pattern. Compare to figure 9.2.

Table 9.1 The Factory Method Design Pattern as applied by the example application

Design pattern	Applied by the example application
Class `Product`	Superclass `Sport`
Class `ConcreteProduct`	`Sport` subclasses `VarsityBaseball`, `VarsityFootball`, `IntramuralBaseball`, `IntramuralFootball`, and `IntramuralVolleyball`
Class `Creator`	Superclass `AthleticsDept`

Table 9.1   The Factory Method Design Pattern as applied by the example application (*continued*)

Design pattern	Applied by the example application
Class `ConcreteCreator`	Subclasses `VarsityDept` and `IntramuralDept`
`factory_method()`	Methods `VarsityDept.create_sport()` and `IntramuralDept.create_sport()`
`operate_on_product()`	Method `AthleticsDept.generate_report()`

9.2   *The Abstract Factory Design Pattern creates families of objects*

Let's think back to our example of the automobile engine manufacturer and consider how an engine is made of many parts, and therefore the manufacturer is a creator of families of engine parts. A Ford engine consists of one family of parts, and a GM engine consists of another family of parts. Some parts are standard and belong to both families. But the manufacturer must neither include Ford-only parts in a GM engine nor include GM-only parts in a Ford engine. If our engine manufacturing application must include the concept of families of objects, the Abstract Factory Design Pattern provides a model to solve this architecture problem.

9.2.1   *Before using Abstract Factory*

We saw in the previous version of our sports application that the `VarsityDept` subclass and the `IntramuralDept` subclass are factory classes that create `Sport` objects for their superclass `AthleticsDept`. But logically, there is no way to prevent us from making a coding error that mixes up the objects that the factories created. The varsity baseball team does not want to play in the open field, and it would not be wise to have football players on the volleyball team. Can we further refine the application to help prevent such logic errors?

If we reexamine figure 9.2, we can consider the players and venue for varsity sports to be one family of objects, and the players and venue for intramural sports to be another family of objects. We don't want to mix up families: the varsity player and venue objects belong together for a varsity sport, and the intramural player and venue objects belong together for an intramural sport.

9.2.2   *After using Abstract Factory*

The Abstract Factory Design Pattern provides a model for an architecture design that creates families of objects (figure 9.4). We've added the use of the pattern as an increment to the previous version of the application.

The abstract `ProvisionsFactory` class is the interface for two factory classes. Factory class `VarsityFactory` creates player and venue objects from the varsity family, and factory class `IntramuralFactory` creates player and venue objects from the intramural family.

The `VarsityDept` subclass of superclass `AthleticsDept` requires the varsity family of `Sport` objects, so it must use `VarsityFactory`. Similarly, the `IntramuralDept` subclass requires the intramural family of `Sport` objects, so it must use `IntramuralFactory`. The two factory classes relieve VarsityDept and IntramuralDept of the responsibility of creating objects within the appropriate families, and neither subclass needs to have knowledge of how the factories accomplish their tasks.

The Abstract Factory Design Pattern

"Provide an interface for creating families of related or dependent objects without specifying their concrete classes." (GoF p. 87)

It's all about families: the Strategy Design Pattern models a software architecture that manages a family of algorithms, and the Abstract Factory Design Pattern models a software architecture that creates families of objects.

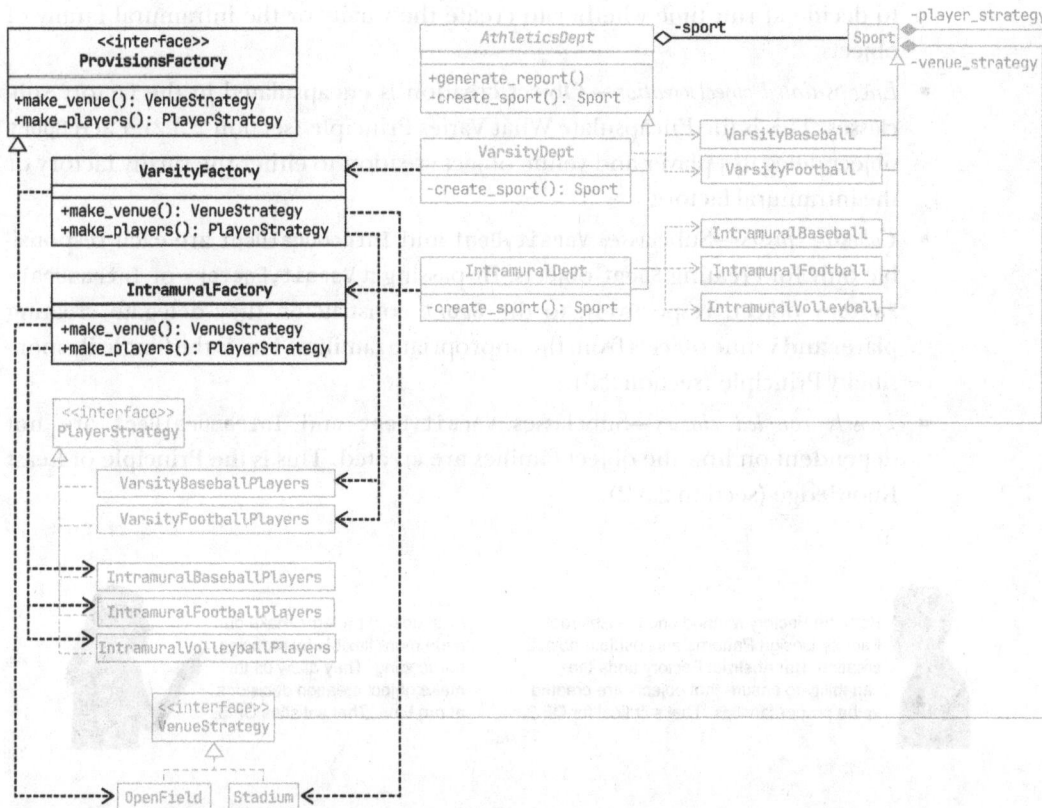

Figure 9.4   **This version of the application is modeled from the Abstract Factory Design Pattern. Interface ProvisionsFactory is the abstract factory whose implementor classes are used by the Sport subclasses. Implementor class VarsityFactory creates the varsity family of player and venue objects, and therefore, VarsityDept uses VarsityFactory. Implementor class IntramuralFactory creates the intramural family of player and venue objects, and therefore, IntramuralDept uses IntramuralFactory. The grayed-out portions of the diagram have not changed logically from figure 9.2.**

How will this work? As before, the `AthleticsDept` subclass `VarsityDept` creates varsity `Sport` objects. In this version of the application, the `create_sport()` method passes a `VarsityFactory` object to the `Sport` constructor. The `Sport` constructor then uses the `VarsityFactory` object to create appropriate player and venue objects from the varsity family.

Similarly, the `AthleticsDept` subclass `IntramuralDept` creates intramural `Sport` objects. Its `create_sport()` method passes an `IntramuralFactory` object to the `Sport` constructor. The latter then uses the `IntramuralFactory` object to create appropriate player and venue objects from the intramural family.

Figure 9.4 shows some of the benefits of using the Abstract Factory Pattern:

- *Keeps families together*—Each factory subclass guarantees that the objects it creates are from a single family.

- *Flexibility to choose which family*—There is less hardcoding, which makes it possible to decide at run time whether to create the varsity or the intramural family of objects.

- *Encapsulated object creation*—Object creation is encapsulated in the factory subclasses. This is the Encapsulate What Varies Principle (section 2.3.2). Each `Sport` object delegates player and venue object creation to either the varsity factory or the intramural factory.

- *Cohesive classes*—Subclasses `VarsityDept` and `IntramuralDept` are each responsible only for creating `Sport` objects. By passing a `VarsityFactory` or `Intramural-Factory` object, respectively, to the `Sport` constructor, they delegate creating player and venue objects from the appropriate families. This is the Single Responsibility Principle (section 2.3).

- *Loosely coupled classes*—Subclasses `VarsityDept` and `IntramuralDept` are not dependent on how the object families are created. This is the Principle of Least Knowledge (section 2.3.2).

Both the Factory Method and the Abstract Factory Design Patterns encapsulate object creation. But Abstract Factory adds the capability to ensure that objects are created in the proper families. That's critical for DF 2.

Both design patterns make our code more flexible by reducing hardcoding. They allow us to make object creation decisions at run time. That satisfies DF 3.

Listing 9.8 shows the abstract factory class `ProvisionsFactory` and the classes `Varsity-Factory` and `IntramuralFactory` that implement the interface. These classes must implement methods `make_players()` and `make_venue()` to create player and venue objects, respectively, within each family. Classes `VarsityFactory` and `Intramural-Factory` take full responsibility for creating the player and venue objects. Because

`VarsityFactory` creates only varsity objects and `IntramuralFactory` creates only intramural objects, there's no longer the danger of mixing up the objects.

Listing 9.8 **(Program 9.3 Provisions-AbsFactoryDP) provisions_factory.py**

```python
from abc import ABC, abstractmethod

from sport import SportType
from player_strategy import VarsityBaseballPlayers, \
                            VarsityFootballPlayers, \
                            IntramuralBaseballPlayers, \
                            IntramuralFootballPlayers, \
                            IntramuralVolleyballPlayers
from venue_strategy import Stadium, OpenField

class ProvisionsFactory(ABC):          # ◄── Abstract factory class
    @abstractmethod
    def make_players(self, player_type):   # ◄──
        pass
                                            #  Factory methods to be implemented
                                            #  by the factory subclasses
    @abstractmethod
    def make_venue(self):                   # ◄──
        pass

class VarsityFactory(ProvisionsFactory):    # ◄── Factory class to create and return
    def make_players(self, sport_type):     #     the varsity family of objects
        match sport_type:
            case SportType.BASEBALL:
                return VarsityBaseballPlayers()
            case SportType.FOOTBALL:
                return VarsityFootballPlayers()
            case _:
                return None;

    def make_venue(self):
        return Stadium()

class IntramuralFactory(ProvisionsFactory):   # ◄── Factory class to create and return
    def make_players(self, sport_type):       #     the intramural family of objects
        match sport_type:
            case SportType.BASEBALL:
                return IntramuralBaseballPlayers()
            case SportType.FOOTBALL:
                return IntramuralFootballPlayers()
            case SportType.VOLLEYBALL:
                return IntramuralVolleyballPlayers()
            case _:
                return None;

    def make_venue(self):
        return OpenField()
```

The `Sport` superclass delegates the creation of the sport's family of player and venue objects to the `ProvisionsFactory` object passed to its constructor.

Listing 9.9   (Program 9.3 Provisions-AbsFactoryDP) sport.py

```
...

class Sport:
    _CATEGORY = None
    _SPORT_TYPE = None

    def __init__(self, factory):
        self._player_strategy = factory.make_players(self._SPORT_TYPE)
        self._venue_strategy  = factory.make_venue()

    ...
```

The Sport subclasses are now greatly simplified from listing 9.3. Because classes VarsityFactory and IntramuralFactory are responsible for creating the player and venue objects, each Sport subclass only needs to specify its category and sport type.

Listing 9.10   (Program 9.3 Provisions-AbsFactoryDP) sports.py

```
from sport import Sport, Category, SportType

class VarsityBaseball(Sport):
    _CATEGORY = Category.VARSITY
    _SPORT_TYPE = SportType.BASEBALL

class VarsityFootball(Sport):
    _CATEGORY = Category.VARSITY
    _SPORT_TYPE = SportType.FOOTBALL

class IntramuralBaseball(Sport):
    _CATEGORY = Category.INTRAMURAL
    _SPORT_TYPE = SportType.BASEBALL

class IntramuralFootball(Sport):
    _CATEGORY = Category.INTRAMURAL
    _SPORT_TYPE = SportType.FOOTBALL

class IntramuralVolleyball(Sport):
    _CATEGORY = Category.INTRAMURAL
    _SPORT_TYPE = SportType.VOLLEYBALL
```

In the AthleticsDept subclasses VarsityDept and IntramuralDept, method create_sport() creates and passes the appropriate VarsityFactory or IntramuralFactory object to the constructors of the Sport subclasses to create the correct family of player and venue objects.

Listing 9.11   (Program 9.3 Provisions-AbsFactoryDP) athletics_dept.py

```
from abc import ABC, abstractmethod

from sport import SportType
```

```
from sports import VarsityBaseball, VarsityFootball, \
                   IntramuralBaseball, IntramuralFootball, \
                   IntramuralVolleyball
from provisions_factory import VarsityFactory, IntramuralFactory

class AthleticsDept(ABC):
    @abstractmethod
    def create_sport(self, sport_type):
        pass

    def generate_report(self, sport_type):
        sport = self.create_sport(sport_type)

        print(f'{sport.CATEGORY} {sport.SPORT_TYPE}')
        print(f'  players: {sport.recruit_players()}')
        print(f'    venue: {sport.reserve_venue()}')
        print()

class VarsityDept(AthleticsDept):
    def create_sport(self, sport_type):
        match sport_type:
            case SportType.BASEBALL:
                return VarsityBaseball(VarsityFactory())
            case SportType.FOOTBALL:
                return VarsityFootball(VarsityFactory())
            case _:
                return None;
```

Uses a VarsityFactory to create varsity player and venue objects

```
class IntramuralDept(AthleticsDept):
    def create_sport(self, sport_type):
        match sport_type:
            case SportType.BASEBALL:
                return IntramuralBaseball(IntramuralFactory())
            case SportType.FOOTBALL:
                return IntramuralFootball(IntramuralFactory())
            case SportType.VOLLEYBALL:
                return IntramuralVolleyball(IntramuralFactory())
            case _:
                return None;
```

Uses an IntramuralFactory to create player and venue objects

There are no changes to the test program in this version of the application, and the output remains the same.

9.2.3   *Abstract Factory's generic model*

Figure 9.5 shows the generic model of the Abstract Factory Design Pattern. It is from a design pattern's generic model that we can create a custom solution to an architecture problem. Table 9.2 shows how the example application applies the pattern.

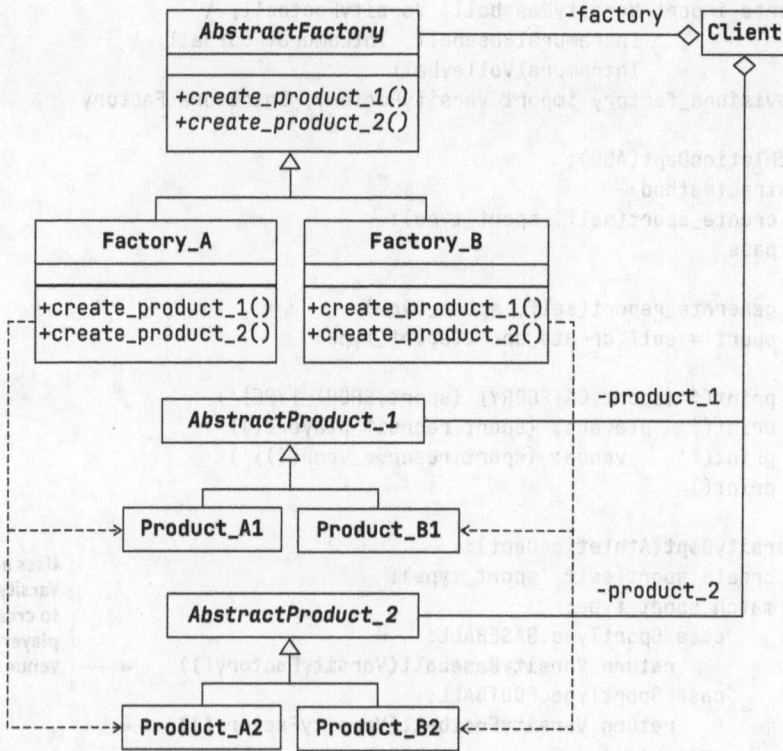

Figure 9.5   The generic model of the Abstract Factory Design Pattern. Compare with figure 9.4.

The factory classes are key. Each one creates objects from only one family.

Using tested factory classes lessens the chance of making coding errors that mix up the objects from different families.

Table 9.2   The Abstract Factory Design Pattern as applied by the example application

Design pattern	Applied by the example application
Client	Superclass AthleticsDept
Superclass AbstractFactory	Interface ProvisionsFactory
Factory subclasses Factory_A and FactoryB	Factory classes VarsityFactory and IntramuralFactory
Methods create_product_1() and create_product_2()	Methods VarsityFactory.make_players(), Varsity-Factory.make_venue(), IntramuralFactory.make_players(), and IntramuralFactory.make_venue()

Table 9.2 The Abstract Factory Design Pattern as applied by the example application (*continued*)

Design pattern	Applied by the example application
Classes `AbstractProduct_1` and `AbstractProduct_2`	Interfaces `PlayerStrategy` and `VenueStrategy`
Subclasses `Product_A1`, `Product_B1`, `Product_A2`, and `Product_B2`	Classes `VarsityBaseballPlayers`, `VarsityFootballPlayers`, `IntramuralBaseballPlayers`, `IntramuralFootballPlayers`, `IntramuralVolleyballPlayers`, `Stadium`, and `OpenField`

Our example application used the Strategy, Factory Method, and Abstract Factory Design Patterns!

A well-designed application may use several patterns, some multiple times. Applications modeled from design patterns will be more cohesive, have less hardcoding, and use good design principles.

9.3 *Choosing between Factory Method and Abstract Factory*

The Factory Method and the Abstract Factory design patterns both involve creating objects, but they serve different purposes. You must decide which pattern is appropriate to solve a particular programming problem.

The Factory Method Design Pattern defines an interface for creating a single object, but there can be different versions of the object. Delegate creating the versions to subclasses. In our example application, subclasses `VarsityBaseBall` and `VarsityFootball` create `VarsityBaseBallPlayers` and `VarsityFootballPlayers` objects, respectively, which are versions of `PlayerStrategy`.

The Abstract Factory Design Pattern is a model for creating families of related objects and reduces the chance of inadvertently mixing objects from different families. In our example, the `VarsityFactory` class creates venue and player objects only for varsity sports, whereas the `IntramuralFactory` class creates venue and player objects only for intramural sports.

Summary

- The Factory Method Design Pattern defines an interface for creating an object but delegates to subclasses to decide which object to create.
- The Abstract Factory Design Pattern provides an interface for creating families of related objects. It helps to prevent coding errors that mix up objects from different families.

The Adapter and Façade Design Patterns

10

This chapter covers

- The Adapter Design Pattern
- The Façade Design Pattern

In this chapter, we tackle an all-too-common problem: working with legacy software. This code can be from a library that we can't modify, or it may be other external code that we don't have access to or otherwise cannot modify.

The Adapter Design Pattern provides a model for a software architecture that needs to integrate external code with code in an existing application. However, the external and application codes weren't originally designed to work together, and we cannot change either of them. The pattern can also help to isolate an application from interface changes in the external code that may be outside of our control. Our example application must generate a report about the attendance and venue of various school sports, but each sport reports that data differently.

The Façade Design Pattern provides a simpler, higher-level interface that makes complex code that we can't modify easier to use. Our example application must interact with multiple organizations to raise funds for school sports.

NOTE Be sure to read the introduction to part 4 of the book for important information about design patterns in general and to learn how this and subsequent chapters teach each pattern.

10.1 The Adapter Design Pattern integrates code

When we develop an application, we may need to incorporate external code, such as code from a library or code that was previously written for some other application. We might not have access to the code's source files or know how it was implemented, and we might not be able to or allowed to change that code. Unfortunately, the external code isn't compatible with our application because it has a different interface. We may also be unable to change our application code due to its having many dependents. The Adapter Design Pattern provides a model for solving this classic architecture problem of integrating multiple pieces of code that were never designed to work together.

An application often needs to import code from libraries and other external sources, but we can't modify the external code.

The Adapter Design Pattern saves the day if the external code's design isn't compatible with the application's code design.

For an example of a code integration challenge, consider developing a drawing application that has various shape objects, such as lines, rectangles, and circles. The shape interface supports drawing operations such as setting the color, size, and orientation of a shape. Now we're asked to add a text object to the application. We find some existing code that edits and displays text and has an interface that supports operations such as setting the text color, font size, and font face. But the text interface isn't compatible with the shape interface, and the text code wasn't designed to work with the shape code. The Adapter Design Pattern provides a model to integrate the shape and text interfaces.

For our concrete example, we'll develop another example application involving sports reporting. As a demonstration, the first version will not use the Adapter Design Pattern, and we'll point out its faults. Then we'll design a second version that uses the Adapter Design Pattern and see that pattern's benefits.

In our example application, a college's athletics department needs to know the venues and average number of fans attending varsity baseball, varsity football, and intramural volleyball games. It gets this game data from the baseball, football, and volleyball organizations.

10.1.1 Desired design features

An application that needs to work with existing external code should have the following features:

- *DF 1*—We should not need to modify our application code or the external code to make them work together.
- *DF 2*—Our application code should be isolated from any interface changes by the external code.
- *DF 3*—It should be straightforward to add another sport to the report.

10.1.2 *Before using Adapter*

Suppose that due to lack of coordination, the three sports organizations report their game data differently, and they don't want to change how they report. Therefore, class `AttendanceReport` requires three overloaded public `print()` methods (figure 10.1),

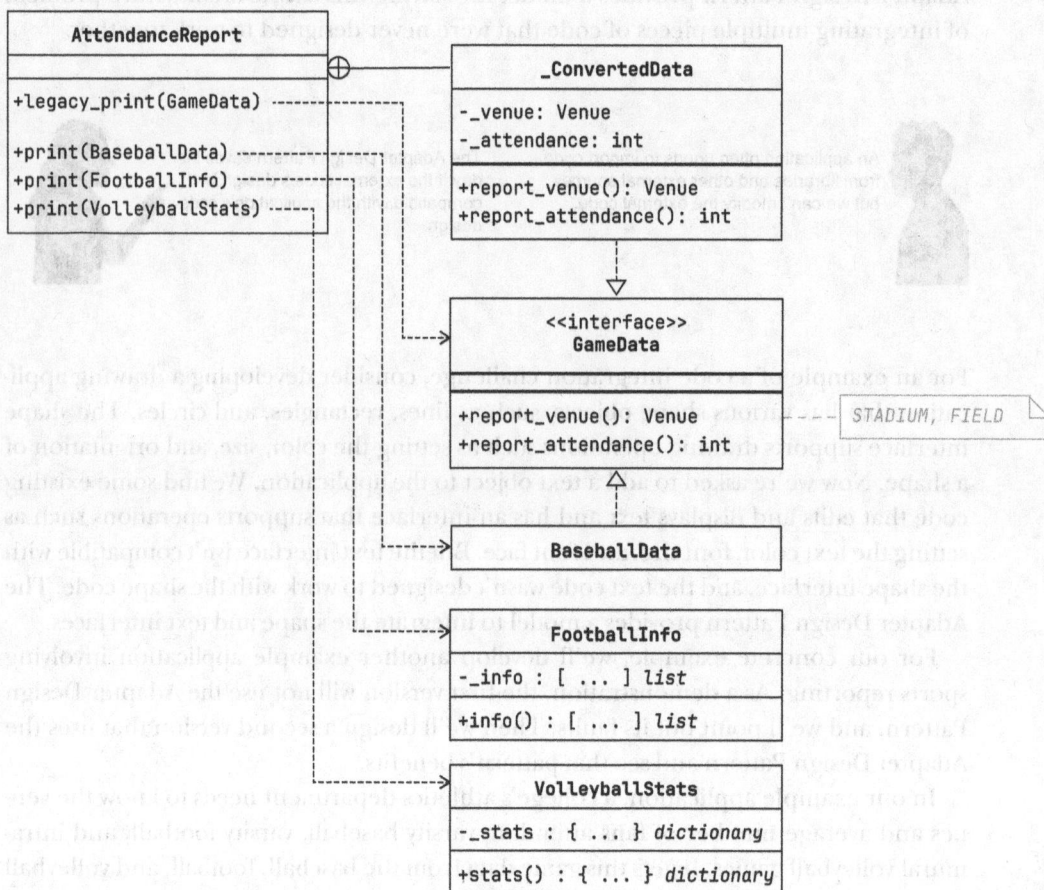

Figure 10.1 In the first version of the application, classes `BaseballData`, `FootballInfo`, and `VolleyballStats` present their venue and attendance data in different ways. Therefore, class `AttendanceReport` has three overloaded public `print()` methods. But the class's legacy method `legacy_print()`, which we cannot change, can only print `GameData` objects. Therefore, the class has a nested private class `_ConvertedData` to convert `FootballInfo` and `VolleyballStats` objects to `GameData` objects. `BaseballData` is already a `GameData` object.

one for each sport. Each of these `print()` functions calls the public `legacy_print()` method that does the actual printing, but it can only accept a `GameData` parameter. Because it's legacy code and other parts of the application may depend on it, we don't want to change the method. Therefore, class `AttendanceReport` contains a nested private class `_ConvertedData` to convert `FootballInfo` and `VolleyballStats` objects to `GameData` objects. `BaseballData` implements `GameData`, and its objects don't require conversion.

Example output from this attendance report application is as follows:

```
Baseball
   Venue.STADIUM: 500

Football
   Venue.STADIUM: 2000

Volleyball
   Venue.FIELD: 150
```

The legacy `legacy_print()` method of class `AttendanceReport` expects venue and attendance data in the form of an `GameData` object. We don't want to modify that method. `GameData` is an interface class that defines two abstract methods: `report_venue()` and `report_attendance()`.

Listing 10.1   (Program 10.1 Fans) game_data.py (poor design before DP)

```python
from enum import Enum
from abc import ABC, abstractmethod

class Venue(Enum):
    STADIUM = 0
    FIELD = 1

class GameData(ABC):
    @abstractmethod
    def report_venue(self): pass

    @abstractmethod
    def report_attendance(self): pass
```

Class `BaseballData` is the only one that is a subclass of `GameData`. To keep this example simple, we'll hardcode the return values of its `report_venue()` and `report_attendance()` methods.

Listing 10.2   (Program 10.1 Fans) baseball_data.py (poor design before DP)

```python
from game_data import GameData, Venue

class BaseballData(GameData):
    def report_venue(self):
```

```
                    return Venue.STADIUM

        def report_attendance(self):
            return 500
```

Classes FootballInfo and VolleyballStats do not implement interface GameData. Perhaps the football and volleyball sports obtained their code from a library, and we have no access to their source files. Class FootballInfo presents its venue and attendance data as a list.

```
from game_data import Venue

class FootballInfo:
    def __init__(self):
        self._info = [Venue.STADIUM, 2000]

    @property
    def info(self):
        return self._info
```

Class VolleyballStats presents its venue and attendance data as a dictionary.

```
from game_data import Venue

class VolleyballStats:
    def __init__(self):
        self._stats = { 'venue' : Venue.FIELD,
                        'attendance' : 150
                      }

    @property
    def stats(self):
        return self._stats
```

Class AttendanceReport requires three overloaded public print() methods (listing 10.5) that take BaseballData, FootballInfo, and VolleyballStats parameters. Each overloaded print() method calls the legacy legacy_print() method, which can only accept a GameData object. We don't want to modify this legacy printing code. Therefore, class AttendanceReport contains a private nested class _ConvertedData that implements interface GameData.

Method print() is overloaded, as designated by the @multimethod decorators (review section 7.1.4). The print() methods for FootballInfo and VolleyballStats must each create a _ConvertedData object to contain their venue and attendance values in a GameData object. The print() method for BaseballData can call the legacy print method directly because BaseballData already implements GameData.

Listing 10.5 (Program 10.1 Fans) attendance_report.py (poor design before DP)

```python
from multimethod import multimethod

from game_data import GameData
from baseball_data import BaseballData
from football_info import FootballInfo
from volleyball_stats import VolleyballStats

class AttendanceReport:
    class _ConvertedData(GameData):
        def __init__(self, venue, attendance):
            self._venue = venue
            self._attendance = attendance

        def report_venue(self):
            return self._venue

        def report_attendance(self):
            return self._attendance

    def legacy_print(self, game_data, title):
        print(title)
        print(f'  {game_data.report_venue()}: ', end='')
        print(f'{game_data.report_attendance()}')
        print()

    @multimethod
    def print(self, data: BaseballData, title):
        self.legacy_print(data, title)

    @multimethod
    def print(self, data: FootballInfo, title):
        venue = data.info[0]
        attendance = data.info[1]
        self.legacy_print(self._ConvertedData(venue, attendance),
                          title)

    @multimethod
    def print(self, data: VolleyballStats, title):
        venue = data.stats['venue']
        attendance = data.stats['attendance']
        self.legacy_print(self._ConvertedData(venue, attendance),
                          title)
```

Nested class for converting game data

Legacy printing method, which cannot change

This is already starting to look ugly! We needed a private internal class ConvertedData to convert data. That violates DF 1. If any sport changes the way it reports its data, we'll have to modify a print() member function in class AttendanceReport. That violates DF 2.

This code will get even uglier if we get more sports and then must print venue and attendance data stored in other incompatible ways. That violates DF 3.

The test program produces the desired reports.

> **Listing 10.6   (Program 10.1 Fans) main.py (poor design before DP)**

```python
from baseball_data import BaseballData
from football_info import FootballInfo
from volleyball_stats import VolleyballStats
from attendance_report import AttendanceReport

if __name__ == '__main__':
    baseball_data = BaseballData()
    football_info = FootballInfo()
    volleyball_stats = VolleyballStats()

    report = AttendanceReport()

    report.print(baseball_data,    'Baseball')
    report.print(football_info,    'Football')
    report.print(volleyball_stats, 'Volleyball')
```

This version of our attendance report application has several major faults, including these:

- *Class with multiple responsibilities*—Class `AttendanceReport` is responsible for both converting data and printing reports.
- *Classes not loosely coupled*—Class `AttendanceReport` must know the internal implementations of classes `FootballInfo` and `VolleyballStats` to convert them to `GameData` objects.
- *Inflexible architecture design*—If there is another source of venue and attendance data, such as for basketball games, it will require changes to class `AttendanceReport`.

Incompatible software is an all-too-common problem!

The software may have been written by multiple programmers at various times for different purposes. Some of the programmers may no longer be around.

10.1.3   *After using Adapter*

Let's see how the Adapter Design Pattern removes these faults. It encapsulates the data conversion code and thereby removes that responsibility from class `AttendanceReport`. The pattern introduces two adapter classes, `FootballData` and `VolleyballData`, each of which implements the `GameData` interface (figure 10.2). Class `FootballData` is the adapter that "wraps" (aggregates) class `FootballInfo`. Similarly, class `VolleyballData` is the adapter that wraps class `VolleyballStats`. Class `AttendanceReport` then needs only the public `legacy_print()` method, which is always passed a `GameData` object.

The Adapter Design Pattern

"Convert the interface of a class into another interface clients expect. Adapter lets classes work together that couldn't otherwise because of incompatible interfaces." (GoF p. 139)

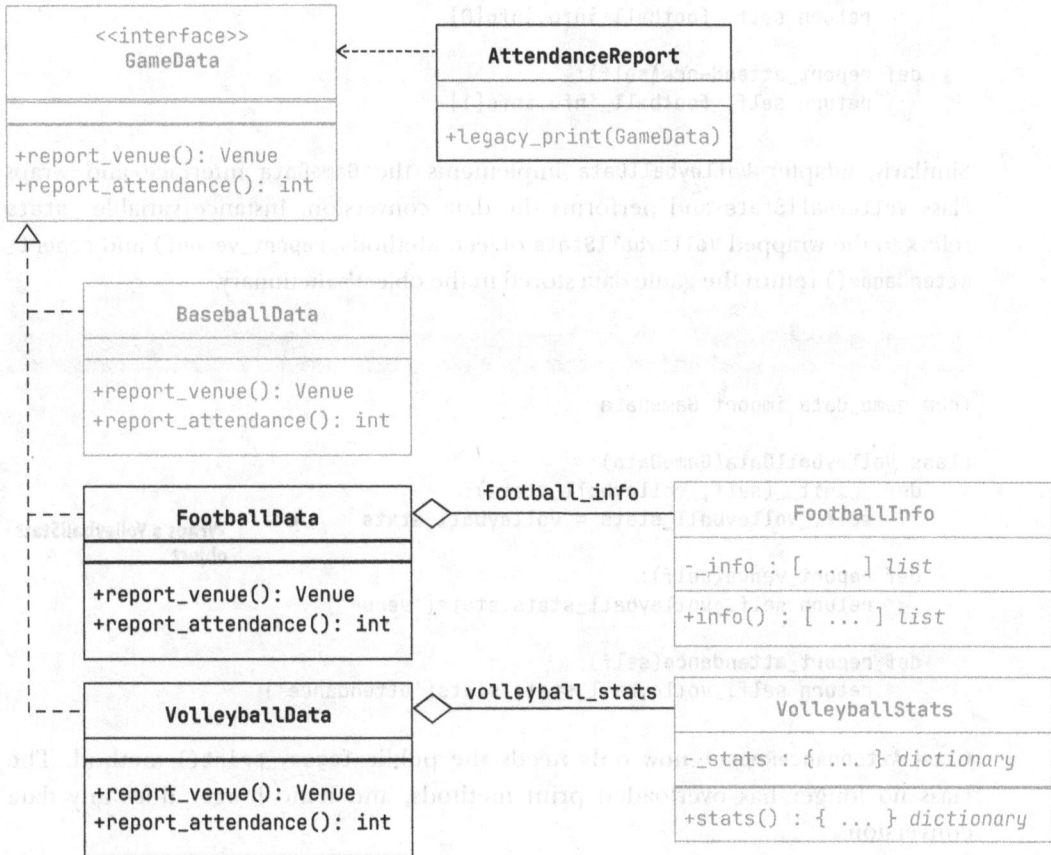

Figure 10.2 This version of the application uses the Adapter Design Pattern. Adapter classes `FootballData` and `VolleyballData` implement the `GameData` interface. Each wraps classes `FootballInfo` and `VolleyballStats`, respectively, and encapsulates the data conversion code. The grayed-out portions of the diagram have not changed logically from figure 10.1.

Adapter `FootballData` implements the `GameData` interface. It wraps class `FootballInfo` and performs the data conversion. Instance variable `_info` refers to the wrapped `FootballInfo` object. Methods `report_venue()` and `report_attendance()` return the game data stored in the object's list.

Listing 10.7   (Program 10.2 Fans-AdapterDP) football_data.py

```python
from game_data import GameData

class FootballData(GameData):
    def __init__(self, football_info):
        self._football_info = football_info

    def report_venue(self):
        return self._football_info.info[0]

    def report_attendance(self):
        return self._football_info.info[1]
```

◀ **Wraps a FootballInfo object**

Similarly, adapter `VolleyballData` implements the `GameData` interface and wraps class `VolleyballStats` and performs the data conversion. Instance variable `_stats` refers to the wrapped `VolleyballStats` object. Methods `report_venue()` and `report_attendance()` return the game data stored in the object's dictionary.

Listing 10.8   (Program 10.2 Fans-AdapterDP) volleyball_data.py

```python
from game_data import GameData

class VolleyballData(GameData):
    def __init__(self, volleyball_stats):
        self._volleyball_stats = volleyball_stats

    def report_venue(self):
        return self._volleyball_stats.stats['venue']

    def report_attendance(self):
        return self._volleyball_stats.stats['attendance']
```

◀ **Wraps a VolleyballStats object**

Class `AttendanceReport` now only needs the public `legacy_print()` method. The class no longer has overloaded print methods, and it no longer does any data conversions.

Listing 10.9   (Program 10.2 Fans-AdapterDP) attendance_report.py

```python
class AttendanceReport:
    def legacy_print(self, game_data, title):
        print(title)
        print(f'  {game_data.report_venue()}: ', end='')
        print(f'{game_data.report_attendance()}')
        print()
```

The test program creates the two adapter classes and arranges each one to adapt its corresponding object. The output is the same as before.

```python
from baseball_data import BaseballData
from football_info import FootballInfo
from football_data import FootballData
from volleyball_stats import VolleyballStats
from volleyball_data import VolleyballData
from attendance_report import AttendanceReport

if __name__ == '__main__':
    baseball_data = BaseballData()
    football_info = FootballInfo()
    volleyball_stats = VolleyballStats()

    football_data = FootballData(football_info)
    volleyball_data = VolleyballData(volleyball_stats)

    report = AttendanceReport()

    report.legacy_print(baseball_data,  'Baseball')
    report.legacy_print(football_data,  'Football')
    report.legacy_print(volleyball_data,'Volleyball')
```

Adapts a FootballInfo object

Adapts a VolleyballStats object

Each class that provides game data is paired with an adapter class if it doesn't already conform to the **GameData** interface.

We can add new game data classes and their adapters without modifying either the data classes or the legacy printing code.

Using the Adapter Design Pattern to model the architecture of the attendance report application has several important benefits:

- *Encapsulated data conversions*—The FootballData and VolleyballData adapter classes encapsulate data conversions from the FootballInfo and Volleyball-Stats classes, respectively. This is the Encapsulate What Varies Principle (section 2.3.2).

- *Single class responsibility*—Class AttendanceReport now only has the responsibility to print the report. It no longer has data conversion responsibilities. This is the Single Responsibility Principle (section 2.3). Each of the adapter classes FootballData and VolleyballData has the single responsibility to convert data.

- *Loosely coupled classes*—By applying the Principle of Least Knowledge (section 2.3.2), class AttendanceReport is loosely coupled with the data classes Football-Info and VolleyballStats. We can add new game data classes and their adapters without changing class AttendanceReport.

10.1.4 Adapter's generic model

Figure 10.3 shows the generic model of the Adapter Design Pattern. From a design pattern's generic model, we can create a custom solution to an architecture problem. Table 10.1 shows how the example application applies the pattern.

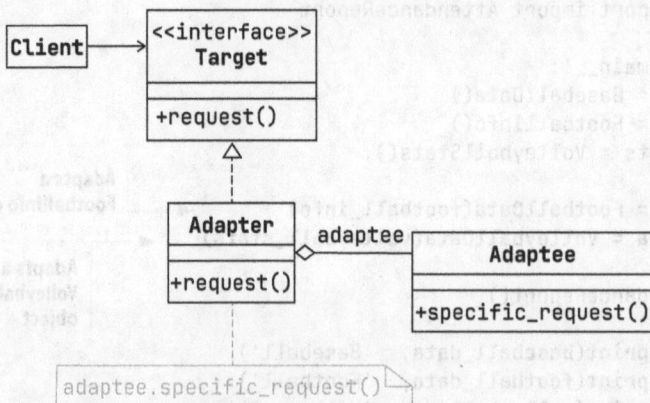

Figure 10.3   The generic model of the Adapter Design Pattern. Compare with figure 10.2. The Adapter class implements the `Target` interface. It adapts an `Adaptee` class by wrapping it so that the latter can work with the `Target` interface.

Table 10.1   The Adapter Method Design Pattern as applied by the example application

Design pattern	Applied by the example application
Interface `Target`	Interface `GameData`
Class `Adapter`	Classes `FootballData` and `VolleyballData`
Class `Adaptee`	Class `FootballInfo` and `VolleyballStats`
Function `request()`	Methods `report_venue()` and `report_attendance()`
Function `specific_request()`	Methods `FootballInfo.info()` and `VolleyballStats.stats()`

10.1.5 An alternative Adapter model

The Adapter Design Pattern has an alternative model that simplifies the adapter classes by relying on multiple inheritance instead of wrapping (figure 10.4). Adapter class `FootballData` implements the `GameData` interface and inherits from the `FootballInfo` class (listing 10.11).

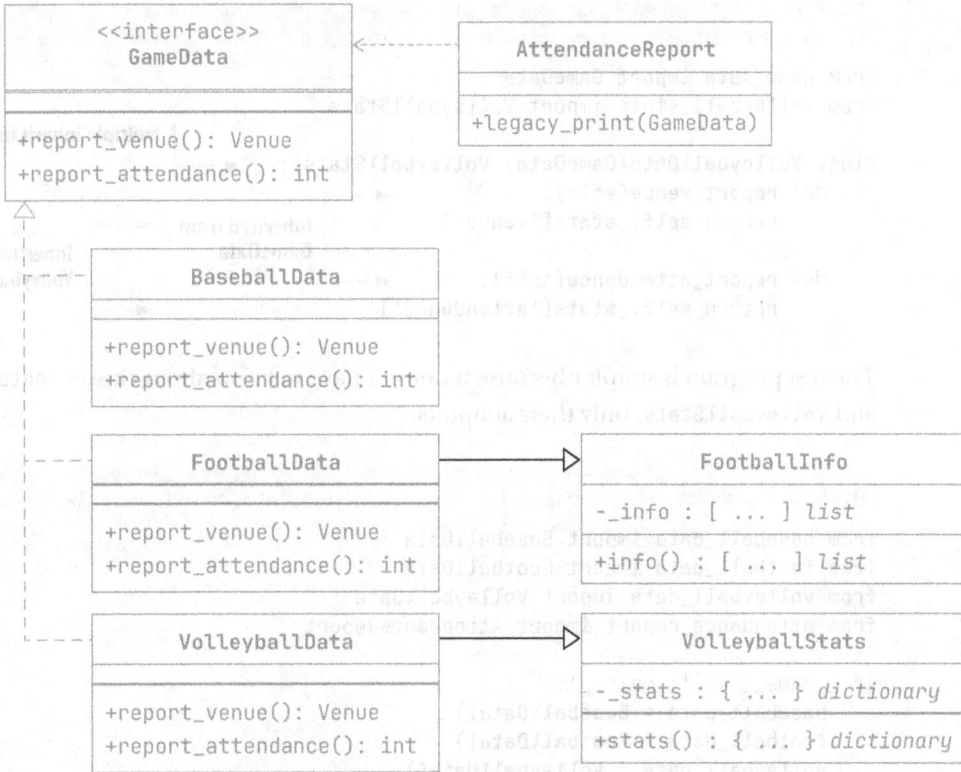

Figure 10.4   In the alternative version of the Adapter Design Pattern, adapter class `FootballData` implements the `GameData` interface and inherits from (rather than aggregates) the `FootballInfo` class. Adapter class `VolleyballData` implements the `GameData` interface and inherits from the `VolleyballStats` class. Neither adapter class does wrapping. The grayed-out portions of the diagram have not changed logically from figure 10.2.

Listing 10.11   (Program 10.3 Fans-AdapterDPx) football_data.py

```python
from game_data import GameData
from football_info import FootballInfo

class FootballData(GameData, FootballInfo):      ← Multiple inheritance
    def report_venue(self):                       ← Inherited from
        return self._info[0]                         GameData
                                                                   ← Inherited from
    def report_attendance(self):                  ←                  FootballInfo
        return self._info[1]                      ←
```

Similarly, adapter class `VolleyballData` implements the `GameData` interface and inherits from the `VolleyballStats` class.

Listing 10.12   (Program 10.3 Fans-AdapterDPx) volleyball_data.py

```python
from game_data import GameData
from volleyball_stats import VolleyballStats

class VolleyballData(GameData, VolleyballStats):
    def report_venue(self):
        return self._stats['venue']

    def report_attendance(self):
        return self._stats['attendance']
```

Multiple inheritance

Inherited from GameData

Inherited from VolleyballStats

The test program is simpler because it doesn't have to know about classes FootballInfo and VolleyballStats, only their adapters.

Listing 10.13   (Program 10.3 Fans-AdapterDPx) main.py

```python
from baseball_data import BaseballData
from football_data import FootballData
from volleyball_data import VolleyballData
from attendance_report import AttendanceReport

if __name__ == '__main__':
    baseball_data = BaseballData()
    football_data = FootballData()
    volleyball_data = VolleyballData()

    report = AttendanceReport()

    report.legacy_print(baseball_data,   'Baseball')
    report.legacy_print(football_data,   'Football')
    report.legacy_print(volleyball_data, 'Volleyball')
```

Figure 10.5 shows the model of the alternative version of the Adapter Design Pattern.

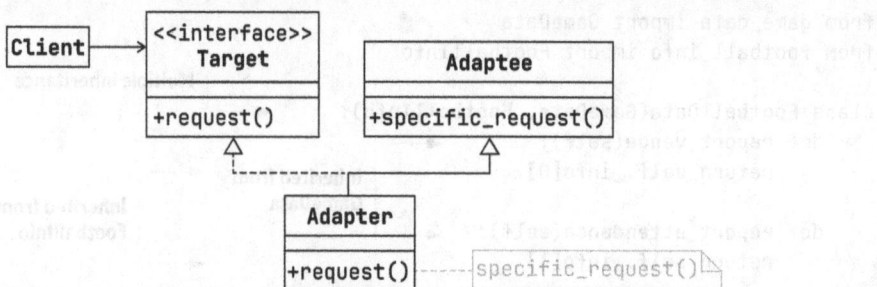

Figure 10.5   The model of the alternative version of the Adapter Design Pattern. Compare with figure 10.4. The Adapter class relies on multiple inheritance.

The `Adapter` class in figure 10.3 relies on object composition (wrapping) and is called an *object adapter*. The `Adapter` class in figure 10.5 relies on multiple inheritance and is called a *class adapter*.

> There are two types of adapters! How do I know which type to use?
>
> It depends on what your application needs. Often it doesn't matter which type you use, so use whichever one is more convenient for you to program.

We should decide which type of adapter to use based on the needs of our application. We can share an object adapter. If several adaptee classes have the same interface, multiple instances of the same object adapter can each wrap an adaptee. Because it aggregates the adaptee class, an object adapter also wraps any adaptee subclasses. On the other hand, with a class adapter, the client doesn't have to know about the adaptee class. Because it uses inheritance, a class adapter can override an adaptee's methods. If these features of the two types of adapters don't matter for an application, either type of adapter will do.

10.2 *The Façade Design Pattern hides a subsystem of interfaces*

Another common problem that we may encounter with a body of existing code is that it's complex and hard to use. The Façade Design Pattern provides a model for an application architecture that hides a subsystem of multiple interfaces. The application accomplishes this feat by "fronting" the subsystem interfaces with a simpler interface. This is a pattern we often use in our daily lives.

Consider starting a trip by car. We must interact with several components of the car:

1 Open the car door.
2 Sit in the driver's seat.
3 Close the car door.
4 Step on the brake.
5 Start the ignition.
6 Shift the gear.
7 Release the parking brake.
8 Step on the accelerator.

But we normally don't think of each step every time we start a trip. Instead, we have a "start the car" habit that allows us to do all the steps in order without thinking. This habit is our façade that hides all the steps. We simply start the car.

For our concrete programming example of using the Façade Design Pattern, consider a college athletics department that must do fundraising for its sports several times a year. It must solicit alumni for money, schedule fundraising meetings with booster clubs, and collect student fees. Let's suppose that the university administration also helps with the fundraising. We'll design two versions of this fundraising application. The first version doesn't use the Façade Design Pattern, and it will have several faults. The second version will use the pattern, and we'll see the benefits.

10.2.1   Desired design features

Design features for such an application should include the following:

- *DF 1*—The application should not depend on the interfaces or the implementations of any of its multiple components.
- *DF 2*—The application should not be concerned with the order that its components perform their tasks.
- *DF 3*—The application needs to interact with only a single interface to manage its components.

10.2.2   Before using Façade

Classes `AthleticsDept` and `Administration` each perform fundraising, so each class must interact with classes `Alumni`, `BoosterClubs`, and `Students` (figure 10.6). Classes `AthleticsDept` and `Administration` each call the `send_solicitations()` method of class `Alumni`, the `schedule_meetings()` method of class `BoosterClubs`, and the `collect_fees()` method of class `Students`.

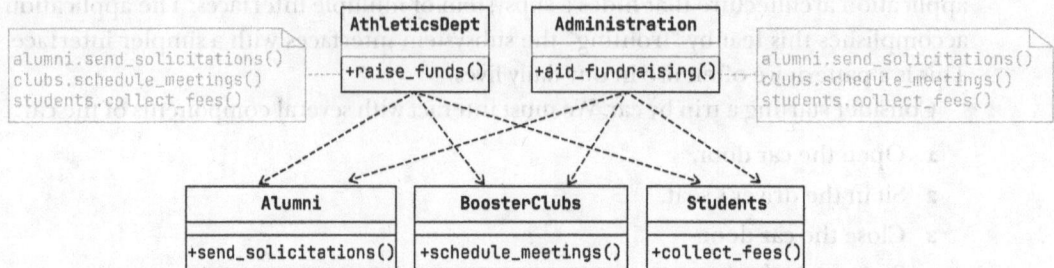

Figure 10.6   To perform fundraising, classes `AthleticsDept` and `Administration` each must call the appropriate methods of classes `Alumni`, `BoosterClubs`, and `Students`.

Method `send_solicitations()` of class `Alumni` is part of fundraising.

Listing 10.14   (Program10.4 Funds) alumni.py (poor design before DP)

```python
class Alumni:
    def send_solicitations(self):
        print('Send solicitations to alumni.')
```

Method `schedule_meetings()` of class `BoosterClubs` is also part of fundraising.

Listing 10.15   (Program10.4 Funds) booster_clubs.py (poor design before DP)

```python
class BoosterClubs:
    def schedule_meetings(self):
        print('Schedule meetings with booster clubs.')
```

Finally, method `collect_fees()` of class `Students` is another part of fundraising.

Listing 10.16   (Program10.4 Funds) students.py (poor design before DP)

```python
class Students:
    def collect_fees(self):
        print('Collect student fees.')
```

To perform fundraising, method `raise_funds()` of class `AthleticsDept` calls the methods of classes `Alumni`, `BoosterClubs`, and `Students`.

Listing 10.17   (Program10.4 Funds) athletics_dept.py (poor design before DP)

```python
from alumni import Alumni
from booster_clubs import BoosterClubs
from students import Students

class AthleticsDept:
    def raise_funds(self):
        alumni = Alumni()
        clubs = BoosterClubs()
        students = Students()

        print()
        print('ATHLETICS DEPARTMENT')

        alumni.send_solicitations()
        clubs.schedule_meetings()
        students.collect_fees()
```

To help with fundraising, method `aid_fundraising()` of class Administration calls the same methods.

Listing 10.18   (Program10.4 Funds) administration.py (poor design before DP)

```python
from alumni import Alumni
from booster_clubs import BoosterClubs
from students import Students

class Administration:
    def aid_fundrasing(self):
        alumni = Alumni()
        clubs = BoosterClubs()
```

```
    students = Students()

    print()
    print('SCHOOL ADMINISTRATION')

    alumni.send_solicitations()
    clubs.schedule_meetings()
    students.collect_fees()
```

Each of the classes **Alumni**, **BoosterClub**, and **Students** has its own fundraising interface. Therefore, classes **AthleticsDept** and **Administration** must know how to call the different fundraising functions. That violates DF 1 and DF 3.

Also, classes **AthleticsDept** and **Administration** each must know in what order to call call the fundraising functions. That violates DF 2.

The test program calls on classes AthleticsDept and Administration to do fundraising.

Listing 10.19   (Program10.4 Funds) main.py (poor design before DP)

```
from athletics_dept import AthleticsDept
from administration import Administration

if __name__ == '__main__':
    athletics = AthleticsDept()
    athletics.raise_funds();

    administration = Administration()
    administration.aid_fundraising()
```

The output of the application is as follows:
```
ATHLETICS DEPARTMENT
Send solicitations to alumni.
Schedule meetings with booster clubs.
Collect student fees.

SCHOOL ADMINISTRATION
Send solicitations to alumni.
Schedule meetings with booster clubs.
Collect student fees.
```

Faults of this version of the fundraising application include these:

- *Duplicated code*—In classes AthleticsDept and Administration, duplicate code calls the fundraising methods of classes Alumni, BoosterClubs, and Students.

- *Inflexible code*—If we add more classes for fundraising, both the AthleticsDept and Administration classes will need to change.

10.2.3 *After using Façade*

The Façade Design Pattern reduces the duplicated code and hides the fundraising interfaces behind façade class FundRaiser. The façade class presents a simpler and higher-level interface than the interfaces provided by classes Alumni, BoosterClubs, and Students.

The Façade Design Pattern

"Provide a unified interface to a set of interfaces in a subsystem. Façade defines a higher-level interface that makes the interface easier to use." (GoF p. 183)

The raise_funds() method of class AthleticsDept and the aid_fundraising() method of class Administration each only has to call method do_fund_raising() of class FundRaiser (figure 10.7).

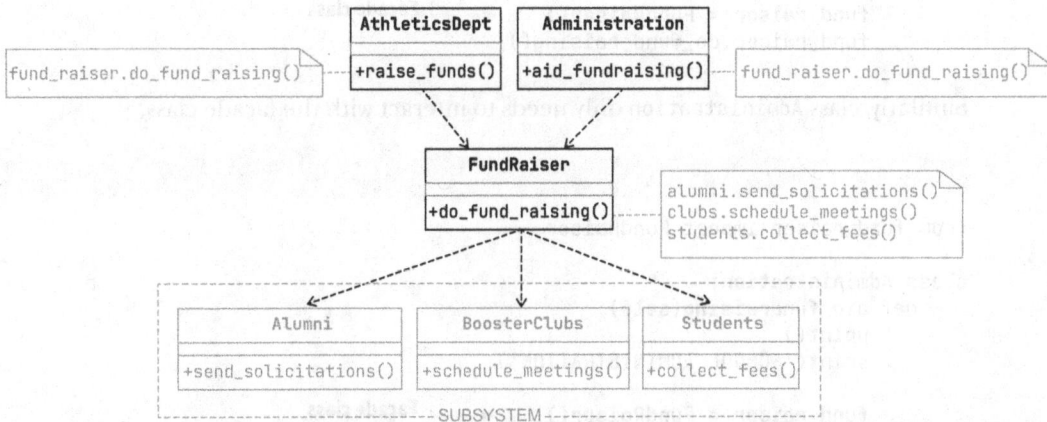

Figure 10.7 The architecture modeled from the Façade Design Pattern hides the details of fundraising behind the façade class FundRaiser, which presents a higher-level interface that simplifies using the subsystem consisting of classes Alumni, BoosterClubs, and Students.

Method do_fund_raising() of the façade class FundRaiser interacts with classes Alumni, BoosterClubs, and Students by calling their methods.

Listing 10.20   (Program 10.5 Funds-FaçadeDP) fund_raiser.py

```python
from alumni import Alumni
from booster_clubs import BoosterClubs
from students import Students

class FundRaiser:
    def do_fund_raising(self):
        alumni = Alumni()
        clubs = BoosterClubs()
        students = Students()
```

```
alumni.send_solicitations()
clubs.schedule_meetings()
students.collect_fees()
```

Class AthleticsDept only needs to interact with the façade class by calling its do_fund_raising() method.

> **Listing 10.21   (Program 10.5 Funds-FaçadeDP) athletics_dept.py**

```
from fund_raiser import FundRaiser

class AthleticsDept:
    def raise_funds(self):
        print()
        print('ATHLETICS DEPARTMENT')

        fund_raiser = FundRaiser()        ◄——┤ Façade class
        fund_raiser.do_fund_raising()
```

Similarly, class Administration only needs to interact with the façade class.

> **Listing 10.22   (Program 10.5 Funds-FaçadeDP) administration.py**

```
from fund_raiser import FundRaiser

class Administration:
    def aid_fundraising(self):
        print()
        print('SCHOOL ADMINISTRATION')

        fund_raiser = FundRaiser()        ◄——┤ Façade class
        fund_raiser.do_fund_raising()
```

Very nice! Now the AthleticsDept and Administration classes only need to interact with the FundRaiser class.

We can create another façade class if the athletics department and the administration want to send out thank-you messages.

Modeling the architecture from the Façade Design Pattern has several key benefits:

- *Reduced code duplication*—The façade class encapsulates all the fundraising operations, and that code needs to appear only once. This is the Don't Repeat Yourself (DRY) Principle (section 2.3.3).
- *Loosely coupled classes*—The AthleticsDept and Administration classes have no dependencies on the Alumni, BoosterClubs, and Students classes. This is the Principle of Least Knowledge (section 2.3.2).

- *More flexible code*—If we add another class for fundraising, such as Corporate-Sponsors, only the façade class will need to change. This is the Encapsulate What Varies Principle (section 2.3.2).

- *Easier-to-use subsystem*—The façade class makes the Alumni, BoosterClubs, and Students subsystem easier to use with a simple interface that hides the subsystem interfaces.

10.2.4 Façade's generic model

Figure 10.8 shows the generic model of the Façade Design Pattern. Recall that it is from the design pattern's generic model that we can create a custom solution to an architecture problem (section 8.1.3). Table 10.2 shows how the example application applies the pattern.

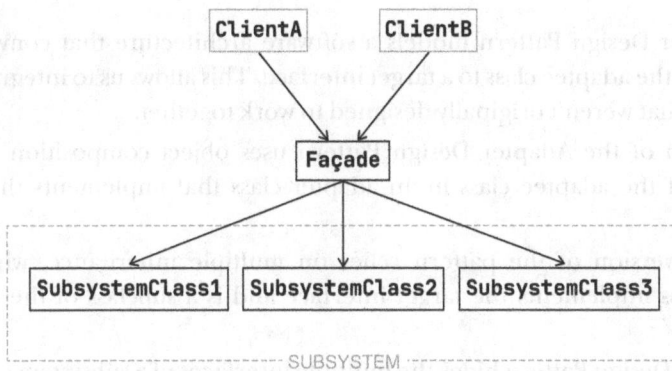

Figure 10.8 The generic model of the Façade Design Pattern. Compare with figure 10.7. The Façade class hides the interfaces of the subsystem classes and makes the subsystem consisting of classes Alumni, BoosterClubs, and Students easier to use.

Table 10.2 The Façade Method Design Pattern as applied by the example application

Design pattern	Applied by the example application
Classes ClientA, ClientB, etc.	Classes AthleticsDept and Administration
Class Façade	Class FundRaiser
Classes SubsystemClass1, SubsystemClass2, etc.	Classes Alumni, BoosterClubs, and Students

The Adapter Design Pattern models an architecture where an adaptee interface is adapted to be compatible with a target interface. It's the pattern for integrating library code with legacy application code.

The Façade Design Pattern models an architecture where a simpler higher-level interface hides a subsystem of interfaces. Both make an application with multiple components easier to use.

10.3   *Choosing between Adapter and Façade*

The Adapter Design Pattern and the Façade Design Pattern both model ways to simplify using code that you can't or don't want to modify. But the models are appropriate for different situations.

Use the Adapter Design Pattern when you have a desired interface, and you must adapt classes you can't change by converting them to that interface. In our example, our legacy printing routine could only accept GameData objects, so we had to convert FootballInfo and VolleyballStats objects.

Use the Façade Design Pattern model to create a "fronting" façade class that hides the complexity of a subsystem of classes. The façade class has a simpler set of methods to call, and each method hides the calls it makes to methods of the subsystem classes. In our example, method do_fund_raising() of the façade class FundRaiser makes calls to methods of the Alumni, BoosterClubs, and Students subsystem classes.

Summary

- The Adapter Design Pattern models a software architecture that converts the interface of the adaptee class to a target interface. This allows us to integrate bodies of code that weren't originally designed to work together.

- One version of the Adapter Design Pattern uses object composition to wrap an object of the adaptee class in an adapter class that implements the target interface.

- The other version of the pattern relies on multiple inheritance, where the adapter class implements the target interface and is a subclass of the adaptee class.

- The Façade Design Pattern hides the multiple interfaces of a subsystem of classes with a simpler and higher-level interface, thereby making the subsystem easier to use.

The Iterator and
Visitor Design Patterns

This chapter covers
- The Iterator Design Pattern
- The Visitor Design Pattern

The two design patterns discussed in this chapter provide models for applications that must flexibly access data stored in various data structures such as lists, tuples, dictionaries, and trees. The example applications continue the theme of generating sports reports.

The Iterator Design Pattern enables a single algorithm to iterate over different sequential collections of objects without needing to know how the collections are implemented. Our first example application is modeled on this design pattern. The application's algorithm can generate a report about the players on several baseball teams, even though each team stores its player data in a different type of sequential collection.

The Visitor Design Pattern works with a single data collection that contains different types of data. The collection is often structured as a tree. The pattern encapsulates different algorithms that are each designed to process the tree nodes. Our second example program is modeled on this design pattern. The application's algorithms can generate different reports from the same collection of intramural games data.

The Iterator Design Pattern is appropriate for applications that have a *single algorithm* that must work on *different types of sequential data collections*.

The Visitor Design Pattern is appropriate for applications that have *different algorithms* that must work on a *single data collection*.

NOTE   Be sure to read the introduction to part 4 of the book for important information about design patterns in general and to learn how this and subsequent chapters teach each pattern.

11.1   The Iterator Design Pattern: One algorithm operates on different sequential data collections

We often must write code that iterates over sequential collections of objects and performs an operation on each object. The types of collections are different. For example, an application might have to work with a list, a generator, and a dictionary of employee objects. No matter what type of sequential collection the objects are stored in, the application must be able to access each object in turn and execute an algorithm to calculate the corresponding employee's pay.

This section demonstrates using the Iterator Design Pattern, which allows an application to iterate over sequential collections of objects without knowing how the collections are implemented. A sequential collection of objects either is empty or must have these properties:

- One of the objects is the first object, and one of the objects is the last object. If there is only one object in the collection, then that object is both the first and the last of the sequence.
- Each object except the last is followed by a unique next object.
- We can access the objects in the collection one at a time in order from the first one through the last one.
- We can tell when we've accessed all the objects in the sequence: i.e., when we've reached the end of the collection.

Lists, tuples, and generators are examples of sequential collections. We can even treat a dictionary as a sequential collection by accessing its keys sequentially to obtain the corresponding values.

As a concrete example, suppose the athletics department wants to print lists of the players on each intramural baseball team. The department doesn't care about the particular order of the players in each list, as long as it includes every player's student ID and name. Here's an example set of printed lists for Team 1, Team 2, and Team 3:

```
TEAM 1
12436 Alwin, Jim
26410 Bond, Bob
14306 Charles, Ronda
61835 Dunn, Fred
30437 Edwards, Gina
76517 Fanning, Pat
98734 Galway, Leslie
14998 Hiroshi, Scott
47303 Ingles, Mary

TEAM 2
63421 Jackson, Tammy
44551 Killebrew, Wally
14306 Lamprey, Roberta
61835 Mays, Serena
30437 Norton, Donna
76517 OBrien, George
98734 Paulson, Marsha
14998 Quark, John
47303 Rogers, Jena

TEAM 3
46841 Smith, Ken
98765 Terrance, Laura
10547 Ulster, Doug
38331 Vicks, Ron
47781 Wong, Henrietta
57974 Xavier, Nancy
56712 Yonnick, Billy
72288 Aaron, Patricia
```

Further suppose that due to a lack of coordination, each team stores its player data in a different type of sequential data collection. Team 1 uses a list, Team 2 uses a generator, and Team 3 uses a dictionary.

11.1.1 Desired design features

An application with an algorithm that must work with different types of sequential collections of objects should have these design features:

- *DF 1*—The application should be able to execute an algorithm that processes the objects without knowing how the sequential collections are implemented.
- *DF 2*—The collections should be independent of one another.
- *DF 3*—It should be possible to add new sequential collections without modifying the application's algorithm code.

11.1.2 Before using Iterator

It is not an unreasonable architecture for the first version of our example team report application to have three Team subclasses to generate the player lists—one subclass per type of collection (figure 11.1)—and a print method for each collection type.

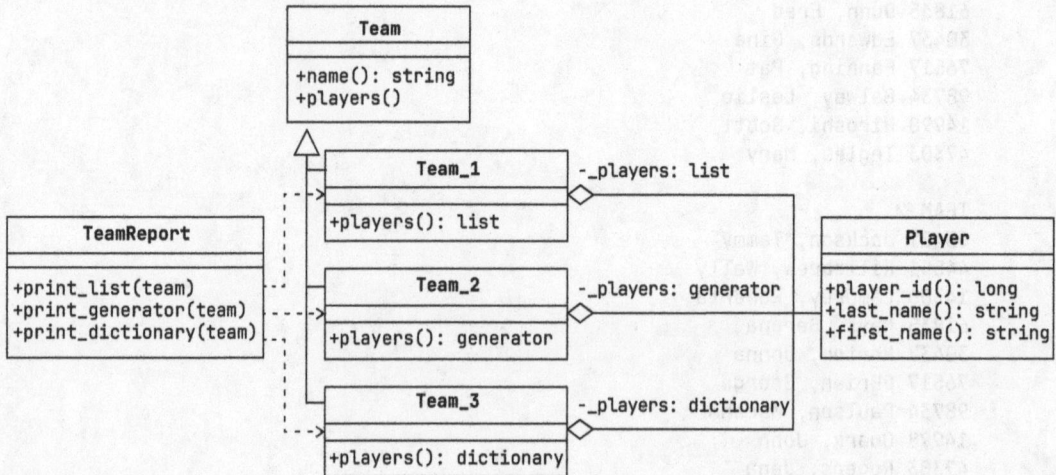

Figure 11.1   Each Team **subclass stores its** Player **objects in a different type of sequential data collection: list, generator, or dictionary. Therefore, class** TeamReport **has three print methods, one for each type of collection.**

Class Player has each player's ID, last name, and first name. A baseball team consists of nine active players, so for simplicity, we'll hardcode the collection sizes to nine.

Listing 11.1   (Program 11.1 Players) player.py (poor design before DP)

```
class Player:
    def __init__(self, player_id, last, first):
        self._player_id = player_id
        self._last_name = last
        self._first_name = first

    @property
    def player_id(self):
        return self._player_id

    @property
    def last_name(self):
        return self._last_name

    @property
    def first_name(self):
        return self._first_name
```

Each Team has a name and a sequential collection of players.

Listing 11.2   (Program 11.1 Players) team.py (part 1 of 4, poor design before DP)

```
from player import Player

class Team:
    def __init__(self, name, players):
        self._name = name
        self._players = players

    @property
    def name(self):
        return self._name

    @property
    def players(self):
        return self._players
```

Subclass Team_1 stores its player data as tuples in a list. Each tuple contains data for one player.

Listing 11.3   (Program 11.1 Players) team.py (part 2 of 4, poor design before DP)

```
class Team_1(Team):
    def __init__(self):
        super().__init__('TEAM 1', [
            (12436, 'Alwin', 'Jim'),
            (26410, 'Bond', 'Bob'),
            (14306, 'Charles', 'Ronda'),
            (61835, 'Dunn', 'Fred'),
            (30437, 'Edwards', 'Gina'),
            (76517, 'Fanning', 'Pat'),
            (98734, 'Galway', 'Leslie'),
            (14998, 'Hiroshi', 'Scott'),
            (47303, 'Ingles', 'Mary')
        ])
```

Subclass Team_2 stores its players as a generator that creates Player objects one at a time on demand.

Listing 11.4   (Program 11.1 Players) team.py (3 of 4, poor design before DP)

```
class Team_2(Team):
    def __init__(self):
        super().__init__('TEAM 2', [
            (63421, 'Jackson', 'Tammy'),
            (44551, 'Killebrew', 'Wally'),
            (14306, 'Lamprey', 'Roberta'),
            (61835, 'Mays', 'Serena'),
            (30437, 'Norton', 'Donna'),
            (76517, 'OBrien', 'George'),
```

```
              (98734, 'Paulson', 'Marsha'),
              (14998, 'Quark', 'John'),
              (47303, 'Rogers', 'Jena')
          ])
          self._index = -1

      def __iter__(self):
          return self

      def __next__(self):
          if self._index < len(self._players) - 1:
              self._index += 1
              return Player(*self._players[self._index])   ◄───┐ Creates and returns
          else:                                                 the next Player object
              raise StopIteration   ◄───┐ No more players
```

Each call to the generator's built-in __next__() method creates and returns the next Player object by calling the constructor:

```
Player(*self._players[self._index])
```

The arguments for the constructor are unpacked from the tuple in the list self ._players indexed by self.index.

Subclass Team_3 stores its player data as a dictionary of named tuples of player names, where the player ID is the key.

```
from collections import namedtuple

class Team_3(Team):
    def __init__(self):
        super().__init__('TEAM 3', {})
        Name = namedtuple('Name', ['last_name', 'first_name'])

        self._players[46841] = Name( last_name='Smith',
                                     first_name='Ken')
        self._players[98765] = Name( last_name='Terrance',
                                     first_name='Laura')
        self._players[10547] = Name( last_name='Ulster',
                                     first_name='Doug')
        self._players[38331] = Name( last_name='Vicks',
                                     first_name='Ron')
        self._players[47781] = Name( last_name='Wong',
                                     first_name='Henrietta')
        self._players[57974] = Name( last_name='Xavier',
                                     first_name='Nancy')
        self._players[56712] = Name( last_name='Yonnick',
                                     first_name='Billy')
        self._players[72288] = Name( last_name='Aaron',
                                     first_name='Patricia')
```

It's unfortunate that the three sequential collections are different.

We may be dealing with legacy code, parts of which were written by different programmers at different times for different purposes.

Because of the three different types of sequential data collections of team players, class `TeamReport` has three methods to print the lists. Each print method must iterate over its sequential collection of `Player` objects in a manner appropriate for a list, a generator, or a dictionary, as appropriate.

Listing 11.6   (Program 11.1 Players) report.py (poor design before DP)

```python
from player import Player

class TeamReport:
    def print_list(self, team):
        print()
        print(team.name)

        for t in team.players:
            player = Player(*t)
            print(f'{player.player_id} {player.last_name}, '
                  f'{player.first_name}')

    def print_generator(self, team):
        print()
        print(team.name)

        player_generator = team

        for _ in range(len(team.players)):
            player = next(player_generator)
            print(f'{player.player_id} {player.last_name}, '
                  f'{player.first_name}')

    def print_dictionary(self, team):
        print()
        print(team.name)

        for key in team.players.keys():
            name = team.players[key]
            player = Player(key, name.last_name, name.first_name)
            print(f'{player.player_id} {player.last_name}, '
                  f'{player.first_name}')
```

Method `print_list()` simply iterates over the `team.players` list to create and print each `Player` object in turn. Method `print_generator()` calls the generator's `next()`

method to create and print the next Player object. Method print_dictionary() uses the key values to access the associated named tuples to sequentially create and print the Player objects.

The test program prints the example Player collections as shown at the beginning of this section.

```python
from team import Team_1, Team_2, Team_3
from report import TeamReport

if __name__ == '__main__':
    report = TeamReport()

    team_1 = Team_1()
    report.print_list(team_1)

    team_2 = Team_2()
    report.print_generator(team_2)

    team_3 = Team_3()
    report.print_dictionary(team_3)
```

Class TeamReporter must know how each of the sequential collections are implemented: as a list, a generator, or a dictionary. It requires three print methods. That violates DF 1.

Adding another report with yet another type of sequential collection such as a linked list would require adding another print method. That violates DF 3.

There are several design problems with this version of the list application, especially in class TeamReport:

- *Duplicated code*—Each print method must iterate over its sequential collection of Player objects in a different way depending on the type of the collection. This will become a greater problem if there are more teams and sequential data collections to store players, such as linked lists.

- *Classes not loosely coupled*—Each print method must know how the Player objects are stored to properly iterate over its sequential collection. Therefore, class TeamReport is not loosely coupled with the Team subclasses.

11.1.3 *After using Iterator*

This is an architecture problem that the Iterator Design Pattern can help solve. The key idea is for the client code (class TeamReport in our application) to delegate to iterator classes the task of iterating over the different types of sequential collections of

Player objects. Each iterator class knows how to iterate over a particular type of collection, and it can provide access to the Player objects without exposing to the client code how the objects are stored.

The Iterator Design Pattern

"Provide a way to access the elements of an aggregate object sequentially without exposing its underlying representation." (GoF p. 257)

As suggested by figure 11.2, the goal is to enable a single algorithm to operate over different sequential data collections. The Iterator Design Pattern enables class Team-Report to be loosely coupled with the Team subclasses. Each subclass no longer provides direct access to its sequential collection of Player objects. Therefore, each subclass can hide how it implements its collection. Instead, each subclass has an iterator property that is an Iterator object, which knows how to iterate over that subclass's collection of Player objects.

Iterator Design Pattern
A single algorithm operates on different sequential data collections.

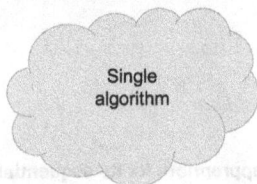

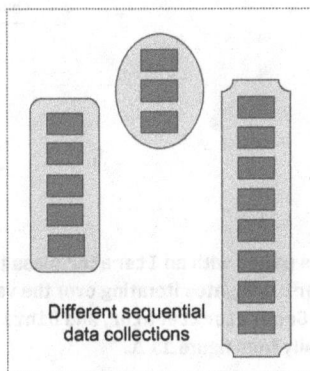

Single algorithm

Different sequential data collections

Figure 11.2 A single algorithm can operate on different sequential data collections.

Class TeamReport lets the Iterator subclasses do the work of iterating over the Player object sequences. There is an Iterator subclass for each type of sequential collection. Therefore, class TeamReport doesn't need to know how each Team subclass implemented its sequential collection (figure 11.3).

Each Iterator class knows how to iterate over its type of sequential collection and has private instance variables to keep track of which Player object the next() method should create and return. Method has_next() returns True if there are more Player objects to create; otherwise, it returns False. Class TeamReport does not know how each Team subclass stores its sequence of Player objects, and therefore it is loosely coupled with the Team subclasses.

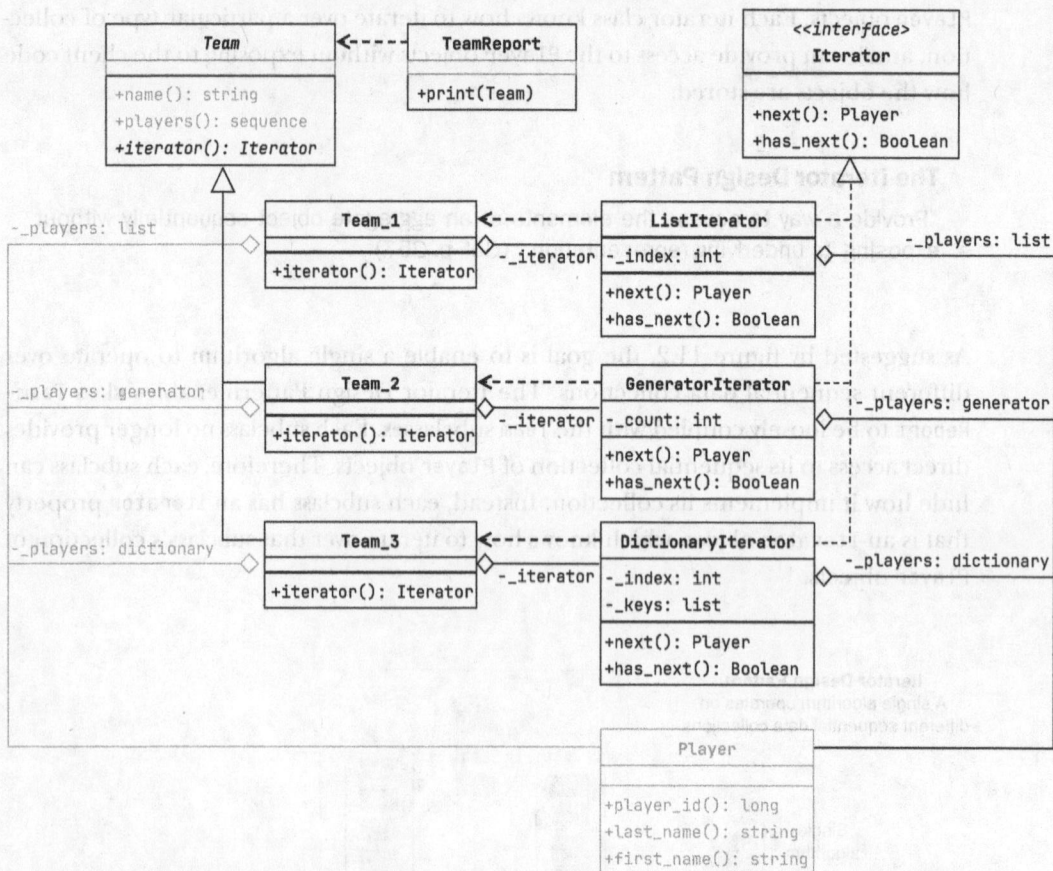

Figure 11.3 Each `Team` subclass is paired with an `Iterator` class that is appropriate for its sequential collection of `Player` objects. Class `TeamReport` delegates iterating over the various types of sequential collections to the `Iterator` classes `ListIterator`, `GeneratorIterator`, and `DictionaryIterator`. The grayed-out portions of the diagram haven't changed logically from figure 11.1.

The Iterator Design Pattern adds more classes when you compare figure 11.1 to figure 11.3.

Yes, using a design pattern can make small applications appear more complex. A good designer must weigh the advantages of using a design pattern versus writing code that may be less flexible and harder to modify.

In listing 11.8, the `Iterator` interface declares two abstract methods: `next()` and `has_next()`. Defined by each `Iterator` class according to the type of sequential data collection, the `next()` method advances to the next `Player` object and returns the object, and the `has_next()` method returns `True` if there are more objects in the sequence or

False otherwise. Each `Iterator` class has private instance variables to keep track of the current `Player` object within its sequence.

Listing 11.8   (Program 11.2 Players-IteratorDP) iterator.py (part 1 of 4)

```python
from abc import ABC, abstractmethod
from player import Player

class Iterator(ABC):
    @abstractmethod
    def next(self):
        pass

    @abstractmethod
    def has_next(self):
        pass
```

Class `ListIterator` uses its `_index` instance variable to keep track of the current `Player` object.

Listing 11.9   (Program 11.2 Players-IteratorDP) iterator.py (part 2 of 4)

```python
class ListIterator(Iterator):
    def __init__(self, team):
        self._players = team.players
        self._index = -1

    def next(self):
        self._index += 1
        t = self._players[self._index]    # Obtains the next tuple of player
        return Player(*t)                 #   data from the team's players list
                                          # Creates and returns the next Player
    def has_next(self):                   #   object by unpacking the tuple
        return self._index < len(self._players) - 1
```

Method next() of class `GeneratorIterator` delegates to method next() of the `Team_2` generator.

Listing 11.10   (Program 11.2 Players-IteratorDP) iterator.py (part 3 of 4)

```python
class GeneratorIterator(Iterator):
    def __init__(self, team):
        self._team = team
        self._players = team.players
        self._player_generator = team
        self._count = 0

    def next(self):
        self._count += 1
        return next(self._player_generator)   # Returns the next Player object
                                              #   created by the generator
    def has_next(self):
        return self._count < len(self._players)
```

Class `DictionaryIterator` iterates over the dictionary keys to sequentially access the
`Player` objects.

Listing 11.11   (Program 11.2 Players-IteratorDP) iterator.py (part 4 of 4)

```python
class DictionaryIterator(Iterator):
    def __init__(self, team):
        self._players = team.players
        self._keys = list(self._players.keys())
        self._index = -1

    def next(self):
        self._index += 1
        key = self._keys[self._index]
        name = self._players[key]
        return Player(key, name.last_name, name.first_name)

    def has_next(self):
        return self._index < len(self._players) - 1
```

> Obtains the next key value of the dictionary

> Creates and returns the Player object associated with the key value

Each `Team` subclass must now create and return an `Iterator` object appropriate for its
type of sequential collection.

Listing 11.12   (Program 11.2 Players-IteratorDP) team.py

```python
from abc import ABC, abstractmethod
from player import Player
from iterator import ListIterator, GeneratorIterator, \
                     DictionaryIterator

class Team(ABC):
    ...

    @property
    @abstractmethod
    def iterator(self):
        pass

class Team_1(Team):
    def __init__(self):
        ...
        self._iterator = ListIterator(self)

    @property
    def iterator(self):
        return self._iterator

class Team_2(Team):
    def __init__(self):
        ...
        self._iterator = GeneratorIterator(self)
        self._index = -1
```

> Team_1 uses a ListIterator.

> Team_2 uses a GeneratorIterator.

```
        @property
        def iterator(self):
            return self._iterator

class Team_3(Team):
    def __init__(self):
        super().__init__('TEAM 3', {})
        ...
        self._iterator = DictionaryIterator(self)   ◀──── Team_3 uses a
                                                            DictionaryIterator.
        @property
        def iterator(self):
            return self._iterator
```

Class TeamReport now reduces to a single, simpler print() method rather than a separate print() method for each type of sequential collection of Player objects. The method delegates the task of iterating over the different collections to each team's Iterator object, which it obtains from the Team object using polymorphism.

Listing 11.13   (Program 11.2 Players-IteratorDP) report.py

```
class TeamReport:
    def print(self, team):
        print()
        print(team.name)
                                             Polymorphism returns
        it = team.iterator   ◀──────────    the appropriate iterator.

        while it.has_next():
            player = it.next()
            print(f'{player.player_id} {player.last_name}, '
                              f'{player.first_name}')
```

The test program generates the same output as before.

Listing 11.14   (Program 11.2 Players-IteratorDP) main.py

```
from team import Team_1, Team_2, Team_3
from report import TeamReport

if __name__ == '__main__':
    report = TeamReport()

    team_1 = Team_1()
    report.print(team_1)

    team_2 = Team_2()
    report.print(team_2)

    team_3 = Team_3()
    report.print(team_3)
```

> Each **Iterator** object is a kind of adapter—one specifically designed to hide the implementation of a sequential collection.

> We can add another form of sequential collection along with its **Iterator** class without modifying the algorithm that generates the team reports.

Using the Iterator Design Pattern provides several important benefits:

- *Delegated iterations*—Class `TeamReport` delegates iterating over the sequential data collections to the `Iterator` classes, which is an application of the Delegation Principle (section 2.3.2).

- *Loosely coupled classes*—Class `TeamReport` no longer needs to know how each `Team` subclass implements its sequential collection, which is an application of the Principle of Least Knowledge (section 2.3.2). Therefore, class `TeamReport` is loosely coupled with the `Team` subclasses.

- *Encapsulated iteration algorithms*—The `Iterator` classes encapsulate the different algorithms to iterate over the various types of sequential collections, which is an application of the Encapsulate What Varies Principle (section 2.3.2).

- *Reduced code duplication*—The iteration algorithms are not duplicated, which is an application of the Don't Repeat Yourself Principle (section 2.3.3).

- *Shareable iteration algorithms*—It will be easy to share the algorithms among similar sequential collections or to add new algorithms for other collections.

11.1.4 Iterator's generic model

Figure 11.4 shows the generic model of the Iterator Design Pattern. From a design pattern's generic model, we can create a custom solution to an architecture problem. Table 11.1 shows how the example application applies the pattern.

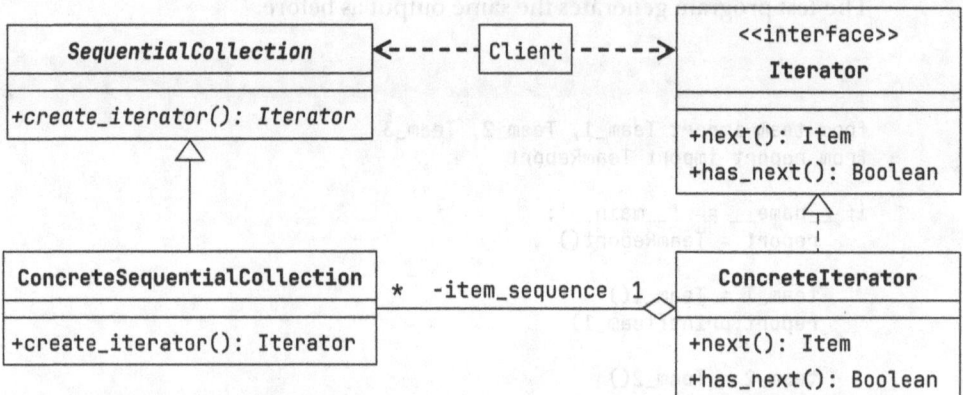

Figure 11.4 The generic model of the Iterator Design Pattern. Compare with figure 11.3. The client delegates iterating over the sequential collections to the `Iterator` subclasses, and thus the client is loosely coupled with the collections.

Table 11.1   The Iterator Design Pattern as applied by the example application

Design pattern	Applied by the example application
Client class	Class `TeamReport`
Superclass `SequentialCollection`	Superclass `Team`
Concrete sequential collections	Subclasses `Team_1`, `Team_2`, and `Team_3`
Interface `Iterator`	Interface `Iterator`
Concrete iterators	Classes `ListIterator`, `GeneratorIterator`, and `DictionaryIterator`
Method `create_iterator()`	`Team` classes' `iterator` properties
Item	`Player` object

> ### Why not use Python iterators?
>
> Certain Python classes, such as lists, tuples, and strings, can implement built-in iterators using the `__iter__()` and `__next()__` methods. Method `__iter__()` returns the iterator. Method `__next()__` advances to the next object in the sequence or raises the `StopIteration` exception after reaching the end of the sequence.
>
> These built-in iterators do not fully conform to the Iterator Design Pattern. They have no iterator superclass, so we can't use the Code to the Interface Principle and write code that uses polymorphism to obtain an appropriate iterator at run time, as we did in the `print()` method of class `TeamReport` (listing 11.13). Because a built-in iterator is specific to a type of sequential collection, we wouldn't be able to hide its implementation.
>
> If we need to take advantage of polymorphism to iterate over different types of sequential collections, the Iterator Design Pattern can be a good wrapper for the built-in iterators, and we used that approach in class `GeneratorIterator` (listing 11.10).

11.2   *The Visitor Design Pattern: Different algorithms operate on a single data collection*

The Visitor Design Pattern works with different algorithms that operate on an application's data collection. The pattern is often used to provide a model for an architecture in which the data is hierarchical and therefore the collection is a tree data structure. The objects are nodes of the tree, and they can be instantiated from different classes, so the nodes' data can be of different datatypes. The node at the top of the tree is the root node. (Trees often grow upside down in software.)

At run time, the application makes multiple "passes" over the tree. Each pass employs an algorithm that "visits" (accesses) each node starting at the root and working its way down. During a visit, the algorithm performs an appropriate operation on the node's data based on the datatype. There can be a different algorithm for each pass. The Visitor Design Pattern encapsulates the different algorithms.

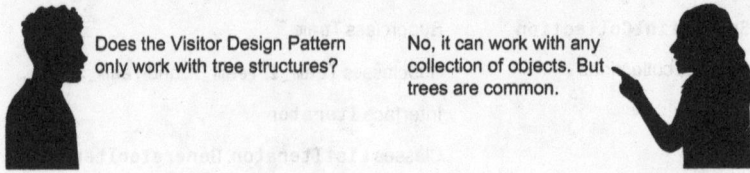

Does the Visitor Design Pattern only work with tree structures?

No, it can work with any collection of objects. But trees are common.

Figure 11.5 is an example of a collection of data in the form of a hierarchical tree structure that represents the products sold in a store. The Store node at the top is the root node. The tree nodes include three departments: Produce, Soups, and Soaps. The Produce department has Vegetables and Fruits categories. The Soaps department has Bar, Dish, and Laundry categories. At the bottom of the tree, the leaf nodes (shaded in gray) represent the products.

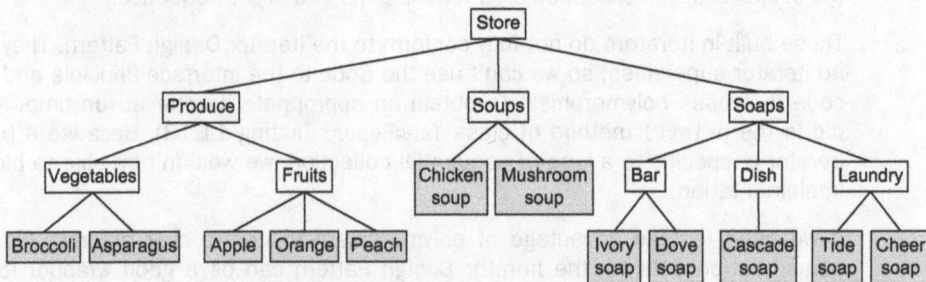

Figure 11.5 An example tree data structure of hierarchical data for a store. Store is the root node. The product nodes at the bottom (shaded in gray) are the leaf nodes.

The store application can make several passes over the tree and execute a different algorithm for each pass. For example, the first pass's algorithm can simply print the data hierarchically by department and category. If each product node contains the unit price and the number of units sold, the second-pass algorithm can print how many units of each product were sold, and the third-pass algorithm can calculate and print the revenue each department earned from selling these products.

For a concrete example, we'll continue our theme of the athletics department printing reports. Suppose the department wants an application that prints reports about intramural games played during a weekend. Residence halls named North, South, East, and West have teams that play baseball, football, and volleyball. We can represent the data collection as a hierarchical tree structure (figure 11.6).

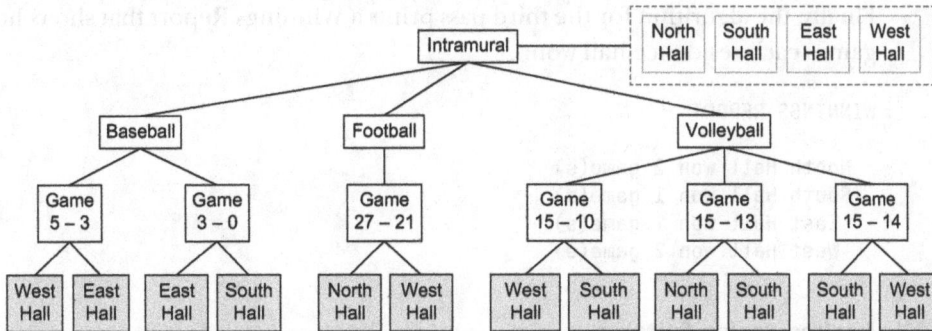

Figure 11.6 A data collection as a hierarchical tree structure that represents intramural baseball, football, and volleyball games played by teams from residence halls. The Intramural node is the root node, and it also has a separate list of residence hall objects. The residence hall objects at the bottom (shaded in gray) representing the winner and loser of each game are the tree's leaf nodes.

The Intramural node is the tree root, and it references the sport nodes. It also has a separate list of residence hall objects that is not part of the games hierarchy. Each of the sport nodes—Baseball, Football, and Volleyball—references Game nodes that represent games played in that sport. Each Game node references leaf Hall nodes that represent the winning and losing residence halls of each game. The Game nodes also contain the number of points scored by the winning and losing teams in each game.

Our intramural reports application makes three passes over this tree. Each pass uses a different algorithm to print a particular report. The algorithm for the first pass prints a Scores Report containing the game results:

```
SCORES REPORT

    baseball
        West Hall beat  East Hall  5 to  3
        East Hall beat South Hall  3 to  0

    football
        North Hall beat  West Hall 27 to 21

    volleyball
        West Hall beat South Hall 15 to 10
        North Hall beat South Hall 15 to 13
        South Hall beat  West Hall 15 to 14
```

The algorithm for the second pass prints an Activities Report that shows how many games were played in each sport:

```
ACTIVITIES REPORT

        baseball: 2 game(s)
        football: 1 game(s)
        volleyball: 3 game(s)
```

Finally, the algorithm for the third pass prints a Winnings Report that shows how many games each residence hall won:

```
WINNINGS REPORT

  North Hall won 2 game(s)
  South Hall won 1 game(s)
   East Hall won 1 game(s)
   West Hall won 2 game(s)
```

11.2.1 Desired design features

An application that makes multiple passes over a data collection with a different algorithm for each pass should have these design features:

- *DF 1*—The pass algorithms should be independent of each other.
- *DF 2*—The data collection and the algorithms that operate on the collection should be independent of each other.
- *DF 3*—Adding new passes and their algorithms should not require modifying the data collection.

11.2.2 Before using Visitor

As a demonstration, the first version of the application will not use the Visitor Design Pattern, and it will have some major faults. Afterward, we'll refactor the code to be modeled after the pattern and highlight the benefits of using the pattern.

Figure 11.7 shows how we can implement this hierarchical data collection as a tree with four classes: Intramural, Sport, Game, and Hall. Each class except Hall (which

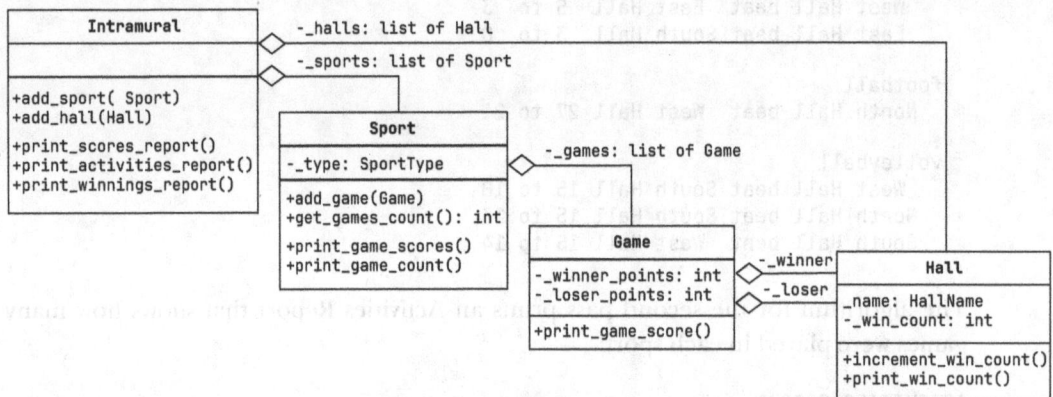

Figure 11.7   The four major classes of the first version of the intramural sports reports application. To implement the hierarchical tree structure, each class except Hall aggregates the class that is at the next-lower level in the hierarchy. The Intramural class's list of Hall objects is not part of the hierarchical tree structure.

represents the leaf nodes) aggregates the class that is at the next-lower level in the hierarchy. Each class has instance variables and methods to implement the three report generation algorithms.

Listing 11.15 shows the leaf `Hall` class, whose objects represent the winning and losing residence hall, respectively, of a game. Private instance variable `_win_count` records the number of times the hall won a game. Method `increment_win_count()` bumps the count up by one. Method `print_win_count()` prints one line that includes the count in the Winnings Report. For example, it can print

```
North Hall won 2 game(s)
```

Listing 11.15 (Program 11.3 Results) hall.py (poor design before DP)

```python
from enum import Enum

class HallName(Enum):
    NORTH = 1
    SOUTH = 2
    EAST  = 3
    WEST  = 4

    def __str__(self):
        return (self.name.lower().capitalize() + ' Hall')

class Hall:
    def __init__(self, name):
        self._name = name
        self._win_count = 0          ◀────┐ How many games
                                           │ the hall won
    @property
    def name(self):
        return self._name

    def increment_win_count(self):
        self._win_count += 1
                                           ┌ Prints one line of the
    def print_win_count(self):       ◀────┘ Winnings Report
        print(f'{self._name:>12s} won '
              f'{self._win_count} game(s)')
```

`Hall` objects are also in the list that is not part of the game hierarchy referenced by the `Intramural` class.

Each `Game` object represents a single intramural game between two residence halls. The class's two private instance variables `_winner` and `_loser` refer to `Hall` objects at the lowest level of the hierarchy. These `Hall` objects represent the winner and loser of the game, respectively. The `Game` object also records each game's score with private instance variables `_winner_points` and `_loser_points`. Method `print_game_score()` prints the result of a single game as part of the Scores Report. For example, it can print

```
West Hall beat East Hall 5 to 3
```

```python
class Game:
    def __init__(self, winner, winner_points,
                       loser, loser_points):
        self._winner = winner
        self._winner_points = winner_points
        self._loser = loser
        self._loser_points = loser_points

        winner.increment_win_count()

    def print_game_score(self):
        print(f'{self._winner.name:>14s} beat '
              f'{self._loser.name:>10s}'
              f'{self._winner_points:3d} to '
              f'{self._loser_points:2d}')
```

Prints one line of the
Scores Report

Each Sport object represents a type of sport: baseball, football, or volleyball. The class's
private instance variable _games is a list of Game objects at the next lower level of the
hierarchy. These Game objects represent games of that sport type that were played.
Method add_game() appends a Game object to the end of the list.

```python
from enum import Enum

class SportType(Enum):
    BASEBALL   = 1
    FOOTBALL   = 2
    VOLLEYBALL = 3

    def __str__(self):
        return self.name.lower()

class Sport:
    def __init__(self, sport_type):
        self._type = sport_type
        self._games = []

    def add_game(self, game):
        self._games.append(game)

    def print_game_scores(self):
        print()
        print(' ', self._type)

        for game in self._games:
            game.print_game_score()

    def print_game_count(self):
        print(f'{self._type:>12s}: '
              f'{len(self._games)} game(s)')
```

List of games of the
sport that were played

Prints one line of
the Scores Report

Prints one line of the
Activities Report

Method `print_game_scores()` prints the sport type and then iterates over the games list to print the scores of all the games of that type. This output is part of the Scores Report. For example, the method can print

```
volleyball
    West Hall beat South Hall 15 to 10
    South Hall beat North Hall 15 to 13
    South Hall beat  West Hall 15 to 14
```

Method `print_game_count()` prints the number of games of the sport type that were played. This count will appear in one line of the Activities Report. For example,

```
baseball: 2 game(s)
```

Class `Intramural` is the root of the tree. Its private instance variable `_sports` is a list of `Sport` objects at the next-lower level of the hierarchy. These `Sport` objects represent the sports that were played. Class `Intramural` also has private instance variable `_halls`, a list of all the residence halls. This list is not part of the tree hierarchy. We can't simply rely on having all the `Hall` objects uniquely referenced by the `Game` objects because a residence hall may participate in more than one (or zero) games. Methods `add_sport()` and `add_hall()` append `Sport` and `Hall` objects to their lists.

Listing 11.18   (Program 11.3 Results) intramural.py (poor design before DP)

```
class Intramural:
    def __init__(self):
        self._sports = []          ◄──── List of sports
        self._halls  = []          ◄──── List of halls

    def add_sport(self, sport):
        self._sports.append(sport)

    def add_hall(self, hall):
        self._halls.append(hall)

    def print_scores_report(self):
        print()
        print('SCORES REPORT')

        for sport in self._sports:        Prints each sport in
            sport.print_game_scores()     the Scores Report

    def print_activities_report(self):
        print()
        print('ACTIVITIES REPORT')
        print()

        for sport in self._sports:        Prints each sport in
            sport.print_game_count()      the Activities Report

    def print_winnings_report(self):
```

```
print()
print('WINNINGS REPORT')
print()

for hall in self._halls:          | Prints each hall in the
    hall.print_win_count()        | Winnings Report
```

The public printing methods of class `Intramural` generate the three intramural sports reports:

- *Scores Report*—Method `print_scores_report()` iterates over the `Sport` objects and calls method `print_game_scores()` on each object.

- *Activities Report*—Method `print_activities_report()` iterates over the `Sport` and calls method `print_game_count()` on each object.

- *Winnings Report*—Method `print_winnings_report()` iterates over the `Hall` objects and calls method `print_win_count()` on each object.

Scores Report
```
Intramural.print_scores_report()
  ➡ Sport.print_game_scores()
       ➡ Game.print_game_score()
```

Activities Report
```
Intramural.print_activities_report()
  ➡ Sport.print_game_count()
```

Winnings Report
```
Intramural.print_winnings_report()
  ➡ Hall.print_win_count()
```

Generating each report requires a call chain among the methods of the main classes (figure 11.8).

To generate sample data, the test program first calls function `build_tree()`, which hardcodes building a tree data structure and returns a reference to the tree root. Then the program calls the methods of the root `Intramural` node to print the three intramural reports.

Figure 11.8 We use a call chain through the methods of the main classes to generate each report.

Listing 11.19   (Program 11.3 Results) main.py (poor design before DP)

```python
from intramural import Intramural
from sport import SportType, Sport
from game import Game
from hall import HallName, Hall

def build_tree():
    intramural = Intramural()

    baseball   = Sport(SportType.BASEBALL)       |
    football   = Sport(SportType.FOOTBALL)        | Creates the sports
    volleyball = Sport(SportType.VOLLEYBALL)      |

    intramural.add_sport(baseball)
    intramural.add_sport(football)
    intramural.add_sport(volleyball)

    north = Hall(HallName.NORTH)        | Creates the residence halls
    south = Hall(HallName.SOUTH)        |
```

```
    east  = Hall(HallName.EAST)
    west  = Hall(HallName.WEST)
```
↑ **Creates the residence halls**

```
    intramural.add_hall(north)
    intramural.add_hall(south)
    intramural.add_hall(east)
    intramural.add_hall(west)

    baseball.add_game(Game(west, 5, east,  3))
    baseball.add_game(Game(east, 3, south, 0))

    football.add_game(Game(north, 27, west, 21))
```
Creates the games
```
    volleyball.add_game(Game(west,  15, south, 10))
    volleyball.add_game(Game(north, 15, south, 13))
    volleyball.add_game(Game(south, 15, west,  14))

    return intramural

if __name__ == '__main__':
    intramural = build_tree()

    intramural.print_scores_report()
    intramural.print_activities_report()
    intramural.print_winnings_report()
```
Prints the reports

The algorithms for generating the three intramural reports are implemented in bits and pieces among the tree node classes **Intramural**, **Sport**, **Game**, and **Hall**. That violates DF 2.

This will become a major nightmare if we need to add more reports or sport types. That violates DF 3.

The application suffers from many faults. The two most egregious are as follows:

- *Classes with multiple responsibilities*—Classes Intramural, Sport, and Game have two primary responsibilities. Each class must have instance variables and methods to implement the data collection as a tree structure. And each class must also have instance variables and methods to implement the three report generation algorithms.

- *Inflexible application architecture*—If we decide to modify a report's content or add a new report, we will need to make changes throughout the classes.

11.2.3 *After using Visitor*

The Visitor Design Pattern removes these faults. It models a software architecture for our example intramural reports application that separates the algorithm code for generating reports from the code that maintains the tree-structured data collection. Our refactored application has three Visitor classes, each of which encapsulates a report generation algorithm. Visitor is an interface, and each class that implements the interface must implement methods that visit the different types of tree nodes to execute the class's algorithm. In our application, the three Visitor classes are Scores-ReportVisitor, ActivitiesReportVisitor, and WinningsReportVisitor. They implement the algorithms to generate the Scores Report, the Activities Report, and the Winnings Report, respectively. We'll be able to modify or add new Visitor classes and their algorithms without affecting the data collection.

The Visitor Design Pattern

"Represent an operation to be performed on the elements of an object structure. Visitor lets you define a new operation without changing the classes of the elements on which it operates." (GoF p. 331)

As suggested by figure 11.9, the goal is to enable multiple algorithms to operate on a single data collection. Figure 11.10 shows how our team reporting application can implement the Visitor Design Pattern: the Visitor classes ScoresReportVisitor, Activities-ReportVisitor, and WinningsReportVisitor each encapsulate a different report generation algorithm. The Visitor classes implement methods visit_Intramural(), visit_Sport(), visit_Game(), and visit_Hall() , which visit the Intramural, Sport, Game, and Hall nodes of the tree data structure, respectively.

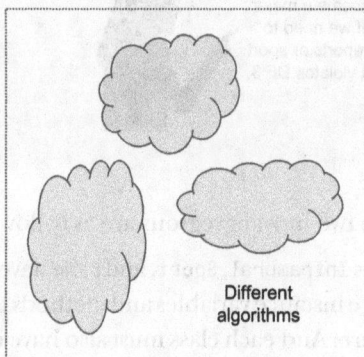

Visitor Design Pattern
Different algorithms operate on a single data collection.

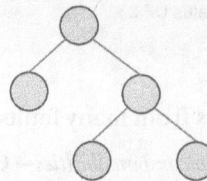

Different algorithms

Single data collection

Figure 11.9   Different algorithms can operate on a single data collection.

Listing 11.20   (Program 11.4 Results-VisitorDP) visitor.py

```python
from abc import ABC, abstractmethod

class Visitor(ABC):

    @abstractmethod
    def visit_intramural(self, node):
        pass
```

```
@abstractmethod
def visit_sport(self, node):
    pass

@abstractmethod
def visit_game(self, node):
    pass

@abstractmethod
def visit_hall(self, node):
    pass
```

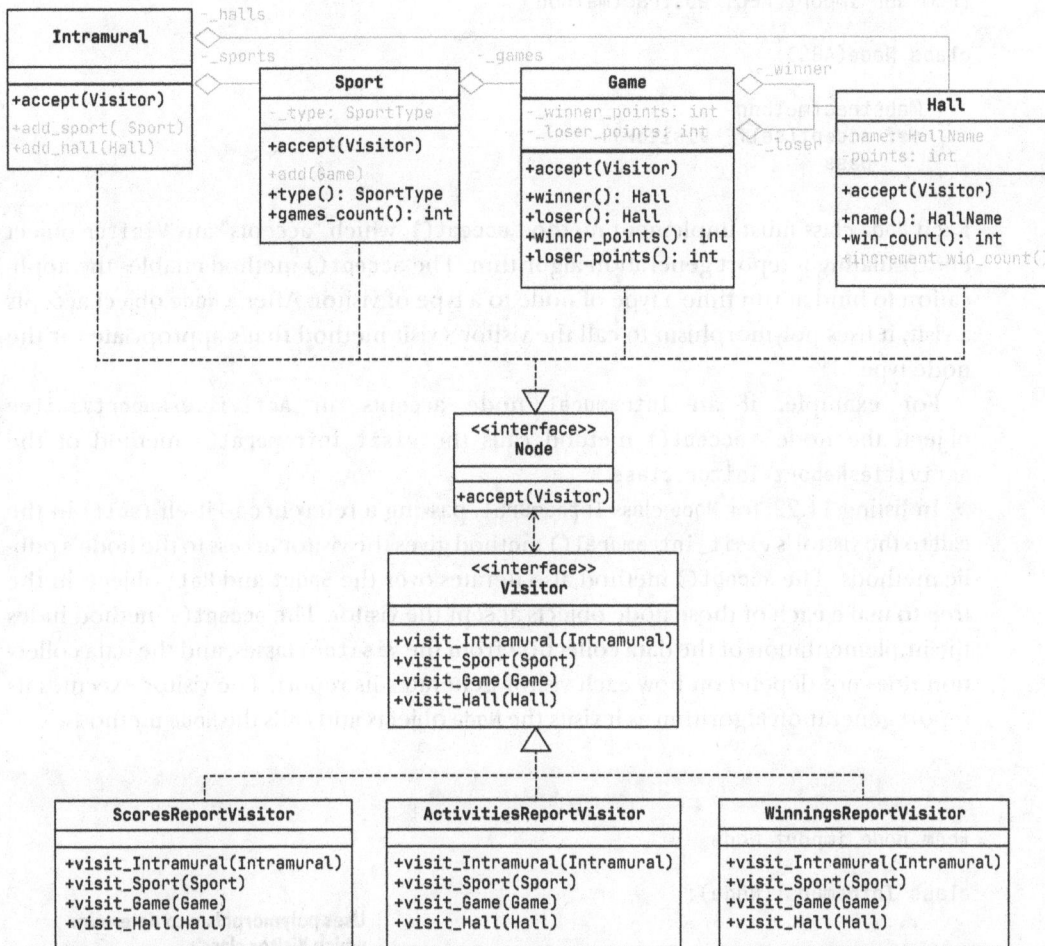

Figure 11.10 **The parts that haven't changed logically from figure 11.7 are shown in gray. Now each of the tree node classes** Intramural, Sport, Game, **and** Hall **implements interface** Node. **The three visitor classes** ScoresReportVisitor, ActivitiesReportVisitor, **and** WinningsReportVisitor **each implement interface** Visitor **and encapsulate a report generation algorithm.**

Why are there separate names for the **Visitor** member functions? Can't we use type hints and overloading and thereby have only one name, like **visit(node: Intramural)**, **visit(node: Sport)**, etc.?

It's your choice! You may find that naming each **Visitor** member function after a **Node** class makes it easier to see which type of node each member function can visit.

Intramural, Sport, Game, and Hall now implement interface Node.

```python
from abc import ABC, abstractmethod

class Node(ABC):

    @abstractmethod
    def accept(self, visitor):
        pass
```

Each Node class must implement method accept(), which "accepts" any Visitor object encapsulating a report generation algorithm. The accept() method enables the application to bind at run time a type of node to a type of visitor. After a Node object accepts a visit, it uses polymorphism to call the visitor's visit method that's appropriate for the node type.

For example, if an Intramural node accepts an ActivitiesReportVisitor object, the node's accept() method calls the visit_intramural() method of the ActivitiesReportVisitor.class.

In listing 11.22, for Node class Intramural, passing a reference to itself (self) in the call to the visitor's visit_intramural() method gives the visitor access to the node's public methods. The accept() method also iterates over the Sport and Hall objects in the tree to make each of those node objects accept the visitor. The accept() method hides the implementation of the data collection from the Visitor classes, and the data collection does not depend on how each visitor generates its report. The visitor executes its report generation algorithm as it visits the Node objects and calls the Node methods.

```python
from node import Node

class Intramural(Node):
    ...

    def accept(self, visitor):
        visitor.visit_intramural(self)    ◄── Uses polymorphism to determine
                                               which Visitor class's
                                               visit_Intramural() method to call

        for sport in self._sports:
            sport.accept(visitor)    ◄── Makes each Sport object
                                         accept the same visitor
```

```
for hall in self._halls:
    hall.accept(visitor)
```
Makes each Hall object accept the same visitor

Each **Visitor** class implements the algorithm to generate a particular report. Each type of **Node** object has an **accept()** method that accepts a **Visitor** object. The **accept()** method then calls the **Visitor** object's visit method that corresponds to the type of the **Node** object. At run time, polymorphism determines which **Visitor** class's visit method is called, depending on which report is being generated.

Each **Visitor** class has methods that visit **Node** objects, one method for each type of node. These methods together execute the **Visitor** class's algorithm as they visit the nodes one after another. This design pattern effectively separates the data collection from the report generation algorithms.

Similarly, Node class Sport implements method accept(), which then uses polymorphism to determine which Visitor class's visit_Sport() method to call. It iterates over the Game objects to make each one accept the visitor.

Because the accept() method passes a reference to the node (self) to the visitor's visit_Sport() method, the visitor will be able to call the Sport node's public type() and games_count() property methods.

Listing 11.23   (Program 11.4 Results-VisitorDP) sport.py

```
from node import Node

class Sport(Node):
    ...

    @property
    def type(self):
        return self._type

    @property
    def games_count(self):
        return len(self._games)

    def accept(self, visitor):
        visitor.visit_sport(self)

        for game in self._games:
            game.accept(visitor)
```
Uses polymorphism to determine which Visitor class's visit_sport() method to call

Makes each Game object accept the same visitor

Likewise, the Game node has public property methods winner(), loser(), winner_points(), and loser_points() that the visitor's visit_Game() method can call.

Listing 11.24   (Program 11.4 Results-VisitorDP) game.py

```
from node import Node

class Game(Node):
    ...
```

```python
@property
def winner(self):
    return self._winner

@property
def winner_points(self):
    return self._winner_points

@property
def loser(self):
    return self._loser

@property
def loser_points(self):
    return self._loser_points

def accept(self, visitor):
    visitor.visit_game(self)
```

Uses polymorphism to determine which Visitor class's visit_Game() method to call

The **Node** classes had to expose some of their internal properties to allow access by the **Visitor** objects.

This is a drawback of the Visitor Design Pattern. A software designer must weigh the pros and cons of each design pattern.

The Node class `Hall` has public property methods `name()` and `win_count()` that the visitor's `visit_Hall()` method can call.

```python
from node import Node

class Hall(Node):
    ...
    @property
    def name(self):
        return self._name

    @property
    def win_count(self):
        return self._win_count

    def accept(self, visitor):
        visitor.visit_hall(self)
```

Uses polymorphism to determine which Visitor class's visit_Hall() method to call

Each Visitor class encapsulates the algorithm to generate a particular report. Class `ScoresReportVisitor` implements the algorithm to generate the Scores Report. After the visitor object is first accepted by the `Intramural` node, the visitor visits nodes of the other types in turn, and it calls the node's public property methods to print part of the report.

Listing 11.26   (Program 11.4 Results-VisitorDP) scores_report_visitor.py

```python
from visitor import Visitor

class ScoresReportVisitor(Visitor):
    def visit_intramural(self, intramural):
        print()
        print('SCORES REPORT')

    def visit_sport(self, sport):
        print()
        print(' ', sport.type)

    def visit_game(self, game):
        winner = game.winner
        winner_points = game.winner_points
        loser = game._loser
        loser_points  = game._loser_points

        print(f'{winner.name:>14s} beat '
              f'{loser.name:>10s}'
              f'{winner_points:3d} to '
              f'{loser_points:2d}')

    def visit_hall(self, hall):
        return
```

The visit methods of class `ScoresReportVisitor` encapsulate the algorithm to produce the Scores Report:

1 Method `visit_Intramural()` prints the report title, `SCORES REPORT`.

2 Method `visit_Sport()` prints the name of the sport type.

3 Method `visit_Game()` prints the results of a game.

4 Method `visit_Hall()` does nothing.

Because each visitor class implements interface `Visitor`, it must implement each visit method—even the methods that do nothing. In this version of our sports reports application, `Visitor` class `ScoresReportVisitor` encapsulates all the code to generate the reports that was previously scattered among the `Intramural`, `Sport`, and `Game` classes (table 11.2).

Table 11.2 Visitor class `ScoresReportVisitor` encapsulates the algorithm to generate the Scores Report

First version	Version with class ScoresReportVisitor
Intramural.print_scores_report()	visit_Intramural()
Sport.print_game_scores()	visit_Sport()
Game.print_game_score()	visit_Game()

Similarly, class `ActivitiesReportVisitor` implements the algorithm to generate the Activities Report.

Listing 11.27　(Program 11.4 Results-VisitorDP) activities_report_visitor.py

```python
from visitor import Visitor

class ActivitiesReportVisitor(Visitor):
    def visit_intramural(self, intramural):
        print()
        print('ACTIVITIES REPORT')
        print()

    def visit_sport(self, sport):
        print(f'{sport.type:>12s}: '
              f'{sport.games_count} game(s)')

    def visit_game(self, game):
        return

    def visit_hall(self, hall):
        return
```

The visit methods of the Visitor class `ActivitiesReportVisitor` encapsulate all the code to generate the Sports Report that formerly resided in the Intramural and Sport classes (table 11.3).

Table 11.3　Visitor class `ActivitiesReportVisitor` encapsulates the algorithm to generate the Activities Report

First version	Version with class ActivitiesReportVisitor
Intramural.print_activities_report()	visit_Intramural()
Sport.print_game_count()	visit_Sport()

The visit methods of subclass `ActivitiesReportVisitor` implement the algorithm to produce the Sports Report:

1　Method `visit_Intramural()` prints the report title, ACTIVITIES REPORT.
2　Method `visit_Sport()` prints the number of games of the sport type.
3　Method `visit_Game()` does nothing.
4　Method `visit_Hall()` does nothing.

Finally, the visit methods of Visitor class `WinningsReportVisitor` implement the algorithm to produce the Winnings Report.

Listing 11.28　(Program 11.4 Results-VisitorDP) winnings_report_visitor.py

```python
from visitor import Visitor

class WinningsReportVisitor(Visitor):
```

```python
def visit_intramural(self, intramural):
    print()
    print('WINNINGS REPORT')
    print()

def visit_sport(self, sport):
    return

def visit_game(self, game):
    return

def visit_hall(self, hall):
    print(f'{hall.name:>12s} won '
          f'{hall.win_count} game(s)')
```

The visit methods of the Visitor class WinningsReportVisitor encapsulate all the code to generate the Winnings Report that formerly resided in the Intramural and Sport classes (table 11.4).

Table 11.4 Visitor class WinningsReportVisitor encapsulates the algorithm to generate the Winnings Report

First version	Version with class WinningsReportVisitor
Intramural.print_halls_report()	visit_Intramural()
Sport.print_game_count()	visit_Sport()

The visit methods of subclass WinningsReportVisitor implement the algorithm to produce the Residence Halls Report:

1 Method visit_Intramural() prints the report title, WINNINGS REPORT.

2 Method visit_Sport() does nothing.

3 Method visit_Game() does nothing.

4 Method visit_Hall() prints a residence hall's number of wins.

Several of the visit methods don't do anything.

We can make **Visitor** into a superclass where the default implementation of each member function does nothing. Then a **Visitor** subclass needs to override only the member functions that do something.

After building the example tree data structure, the test program creates the Scores-ReportVisitor, ActivitiesReportVisitor, and WinningsReportVisitor objects. Then it generates each report by calling intramural_node (the tree root) to accept each visitor object in turn.

Listing 11.29   (Program 11.4 Results-VisitorDP) main.py

```
from intramural import Intramural
from sport import SportType, Sport
from game import Game
from hall import HallName, Hall
from activities_report_visitor import ActivitiesReportVisitor
from scores_report_visitor import ScoresReportVisitor
from winnings_report_visitor import WinningsReportVisitor

def build_tree():
    ...

if __name__ == '__main__':
    intramural_node = build_tree()

    scores_report_visitor    = ScoresReportVisitor()
    activities_report_visitor = ActivitiesReportVisitor()
    winnings_report_visitor   = WinningsReportVisitor()

    intramural_node.accept(scores_report_visitor)
    intramural_node.accept(activities_report_visitor)
    intramural_node.accept(winnings_report_visitor)
```

Prints the Scores Report

Prints the Activities Report

Prints the Winnings Report

The key benefits of using the Visitor Design Pattern to model the architecture of the second version of our intramural games reports application include the following:

- *Encapsulated algorithms*—The algorithms to generate and print the Scores Report, the Activities Report, and the Winnings Report are each encapsulated in the Visitor classes ScoresReportVisitor, ActivitiesReportVisitor, and Winnings-ReportVisitor, respectively. This is the Encapsulate What Varies Principle (section 2.3.2). It will be possible to modify or delete a report generation algorithm or add new ones without affecting other classes.

- *Classes with single responsibility*—The Node classes Intramural, Sport, Game, and Hall are each responsible only for maintaining the tree data structure. The Visitor classes are each responsible only for their report generation algorithm. This is the Single Responsibility Principle (section 2.3).

- *Loose coupling*—The tree data structure is loosely coupled with the report generation algorithms, and the algorithms are loosely coupled with each other. The Node classes do not know what the report generation algorithms are or how they're implemented by the Visitor classes. This is the Principle of Least Knowledge (section 2.3.2). We will be able to modify or delete algorithms or add new algorithms without modifying the data structure or the existing algorithms.

11.2.4 Visitor's generic model

Figure 11.11 shows the generic model of the Visitor Design Pattern. It is from a design pattern's generic model that we can create a custom solution to an architecture problem. Table 11.5 shows how the example application applies the pattern.

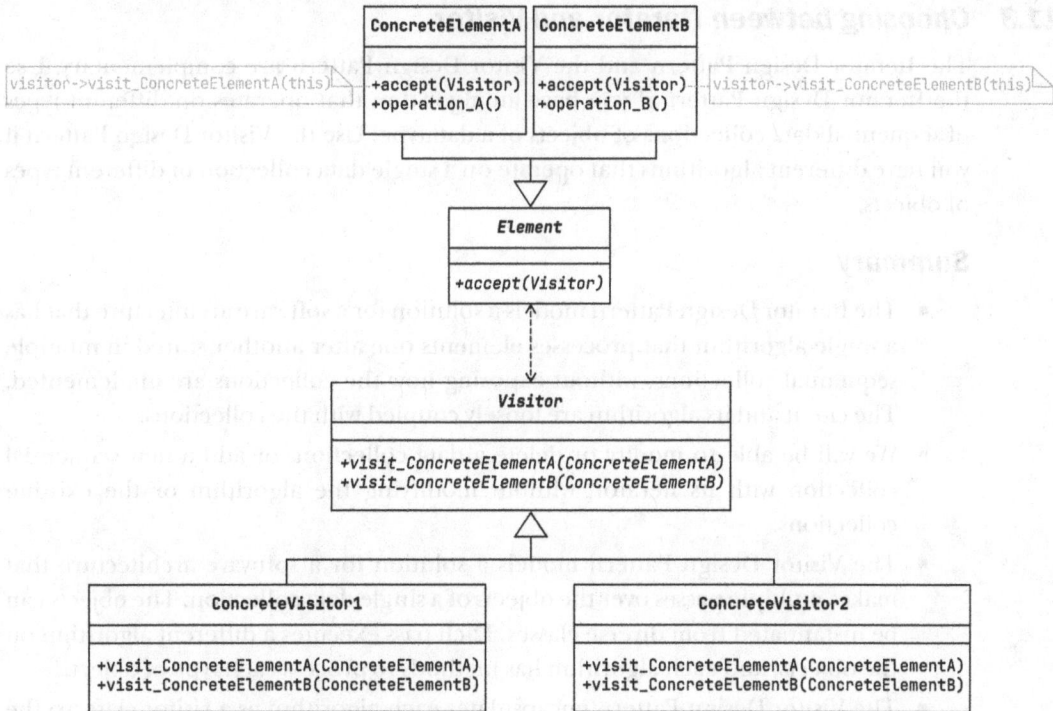

Figure 11.11 **The generic model of the Visitor Design Pattern. Compare with figure 11.10. Each Visitor class encapsulates an algorithm. To execute an algorithm during a pass of the Element objects, each Element object accepts a Visitor object. The accept() function of each concrete Element object calls the visit method that corresponds to that Element object. The visit methods together execute the Visitor class's algorithm as they visit the Element objects one after another.**

Table 11.5 **The Visitor Method Design Pattern as applied by the example application**

Design pattern	Applied by the example application
Superclass Element	Interface Node
Subclasses ConcreteElementA and ConcreteElementB	Classes Intramural, Sport, Game, and Hall
Superclass Visitor	Interface Visitor
Subclasses ConcreteVisitor1 and ConcreteVisitor2	Classes ScoresReportVisitor, Activities-ReportVisitor, and WinningsReportVisitor
Methods visit_ConcreteElementA() and visit_ConcreteElementB()	Methods visit_Intramural(), visit_Sport(), visit_Game(), and visit_Hall()

11.3   *Choosing between Iterator and Visitor*

The Iterator Design Pattern and the Visitor Design Pattern are complementary. Use the Iterator Design Pattern if you have an algorithm that operates on different types of sequential data collections of objects of a datatype. Use the Visitor Design Pattern if you have different algorithms that operate on a single data collection of different types of objects.

Summary

- The Iterator Design Pattern models a solution for a software architecture that has a single algorithm that processes elements one after another stored in multiple sequential collections, without exposing how the collections are implemented. The client and its algorithm are loosely coupled with the collections.

- We will be able to modify or delete a data collection, or add a new sequential collection with its iterator, without modifying the algorithm or the existing collections.

- The Visitor Design Pattern models a solution for a software architecture that makes multiple passes over the objects of a single data collection. The objects can be instantiated from diverse classes. Each pass executes a different algorithm on the objects, and each algorithm has methods to process each type of object.

- The Visitor Design Pattern encapsulates each algorithm as a visitor class, so the algorithms are loosely coupled with the data collection, and the algorithms are loosely coupled with each other. We will be able to modify or delete algorithms or add new algorithms without modifying the data collection or the existing algorithms.

The Observer Design Pattern

This chapter covers

- The Observer Design Pattern

In this chapter, we continue the theme of sports reports generated by a college athletics department. The Observer Design Pattern supports the publisher–subscriber model, where the publisher component creates data objects that subscriber components individually process, each in its own way. The publisher component doesn't know how the subscriber components are implemented, nor does it care what the subscribers do with the data.

Our example application monitors the progress of a baseball game. It prints game statistics both while the game is in progress and after the game is over.

NOTE Be sure to read the introduction to part 4 of the book for important information about design patterns in general and to learn how this and subsequent chapters teach each pattern.

12.1 *The Observer Design Pattern: Publish data for multiple subscribers*

The Observer Design Pattern represents the publisher–subscriber model. A good example of this model is an online news streaming service. People who are interested in news stories subscribe to the service. As each news story becomes available, the streaming service notifies each subscriber by providing the story's headline. Then each subscriber can decide independently whether to request the story from the service by clicking the headline. The streaming service is therefore the publisher of the stories. Different people can subscribe and unsubscribe at any time. Each subscriber can do whatever they wish with the stories: read or ignore them, only scan the headlines, archive stories about a favorite topic, perform sentiment analysis, etc. The streaming service doesn't care what each subscriber does with the stories. It only needs to keep track of who is currently subscribed, notify each subscriber when a story becomes available, and provide the means to obtain the story.

The publisher–subscriber model is also known as the producer–consumer model, where the publisher is the producer of content, and the subscribers are the consumers. The content is also called the subject, and the consumers are the observers of the subject.

For a concrete example, let's suppose a college athletics department wants to generate three different reports about the performance of one team during a given baseball game. The reports are based on the team's hit events. A hit event made by a player on the team is either a hit (single, double, triple, or homer) or an out. A baseball reporter present at the game reports on the hit events as they occur. The three report generators are subscribers of the hit events:

- The logger generates a running log of the players' hits or outs as they occur during the game.

- The table generator prints its report after the game completes. It consists of a table that shows what hits and outs each player made during the game.

- The graph generator also prints its report after the game completes. It consists of a bar chart of the types of hits made during the game.

The baseball reporter publishes each hit event as it occurs by sending it to the subscriber components, which consume the events (figure 12.1). The logger updates its log report immediately after it consumes each event. The table and graph generators must accumulate the event data that they consume, and then each generates its report after the game is over.

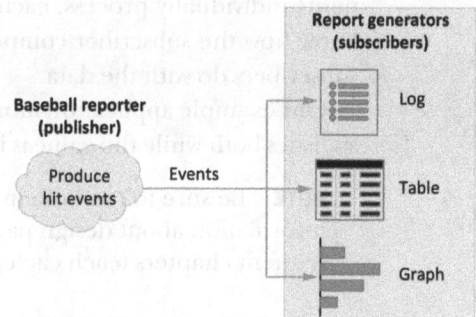

Figure 12.1 An example of the publisher–subscriber model. The publisher component produces hit events that are consumed as they occur by the subscriber components to generate the various reports.

An example of a baseball game log report that is generated line by line during the game as each hit event occurs is as follows:

```
GAME HITS LOG

 1 Al      hit an out
 2 Beth    hit an out
 3 Carl    hit a double
 4 Donna   hit a double
 5 Ed      hit a triple
 6 Fran    hit an out
 7 George  hit a single
 8 Heidi   hit a single
 9 Ivan    hit a triple
10 Al      hit a double
...
56 Beth    hit a single
57 Carl    hit a double
58 Donna   hit an out
59 Ed      hit a single
60 Fran    hit an out
```

Here's an example of a table report generated after a baseball game is over that shows what hits and outs each player made in the game:

```
GAME HITS TABLE

Player   Outs  Singles Doubles Triples Homers
-------------------------------------------------
Al       1     3       2               1
Beth     6     1
Carl     2     2       3
Donna    3             3               1
Ed       3     3               1
Fran     5     2
George   2     2                2
Heidi    2     4
Ivan     3     1               1       1
```

Figure 12.2 is an example of a graph report generated after a baseball game is over. It displays a bar chart of the types of hits that occurred in the game.

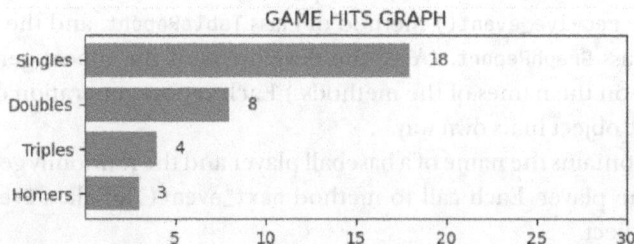

Figure 12.2 An example graph report showing a bar chart

These reports represent three
different visualizations of the
same data.

The report generators consume
each hit event sent by the
baseball reporter as it occurs.

12.1.1 Desired design features

Based on how the publisher–subscriber model works, here are some desired design features for a software solution:

- *DF 1*—The publisher can create content at arbitrary times.
- *DF 2*—The publisher immediately notifies all of its subscribers as soon as it has new content.
- *DF 3*—Once notified, a subscriber can choose to ask for the new content.
- *DF 4*—The publisher provides any new content to a subscriber that asks for it, but otherwise the publisher doesn't care about or have any control over what the subscriber does with the content.
- *DF 5*—A subscriber can do whatever it wants with the content.
- *DF 6*—Consumers can subscribe and unsubscribe at arbitrary times. Without any code changes, the publisher can acquire a new subscriber, or an existing subscriber can unsubscribe.
- *DF 7*—The publisher has no knowledge of how any of its subscribers are implemented, nor do the subscribers know how the publisher is implemented.

12.1.2 Before using Observer

To test the first version of our baseball game reports application (figure 12.3), class EventMaker (listing 12.1) uses a random number generator to generate hit events. A hit event is represented by an Event object that is created and returned by each call to method next_event(). Each Event object consists of a player's name and a randomly generated out or a single, double, triple, or homer (integer value 0, 1, 2, 3, or 4, respectively).

The BaseballReporter class's method report_hits() repeatedly calls next_event() in a loop to obtain Event objects as content until the game is over after 27 outs (listing 12.2). The method publishes each Event object by passing it to the log_event() method of class LogReport, the receive_event() method of class TableReport, and the handle_event() method of class GraphReport. (Alas, the developers of the report generation classes couldn't agree on the names of the methods.) Each report generation class can then process the Event object in its own way.

Each Event object contains the name of a baseball player and the randomly generated hit or out made by the player. Each call to method next_event() of class EventMaker returns a new Event object.

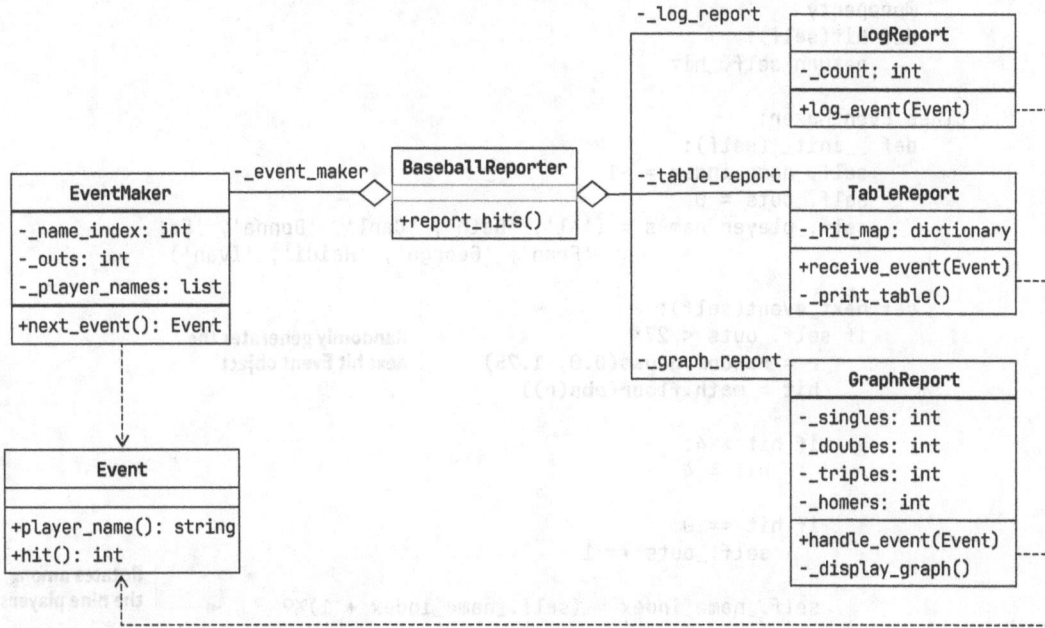

Figure 12.3 **The initial architecture of the baseball game reports application. Method** `report_hits()` **of class** `BaseballReporter` **repeatedly calls the** `next_event()` **method of class** `EventMaker` **to obtain new** `Event` **objects one at a time. It passes each** `Event` **object to the** `log_event()`**,** `handle_event()`**, and** `receive_event()` **methods of the report generation classes. Each report generation class can process the** `Event` **object in its own way.**

In our application, class **BaseballReporter** is the publisher. It calls member function **next_event()** of class **EventMaker** to create the next random **Event** object.

A random data generator is a good way to test our publisher–subscriber model.

Listing 12.1 **(Program 12.1 Stats) event.py (poor design before DP)**

```
import math
import random

class Event:
    def __init__(self, player_name, hit):
        self._player_name = player_name
        self._hit = hit

    @property
    def player_name(self):
        return self._player_name
```

```
        @property
        def hit(self):
            return self._hit

    class EventMaker:
        def __init__(self):
            self._name_index = -1
            self._outs = 0
            self._player_names = ('Al', 'Beth', 'Carl', 'Donna', 'Ed',
                                  'Fran', 'George', 'Heidi', 'Ivan')

        def next_event(self):
            if self._outs < 27:
                r = random.gauss(0.0, 1.75)          Randomly generates the
                hit = math.floor(abs(r))             next hit Event object

                if hit > 4:
                    hit = 4

                if hit == 0:
                    self._outs += 1
                                                              Rotates among
                self._name_index = (self._name_index + 1)%9   the nine players

                return Event(self._player_names[self._name_index],
                             hit)
            else:
                return None
```

Publisher class `BaseballReporter` aggregates the subscriber classes `EventMaker`, `Log-Report`, `GraphReport`, and `TableReport`.

```
from event import EventMaker
from log_report import LogReport
from table_report import TableReport
from graph_report import GraphReport

class BaseballReporter:
    def __init__(self):
        self._event_maker  = EventMaker()
        self._log_report   = LogReport()
        self._table_report = TableReport()
        self._graph_report = GraphReport()

    def report_hits(self):                            Gets the next hit
        event = self._event_maker.next_event()        Event object

        while event is not None:
            self._log_report.log_event(event)
            self._table_report.receive_event(event)   Passes the event to the
            self._graph_report.handle_event(event)    report generators' methods
```

```
event = self._event_maker.next_event()

self._log_report.log_event(None)          Passes None after the
self._table_report.receive_event(None)    game's completion
self._graph_report.handle_event(None)
```

Method `report_hits()` loops to repeatedly acquire new hit `Event` objects one at a time by calling the `next_event()` method of class `EventMaker` until the game has completed (27 outs have occurred) and therefore there are no more hits. It passes each `Event` object to the appropriate method of each report generator object. After the game has completed, the method passes `None` to each report generator as the end sentinel.

There's a serious design flaw here. Publisher **BaseballReporter** must know what method to call on each subscribed report generator in order to pass it a hit **Event** object or **None**.

That violates **DF 7**.

Method `log_event()` of class `LogReport` receives and logs each `Event` object. As soon as it receives the object, it immediately updates the log report by printing its contents.

Listing 12.3   (Program 12.1 Stats) log_report.py (poor design before DP)

```
class LogReport:
    def __init__(self):
        self._count = 0

        print('GAME HITS LOG')
        print()
                                              Receives and logs a
    def log_event(self, event):         ◄──── hit Event object
        if event is not None:
            player_name = event.player_name
            hit = event.hit

            if hit == 0:
                what = 'an out'
            elif hit == 1:
                what = 'a single'
            elif hit == 2:
                what = 'a double'
            elif hit == 3:
                what = 'a triple'
            else:
                what = 'a homer'

            self._count += 1
            print(f'{self._count:2d} {player_name:7s}'
                  f' hit {what}')                        Prints a line of the log
```

Method `receive_event()` of class `TableReport` receives each hit Event object. It uses a private dictionary `_hit_map` to record what hits and outs each player made during the game. The dictionary is keyed by the players' names, and each value is a list of five integer values that record the numbers of outs, singles, doubles, triples, and homers, respectively, for the corresponding player. As soon as the game is over (`None` is received), private method `_print_report()` prints the report.

Listing 12.4   (Program 12.1 Stats) table_report.py (poor design before DP)

```python
class TableReport:
    def __init__(self):
        self._hit_map = {}        ◄──── Dictionary for recording
                                         each player's hits

    def _print_table(self):
        print()
        print('GAME HITS TABLE')
        print()
        print('Player     Outs   Singles Doubles Triples Homers')
        print('--------------------------------------------------')

        for player_name, hits in self._hit_map.items():
            print(f'{player_name:6s}', end='')

            for hit in hits:
                if hit > 0:
                    print(f'{hit:8d}', end='')
                else:
                    print('        ', end='')
            print()

    def receive_event(self, event):      ◄──── Receives a hit Event object
        if event is not None:
            player_name = event.player_name
            hit = event.hit

            if not player_name in self._hit_map:        Creates a new list of outs
                self._hit_map[player_name] = 5*[0]    ◄── and hits for a player

            self._hit_map[player_name][hit] += 1    ◄── Records a hit or an
        else:                                           out for a player
            self._print_table()     ◄──── Game completeda
```

Method `handle_event()` of class `GraphReport` receives each hit Event object. It keeps track of the numbers of outs, singles, doubles, triples, and homers of all the players. As soon as the game is over, method `_display_graph()` displays the bar chart.

Listing 12.5   (Program 12.1 Stats) graph_report.py (poor design before DP)

```python
import matplotlib.pyplot as plt

class GraphReport:
```

```python
    def __init__(self):
        self._singles = 0
        self._doubles = 0
        self._triples = 0
        self._homers  = 0

    def _display_graph(self):
        hits = [self._homers,  self._triples,
                self._doubles, self._singles]
        what = ['Homers',  'Triples',
                'Doubles', 'Singles']

        _, ax = plt.subplots(figsize=(6, 2))
        ax.barh(what, hits, height=0.75)

        plt.title('GAME HITS GRAPH')
        plt.xticks([5, 10, 15, 20, 25, 30],
                   ['5', '10', '15', '20', '25', '30'])

        for i in range(len(what)):
            ax.text(hits[i] + 1, i, str(hits[i]),
                    fontsize=10,
                    ha='left', va='center')

        plt.show()

    def handle_event(self, event):
        if event is not None:
            hit = event.hit

            if hit == 1:
                self._singles += 1
            elif hit == 2:
                self._doubles += 1
            elif hit == 3:
                self._triples += 1
            elif hit == 4:
                self._homers += 1
        else:
            self._display_graph()
```

- `ax.barh(what, hits, height=0.75)` → **Creates a horizontal bar chart**
- `plt.xticks(...)` → **X-axis values and labels**
- `ax.text(...)` → **Hit counts to the right of each bar**
- `def handle_event(self, event):` → **Receives a hit Event object**
- `self._display_graph()` → **Game completed**

None of the subscribers is given the option to ask for the content represented by the **Event** objects. They always get all the content each time.

That violates **DF 3**. What if a particular player's fan club only wanted reports about that player?

The test program outputs the three baseball game reports shown at the beginning of this section.

Listing 12.6   (Program 12.1 Stats) main.py (poor design before DP)

```
from baseball_reporter import BaseballReporter

if __name__ == '__main__':
    reporter = BaseballReporter()
    reporter.report_hits()
```

This software architecture will not scale well! The subscribers are all hardcoded in the publisher **BaseballReporter**.

It won't be possible able to add or remove a subscriber without modifying class **BaseballReporter**. That's a serious violation of **DF 6**.

Although it generates the correct baseball game reports, this version of the application has major architectural problems, including the following

- *Hardcoded subscribers*—Class BaseballReporter hardcodes the three report generators. In the publisher–subscriber model, it should be easy to add and remove subscribers.

- *Classes not loosely coupled*—Class BaseballReporter must know how each subscriber is implemented. Its report_hits() method must know to call log_event() for the log report, handle_event() for the graph report, and receive_event() for the table report. Therefore, class BaseballReporter is not loosely coupled with the report classes.

12.1.3 *After using Observer*

Let's see how the Observer Design Pattern overcomes these shortcomings. The model defines superclass Subject to represent the publisher and interface Observer to represent the subscribers. The key idea is that the publisher produces and publishes the subject content, and there can be multiple subscribers who observe the content. Therefore, in the version of our application modeled from the pattern, the publisher of the Event content, class BaseballReporter, inherits from superclass Subject. The subscribers of the content, report generation classes LogReport, GraphReport, and TableReport, each implement interface Observer (figure 12.4).

The Observer Design Pattern

"Define a one-to-many dependency between objects so that when one object changes state, all its dependents are notified and updated automatically." (GoF p. 293)

Each time the BaseballReporter object gets a new hit Event object from the EventMaker object, it sets its private instance variable _current_event to reference the Event object.

Subject

+attach(Observer)
+detach(Observer)
+notify()

-_observers: list

<<interface>>
Observer

+update()

LogReport

-_count: int

+update(player_name)

EventMaker

-_name_index: int
-_outs: int
-_player_names: list

+next_event(): Event

-event_maker

-current_event

BaseballReporter

+report_hits()
+current_event()

TableReport

outs: int
hit_map: dictionary

+update(player_name)
-_print_table()

Event

+player_name(): string
+hit(): int

GraphReport

outs: int
singles: int
doubles: int
triples: int
homers: int

+update(player_name)
-_display_graph()

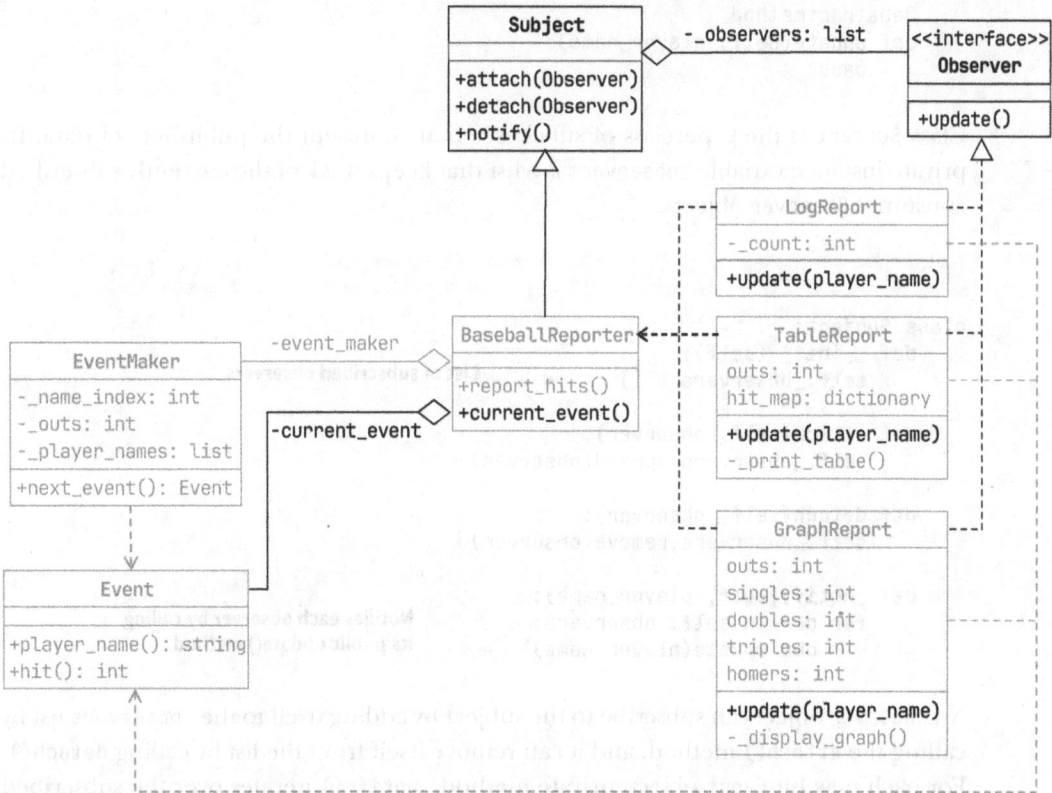

Figure 12.4 This version of the application is modeled from the Observer Design Pattern. The content publisher BaseballReporter is a subclass of Subject, and the report generation classes each implement the interface Observer. The Subject superclass's private instance variable _observers is a list of subscribed observers. The grayed-out portions of the diagram have not changed logically from figure 12.3.

Then it calls the notify() method inherited from superclass Subject to iterate over the _observers list and call the update() method of each subscribed report generator observer, passing the name of the player who made the hit or out. Each observer can then choose to use the player name to decide whether to call the BaseballReporter class's current_event() method to get the current Event object. Classes Event and EventMaker have not changed from Program 12.1 (listing 12.1).

The following listing is the eponymous Observer interface. Classes that implement Observer represent the subscribed consumers of the data. Each of them must implement the public update() method.

Listing 12.7   (Program 12.2 Stats-ObserverDP) observer.py

```
from abc import ABC, abstractmethod

class Observer(ABC):
```

```
@abstractmethod
def update(self, player_name):
    pass
```

Class Subject is the superclass of subclasses that represent the publishers of data. Its private instance variable _observers is a list that keeps track of the currently subscribed consumer Observer objects.

Listing 12.8   (Program 12.2 Stats-ObserverDP) subject.py

```
class Subject:
    def __init__(self):
        self._observers = []       ◀──┤ List of subscribed observers

    def attach(self, observer):
        self._observers.append(observer)

    def detach(self, observer):
        self._observers.remove(observer)

    def _notify(self, player_name):
        for obs in self._observers:           ┌ Notifies each observer by calling
            obs.update(player_name)    ◀──────┤ its public update() method
```

An Observer object can subscribe to the subject by adding itself to the _observers list by calling the attach() method, and it can remove itself from the list by calling detach(). For each new hit Event object, private method _notify() iterates over the subscribed Observer objects in the list and uses polymorphism to call the public update() method of each one and pass the name of the player. Therefore, each subscribed consumer is notified whenever there is a new Event object. This is a use of the Code to the Interface Principle (section 2.3.3).

Class BaseballReporter is the publisher, and therefore it is a subclass of Subject. After a subscribed Observer object is notified of a new event, if the observer is interested in the event's content, it can call the public current_event() property method to get the current hit Event object. Each subscribed consumer can process the event in its own way.

Listing 12.9   (Program 12.2 Stats-ObserverDP) baseball_reporter.py

```
from subject import Subject
from event import EventMaker

class BaseballReporter(Subject):
    def __init__(self):
        super().__init__()
        self._event_maker = EventMaker()
        self._current_event = None

    @property
```

```
    def current_event(self):
        return self._current_event

    def report_hits(self):
        self._current_event = \
            self._event_maker.next_event()

        while self._current_event != None:
            self._notify(self._current_event.player_name)

            self._current_event = \
                self._event_maker.next_event()

        self._notify(None)
```

> Notifies each observer that a new hit Event is available

> Notifies each observer that the game has completed

For testing purposes, as in Program 12.1, method report_hits() repeatedly acquires one new Event object at a time by calling the next_event() method of class EventMaker until the game has completed. Private instance variable current_event is the latest hit Event object. A call to the superclass method _notify() notifies each subscribed observer object that a new hit Event object is available, using the name of the player who made the hit or out. Method report_hits() reports the end of the game using None.

Consumer class LogReport implements interface Observer, and therefore it implements method update(). The __init__() method sets private instance variable _reporter to the publisher, the BaseballReporter object. To subscribe to Event objects, it registers the LogReport object with the publisher by calling its attach() method.

Listing 12.10   (Program 12.2 Stats-ObserverDP) log_report.py

```
from observer import Observer

class LogReport(Observer):
    def __init__(self, reporter):
        self._reporter = reporter
        self._count = 0
        reporter.attach(self)

        print('GAME HITS LOG')
        print()

    def update(self, player_name):
        event = self._reporter.current_event
        hit = event.hit

        if hit == 0:
            what = 'an out'
        elif hit == 1:
            what = 'a single'
        elif hit == 2:
            what = 'a double'
        elif hit == 3:
            what = 'a triple'
```

> Subscribes by registering with publisher BaseballReporter

> Called whenever a new hit Event is available

> Fetches the current hit Event object

```
else:
    what = 'a homer'

self._count += 1
print(f'{self._count:2d} {player_name:7s}'      │ Prints a line of the
      f' hit {what}')                            │ log report
```

The BaseballReporter publisher notifies the log report generator whenever a new hit
Event object becomes available by calling the latter's update() method. The update()
method fetches the current hit Event object from the publisher's current_event property and uses the object to perform its logging operation.

In this example program, we could have given the update() method a parameter
that's the current Event object, and then it wouldn't be necessary to use the current_
event property of class BaseballReporter. But we want to demonstrate choosing
whether to request the hit Event content based on the player's name. Being able to
choose can be important in an actual application if the content is a large amount of
data that we don't want to obtain if it isn't wanted. A new subscriber introduced later,
FanClubReport, takes advantage of having this choice.

Observer class TableReport is another implementor of interface Observer, so it implements method update(). As in class LogReport, the __init__() method sets the private
instance variable _reporter to the BaseballReporter publisher object and calls the publisher's attach() method. Then the publisher can notify the table report generator whenever a new hit Event object becomes available by calling the latter's update() method.

Listing 12.11   (Program 12.2 Stats-ObserverDP) table_reporter.py

```
from observer import Observer

class TableReport(Observer):
    def __init__(self, reporter):
        self._reporter = reporter
        self._hit_map = {}

        reporter.attach(self)   ◀──┐ Subscribes by registering with
                                    │ publisher BaseballReporter

    def _print_table (self):
        ...
                                           ┌ Called whenever a new
                                           │ hit Event is available
    def update(self, player_name):   ◀─────┘
        event = self._reporter.current_event   ◀──┐ Fetches the current
                                                   │ hit Event object
        if player_name is not None:
            hit = event.hit

            if not player_name in self._hit_map:
                self._hit_map[player_name] = 5*[0]

            self._hit_map[player_name][hit] += 1   ◀──┐ Records a player's hit or out
        else:
            self._print_table()   ◀──┐ Prints the table after the game ends
```

Method update() fetches the current hit Event object from the publisher's current_event property and uses the object to record a player's hits. After the game completes, it calls private method _print_table() to print the table.

Subscriber class GraphReport also implements interface Observer, so it implements method update(). As in classes LogReport and TableReport, method __init__() sets private instance variable _reporter to the BaseballReporter object publisher object and calls the publisher's attach() method. Then the publisher can notify the graph report generator whenever a new hit Event object becomes available by calling the latter's update() method.

Listing 12.12   (Program 12.2 Stats-ObserverDP) graph_report.py

```python
import matplotlib.pyplot as plt
from observer import Observer

class GraphReport(Observer):
    def __init__(self, reporter):
        self._reporter = reporter
        self._singles = 0
        self._doubles = 0
        self._triples = 0
        self._homers  = 0

        reporter.attach(self)          ◄──┐ Subscribes by registering with
                                           │ publisher BaseballReporter

    def _display_graph(self):
        ...
                                           ┌─ Called whenever a new
    def update(self, player_name):    ◄────┘  hit Event is available
        if player_name is not None:
            event = self._reporter.current_event   ◄──┐ Fetches the current
            hit = event.hit                            │ hit Event object

            if hit == 1:
                self._singles += 1
            elif hit == 2:
                self._doubles += 1
            elif hit == 3:
                self._triples += 1
            elif hit == 4:
                self._homers += 1
        else:                                 ┌─ Displays the graph
            self._display_graph()      ◄──────┘  after the game ends
```

Method update() fetches the current hit Event object from the publisher's current_event property and uses the object to count the number of each type of hit. After the game completes, it calls private method _display_graph() to display the bar chart.

To demonstrate how easy it is to add a new Observer class, FanClubReport prints a short report about the performance of one of the players, the club's idol.

Listing 12.13   (Program 12.2 Stats-ObserverDP) fan_club_report.py

```
from observer import Observer

class FanClubReport(Observer):
    def __init__(self, reporter, idol):
        self._reporter = reporter
        self._idol = idol
        self._what = None

        reporter.attach(self)        ◄──── Subscribes by registering with
                                           publisher BaseballReporter

    def print_bulletin(self):
        print()
        print('FAN CLUB BULLETIN')
        print(f'The first at-bat by {self._idol}'
            f' resulted in {self._what}.')
                                           Called whenever a new
                                           hit Event is available
    def update(self, player_name):   ◄────
        if player_name == self._idol:    ◄──── Reports only for the idol
            event = self._reporter.current_event  ◄──
            hit = event.hit
                                           Fetches the current
            if hit == 0:                   hit Event object
                self._what = 'an out'
            elif hit == 1:
                self._what = 'a single'
            elif hit == 2:
                self._what = 'a double'
            elif hit == 3:
                self._what = 'a triple'
            else:
                self._what = 'a homer'
                                           Unsubscribes after the
        self._reporter.detach(self)  ◄──── idol's first Event object
```

The class's update() method only obtains and processes the hit Event object of the player whose name matches the name of the club's idol. It only prints the idol's first attempt. After getting that first attempt's content, the FanClubReport object unsubscribes by detaching itself from the BaseballReporter object. Then it will no longer receive update notifications.

An example fan club report (for idol George) is

```
FANCLUB BULLETIN
The at-bat by George resulted in an out.
```

The test program creates a publisher BaseballReporter object, which it passes to each subscriber report generator class's constructor. Each constructor attaches the subscriber to the publisher. The program then calls method report_hits() of class BaseballReporter to start the stream of random Event objects. This will generate three baseball game reports similar to those shown at the start of this section. The call to method `print_bulletin()` prints the fan club report for player George.

Listing 12.14   (Program 12.2 Stats-ObserverDP) main.py

```python
from baseball_reporter import BaseballReporter
from log_report import LogReport
from table_report import TableReport
from graph_report import GraphReport
from fan_club_report import FanClubReport


if __name__ == '__main__':
    reporter = BaseballReporter()

    log   = LogReport(reporter)
    table = TableReport(reporter)
    graph = GraphReport(reporter)
    club  = FanClubReport(reporter, 'George')

    reporter.report_hits()
    club.print_bulletin()
```

Calls the baseball reporter to report hit events

Calls the fan club to print its bulletin

Using the Observer Design Pattern to model the architecture of the baseball game reports application gave us several important benefits:

- *Less hardcoding*—Subject class `BaseballReporter` no longer hardcodes the baseball game report generators. We can add new `Observer` report generator objects to the `Subject` superclass's private `_observers` list at run time or remove existing report generator objects.

- *More flexible code*—It will be easy to create new `Observer` report generator classes or delete ones we no longer need. This supports the Encapsulate What Varies Principle (section 2.3.2).

- *Loosely coupled classes*—Subject class `BaseballReporter` only knows that each of its subscribers implements interface `Observer` and therefore has a public `update()` method. It does not otherwise know how each observer is implemented. Class `BaseballReporter` must provide a `current_event` property to enable an observer to fetch the current hit `Event` content if the observer so chooses. This supports the Principle of Least Knowledge (section 2.3.2) and therefore, class `Baseball-Reporter` and the observer report generator classes are loosely coupled from each other.

- *Single responsibility*—Whenever a new hit `Event` object arrives, each `Observer` report generator can choose to process the object or ignore the event entirely. Each observer is solely responsible for generating a report in its own way. Subject class `BaseballReporter` is only responsible for generating the hit `Event` objects, and it doesn't know or care what the observers do with the events. Subject class `BaseballReporter` and the `Observer` report generator classes support the Single Responsibility Principle (section 2.3).

> The publisher knows nothing about its subscribers other than that it needs to keep track of them and notify each one whenever new content becomes available.

> The publisher also must allow each subscriber to obtain the new content. But otherwise, it doesn't care what the subscribers do with that content.

12.1.4 *The Observer's generic model*

Figure 12.5 shows the generic model of the Observer Design Pattern. From a design pattern's generic model, we can create a custom solution to an architecture problem. Table 12.1 shows how the example application applies the pattern.

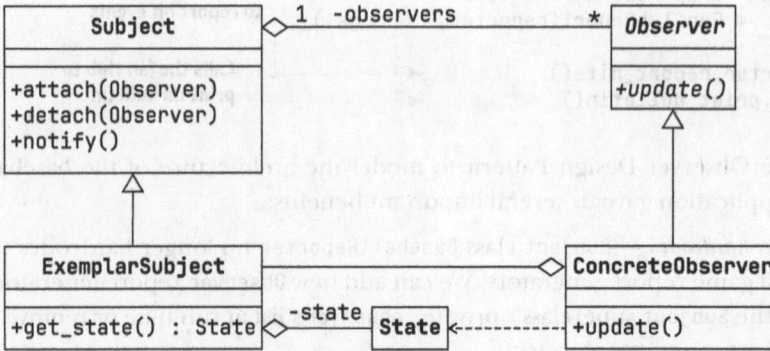

Figure 12.5   The generic model of the Observer Design Pattern. Compare with figure 12.3. During run time, we can add subscriber `Observer` objects to or remove them from the publisher `Subject` class's collection of `Observer` objects. Whenever an `ExemplarSubject` changes state, the `Subject` class's `notify()` method iterates over the observers collection and calls method `update()` of each `ConcreteObserver` object. Each `ConcreteObserver` can then choose to call the `get_state()` method of the `ExemplarSubject` class to get the new state.

Table 12.1   The Observer Method Design Pattern as applied by the example application

Design pattern	Applied by the example application
Subclass `ExemplarSubject`	Subclass `BaseballReporter`
Collection `observers`	List `_observers` in class `Subject`
Class `State`	Class `Event`
Method `get_state()`	Property `current_event` in class `BaseballReporter`
Class `State`	Class `Event`
Subclass `ConcreteObserver`	Classes `LogReport`, `GraphReport`, and `TableReport`

Summary

- The Observer Design Pattern implements the publisher–subscriber model by defining a one-to-many dependency between a subject object (the publisher) and a set of observer objects (the subscribers) so that when the subject object changes state, all the observer objects are notified automatically.

- Once notified, an observer can choose whether to fetch the contents of the new state.

- The publisher is loosely coupled with the subscribers, and the publisher doesn't know or care what the subscribers do with the state changes.

- We can add or remove subscribers without changing the publisher's code.

Summary

The Observer Design Pattern implements the publisher-subscriber model by defining a one-to-many dependency between a subject object (the publisher) and a set of observer objects (the subscribers) so that when the subject object changes state, all the observer objects are notified automatically.

Observers can register and choose whether to track the concern of the publisher.

The publisher is loosely coupled with the subscribers, and the publisher doesn't now care which the subscriber do with the state change.

We can add different subscribers without touching the publisher's code.

The State Design Pattern

This chapter covers

- The State Design Pattern

In chapter 12, we saw how the Observer Design Pattern provides a model for an application in which the subject object (the publisher) plays a key role in the operation of the application by providing content data for the observer objects (the subscribers). In this chapter, an object also plays a key role. We must monitor the runtime state changes of this object because its behavior, which depends on its current state, is critical to the operation of the application.

As we saw in section 4.4, events that change the values of the object's instance variables can cause an object to make a transition from one state to another. The object can behave differently according to its current state. The State Design Pattern provides a model for managing an object's states, the state transitions, and the different behaviors in each state.

NOTE Be sure to read the introduction to part 4 of the book for important information about design patterns in general and to learn how this and subsequent chapters teach each pattern.

13.1 *The State Design Pattern models state transitions*

Here's an analogy. Your car is a complex object that can be in one of several states, but in only one state at a time. For example, it can be turned off, idling, moving, or stopped. When the car is in the off state, you can start it. When it's in the idling state, you can transition it to the moving state by stepping on the accelerator. When it's moving, you can transition it to the stopped state by stepping on the brake. Therefore, in each state, you can perform actions that correctly cause your car to make a reasonable transition to another state. Your car has different behaviors depending on which state it is in. For example, when it's in the moving state, it can be going forward.

But your car must also handle unreasonable or useless actions. For example, if your car is stopped, stepping on the brake has no effect. If an older car is already moving forward, turning the key in the ignition will cause a horrible grinding noise.

In software, the State Design Pattern provides a model for a software application that must manage an object's runtime states and behaviors. The application must handle all the actions, reasonable or not, that can cause the object to transition from one state to another.

Recall that the state of an object during run time is uniquely determined by the set of values of its instance variables. We may have an object in our application whose current state is critical to monitor, and the application's overall operation heavily depends on that object's current state and how it behaves. A useful design tactic is to explicitly name the states to make it easier to refer to each one.

For our concrete example, consider an automatic ticket machine at a sports stadium. At any moment, the machine can be in any one of several named states (figure 13.1):

- READY—The machine is ready to accept a customer's credit card.
- VALIDATING—The machine is validating a customer's credit card.
- TICKET_SOLD—The machine has sold a ticket to a customer.
- SOLD_OUT—The game is sold out, and the machine cannot sell any more tickets.

The instance variables whose values determine the current state of the machine are

- count (integer)—The number of tickets left in the machine
- card_inserted (True or False)—Whether or not a customer's credit card is inserted
- card_validity: (YES, NO, or UNKNOWN)—The validity of the credit card

Customer actions can change the values of the instance variables and thereby cause state transitions. But there can also be times when the machine can act by itself to cause a state transition. If the ticket machine is in the READY state, a customer's action of inserting a credit card causes the machine to transition to the VALIDATING state. In that state, the machine can perform the action of checking whether the credit card was validated. If the card is valid, the machine transitions to the TICKET_SOLD state, where the customer can perform the action of taking the ticket. But if the card is invalid, the machine transitions back to the READY state. The customer can remove the card before it is validated, which forces the machine back to the READY state. The customer taking a sold ticket also causes the machine to transition back to the READY state. But if the customer took the machine's last ticket, the machine transitions to the SOLD_OUT state. Upon return to the READY state, the customer can perform the action of removing the credit card. There are no transitions out of the SOLD_OUT state.

Therefore, the possible actions by the customer and the ticket machine are as follows:

1 Insert a credit card. (Performed by the customer.)
2 Check the credit card's validation status. (Performed by the ticket machine but triggered by the customer in this application.)
3 Take a purchased ticket. (Performed by the customer.)
4 Remove the credit card. (Performed by the customer.)

While in any state, the ticket machine has no control over the actions a customer can take, even if the actions are unexpected. For example, a customer may remove a credit card before the card is validated, or a customer may try to take a ticket before paying for it. Therefore, the machine must also support customer actions that we'll deem to be unreasonable. The machine must handle all possible actions in every state (figure 13.1).

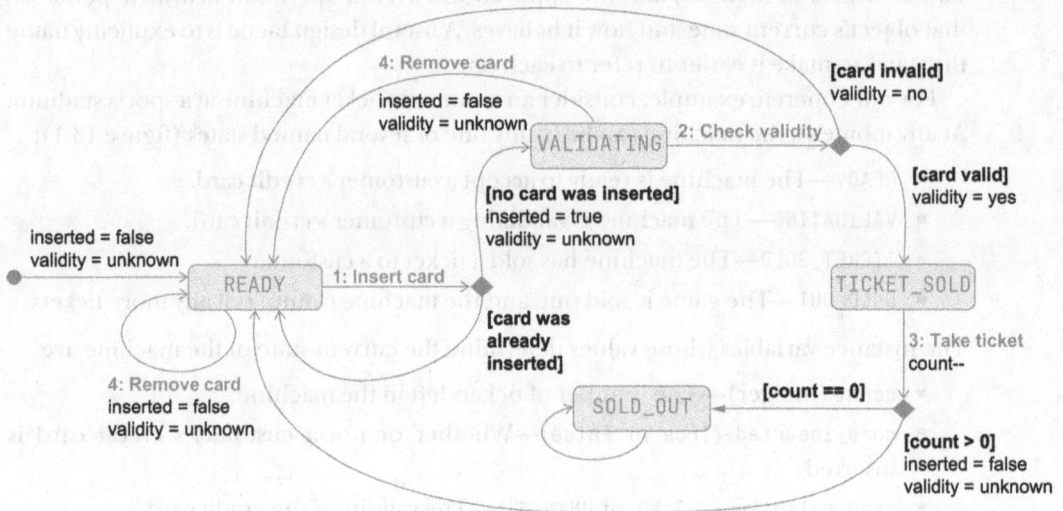

Figure 13.1 A UML state diagram showing the four states and the state transitions of an automatic ticket machine. The machine keeps track of the number of tickets it has, whether a credit card is inserted, and the validity status of the card. Customer and machine actions (numbered, such as *1: Insert card*) and certain conditions (in square brackets, such as *[card invalid]*) can cause transitions from one state to another. This figure only shows actions that cause transitions.

To keep it as simple as possible, the figure only shows actions that cause transitions. It does not show unreasonable actions such as inserting a credit card into the machine while it is in the TICKET_SOLD state when a card is still in the machine. We can assume that an unreasonable action will not cause a state transition and therefore the machine stays in its current state.

Our example application is a simple simulation of the ticket machine. The machine will have only three tickets. To interact with the application, we cause actions by playing the role of the customer or the machine. In response to each Command? prompt, we can enter a number:

- 1 to insert a credit card
- 2 to validate the card
- 3 to take a ticket
- 4 to remove our credit card
- 0 to terminate the program

The application internally keeps track of the ticket machine's current state, and it must behave properly for each action according to the state.

To aid testing and debugging, before each command prompt, the application prints in square brackets the current state of the ticket machine, the number of tickets left, whether a credit card is inserted, and the validity of the card. For example,

```
[TICKET_SOLD 2 True YES]
```

means the ticket machine is in the TICKET_SOLD state, two tickets remain, a credit card is inserted (True), and the card is valid (YES).

The following are examples of interactions with the ticket machine application. The application must be able to handle all actions while in each state. Our inputs (1, 2, 3, 4, or 0) are in **bold**:

- We successfully purchase a ticket, and the machine returns to the READY state to await the next customer action:

```
1: insert card, 2: check card validity
3: take ticket, 4: remove card, 0: quit
[READY 3 False UNKNOWN]
Command? 1
Validating your credit card.

1: insert card, 2: check card validity
3: take ticket, 4: remove card, 0: quit
[VALIDATING 3 True UNKNOWN]
Command? 2
Your credit card is validated.
Take your ticket.

1: insert card, 2: check card validity
3: take ticket, 4: remove card, 0: quit
[TICKET_SOLD 3 True YES]
Command? 3
```

```
Remove your credit card.
Enjoy the game!

1: insert card, 2: check card validity
3: take ticket, 4: remove card, 0: quit
[READY 2 True YES]
Command? 4
You've removed your credit card.

1: insert card, 2: check card validity
3: take ticket, 4: remove card, 0: quit
[READY 2 False UNKNOWN]
Command?
```

- We attempt to purchase a ticket when the machine is sold out. The machine remains in the SOLD_OUT state:

```
1: insert card, 2: check card validity
3: take ticket, 4: remove card, 0: quit
[SOLD_OUT 0 False UNKNOWN]
Command? 1
*** Machine sold out. ***
Remove your credit card

1: insert card, 2: check card validity
3: take ticket, 4: remove card, 0: quit
[SOLD_OUT 0 True UNKNOWN]
Command? 4
You've removed your credit card.

1: insert card, 2: check card validity
3: take ticket, 4: remove card, 0: quit
[SOLD_OUT 0 False UNKNOWN]
Command?
```

- We change our mind and remove a card while its validity is being checked. The machine returns to the READY state:

```
1: insert card, 2: check card validity
3: take ticket, 4: remove card, 0: quit
[READY 3 False UNKNOWN]
Command? 1
Validating your credit card.

1: insert card, 2: check card validity
3: take ticket, 4: remove card, 0: quit
[VALIDATING 3 True UNKNOWN]
Command? 4
You removed your credit card before it was validated.
No sale.

1: insert card, 2: check card validity
```

```
3: take ticket, 4: remove card, 0: quit
[READY 3 False UNKNOWN]
Command?
```

- The machine fails to validate the credit card and rejects the card. After we remove the credit card, the machine returns to the READY state:

```
1: insert card, 2: check card validity
3: take ticket, 4: remove card, 0: quit
[READY 1 False UNKNOWN]
Command? 1
Validating your credit card.

1: insert card, 2: check card validity
3: take ticket, 4: remove card, 0: quit
[VALIDATING 1 True UNKNOWN]
Command? 2
*** Credit card rejected. ***
Remove your card.

1: insert card, 2: check card validity
3: take ticket, 4: remove card, 0: quit
[READY 1 True NO]
Command? 4
You've removed your credit card.

1: insert card, 2: check card validity
3: take ticket, 4: remove card, 0: quit
[READY 1 False UNKNOWN]
Command? 1
```

- We try to take a ticket while the machine is still checking our credit card's validity. This is an unreasonable action, and the machine remains in its current VALIDATING state:

```
1: insert card, 2: check card validity
3: take ticket, 4: remove card, 0: quit
[READY 2 False UNKNOWN]
Command? 1
Validating your credit card.

1: insert card, 2: check card validity
3: take ticket, 4: remove card, 0: quit
[VALIDATING 2 True UNKNOWN]
Command? 3
Still checking your credit card's validity.

1: insert card, 2: check card validity
3: take ticket, 4: remove card, 0: quit
[VALIDATING 2 True UNKNOWN]
Command?
```

- Here are some other unreasonable actions to which the machine must respond appropriately:

```
1: insert card, 2: check card validity
3: take ticket, 4: remove card, 0: quit
[READY 3 False UNKNOWN]
Command? 1
Validating your credit card.

1: insert card, 2: check card validity
3: take ticket, 4: remove card, 0: quit
[VALIDATING 3 True UNKNOWN]
Command? 2
Your credit card is validated.
Take your ticket.

1: insert card, 2: check card validity
3: take ticket, 4: remove card, 0: quit
[TICKET_SOLD 3 True YES]
Command? 1
Take the ticket you've already bought.

1: insert card, 2: check card validity
3: take ticket, 4: remove card, 0: quit
[TICKET_SOLD 3 True UNKNOWN]
Command? 3
Remove your credit card.
Enjoy the game!

1: insert card, 2: check card validity
3: take ticket, 4: remove card, 0: quit
[READY 2 True UNKNOWN]
Command? 1
Remove the credit card that's already inserted.

1: insert card, 2: check card validity
3: take ticket, 4: remove card, 0: quit
[READY 2 True UNKNOWN]
Command?
```

As a demonstration, the first version of our example ticket machine application will not use the State Design Pattern, and then we will see its major faults. The second version will use the pattern, and we will gain its benefits.

13.1.1 Desired design features

An application that successfully implements states, behaviors, and state transitions should have these design features:

- *DF 1*—It is always clear at run time what the application's current state is.
- *DF 2*—The code for each state, including its behaviors and transitions, should be well encapsulated.

- *DF 3*—The code for each state should handle all the actions, whether reasonable or not, for that state.
- *DF 4*—It should be possible to add, remove, or modify states with minimal code changes.
- *DF 5*—There should be minimal dependencies among the states other than making transitions.

13.1.2 Before using State

For our initial version, we can design our ticket machine simulation application in a straightforward way. We'll see how many of the desired design features it has. Afterward, we'll refactor the application using a design modeled from the State Design Pattern.

Class `TicketMachine` is the heart of the first version of our application (figure 13.2). Enum classes `State` and `Validity` represent the state of the ticket machine and the validity of a credit card, respectively.

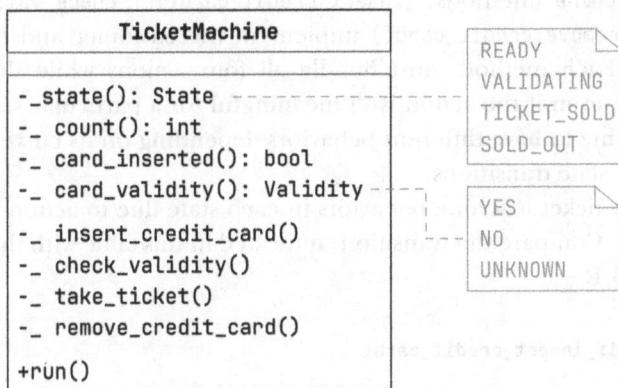

```
TicketMachine
-_state(): State
-_ count(): int
-_ card_inserted(): bool
-_ card_validity(): Validity
-_ insert_credit_card()
-_ check_validity()
-_ take_ticket()
-_ remove_credit_card()
+run()
```

```
READY
VALIDATING
TICKET_SOLD
SOLD_OUT
```

```
YES
NO
UNKNOWN
```

Figure 13.2 Class TicketMachine is the heart of the first version of our ticket machine application. Its private instance variables keep track of the current state of the machine, the number of tickets, whether a credit card is inserted, and the validity of the credit card. The private methods implement the customer and machine actions.

Listing 13.1   (Program 13.1 Tickets) ticket_machine.py (1 of 7, poor design before DP)

```python
import random
from enum import Enum

class State(Enum):
    READY       = 1
    VALIDATING  = 2
    TICKET_SOLD = 3
    SOLD_OUT    = 4

    def __str__(self):
        return self.name

class Validity(Enum):
```

```
YES     = 1
NO      = 2
UNKNOWN = 3

    def __str__(self):
        return self.name
```

The private instance variables of class TicketMachine keep track of the current state of the machine, the count of tickets, whether a credit card is inserted, and the validity of the credit card. The starting machine state is READY.

```
class TicketMachine:
    def __init__(self, count):
        self._state = State.READY        ◀──────┤ The starting machine state
        self._count = count
        self._card_inserted = False
        self._card_validity = Validity.UNKNOWN
```

The private TicketMachine methods _insert_credit_card(), _check_validity(), _take_ticket(), and _remove_credit_card() implement the customer and machine actions (figure 13.1). Each method must handle all four actions while the ticket machine is in any state, even if the action isn't meaningful for a particular state. The actions cause the machine to have different behaviors depending on its current state. Some actions can cause state transitions.

Table 13.1 shows the ticket machine behaviors in each state due to action method _insert_credit_card(). Compare the transitions indicated in this table with the transitions shown in figure 13.1.

Table 13.1   Action method 1: _insert_credit_card()

Ticket machine state	Machine behaviors in each state
READY	If no card is already inserted:
	■ Print "Validating your credit card."
	■ Set _card_inserted to True.
	■ Set _card_validity to UNKNOWN.
	■ *Transition to the* **VALIDATING** *state.*
	Else if the already-inserted card is invalid:
	■ Print "Credit card rejected."
	■ Print "Remove your card."
	Else:
	■ Print "Remove the credit card that's already inserted."
VALIDATING	Print "Still checking your credit card's validity."

Table 13.1 Action method 1: _insert_credit_card() (continued)

Ticket machine state	Machine behaviors in each state
TICKET_SOLD	Print "Take the ticket you've already bought."
	Set _card_inserted to True.
	Set _card_validity to UNKNOWN.
SOLD_OUT	Print "Machine sold out."
	Print "Remove your credit card."
	Set _card_inserted to True.
	Set _card_validity to UNKNOWN.

Method _insert_credit_card() is the starting method for a ticket purchase when the customer inserts a credit card into the ticket machine while the machine is in the READY state. But the method should handle all the actions in all the states. If the machine is in the READY state and we insert a credit card when the machine doesn't already contain a card, the machine transitions to the VALIDATING state.

Listing 13.3 (Program 13.1 Tickets) ticket_machine.py (3 of 7, poor design before DP)

```python
def _insert_credit_card(self):
    match self._state:
        case State.READY:
            if not self._card_inserted:
                print("Validating your credit card.")

                self._card_inserted = True
                self._card_validity = Validity.UNKNOWN
                self._state = State.VALIDATING          ◄─── Transitions to the
                                                             VALIDATING state
            elif self._card_validity == Validity.NO:
                print("*** Credit card rejected. ***")
                print("Remove your card.")

            else:
                print("Remove the credit card that's "
                    "already inserted.")

        case State.VALIDATING:
            print("Remove the credit card that's "
                "already inserted.")

        case State.TICKET_SOLD:
            print("Take the ticket you've "
                "already bought.")

            self._card_inserted = True
            self._card_validity = Validity.UNKNOWN
```

```
        case State.SOLD_OUT:
            print("*** Machine sold out. ***")
            print("Remove your credit card")

            self._card_inserted = True;
            self._card_validity = Validity.UNKNOWN
```

Table 13.2 shows the ticket machine behaviors in each state due to action method _check_validity(). Compare the transitions indicated in this table with the transitions shown in figure 13.1.

Table 13.2 Action method 2: `_check_validity()`

Ticket machine state	Machine behaviors in each state
READY	If no card is inserted:
	■ Print "First insert your credit card."
	Else if the card is valid:
	■ Print "Remove the credit card that's already inserted."
	Else:
	■ Print "Credit card rejected."
	■ Print "Remove your card."
VALIDATING	If the card's validity is unknown:
	■ Randomly set `_card_validity` to either Yes or No
	If the card is valid:
	■ Print "Your credit card is validated."
	■ Print "Take your ticket."
	■ Transition to the TICKET_SOLD state.
	Else:
	■ Print "*** Credit card rejected. ***"
	■ Print "Remove your card."
	■ Transition to the READY state.
TICKET_SOLD	Print "Take the ticket you've already bought."
SOLD_OUT	Print "Machine sold out."
	If a card is inserted:
	■ Print "Remove your credit card."

After we've inserted a credit card and the ticket machine is in the VALIDATING state, method _check_validity() is the machine action of checking whether the machine validated the card. But the method should handle all the actions in all the states. If the card is valid, the machine transitions to the TICKET_SOLD state; otherwise, it returns to the READY state.

```
    def _check_validity(self):
        match self._state:
            case State.READY:
                if not self._card_inserted:
                    print("First insert your credit card.")

                elif self._card_validity == Validity.YES:
                    print("Remove the credit card that's "
                            "already inserted.")

                else:
                    print("*** Credit card rejected. ***")
                    print("Remove your card.")

            case State.VALIDATING:
                if self._card_validity == Validity.UNKNOWN:
                    self._card_validity = Validity.YES \
                        if random.randint(0, 2) < 2 \
                        else Validity.NO

                if self._card_validity == Validity.YES:
                    print("Your credit card is validated.")
                    print("Take your ticket.")

                    self._state = State.TICKET_SOLD          ◄─── Transitions to the
                                                                  TICKET_SOLD state

                else:
                    print("*** Credit card rejected. ***")
                    print("Remove your card.")

                    self._state = State.READY;              ◄─── Transitions back to
                                                                  the READY state

            case State.TICKET_SOLD:
                print("Take the ticket that you've "
                        "already bought.")

            case State.SOLD_OUT:
                print("*** Machine sold out. ***")

                if self._card_inserted:
                    print("Remove your credit card.")
```

Table 13.3 shows the ticket machine behaviors in each state due to action method _take_ticket(). Compare the transitions indicated in this table with the transitions shown in figure 13.1.

Method _take_ticket() is the customer action of taking the newly purchased ticket when the machine is in the TICKET_SOLD state, but it should handle all the actions in all the states. If there are tickets remaining, the machine transitions back to the READY state. Otherwise, it transitions to the SOLD_OUT state.

Table 13.3   Action method 3: _take_ticket()

Ticket machine state	Machine behaviors in each state
READY	If no card is inserted: ■ Print "First insert your credit card." Else if the card's validity is unknown: ■ Print "Still checking your credit card's validity." Else if the card is valid: ■ Print "Take the ticket you've already bought." ■ Print "Remove your credit card." Else: ■ Print "*** Credit card rejected. ***" ■ Print "Remove your card."
VALIDATING	If the card's validity is unknown: ■ Print "Still checking your credit card's validity." Else if the card is valid: ■ Print "Your card is already validated." ■ Print "Take your ticket." Else: ■ Print "*** Credit card rejected. ***" ■ Print "Remove your card."
TICKET_SOLD	Print "Remove your credit card." Print "Enjoy the game!" Decrement the ticket count If the ticket count > 0: ■ *Transition to the READY state.* Else: ■ *Transition to the SOLD_OUT state.*
SOLD_OUT	Print "Machine sold out." If a card is inserted: ■ Print "Remove your credit card."

Table 13.3 shows the machine behaviors in each state due to actions initiated

Listing 13.5   (Program 13.1 Tickets) ticket_machine.py (5 of 7, poor design before DP)

```python
def _take_ticket(self):
    match self._state:
        case State.READY:
            if not self._card_inserted:
                print("First insert your credit card.")
```

```
    elif self._card_validity == Validity.UNKNOWN:
        print("Still checking your "
              "credit card's validity.")

    elif self._card_validity == Validity.YES:
        print("Take the ticket that you've "
              "already bought.")
        print("Remove your card.")

    else:
        print("*** Credit card rejected. ***")
        print("Remove your card.")

case State.VALIDATING:
    if self._card_validity == Validity.UNKNOWN:
        print("Still checking your "
              "credit card's validity.")

    elif self._card_validity == Validity.YES:
        print("Your card is already validated.")
        print("Take your ticket.")

    else:
        print("*** Credit card rejected. ***")
        print("Remove your card.")

case State.TICKET_SOLD:
    print("Remove your credit card.")
    print("Enjoy the game!")

    self._count -= 1

    if self._count > 0:
        self._state = State.READY        ◄──┤ Transitions back to
    else:                                    │ the READY state
        self._state = State.SOLD_OUT     ◄──┤ Transitions to the
case State.SOLD_OUT:                         │ SOLD_OUT state
    print("*** Machine sold out. ***")

    if self._card_inserted:
        print("Remove your credit card.")
```

Table 13.4 shows the ticket machine behaviors in each state due to action method _remove_credit_card(). Compare the transitions indicated in this table with the transitions shown in figure 13.1.

Method _remove_credit_card() is the action when we remove the credit card from the ticket machine when it is in the READY state or the VALIDATING state. But as usual, it should handle all the actions in all the states. If we remove the card when the machine is in the VALIDATING state (the machine hasn't yet validated the card), the machine transitions back to the READY state.

Table 13.4   Action method _remove_credit_card()

Ticket machine state	Machine behaviors in each state
READY	If a card is inserted:
	■ Print "You've removed your credit card."
	Else:
	■ Print "No credit card inserted."
	Set card_inserted to False.
	Set _card_validity to UNKNOWN.
VALIDATING	If no card is inserted:
	■ Print "No credit card inserted."
	Else if the card is invalid:
	■ Print "*** Credit card rejected. ***"
	■ Print "Remove your card."
	Else:
	■ Print "You removed your credit card before it was validated."
	■ PRINT "No sale."
	Set card_inserted to False.
	Set _card_validity to UNKNOWN.
	Transition to the **READY** *state.*
TICKET_SOLD	Print "First take your ticket."
SOLD_OUT	If card inserted:
	■ Print "You've removed your credit card."
	■ Set card_inserted to False.
	■ Set _card_validity to UNKNOWN.
	Else:
	■ Print "No credit card inserted."

Listing 13.6   (Program 13.1 Tickets) ticket_machine.py (6 of 7, poor design before DP)

```
def _remove_credit_card(self):
    match self._state:
        case State.READY:
            if self._card_inserted:
                print("You've removed your credit card.")
            else:
                print("No credit card inserted.")

            self._card_inserted = False
```

```
                    self._card_validity = Validity.UNKNOWN

             case State.VALIDATING:
                 if not self._card_inserted:
                     print("No credit card inserted.")

                 elif self._card_validity == Validity.NO:
                     print("*** Credit card rejected. *** ")
                     print("Remove your card.")

                 else:
                     print("You removed your credit card "
                             "before it was validated.")
                     print("No sale.")

                 self._card_inserted = False
                 self._card_validity = Validity.UNKNOWN
                 self._state = State.READY              ◄———  Transitions back to
                                                              the READY state
             case State.TICKET_SOLD:
                 print("First take your ticket.")

             case State.SOLD_OUT:
                 if self._card_inserted:
                     print("You've removed your credit card.")

                     self._card_inserted = False
                     self._card_validity = Validity.UNKNOWN

                 else:
                     print("No credit card inserted.")
```

Finally, public method run() runs the simulation.

Listing 13.7   (Program 13.1 Tickets) ticket_machine.py (7 of 7, poor design before DP)

```
    def run(self):
        command = -1

        while command != 0:
            print()
            print("1: insert card, 2: check card validity")
            print("3: take ticket, 4: remove card, 0: quit")
            print(f"[{self._state} {self._count}"
                    f" {self._card_inserted}"
                    f" {self._card_validity}]")
            command = int(input("Command? "))

            match command:
                case 1: self._insert_credit_card()
                case 2: self._check_validity()
                case 3: self._take_ticket()
                case 4: self._remove_credit_card()

                case 0:
```

```
                        print()
                        print("Done!")

                case _:
                        print("*** Invalid command. ***")
```

The test program creates a `TicketMachine` object with three tickets and calls the `run()` method.

Listing 13.8   (Program 13.1 Tickets) main.py (poor design before DP)

```
from ticket_machine import TicketMachine

if __name__ == '__main__':
    machine = TicketMachine(3)
    machine.run()
```

Class **TicketMachine** is awfully complicated! Its design is focused on the actions—each action 1, 2, 3, and 4 has its own method function. The state behaviors are scattered among the action functions. Adding, removing, or modifying a state would be difficult. The design violates DF 2, DF 3, and DF 4.

The class has way too many responsibilities! The State Design Pattern will do a much better job of encapsulating the states and their behaviors.

This version of our ticket machine application works correctly. We can interact with it and see proper behaviors. But it has major faults, including the following:

- *Multiple responsibilities*—Class `TicketMachine` not only has to keep track of the machine's state but also is responsible for all the actions that occur in all the states. All the application logic is concentrated in this one class.

- *Poor encapsulation*—The states and their behaviors are not well encapsulated.

- *Inflexible code*—If we need to modify, add, or remove ticket machine states and their actions, we will need to change the `TicketMachine` class.

13.1.3 *After using State*

The State Design Pattern provides a model for a software architecture that eliminates these faults (figure 13.3). Each subclass of superclass `State` represents a ticket machine state, and each `State` subclass encapsulates handling all the customer and machine actions for its state. Class `StatesBlock` aggregates all the `State` subclasses, and its public `initialize()` method returns the ticket machine's initial state. Class `StatesBlock` enables the `State` subclasses to be loosely coupled with each other and class `Ticket-Machine` to be loosely coupled with the `State` subclasses.

Instance variable `state` of class `TicketMachine` is the `State` object that represents the current state of the machine. Through polymorphism, the class defers handling each of its action methods `_insert_credit_card()`, `_check_validity()`, `_take_ticket()`, and _remove_credit_card() to the corresponding action method of the current State object. Each of the State subclass action methods returns a State object that is the next state that the machine should transition to.

The State Design Pattern

"Allow an object to alter its behavior when its internal state changes. The object will appear to change its class." (GoF p. 305)

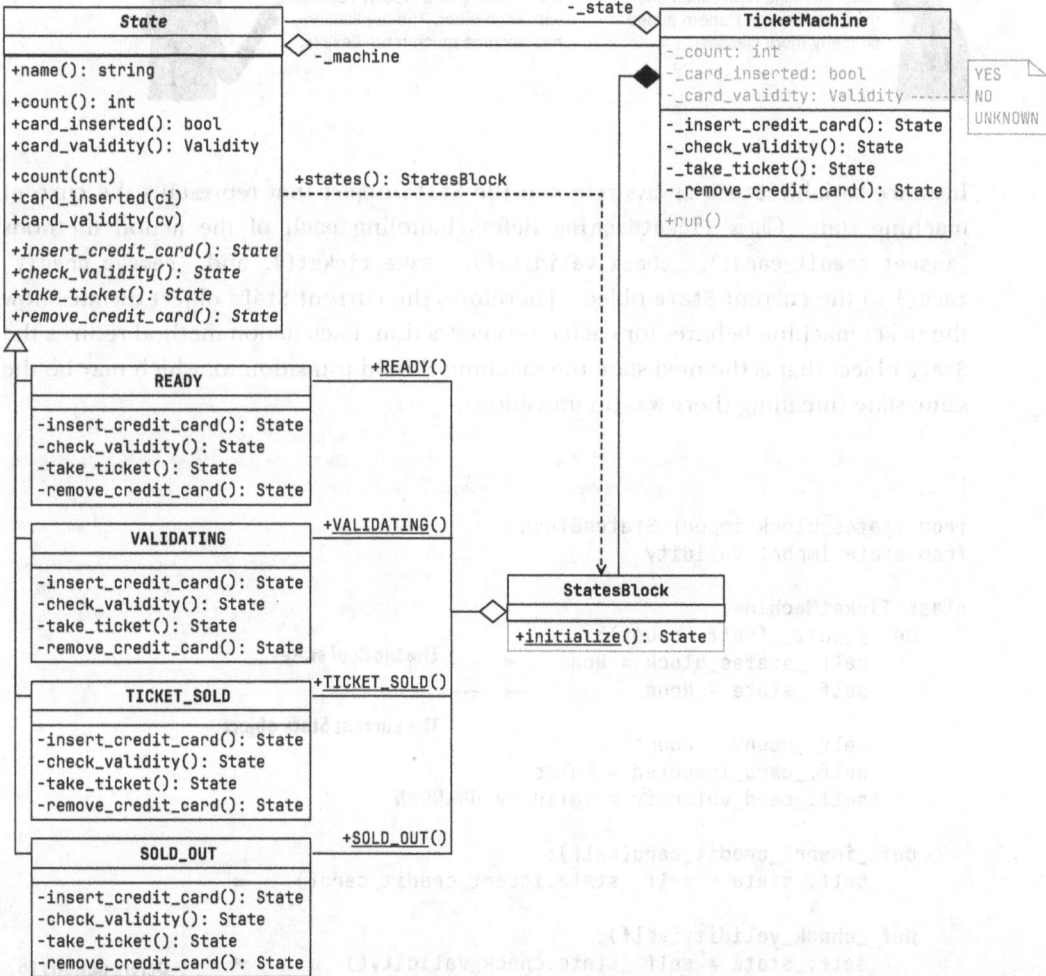

State

+name(): string

+count(): int
+card_inserted(): bool
+card_validity(): Validity

+count(cnt)
+card_inserted(ci)
+card_validity(cv)

+insert_credit_card(): State
+check_validity(): State
+take_ticket(): State
+remove_credit_card(): State

-_machine

+states(): StatesBlock

-_state

TicketMachine

-_count: int
-_card_inserted: bool
-_card_validity: Validity

-_insert_credit_card(): State
-_check_validity(): State
-_take_ticket(): State
-_remove_credit_card(): State

+run()

YES
NO
UNKNOWN

READY

-insert_credit_card(): State
-check_validity(): State
-take_ticket(): State
-remove_credit_card(): State

+READY()

VALIDATING

-insert_credit_card(): State
-check_validity(): State
-take_ticket(): State
-remove_credit_card(): State

+VALIDATING()

StatesBlock

+initialize(): State

TICKET_SOLD

-insert_credit_card(): State
-check_validity(): State
-take_ticket(): State
-remove_credit_card(): State

+TICKET_SOLD()

SOLD_OUT

-insert_credit_card(): State
-check_validity(): State
-take_ticket(): State
-remove_credit_card(): State

+SOLD_OUT()

Figure 13.3 The subclasses of superclass State encapsulate handling the customer and machine actions for each state of the ticket machine. Each action method of the subclasses returns a State object that is the next state for the ticket machine to transition to. By aggregating the State subclasses in class StatesBlock, the subclasses are loosely coupled with each other and with class TicketMachine. Each action method of class TicketMachine defers to the corresponding method of the current State object pointed to by its private _state instance variable.

The code for class `TicketMachine` is much simpler in this version of the application because it no longer has the responsibility of managing the states and their customer and machine actions. As in the previous version of the application, `TicketMachine` has private _count, _card_inserted, and _card_validity instance variables to keep track of the count of remaining tickets, whether a credit card is inserted, and the validity of the card, respectively.

Modeling the new version of the ticket machine application after the State Design Pattern added so many more classes!

Yes, but the added **State** classes are cohesive and loosely coupled with each other. The application has become much more flexible.

Instance variable state always refers to the State object that represents the current machine state. Class `TicketMachine` defers handling each of the action methods _insert_credit_card(), _check_validity(), _take_ticket(), and _remove_credit_card() to the current State object. Therefore, the current State object dictates how the ticket machine behaves for each customer action. Each action method returns the State object that is the next state the machine should transition to, which may be the same state (meaning there was no transition).

Listing 13.9   (Program 13.2 Tickets-StateDP) ticket_machine.py

```
from states_block import StatesBlock
from state import Validity

class TicketMachine:
    def __init__(self, count):
        self._states_block = None        ◄───┤  The block of states
        self._state = None               ◄───

                                              │  The current State object
        self._count = count
        self._card_inserted = False
        self._card_validity = Validity.UNKNOWN

    def _insert_credit_card(self):
        self._state = self._state.insert_credit_card()    ◄───

    def _check_validity(self):
        self._state = self._state.check_validity()    ◄───
                                                           Defers actions to
                                                           the current State
    def _take_ticket(self):                                object and gets
        self._state = self._state.take_ticket()    ◄───    the next state

    def _remove_credit_card(self):
        self._state = self._state.remove_credit_card()    ◄───
```

```
        def run(self):
            self._states_block = StatesBlock()
            self._state = StatesBlock.initialize(self)   ◄──── Initializes the block of
                                                                State objects, which
            command = -1                                        returns the initial state

            while command != 0:
                ...
```

As before, the run() method performs the simulation. It starts by initializing the StatesBlock, which returns the starting state.

Class State is the abstract superclass of subclasses READY, VALIDATING, TICKET_SOLD, and SOLD_OUT. Its constructor receives the name of the subclass and a reference to the TicketMachine object. Properties count, card_inserted, and card_validity access and set the corresponding TicketMachine instance variables.

Listing 13.10   (Program 13.2 Tickets-StateDP) state.py

```
from abc import ABC, abstractmethod
from enum import Enum

class Validity(Enum):
    YES     = 1
    NO      = 2
    UNKNOWN = 3

class State(ABC):
    def __init__(self, name, machine):
        self._name = name
        self._machine = machine

    @property
    def name(self):
        return self._name

    @property
    def states(self):                            ◄──┐
        return self._machine._states_block          │
                                                    │
    @property                                       │
    def count(self):                             ◄──┤
        return self._machine._count                 │
                                                    │
    @count.setter                                   │
    def count(self, new_count):          Accesses and sets
        self._machine._count = new_count  TicketMachine
                                          instance variables
    @property                                       │
    def card_inserted(self):                     ◄──┤
        return self._machine._card_inserted         │
                                                    │
    @card_inserted.setter                           │
    def card_inserted(self, new_card_inserted):  ◄──┘
```

```
                    self._machine._card_inserted = new_card_inserted

        @property
        def card_validity(self):
            return self._machine._card_validity

        @card_validity.setter
        def card_validity(self, new_card_validity):
            self._machine._card_validity = new_card_validity

        @abstractmethod
        def insert_credit_card(self):
            pass

        @abstractmethod
        def check_validity(self):
            pass

        @abstractmethod
        def take_ticket(self):
            pass

        @abstractmethod
        def remove_credit_card(self):
            pass
```

Accesses and sets TicketMachine instance variables

Action methods to be implemented by each State subclass

Each State subclass must implement the customer action methods insert_credit_card(), check_validity(), take_ticket(), and remove_credit_card() to perform the customer and machine action behaviors defined for each state. Each method returns a State object that is the next state for the ticket machine to transition to.

Subclass READY implements the action methods to perform the actions relevant to the ticket machine being in the READY state.

Listing 13.11 (Program 13.2 Tickets-StateDP) READY.py

```python
from state import Validity, State

class READY(State):
    def __init__(self, machine):
        super().__init__('READY', machine)

    def insert_credit_card(self):
        if not self.card_inserted:
            print("Validating your credit card.")

            self.card_inserted = True
            self.card_validity = Validity.UNKNOWN
            return self.states.VALIDATING

        elif self.card_validity == Validity.NO:
            print("*** Credit card rejected. ***")
            print("Remove your card.")
```

```
                        return self

            else:
                print("Remove the credit card that's "
                    "already inserted.")
                return self

    def check_validity(self):
        if not self.card_inserted:
            print("First insert your credit card.")

        elif self.card_validity == Validity.YES:
            print("Remove the credit card that's "
                "already inserted.")
        else:
            print("*** Credit card rejected. ***")
            print("Remove your card.")

        return self

    def take_ticket(self):
        if not self.card_inserted:
            print("First insert your credit card.")

        elif self.card_validity == Validity.UNKNOWN:
            print("Still checking your "
                "credit card's validity.")

        elif self.card_validity == Validity.YES:
            print("Take the ticket that you've "
                "already bought.")
            print("Remove your card.")

        else:
            print("*** Credit card rejected. ***")
            print("Remove your card.")

        return self

    def remove_credit_card(self):
        if self.card_inserted:
            print("You've removed your credit card.")

        else:
            print("No credit card inserted.")

        self.card_inserted = False
        self.card_validity = Validity.UNKNOWN
        return self
```

Each action method returns the next state to transition to, such as

```
return self.states.VALIDATING
```

where states is the states block. If there should be no transition, the method simply returns self to stay in the current state:

```
return self
```

Subclass VALIDATING implements the action methods to perform the actions relevant to the ticket machine being in the VALIDATING state.

Listing 13.12   (Program 13.2 Tickets-StateDP) VALIDATING.py

```python
import random
from state import Validity, State

class VALIDATING(State):
    def __init__(self, machine):
        super().__init__('VALIDATING', machine)

    def insert_credit_card(self):
        print("Still checking your "
            "credit card's validity.")

        return self

    def check_validity(self):
        if self.card_validity == Validity.UNKNOWN:
            self.card_validity = Validity.YES \
                if random.randint(0, 2) < 2 \
                else Validity.NO

        if self.card_validity == Validity.YES:
            print("Your credit card is validated. "
                "Take your ticket.")

            return self.states.TICKET_SOLD;

        else:
            print("*** Credit card rejected. ***")
            print("Remove your card.")

            return self.states.READY;

    def take_ticket(self):
        if self.card_validity == Validity.UNKNOWN:
            print("Still checking your "
                "credit card's validity.")

        elif self.card_validity == Validity.YES:
            print("Your card is already validated.")
            print("Take your ticket.")

        else:
            print("*** Credit card rejected. ***")
            print("Remove your card.")
```

```
        return self

    def remove_credit_card(self):
        if not self.card_inserted:
            print("No credit card inserted.")

        elif self.card_validity == Validity.NO:
            print("*** Credit card rejected. *** ")
            print("Remove your card.")

        else:
            print("You removed your credit card "
                    "before it was validated.")
            print("No sale.")

        self.card_inserted = False
        self.card_validity = Validity.UNKNOWN
        return self.states.READY
```

Subclass `TICKET_SOLD` implements the action methods to perform the actions relevant to the ticket machine being in the `TICKET_SOLD` state.

Listing 13.13   (Program 13.2 Tickets-StateDP) TICKET_SOLD.py

```
from state import Validity, State

class TICKET_SOLD(State):
    def __init__(self, machine):
        super().__init__('TICKET_SOLD', machine)

    def insert_credit_card(self):
        print("Take the ticket you've "
                "already bought.")

        self.card_inserted = True;
        self.card_validity = Validity.UNKNOWN;

        return self

    def check_validity(self):
        print("Take the ticket that you've "
                "already bought.")

        return self

    def take_ticket(self):
        print("Remove your credit card.")
        print("Enjoy the game!")

        self.count -= 1

        if self.count > 0:
            return self.states.READY
        else:
```

```
        return self.states.SOLD_OUT

    def remove_credit_card(self):
        print("First take your ticket.")

        return self
```

Subclass SOLD_OUT implements the action methods to perform the actions relevant to the ticket machine being in the SOLD_OUT state.

Listing 13.14   (Program 13.2 Tickets-StateDP) SOLD_OUT.py

```
from state import Validity, State

class SOLD_OUT(State):
    def __init__(self, machine):
        super().__init__('SOLD_OUT', machine)

    def insert_credit_card(self):
        print("*** Machine sold out. ***")
        print("Remove your credit card")

        self.card_inserted = True;
        self.card_validity = Validity.UNKNOWN;

        return self

    def check_validity(self):
        print("*** Machine sold out. ***")

        if self.card_inserted:
            print("Remove your credit card.")

        return self

    def take_ticket(self):
        print("*** Machine sold out. ***")

        if self.card_inserted:
            print("Remove your credit card.")

        return self

    def remove_credit_card(self):
        if self.card_inserted:
            print("You've removed your credit card.")

            self.card_inserted = False
            self.card_validity = Validity.UNKNOWN

        else:
            print("No credit card inserted.")

        return self
```

In the first version of our application, class **TicketMachine** grouped the behaviors by action first and then by ticket machine state.

By using the State Design Pattern to model the application, we now have a cohesive **State** object representing each machine state, and each **State** object encapsulates action behaviors relevant to its state.

Class **StatesBlock** privately aggregates the **State** subclasses as class variables because only one block is necessary, and once initialized, the block never changes. Aggregating the subclasses in this class allows the subclasses to be loosely coupled with each other and with class **TicketMachine**.

The run() method of class **TicketMachine** calls the initialize() method to create the **State** objects. The method returns a reference to the initial READY state.

Listing 13.15   (Program 13.2 Tickets-StateDP) states_block.py

```python
from READY import READY
from VALIDATING import VALIDATING
from TICKET_SOLD import TICKET_SOLD
from SOLD_OUT import SOLD_OUT

class StatesBlock:
    _READY_state       = None          State subclasses
    _VALIDATING_state  = None          aggregated as private
    _TICKET_SOLD_state = None          class variables
    _SOLD_OUT_state    = None

    @classmethod
    def initialize(cls, machine):
        cls._READY_state       = READY(machine)
        cls._VALIDATING_state  = VALIDATING(machine)
        cls._TICKET_SOLD_state = TICKET_SOLD(machine)
        cls._SOLD_OUT_state    = SOLD_OUT(machine)

        return cls._READY_state          ◄——  The initial state

    @classmethod
    @property
    def READY(cls):
        return cls._READY_state

    @classmethod
    @property
    def VALIDATING(cls):
        return cls._VALIDATING_state

    @classmethod
    @property
    def TICKET_SOLD(cls):
        return cls._TICKET_SOLD_state
```

```
@classmethod
@property
def SOLD_OUT(cls):
    return cls._SOLD_OUT_state
```

There is no change to main.py. The program behaves the same as the first version. But modeling it from the State Design Pattern has the following benefits:

- *Encapsulated customer actions*—Each `State` subclass encapsulates all the customer actions when the ticket machine is in the corresponding state. It will be possible to modify the behavior of a state or to remove or add states without changing the other `State` subclasses or class `TicketMachine`. This is the Encapsulate What Varies Principle (section 2.3.2).
- *Single-responsibility classes*—Class `TicketMachine` only has the responsibility to keep track of the values of its current `state` and the other instance variables. It is no longer responsible for the customer actions of each state. This is the Single Responsibility Principle (section 2.3).
- *Loosely coupled* classes—The `State` subclasses are loosely coupled with each other, and class `TicketMachine` is loosely coupled with the `State` subclasses. Following the Principle of Least Knowledge (section 2.3.2), class `TicketMachine` has no dependencies on any of the `State` subclasses.

13.1.4 *State's generic model*

Figure 13.4 shows the generic model of the State Design Pattern. From a design pattern's generic model, we can create a custom solution to an architecture problem. Table 13.5 shows how the example application applies the pattern.

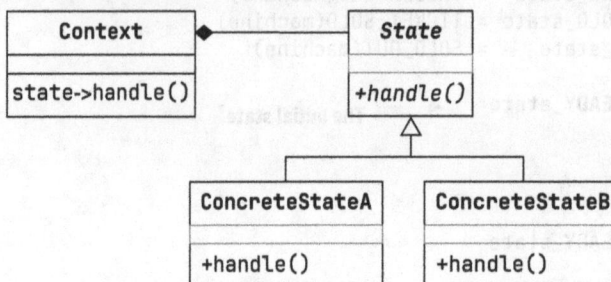

Figure 13.4   The generic model of the State Design Pattern. Compare with figure 13.3. Instead of the `Context` class aggregating the `State` subclasses as shown here, figure 13.3 shows the `State` subclasses encapsulated in the `StatesBlock` class, which allows the `State` subclasses to be loosely coupled with each other and with the `TicketMachine` class. Also in figure 13.3, each of the customer action methods returns the `State` object the ticket machine will transition to.

Table 13.5 The State Method Design Pattern as applied by the example application

Design pattern	Applied by the example application
Class `Context`	Class `TicketMachine` (using class `StatesBlock`)
Superclass `State`	Superclass `State`
Subclasses `ConcreteStateA` and `ConcreteStateB`	Subclasses READY, VALIDATING, TICKET_SOLD, and SOLD_OUT
Method `handle()`	`State` methods `insert_credit_card()`, `check_validity()`, `take_ticket()`, and `remove_credit_card()`

The second version of our ticket machine application goes beyond what the State Design Pattern models, doesn't it?

Yes. By introducing class **statesBlock**, we added the extra feature of making class **TicketMachine** loosely coupled with the **State** classes. Also, each action method returns the next state to transition to.

13.2 *Choosing between State and Visitor*

Both the State Design Pattern and the Visitor Design Pattern share the philosophy of separating the data from operations on the data. The Visitor Design Pattern models an architecture that encapsulates different algorithms that operate on the objects of a data structure according to the different datatypes of the objects. The State Design Pattern models an architecture that encapsulates different object behaviors according to the different states of the object.

Summary

- The State Design Pattern models a solution for a software architecture when it's important to monitor the runtime states of a particular object.
- A set of actions performed on the object causes it to behave in ways according to its current state.
- Some actions cause the object to make state transitions.
- Separate state classes each encapsulate the action behaviors of the object when it is in that state.
- Each state class must implement all the action behaviors.

The Singleton, Composite, and Decorator Design Patterns

This chapter covers

- The Singleton Design Pattern
- The Composite Design Pattern
- The Decorator Design Pattern

This chapter's design patterns provide models for solving architecture problems when we must manage a collection of one or more objects so that the collection behaves in a unified way. Applying the right design pattern can simplify the application's code that works with the objects, and it can also make the code more flexible.

The Singleton Design Pattern models the simplest case of a collection of only one object. Only one instance of its class, the singleton object, can exist during the application's run time.

The Composite Design Pattern provides a model for an application that manages objects stored in a hierarchical tree structure. The application greatly reduces the complexity of its code if it can treat an individual object the same way it treats a composition of objects.

We may want our application to add responsibilities to an object in the form of attributes and behaviors at run time, but without changing the object's code. These additional responsibilities, in the form of objects, are called *decorations* by the Decorator Design Pattern. The pattern models handling an object's decorations in a flexible manner.

> **NOTE** Be sure to read the introduction to part 4 of the book for important information about design patterns in general and to learn how this and subsequent chapters teach each pattern.

14.1 The Singleton Design Pattern ensures that a class has only one object

Suppose an application needs to print to one or more printers. Whenever the application wants to print something, it must access a `PrintSpooler` object. The application doesn't know whether the spooler object already exists. If the object doesn't exist, one is created without the application knowing it happened. Each time the application wants to print, it accesses the same `PrintSpooler` object, so at most one `PrintSpooler` object exists. Therefore, the object is a *singleton* object. The Singleton Design Pattern provides a model for a software architecture that supports such an object.

For our concrete example, assume that the college sports stadium has an executive suite that's available for use only during certain sporting events. There is only one pass that allows its holder to use the suite whenever it's available. The pass is a singleton object, and there can be at most one of them.

14.1.1 Desired design features

An application that can have at most one instance of a particular class should have the following design features:

- *DF 1*—There must be a way for the application to access the singleton object.
- *DF 2*—Whenever the application needs the singleton object, it must always access the same object.
- *DF 3*—If the singleton object doesn't already exist, one must be created without any action by the application.
- *DF 4*—The singleton object doesn't need to exist if the application never accesses the object.
- *DF 5*—There can never be more than one instance of the singleton object.
- *DF 6*—If the singleton object is deleted, then a new instance of the singleton can be created.

14.1.2 Before using Singleton

The first version of our application will not use the Singleton Design Pattern, and it will fail to have all the desired design features. Then we'll refactor that application using the design pattern.

A common but inadequate solution to having a singleton object is to make it the value of a global variable. We'll do so in the first version of our application, where class ExecutivePass is a straightforward implementation of the executive pass (figure 14.1).

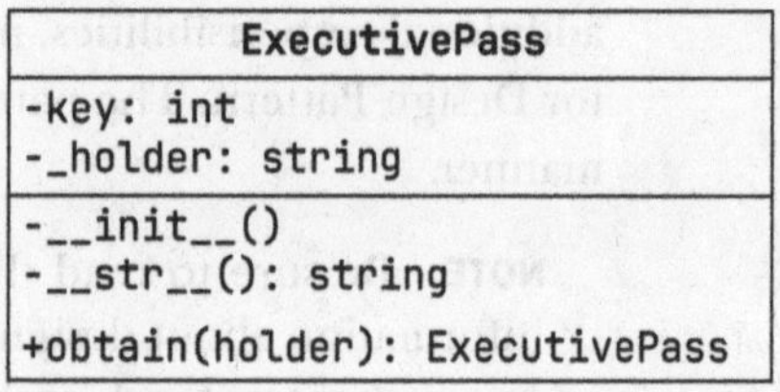

ExecutivePass
-_key: int -_holder: string
-__init__() -__str__(): string +obtain(holder): ExecutivePass

The pass uses a randomly generated four-digit key as its unique identifier. Public class method obtain() allows the caller to obtain a reference to the pass object. The method sets

Figure 14.1   An unsuccessful attempt at a singleton class

the object's private _holder instance variable to the name of the person holding the pass. Each time an ExecutivePass object is created, the application prints a line that identifies the pass. For example,

```
** Executive pass created, key = 569
```

Listing 14.1   (Program 14.1 ExecPass) executive_pass.py (poor design before DP)

```
import random

class ExecutivePass:
    def __init__(self):
        self._key = random.randint(1, 999)    ◄──── Generates a random key
        self._holder = None

        print("** Executive pass created, "
              f"key = {self._key}")
        print()

    def __str__(self):
        return (f'pass holder is {self._holder}, '
                f'key = {self._key}')

    def obtain(self, holder):    ◄──── Obtains the executive pass
        self._holder = holder
        return self
```

In the test program, the value of the global variable global_pass is the ExecutivePass object.

Listing 14.2   (Program 14.1 ExecPass) main.py (poor design before DP)

```
from copy import copy
from executive_pass import ExecutivePass

global_pass = ExecutivePass()    ◄────┐
                                       │  The global
                                       │  ExecutivePass object
def run_app():                         │
    global global_pass         ◄───────┘
```

```
ron_pass = global_pass.obtain("Ron")            ◄──── Ron obtains the global pass.
print("Ron takes hold of the global pass")
print(f"  Ron's pass: {ron_pass}")

print()

sal_pass = ron_pass.obtain("Sal")               ◄──── Sal obtains the global
print("Sal takes the global pass from Ron")           pass from Ron.
print(f"  Sal's pass: {sal_pass}")

print()

copy_pass = copy(sal_pass)                       │ Bob obtains a copy
bob_pass = copy_pass.obtain("Bob")               │ of the global pass.
print("Bob makes a copy of Sal's global pass")
print(f"  Bob's pass: {bob_pass}")
print("But Sal still holds the original global pass")
print(f"  Sal's pass: {sal_pass}")

print()

another_pass = ExecutivePass()                   │ Tim obtains another
tim_pass = another_pass.obtain("Tim")            │ global pass.
print("Create another executive pass for Tim")
print(f"  Tim's pass: {tim_pass}")
print("But Sal still holds the original global pass")
print(f"  Sal's pass: {sal_pass}")
print("And Bob still holds his copy")
print(f"  Bob's pass: {bob_pass}")

if __name__ == '__main__':
    run_app()
```

An example of the program's output is as follows:

```
** Executive pass created, key = 575

Ron takes hold of the global pass
  Ron's pass: pass holder is Ron, key = 575

Sal takes the global pass from Ron
  Sal's pass: pass holder is Sal, key = 575

Bob makes a copy of Sal's global pass
  Bob's pass: pass holder is Bob, key = 575
But Sal still holds the original global pass
  Sal's pass: pass holder is Sal, key = 575

** Executive pass created, key = 158

Create another executive pass for Tim
  Tim's pass: pass holder is Tim, key = 158
But Sal still holds the original global pass
  Sal's pass: pass holder is Sal, key = 575
And Bob still holds his copy
  Bob's pass: pass holder is Bob, key = 575
```

Obviously, simply making an object global is insufficient to make it a singleton. This version of our application has failed to have only a single executive pass. Bob was able to make a copy of Sal's executive pass (key 575), and Tim obtained a second global pass (key 158). The application created two different "singleton" ExecutivePass objects. One of the two passes (key 575) had two people (Sal and Bob) claiming to hold it at the same time.

Because the executive pass is a global object, it's automatically created when the application starts. Therefore, it exists even if it's never accessed. That violates DF 3 and DF 4.

It's easy to forget about making copies of an object that's supposed to be a singleton. We ended up with multiple copies of the singleton object. That violated DF 2 and DF 5.

Here are the major faults of the first version of our application:

- *Use of a global variable*—We should not have global variables in a well-designed application. Different parts of the application can access a global variable. One part can change the variable's value unbeknownst to other parts that weren't expecting the change, resulting in unwanted surprises and possible logic errors. An exception to this rule is the special case in which a global variable such as PI represents a constant value.

- *Order of creation*—If different global objects declared in different source files depend on each other, logic errors can occur because the order in which the objects are created when the application starts is undefined.

- *The object is always present*—In our example, the executive suite is not open for every sporting event. Because we defined the pass globally, it is always present. This can be a problem if the singleton object is costly to construct or consumes many resources. We can't delete the global object in order to create a new one.

- *We can copy the singleton object*—These operations will create more instances of the supposedly singleton object.

14.1.3   *After using Singleton*

We can fix the problems with class ExecutivePass by refactoring the code to model it after the Singleton Design Pattern.

The Singleton Design Pattern

"Ensure a class has only one instance, and provide a global point of access to it." (GoF p. 127)

We must make several significant changes (figure 14.2):

- *Private class variable* `_instance` is static and refers to the one and only singleton object if it exists. Otherwise, the variable's value is `None`.

- A *public class method* `obtain()` returns a reference to the singleton object. The method creates the object if it doesn't already exist. `ExecutivePass.obtain()` is the global point of access to the singleton object.

- *Deleting the singleton object* enables us to create a new one later.

- *Control creating the singleton object.* We must control the creation of a singleton pass object, because we create it only when it's needed (lazy construction). Disallow an attempt to create a singleton object when one already exists.

- *Disallow making copies of the singleton object.* We must control the creation of a singleton pass object and disallow making copies of it.

ExecutivePass
-_instance: ExecutivePass -_key: int -_holder: string
+obtain(holder): ExecutivePass +delete()
-__str__(): string
-__new__(): Exception -__copy__(): Exception -__ deepcopy__(): Exception

Figure 14.2   A well-designed singleton object. The private class variable _instance is a reference to the singleton object if it exists, or None otherwise. The public class method obtain() returns a reference to the singleton object. It first creates the singleton if it doesn't already exist.

Private class variable `_instance` refers to the singleton object if it exists; otherwise, its value is `None`. Class method `obtain()` will be the only way for an application to get a reference to the singleton `ExecutivePass` object. Class method `delete()` deletes the singleton object by setting `_instance` to `None`, which will allow us to create a new singleton object later.

Listing 14.3   (Program 14.2 ExecPass-SingletonDP) executivePass.py

```
import random

class ExecutivePass(object):        ◀── The singleton
    _instance = None                    ExecutivePass object

    @classmethod                     ◀── Obtains the
    def obtain(cls, holder):             ExecutivePass object
        if cls._instance is None:                        ◀── Creates the singleton
            cls._instance = super().__new__(cls)             object if it doesn't
            cls._instance._key = random.randint(1, 999)      already exist

            print("** Executive pass created, "
                  f"key = {cls._instance._key}")
            print()

        cls._instance._holder = holder
```

```
            return cls._instance          ◄─── Returns the new or existing
                                                singleton object
        @classmethod
        def delete(cls):                          ◄─── Deletes the singleton object
            print("** Executive pass deleted, "
                  f"key = {cls._instance._key}")

            cls._instance = None
            return None

        def __str__(self):
            return (f'holder is {self._holder}, '
                    f'key = {self._key}')
                                               ◄─── Can't explicitly create
                                                    a singleton object
        def __new__(cls):
            raise NotImplementedError(
                "Cannot explicitly create a singleton.")

        def __copy__(self):
            raise NotImplementedError("Cannot copy a singleton.")
                                                                    Can't copy a
        def __deepcopy__(self):                                     singleton object
            raise NotImplementedError("Cannot copy a singleton.")
```

We don't want to allow an application to create a singleton ExecutivePass object explicitly by calling the class constructor, so we override the built-in class method __new__() to raise an exception. We also disallow making copies of the singleton object by overriding each of the built-in methods __copy__() and __deepcopy__() to raise an exception. These two methods are automatically called whenever the application calls functions copy() and deepcopy(), respectively.

In a class, built-in method __new__() is responsible for creating an object of the class. Then __new__() calls built-in method __init__() to initialize the object. We usually don't have to define __new__() because its default definition is sufficient. In our example application, we override __new__() to raise an exception. Method __init__() will never be called. Instead, public class method obtain() creates and initializes the singleton object, but only if one doesn't already exist.

The new test program main.py demonstrates that we now have a properly behaving singleton ExecutivePass object. There is at most one singleton object at a time, and it is created only when it is needed and only if it doesn't already exist. Only after an existing singleton object is deleted can we create a new one.

Listing 14.4   (Program 14.2 ExecPass-SingletonDP) main.py

```
from copy import copy
from executive_pass import ExecutivePass

def run_app():
    ron_pass = ExecutivePass.obtain("Ron")
    print("Ron takes hold of the executive pass")
```

```
    print(f"  Ron's pass: {ron_pass}")
    print()

    sal_pass = ExecutivePass.obtain("Sal")
    print("Sal takes the executive pass from Ron")
    print(f"  Sal's pass: {sal_pass}")
    print()

    sal_pass = ExecutivePass.delete()

    pat_pass = ExecutivePass.obtain("Pat")
    print("Successfully created a new executive pass for Pat")
    print(f"  Pat's pass: {pat_pass}")
    print()

    leo_pass = pat_pass                          ◄────┐ Assigns Pat's pass to Leo
    print("Pat's pass is assigned to Leo")
    print("Now Pat and Leo together hold Pat's pass")
    print(f"  Leo's pass: {leo_pass}")
    print(f"  Pat's pass: {leo_pass}")

    print()
    print("Try to explicitly create another executive pass")
    tim_pass = ExecutivePass()
                                                        Disallowed
    print()                                             operations
    print("Try to make a copy of Pat's pass")
    bob_pass = copy(pat_pass)            ◄──────────

if __name__ == '__main__':
    run_app()
```

Example output of this version using the Singleton Design Pattern is as follows:

```
** Executive pass created, key = 717

Ron takes hold of the executive pass
  Ron's pass: holder is Ron, key = 717

Sal takes the executive pass from Ron
  Sal's pass: holder is Sal, key = 717

** Executive pass deleted, key = 717          Creates a new pass only after
** Executive pass created, key = 837          deleting the existing pass

Successfully created a new executive pass for Pat
  Pat's pass: holder is Pat, key = 837

Pat's pass is assigned to Leo
Now Pat and Leo together hold Pat's pass
  Leo's pass: holder is Pat, key = 837
  Pat's pass: holder is Pat, key = 837        Two holders of Pat's pass

Try to explicitly create another executive pass
...
```

```
SingletonDP/main.py", line 30, in run_app
    tim_pass = ExecutivePass()
               ^^^^^^^^^^^^^^^^
SingletonDP/executive_pass.py", line 32, in __new__
    raise NotImplementedError(
NotImplementedError: Cannot explicitly create a singleton.
```

> Cannot explicitly
> create a new pass

At most one singleton ExecutivePass object existed at any time. Only after the singleton object (key 717) was deleted could we create a new one (key 837). An attempt to explicitly create a new ExecutivePass object by calling the constructor raised an exception. Attempting to copy an ExecutivePass object by calling function copy() or deepcopy() also would have raised an exception.

The test program's output demonstrates a shortcoming of this implementation of the Singleton Design Pattern. Ideally, the assignment

```
leo_pass = Pat_pass
```

would make Leo the holder of the pass that Pat held. But Python doesn't have a built-in __assign__() method that would enable us to override the = assignment operator and change the holder. Both Leo and Pat ended up holding Pat's pass.

14.1.4   *Singleton's generic model*

Figure 14.3 shows the generic model of the Singleton Design Pattern. From a design pattern's generic model, we can create a custom solution to an architecture problem. Table 14.1 shows how the example application applies the pattern.

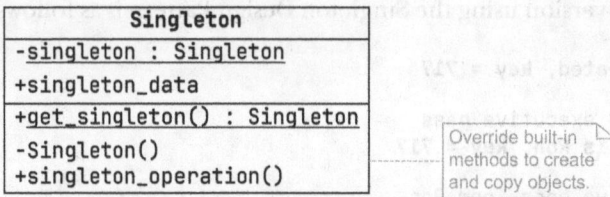

```
┌───────────────────────────────┐
│          Singleton            │
├───────────────────────────────┤
│ -singleton : Singleton        │
│ +singleton_data               │
├───────────────────────────────┤
│ +get_singleton() : Singleton  │
│ -Singleton()                  │
│ +singleton_operation()        │
└───────────────────────────────┘
```

> Override built-in
> methods to create
> and copy objects.

Figure 14.3   The generic model of the Singleton Design Pattern. Compare with figure 14.2. The private static instance variable singleton refers to the Singleton object if it exists; otherwise, its value is null. The private static method get_singleton() returns a reference to the existing Singleton object. If the singleton object doesn't already exist, the function creates and returns a reference to a newly created Singleton object.

Table 14.1   The Singleton Method Design Pattern as applied by the example application

Design pattern	Applied by the example application
Class Singleton	Class ExecutivePass
Static instance variable singleton	Private class variable _instance

Table 14.1 The Singleton Method Design Pattern as applied by the example application (*continued*)

Design pattern	Applied by the example application
Static method `get_singleton()`	Public class method `obtain()`
Private constructor `Singleton()`	Public class method `__new__()`
Public instance variable `singleton_data`	Public property `holder`
Public method `singleton_operation()`	Public methods `__str__()` and `delete()`

Singleton objects and multithreading

We must be extra cautious when creating singleton objects in a multithreaded program. In our example application, method `__new__()` of class `ExecutivePass` first checks whether the singleton object already exists. If it doesn't exist, `__new__()` creates one. But if multiple threads simultaneously execute this method when the singleton object doesn't already exist, more than one thread may test that the value of the class variable `_instance` is `None`, and each of those threads will create a singleton object. Class variable `_instance` will refer to the last one that was created.

Chapter 16 introduces the design of multithreaded programs and how to avoid such *race conditions*.

14.2 The Composite Design Pattern: Treat individual and composite objects uniformly

Many applications keep data in a tree data structure. We saw tree structures in chapter 11 and the Visitor Design Pattern. Data in tree structures often represents part–whole hierarchies. The Composite Design Pattern provides a model for a software architecture to manage such hierarchies. An example of such a hierarchy is the objects that represent the provisions for a baseball player and the cost of each item (figure 14.4).

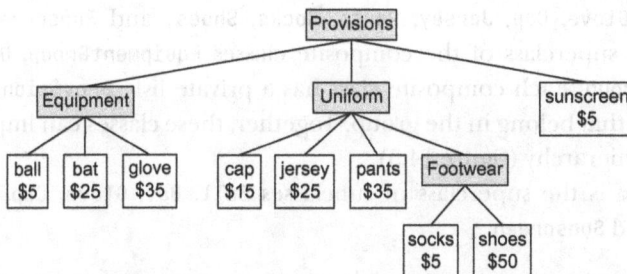

Figure 14.4 The hierarchy of objects in a tree data structure that represents the provisions for a baseball player and the cost of each item. The composite objects are shaded gray.

Suppose the athletics department wants a printout of the cost to outfit a baseball player. The printout should list the cost of each provision item. It should also show the cost subtotals of the equipment, uniform, and footwear composites, and the total cost of all the provisions. For example,

```
PROVISIONS
    EQUIPMENT
            ball cost: $ 5
             bat cost: $25
           glove cost: $35
    EQUIPMENT total: $65
    UNIFORM
             cap cost: $15
          jersey cost: $25
           pants cost: $35
        FOOTWEAR
               shoes cost: $50
               socks cost: $ 5
        FOOTWEAR total: $55
    UNIFORM total: $130
    sunscreen cost: $ 5
PROVISIONS total: $200
```

14.2.1 Desired design features

An application with data in a tree structure that represents a part-whole hierarchy should have the following features:

- *DF 1*—The application should be able to treat a composition of parts the same way it treats an individual part.
- *DF 2*—It should be possible at run time to add new parts and compositions of parts.

14.2.2 Before using Composite

The first version of our cost report application does not use the Composite Design Pattern. After examining the design shortcomings of that version, we'll refactor the application using the pattern and see how the pattern simplifies the code.

In the first version of our application, class ProvisionItem is the superclass of subclasses Ball, Bat, Glove, Cap, Jersey, Pants, Socks, Shoes, and Sunscreen. Class ProvisionGroup is the superclass of the composite classes EquipmentGroup, Uniform-Group, and FootwearGroup. Each composite class has a private list _provisions of the ProvisionItem objects that belong in the group. Together, these classes can implement a tree-structured data hierarchy (figure 14.5).

Class ProvisionItem is the superclass of subclasses Ball, Bat, Glove, Cap, Jersey, Pants, Socks, Shoes, and Sunscreen.

Listing 14.5   (Program 14.3 CostReport) provision_item.py (poor design before DP)

```
class ProvisionItem:
    def __init__(self, name, cost):
        self._name = name
```

```
        self._cost = cost

    @property
    def name(self):
        return self._name

    @property
    def cost(self):
        return self._cost

    def print_item(self):
        print(f'{self._name:>6s} cost: ${self.cost:2d}')
```

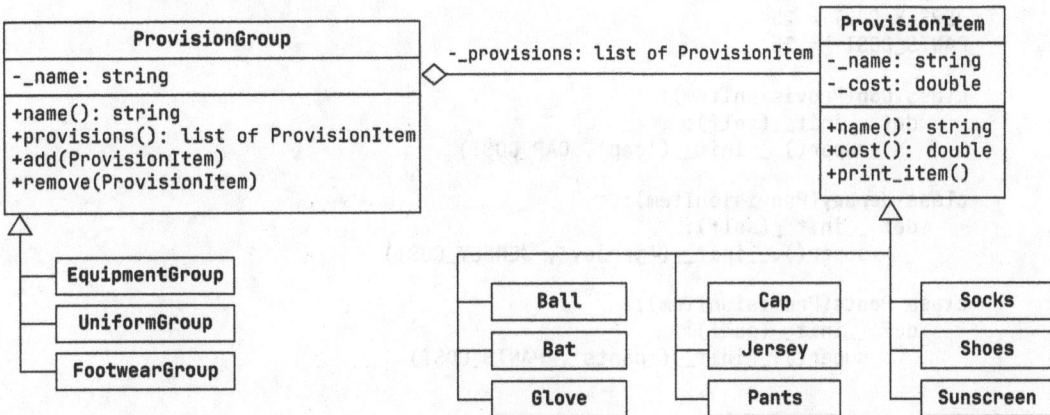

Figure 14.5 Classes Ball, Bat, Glove, Cap, Jersey, Pants, Socks, Shoes, and Sunscreen are subclasses of class ProvisionItem. Composite classes EquipmentGroup, UniformGroup, and FootwearGroup are subclasses of ProvisionGroup, and each has a list of ProvisionItem objects.

The ProvisionItem subclasses Ball, Bat, and Glove represent equipment items. Each subclass's constructor invokes the superclass ProvisionItem constructor and passes its name and cost.

Listing 14.6   (Program 14.3 CostReport) equipment.py (poor design before DP)

```
from provision_item import ProvisionItem

BALL_COST  = 5
BAT_COST   = 25
GLOVE_COST = 35

class Ball(ProvisionItem):
    def __init__(self):
        super().__init__('ball', BALL_COST)

class Bat(ProvisionItem):
```

```
    def __init__(self):
        super().__init__('bat', BAT_COST)

class Glove(ProvisionItem):
    def __init__(self):
        super().__init__('glove', GLOVE_COST)
```

ProvisionItem subclasses Cap, Jersey, and Pants represent uniform items.

Listing 14.7   (Program 14.3 CostReport) uniform.py (poor design before DP)

```
from provision_item import ProvisionItem

CAP_COST    = 15
JERSEY_COST = 25
PANTS_COST  = 35

class Cap(ProvisionItem):
    def __init__(self):
        super().__init__('cap', CAP_COST)

class Jersey(ProvisionItem):
    def __init__(self):
        super().__init__('jersey', JERSEY_COST)

class Pants(ProvisionItem):
    def __init__(self):
        super().__init__('pants', PANTS_COST)
```

ProvisionItem subclasses Socks and Shoes represent footwear items.

Listing 14.8   (Program 14.3 CostReport) footwear.py (poor design before DP)

```
from provision_item import ProvisionItem

SHOES_COST = 50
SOCKS_COST = 5

class Shoes(ProvisionItem):
    def __init__(self):
        super().__init__('shoes', SHOES_COST)

class Socks(ProvisionItem):
    def __init__(self):
        super().__init__('socks', SOCKS_COST)
```

And ProvisionItem subclass Sunscreen represents a sunscreen item.

Listing 14.9   (Program 14.3 CostReport) sunscreen.py (poor design before DP)

```
from provision_item import ProvisionItem

SUNSCREEN_COST = 5
```

```python
class Sunscreen(ProvisionItem):
    def __init__(self):
        super().__init__('sunscreen', SUNSCREEN_COST)
```

Classes EquipmentGroup, UniformGroup, and FootwearGroup are subclasses of superclass ProvisionGroup. The superclass provides the common properties name and _provisions, the name of the group, and a list of ProvisionItem objects, respectively.

Listing 14.10   (Program 14.3 CostReport) provision_group.py (poor design before DP)

```python
class ProvisionGroup:
    def __init__(self, name):
        self._name = name
        self._provisions = []          ◀───┐ List of ProvisionItem objects

    @property
    def name(self):
        return self._name

    @property
    def provisions(self):
        return self._provisions

    def add(self, item):
        self._provisions.append(item)

    def remove(self, item):
        self._provisions.remove(item)

class EquipmentGroup(ProvisionGroup):
    def __init__(self):
        super().__init__('EQUIPMENT')

class UniformGroup(ProvisionGroup):
    def __init__(self):
        super().__init__('UNIFORM')

class FootwearGroup(ProvisionGroup):
    def __init__(self):
        super().__init__('FOOTWEAR')
```

Class CostReport generates the report. Its constructor is passed EquipmentGroup, UniformGroup, and FootwearGroup objects, along with a Sunscreen object. Private method _compute_group_costs() computes the total cost of each ProvisionGroup object by summing the costs of its aggregated ProvisionItem objects. Private method _print_costs() prints the costs.

Listing 14.11   (Program 14.3 CostReport) cost_report.py (poor design before DP)

```python
class CostReport:
    def __init__(self, equipment, uniform,
                 footwear, sunscreen):
```

```
            self._equipment = equipment
            self._uniform   = uniform
            self._footwear  = footwear
            self._sunscreen = sunscreen

            self._equipment_cost = 0
            self._uniform_cost   = 0
            self._footwear_cost  = 0

    def _compute_group_costs(self):
        for item in self._equipment.provisions:
            self._equipment_cost += item.cost

        for item in self._uniform.provisions:
            self._uniform_cost += item.cost

        for item in self._footwear.provisions:
            self._footwear_cost += item.cost

        self._uniform_cost += self._footwear_cost

    def _print_costs(self):
        print('PROVISIONS')

        print(f'    {self._equipment.name}')
        for item in self._equipment.provisions:
            print('        ', end='')
            item.print_item()

        print(f'    {self._equipment.name}'
              f' total: ${self._equipment_cost:2d}')

        print(f'    {self._uniform.name}')
        for item in self._uniform.provisions:
            print('          ', end='')
            item.print_item()

        print(f'        {self._footwear.name}')
        for item in self._footwear.provisions:
            print('              ', end='')
            item.print_item()

        print(f'        {self._footwear.name}'
              f' total: ${self._footwear_cost:2d}')

        print(f'    {self._uniform.name}'
              f' total: ${self._uniform_cost:2d}')

        print('    ', end='')
        self._sunscreen.print_item()

        all_provisions_total = (  self._equipment_cost
                                + self._uniform_cost
                                + self._sunscreen.cost)
        print(f'ALL PROVISIONS total: ${all_provisions_total}')
```

Computes the cost of each composite ProvisionGroup

Prints the costs

```
    def generate_report(self):
        self._compute_group_costs()
        self._print_costs()
```

In the test program main.py, method `build_provisions_tree()` builds branches of the example provisions tree and returns the `ProvisionGroup` objects and the `Sunscreen` object in a tuple. Then the program passes the unpacked tuple `*tree` to construct a `CostReport` object and generate the report.

Listing 14.12   (Program 14.3 CostReport) main.py

```
from provision_group import EquipmentGroup, UniformGroup, \
                            FootwearGroup
from equipment   import Ball, Bat, Glove
from uniform     import Cap, Jersey, Pants
from footwear    import Shoes, Socks
from sunscreen   import Sunscreen
from cost_report import CostReport


def build_provisions_tree():
    equipment = EquipmentGroup()
    uniform   = UniformGroup()
    footwear  = FootwearGroup()

    equipment.add(Ball())
    equipment.add(Bat())
    equipment.add(Glove())

    uniform.add(Cap())
    uniform.add(Jersey())
    uniform.add(Pants())

    footwear.add(Shoes())
    footwear.add(Socks())

    sunscreen = Sunscreen()

    return equipment, uniform, footwear, sunscreen   ◄──┐ Returns a tuple


if __name__ == '__main__':
    tree = build_provisions_tree()          ┌ Unpacks the tuple to
    report = CostReport(*tree)         ◄──── create the cost report
    report.generate_report()
```

The application does produce the desired report. But member function **generate_report()** treats **ProvisionGroup** and **ProvisionItem** objects differently. That violates DF 1.

Member function **generate_report()** is hardcoded to handle only these particular **ProvisionGroup** and **ProvisionItem** objects. It won't be easy to add new items or groups. That violates DF 2.

Indeed, problems with this version of the application include the following:

- *Complicated report generator*—Method `generate_report()` of class `CostReport` is complicated and dependent on the cost tree structure. It will be hard to change if we change the organization of the data.

- *Individual and composite objects treated differently*—We want objects at all levels of the tree, individual or composite, to be treated the same. Method `generate_report()` treats them differently to compute and print their costs.

- *Hardcoded report generator*—Method `generate_report()` is hardcoded to print only one report.

- *Incomplete tree*—We did not build the complete tree data structure. For example, footwear wasn't made part of the uniform. An incomplete tree isn't a problem for generating the cost report in this version of the application, but other applications may need the complete tree.

14.2.3   *After using Composite*

We can refactor the first version of our cost report application to an architecture modeled from the Composite Design Pattern. The goal of the Composite Design Pattern is to treat the individual objects the same way as the composite objects to compute and print their costs. We want all the leaf classes of the data tree—`Ball`, `Bat`, `Glove`, `Cap`, `Jersey`, `Pants`, `Socks`, `Shoes`, and `Sunscreen`—and the composite classes `Equipment`, `Uniform`, and `Footwear` to present the same interface.

> **The Composite Design Pattern**
>
> "Compose objects into tree structures to represent part-whole hierarchies. Composite lets its clients treat individual objects and compositions of objects uniformly." (GoF p. 163)

The key to using this model is to make class `ProvisionGroup` also a subclass of class `ProvisionItem`. Doing so ultimately makes the composite classes `EquipmentGroup`, `UniformGroup`, and `FootwearGroup` subclasses of `ProvisionItem`. Classes `Ball`, `Bat`, `Glove`, `Cap`, `Jersey`, `Pants`, `Socks`, `Shoes`, and `Sunscreen` remain subclasses of `ProvisionItem`, and as before, class `ProvisionGroup` maintains a list of `ProvisionItem` objects (figure 14.6).

Class `ProvisionGroup` is now a subclass of class `ProvisionItem`. These two classes have common methods, including `provisions()`, `add()`, and `remove()`. But because these methods don't make sense for the individual `ProvisionItem` objects, each method throws an "invalid operation" exception. The `ProvisionGroup` subclasses `EquipmentGroup`, `UniformGroup`, and `FootwearGroup` override those methods with appropriate behaviors.

As in the previous version of the application, the `cost()` method of a `ProvisionItem` object returns the cost of that individual item. Also see listing 14.13.

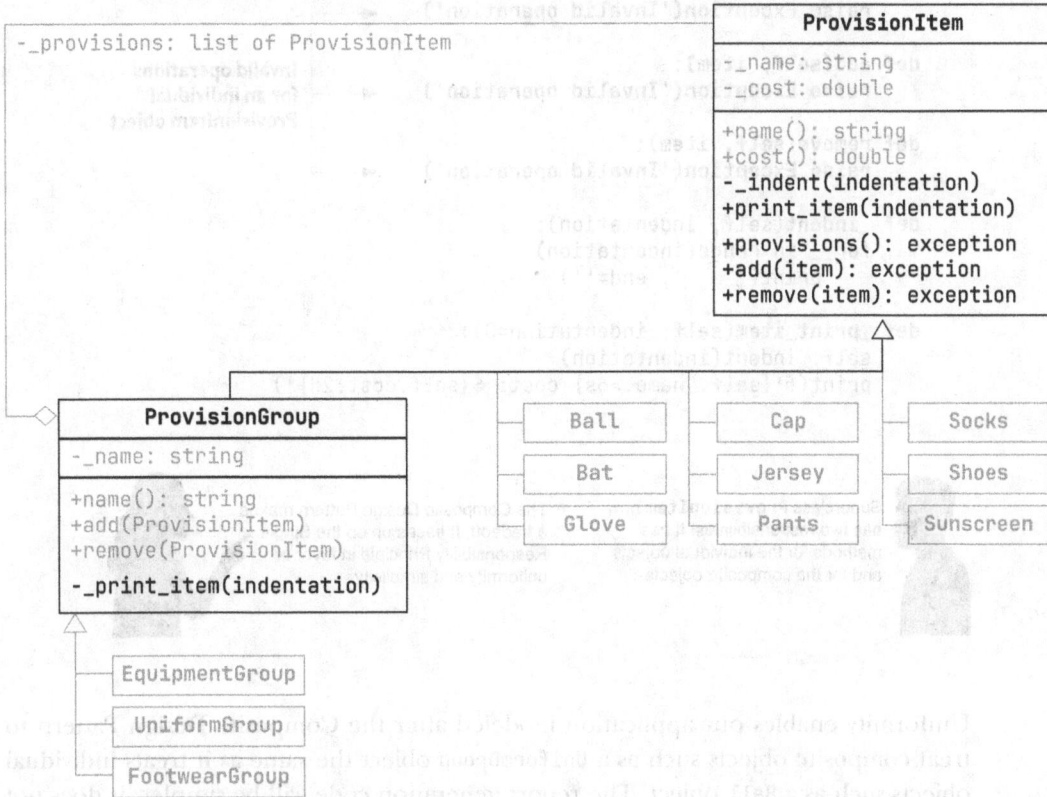

Figure 14.6 In the second version of our cost report application, modeled from the Composite Design Pattern, class ProvisionGroup is now itself a subclass of class ProvisionItem. UniformGroup now aggregates FootwearGroup. The grayed-out portions of the diagram haven't changed logically from figure 14.5.

Listing 14.13 (Program 14.4 CostReport-CompositeDP) provision_item.py

```python
class ProvisionItem:
    def __init__(self, name, cost):
        self._name = name
        self._cost = cost
        self._provisions = None

    @property
    def name(self):
        return self._name

    @property
    def cost(self):
        return self._cost          ◄—— Returns the cost of this
                                        individual ProvisionItem object

    @property
    def provisions(self):
```

```
            raise Exception('Invalid operation')   ◄─────┐

    def add(self, item):                                 │   Invalid operations
        raise Exception('Invalid operation')   ◄─────────┤   for an individual
                                                         │   ProvisionItem object
    def remove(self, item):                              │
        raise Exception('Invalid operation')   ◄─────────┘

    def _indent(self, indentation):
        for _ in range(indentation):
            print('    ', end='')

    def _print_item(self, indentation=0):
        self._indent(indentation)
        print(f'{self._name:>6s} cost: ${self.cost:2d}')
```

Superclass **ProvisionItem** now has two responsibilities! It has methods for the individual objects and for the composite objects.

The Composite Design Pattern makes a tradeoff. It eases up on the Single Responsibility Principle in favor of uniformity and simplicity.

Uniformity enables our application modeled after the Composite Design Pattern to treat composite objects such as a UniformGroup object the same as it treats individual objects such as a Ball object. The report generation code will be simpler: it does not need to know whether it is dealing with an individual object or a composite object to compute and print costs.

Class ProvisionGroup overrides methods cost(), provisions(), add(), and remove() to implement behaviors appropriate for composite objects. The cost() and _print_item() methods iterate over the ProvisionItem objects in the _provisions list to compute the item's cost and to print the item, respectively. Method cost() sums the costs of the objects in the list. Objects in the list can be either individual ProvisionItem objects or composite ProvisionGroup objects, and in either case, the method accesses the objects' cost property. (In this version of the application, the test program will make FootwearGroup one of the items in the provisions list of class UniformGroup.) Similarly, method print_item() calls the print_item() method of each ProvisionItem object in the _provisions list, whether it's an individual item or a group item.

Listing 14.14   (Program 14.4 CostReport-CompositeDP) provision_group.py

```python
from provision_item import ProvisionItem

class ProvisionGroup(ProvisionItem):
    def __init__(self, name):
        self._name = name
        self._provisions = []
```

```
    @property
    def name(self):
        return self._name

    @property
    def provisions(self):
        return self._provisions

    @property
    def cost(self):
        cost = 0

        for item in self._provisions:          Sums the cost
            cost += item.cost                    of each item

        return cost

    def add(self, item):
        self._provisions.append(item)

    def remove(self, item):
        self._provisions.remove(item)

    def print_item(self, indentation=0):
        self._indent(indentation)
        print(self._name)

        for item in self._provisions:                        Prints each item
            item._print_indented(indentation + 1)

        self._indent(indentation)
        print(f'{self._name} total: ${self.cost}')

class EquipmentGroup(ProvisionGroup):
    ...

class UniformGroup(ProvisionGroup):
    ...

class FootwearGroup(ProvisionGroup):
    ...
```

Class `CostReport` is now much simpler. Its constructor is passed a reference to the root of the cost tree. Method `generate_report()` method simply calls `print_item()` on the tree root. Because each `ProvisionGroup` object in turn calls `print_item()` on each provision object that it aggregates, the entire report will be printed.

Listing 14.15   (Program 14.4 CostReport-CompositeDP) cost_report.py

```
class CostReport:
    def __init__(self, tree_root):
        self._tree_root = tree_root        ◄─── Root of the provisions tree

    def generate_report(self):
        self._tree_root.print_item()       ◄─── Starts printing at the root
```

ProvisionItem subclasses Ball, Bat, Glove, Cap, Jersey, Pants, Socks, Shoes, and Sunscreen have not changed in this version of the application.

As in the previous version of the application, function build_cost_tree() of the test program main.py builds the example cost tree. This time, we add the composite class Footwear object to the provisions list of the UniformGroup object. We also create a tree_root object whose branches are the equipment, uniform, and sunscreen objects.

Listing 14.16   (Program 14.4 CostReport-CompositeDP) main.py

```
from provision_group import EquipmentGroup, UniformGroup, \
                            FootwearGroup
from equipment    import Ball, Bat, Glove
from uniform      import Cap, Jersey, Pants
from footwear     import Shoes, Socks
from sunscreen    import Sunscreen
from cost_report import CostReport

def build_cost_tree():
    equipment = EquipmentGroup()
    uniform   = UniformGroup()
    footwear  = FootwearGroup()

    equipment.add(Ball())
    equipment.add(Bat())
    equipment.add(Glove())

    footwear.add(Shoes())
    footwear.add(Socks())

    uniform.add(Cap())
    uniform.add(Jersey())
    uniform.add(Pants())
    uniform.add(footwear)         ◄──  Adds the FootwearGroup
                                       object to the UniformGroup's
                                       provisions list

    sunscreen = Sunscreen()

    tree_root = ProvisionGroup("PROVISIONS")
    for item in (equipment, uniform, sunscreen):    │ Creates the tree root
        tree_root.add(item)

    return tree_root

if __name__ == '__main__':
    report = CostReport(build_cost_tree())     │ Creates and prints the report
    report.generate_report()
```

To create and print the report, we pass the tree root to the constructor of class CostReport and call the latter's generate_report() method.

The primary benefits we've gained from using the Composite Design Pattern are as follows:

- *Uniformity*—The class for individual objects and the class for composite objects share an interface. Therefore, our code can treat individual objects the same way it treats composite objects.

- *Simplicity*—Code that performs operations on the components of the tree, such as computing costs and printing, is simpler.

- *Encapsulation*—Calculating costs and printing become the responsibilities of the `ProvisionItem` and `ProvisionGroup` classes. Class `CostReport` has no dependencies on those classes or on the tree structure.

- *Flexibility*—It won't be hard to add new `ProvisionItem` and `ProvisionGroup` objects or remove existing ones.

14.2.4 Composite's generic model

Figure 14.7 shows the generic model of the Composite Design Pattern. It is from a design pattern's generic model that we can create a custom solution to an architecture problem. Table 14.2 shows how the example application applies the pattern.

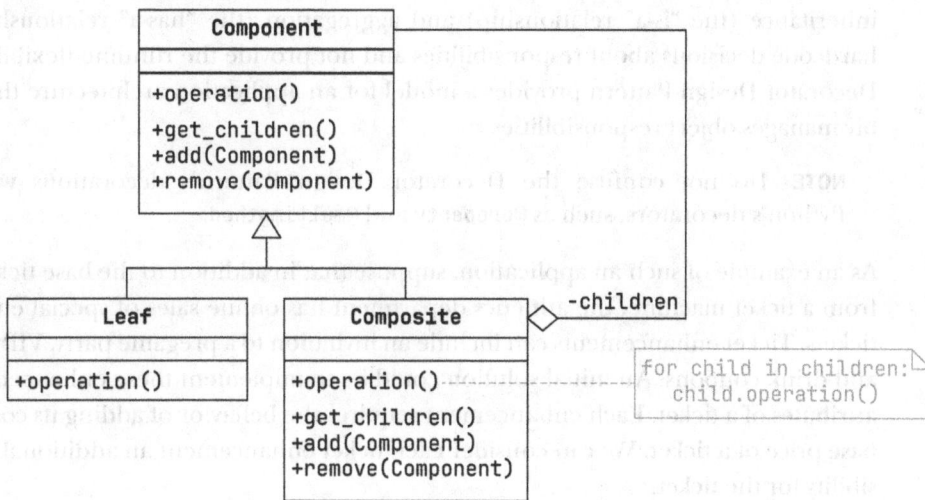

Figure 14.7 The generic model of the Composite Design Pattern. Compare with figure 14.6. Both the individual `Leaf` class and the `Composite` class inherit from the `Component` superclass.

Table 14.2 The Composite Design Pattern as applied by the example application

Design pattern	Applied by the example application
Superclass `Component`	*Superclass* `ProvisionItem`
Class `Composite`	*Class* `ProvisionGroup`

Table 14.2   The Composite Design Pattern as applied by the example application (*continued*)

Design pattern	Applied by the example application
Class Leaf	Classes Ball, Bat, Glove, Cap, Jersey, Pants, Socks, Shoes, and Sunscreen
Operation	Methods add(), remove(), and print_item(); properties name and cost
Children	The _provisions list of class ProvisionGroup

14.3   *The Decorator Design Pattern: Dynamically add object responsibilities*

Classes have instance variables whose runtime values are the attributes of their objects. As chapter 2 emphasized, managing object attributes is an important aspect of application design. Classes also have methods that control their objects' runtime behaviors. Instance variables and methods implement the responsibilities of a class, and good design assigns a primary responsibility to each class. But what if we need the flexibility to dynamically add more responsibilities to a class's objects during run time? Both inheritance (the "is-a" relationship) and aggregation (the "has-a" relationship) will hardcode decisions about responsibilities and not provide the runtime flexibility. The Decorator Design Pattern provides a model for an application architecture that flexibly manages object responsibilities.

> **NOTE** Do not confuse the Decorator Design Pattern's decorations with Python's decorators, such as @property and @multimethod.

As an example of such an application, suppose that in addition to the base tickets sold from a ticket machine, the athletics department has online sales of special enhanced tickets. Ticket enhancements can include an invitation to a pregame party, VIP seating, and drink coupons. An initial solution could be to implement these enhancements as attributes of a ticket. Each enhancement requires the behavior of adding its cost to the base price of a ticket. We can consider each ticket enhancement an additional responsibility for the ticket.

14.3.1   *Desired design features*

An application should have the following features to be able to dynamically add responsibilities to an existing class:

- *DF 1*—We should not need to modify the class to which we add new responsibilities.
- *DF 2*—We should be able to dynamically add any number of responsibilities in any order and combination during run time.
- *DF 3*—The class should not have dependencies on the implementations of the responsibilities.

- *DF 4*—It should be possible to add, delete, or modify responsibilities without modifying the classes that have them.
- *DF 5*—Code that uses an object that can acquire additional responsibilities should not treat the object any differently based on the number (including none), order, or combination of additional responsibilities.

14.3.2 *Before using Decorator*

We'll develop two versions of our enhanced ticket application. The first version implements the ticket attributes and behaviors in an obvious way, as instance variables and methods of the Ticket class. But that implementation will have some major shortcomings. Then we'll model the design of the second version of our application from the Decorator Design Pattern, which will greatly increase the flexibility of managing the additional ticket behaviors.

The first version of our ticket application simply makes the cost of each ticket enhancement a constant attribute of the Ticket class (figure 14.8). The Ticket class's private instance variables _pregame_party, _vip_seating, and _drink_coupons implement the ticket enhancements. Method cost() calculates and returns the total cost of a ticket. The responsibility of a Ticket object is to manage a ticket's enhancements and compute its total cost.

Ticket
+<u>BASE_PRICE</u>:   double = 30   +<u>PARTY_PRICE</u>:   double = 25   +<u>VIP_PRICE</u>:   double = 20   +<u>COUPON_PRICE</u>:   double = 5
-_pregame_party: bool   -_vip_seating: bool   -_drink_coupons: int
+cost(): double

Figure 14.8 We implement the enhancements to a base ticket as instance variables of the Ticket class. Each enhancement has a cost.

Listing 14.17 (Program 14.5 Enhanced) ticket.py (poor design before DP)

```
class Ticket:
    BASE_PRICE   = 30
    PARTY_PRICE  = 25
    VIP_PRICE    = 20
    COUPON_PRICE = 5

    def __init__(self, party=False, vip=False, coupons=0):
        self._pregame_party = party          ┐
        self._vip_seating = vip              │ Ticket enhancements
        self._drink_coupons = coupons        ┘

        self._cost = Ticket.BASE_PRICE

    @property                     ┐ Computes the cost
    def cost(self):               ┘ of each ticket
        if self._pregame_party:
            self._cost += Ticket.PARTY_PRICE

        if self._vip_seating:
            self._cost += Ticket.VIP_PRICE
```

```
                self._cost += self._drink_coupons*Ticket.COUPON_PRICE
                return self._cost

            def print_ticket(self):
                print('   base ticket price: $'
                    f'{Ticket.BASE_PRICE}')

                if self._pregame_party:
                    print('  pregame party price: $'
                        f'{Ticket.PARTY_PRICE}')

                if self._vip_seating:
                    print('    VIP seating price: $'
                        f'{Ticket.VIP_PRICE}')

                if self._drink_coupons > 0:
                    print('   drink coupon price: $'
                        f'{self._drink_coupons*Ticket.COUPON_PRICE}'
                        f' = {self._drink_coupons} x '
                        f'{Ticket.COUPON_PRICE}')
```

A test program creates and prints some sample tickets.

Listing 14.18   (Program 14.5 Enhanced) main.py (poor design before DP)

```
from ticket import Ticket

def print_ticket(name, ticket):
    print()
    print(f"{name}'s ticket:")
    ticket.print_ticket()
    print(f"TOTAL COST: ${ticket.cost}")

if __name__ == '__main__':
    john_ticket = Ticket(True, True, 2)
    print_ticket('John', john_ticket)

    mary_ticket = Ticket(True, False, 3)
    print_ticket('Mary', mary_ticket)

    leslie_ticket = Ticket()                    ◄── Plain ticket without
    print_ticket('Leslie', leslie_ticket)           enhancements

    sidney_ticket = Ticket(False, True, 1)
    print_ticket('Sidney', sidney_ticket)
```

The output is as follows:

```
John's ticket:
    base ticket price: $30
  pregame party price: $25
    VIP seating price: $20
   drink coupon price: $10 = 2 x $5
TOTAL COST: $85
```

```
Mary's ticket:
     base ticket price: $30
  pregame party price: $25
   drink coupon price: $15 = 3 x $5
TOTAL COST: $70

Leslie's ticket:
     base ticket price: $30
TOTAL COST: $30

Sidney's ticket:
     base ticket price: $30
     VIP seating price: $20
   drink coupon price: $ 5 = 1 x $5
TOTAL COST: $55
```

Class **Ticket** implements all the ticket enhancements by itself! That violates DF 1, DF 2, DF 3, and DF 4.

The way it calculates the cost of a ticket depends on how many enhancements the ticket has. That violates DF 5.

Indeed, inflexibility is the major fault of this design:

- *Inflexible code*—Hardcoding the kinds of ticket enhancements means it won't be possible to add, remove, or modify enhancements without needing to modify the Ticket class.
- *Enhancement implementations not hidden*—Class Ticket has intimate knowledge of how the ticket enhancements are implemented and treats tickets (i.e., computes their costs) differently depending on the enhancements.

14.3.3 After using Decorator

The Decorator Design Pattern treats each ticket enhancement as a "decoration" that conceptually wraps the base ticket and any prior enhancements. Figure 14.9 shows a base ticket decorated with a pregame party enhancement, a VIP seating enhancement, and two drink coupons. Each enhancement adds the responsibility to the ticket to include the enhancement cost in the total ticket price. Each enhancement and the base ticket have a cost() function. Each enhancement returns its own cost plus the total cost of whatever it wraps.

To implement this nested wrapping architecture, we make each enhancement an object, and we link the enhancement objects together in the order in which they wrap each other. The enhancements can wrap in any order. The last enhancement in the chain links with the base ticket object (figure 14.10). Therefore, the base ticket itself is wrapped the most deeply.

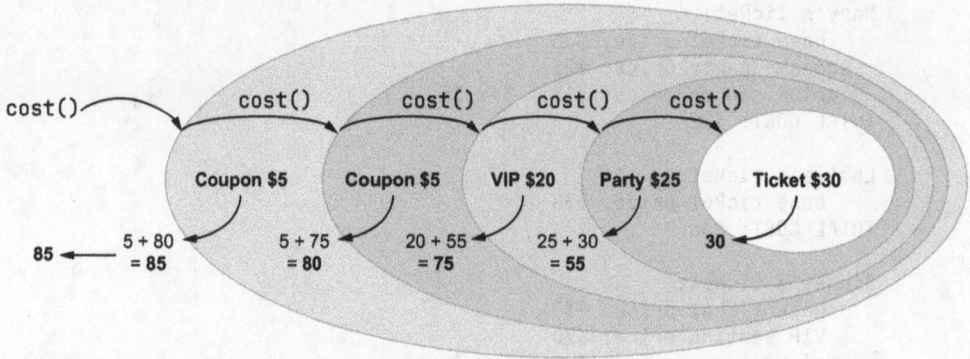

Figure 14.9 An enhanced ticket is conceptually wrapped by any number of pregame party, VIP seating, and drink coupon enhancement decorators. Each decorator wraps the base ticket and any prior wrappers. To calculate the cost of an enhanced ticket, each decorator calls the `cost()` method of whatever it wraps (either another decorator or the base ticket). Each return value is the cost of the decorator plus the total cost of whatever it wraps.

Figure 14.10 Each decorator object, except the last one in the chain, points to the enhancement object that it wraps. The last enhancement object in the chain points to the base ticket object.

There's an additional requirement: no matter how many additional responsibilities a ticket has from its enhancements, it's still a ticket. Our application code should treat an enhanced ticket no differently than an unenhanced base ticket. To meet this requirement, we need each enhancement class to be a subclass of the Ticket superclass (figure 14.11). We accomplish this with class Enhancement, which is both a subclass of Ticket and a superclass of the subclasses Party, VIP, and Coupon. The Enhancement instance variable _ticket will link to the next Ticket object, which could be a base ticket or an enhanced ticket.

The Decorator Design Pattern

"Attach additional responsibilities to an object dynamically. Decorators provide a flexible alternative to subclassing for extending functionality." (GoF p. 175)

Abstract class Ticket is the superclass of class BaseTicket and superclass Enhancement. Its abstract cost() method must be implemented by BaseTicket and by Enhancement. Each BaseTicket object represents a ticket before any enhancements. Its cost is BaseTicket.BASE_PRICE. Also see listing 14.19.

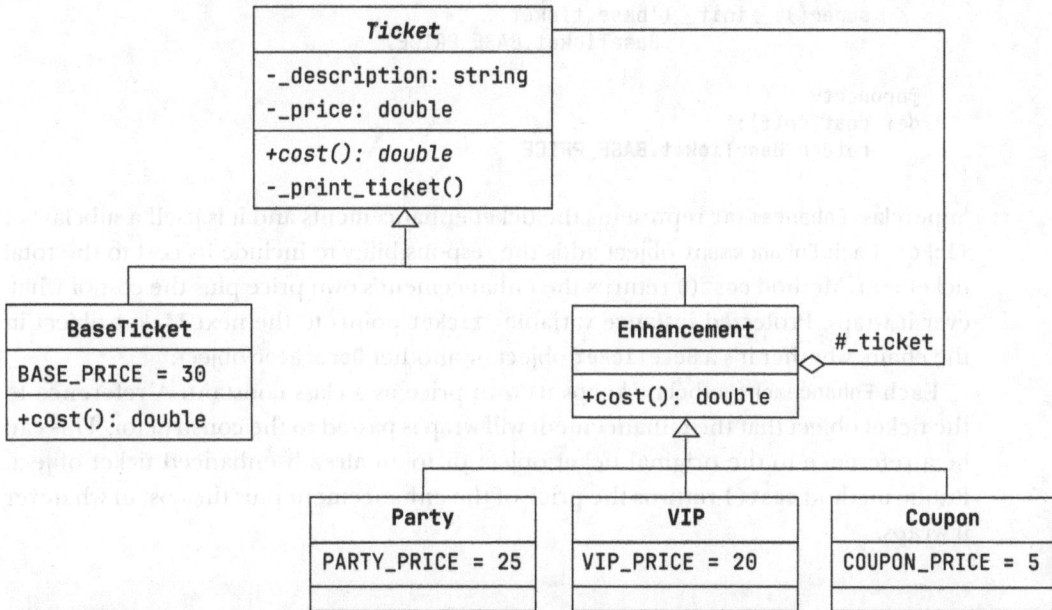

Figure 14.11 Abstract superclass Ticket has subclasses that represent a base ticket or a ticket wrapped with enhancements. The Enhancement superclass has a protected link to the next Enhancement object or to the BaseTicket object. Party, VIP, and Coupon are enhancements. One or more of their objects can wrap a BaseTicket object. Each Enhancement object adds the responsibility to include its cost to the total ticket cost.

Listing 14.19   (Program 14.6 Enhanced-DecoratorDP) ticket.py

```python
from abc import ABC, abstractmethod

class Ticket(ABC):
    def __init__(self, description, price):
        self._description = description
        self._price = price                    ◄─── Ticket price

        self._print_ticket()

    @property
    @abstractmethod          Cost of a base ticket
    def cost(self):    ◄──── or enhanced ticket
        pass

    def _print_ticket(self):
        print(f'{self._description:>17s} price: $'
              f'{self._price:2d}')

class BaseTicket(Ticket):
    BASE_PRICE = 30

    def __init__(self):
```

```
super().__init__('base ticket',
                 BaseTicket.BASE_PRICE)

@property
def cost(self):
    return BaseTicket.BASE_PRICE
```

Superclass Enhancement represents the ticket enhancements and it is itself a subclass of Ticket. Each Enhancement object adds the responsibility to include its cost to the total ticket cost. Method cost() returns the enhancement's own price plus the cost of whatever it wraps. Protected instance variable _ticket points to the next Ticket object in the chain, whether it's a BaseTicket object or another Decorator object.

Each Enhancement subclass keeps its own price as a class constant. A reference to the ticket object that the enhancement will wrap is passed to the constructor. This can be a reference to the original ticket object or to an already-enhanced ticket object. Public method cost() returns the price of the enhancement plus the cost of whatever it wraps.

Listing 14.20   (Program 14.6 Enhanced-DecoratorDP) enhancement.py

```
from ticket import Ticket

class Enhancement(Ticket):
    def __init__(self, description, price, ticket):
        super().__init__(description, price)
        self._ticket = ticket          ◄──── The ticket object that this
                                              enhancement object will wrap

    @property
    def cost(self):
        return self._price + self._ticket.cost   ◄──── Enhancement price +
                                                        cost of what it wraps

class Party(Enhancement):
    PARTY_PRICE = 25

    def __init__(self, ticket):
        super().__init__('pregame party',
                         Party.PARTY_PRICE, ticket)

class VIP(Enhancement):
    VIP_PRICE = 20

    def __init__(self, ticket):
        super().__init__('VIP seating',
                         VIP.VIP_PRICE, ticket)

class Coupon(Enhancement):
    COUPON_PRICE = 5

    def __init__(self, ticket):
        super().__init__('drink coupon',
                         Coupon.COUPON_PRICE, ticket)
```

The test program creates BaseTicket objects and decorates each one by wrapping it with any number and combination of Enhancement objects in any order. If a ticket includes multiple drink coupons, we decorate the ticket by wrapping it with multiple Coupon objects.

Listing 14.21   (Program 14.6 Enhanced-DecoratorDP) main.py

```python
from ticket import BaseTicket
from enhancement import Party, VIP, Coupon

def print_ticket(name, ticket):
    print()
    print(f"{name:>8s}'s ticket TOTAL: $"
          f"{ticket.cost:2d}")
    print("---------------------------")

if __name__ == '__main__':
    john_ticket = BaseTicket()
    john_ticket = Party(john_ticket)
    john_ticket = VIP(john_ticket)
    john_ticket = Coupon(john_ticket)
    john_ticket = Coupon(john_ticket)
    print_ticket('John', john_ticket)

    mary_ticket = BaseTicket()
    mary_ticket = Coupon(mary_ticket)
    mary_ticket = Coupon(mary_ticket)
    mary_ticket = Party(mary_ticket)
    mary_ticket = Coupon(mary_ticket)
    print_ticket('Mary', mary_ticket)

    leslie_ticket = BaseTicket()
    print_ticket('Leslie', leslie_ticket)

    sidney_ticket = BaseTicket()
    sidney_ticket = Coupon(sidney_ticket)
    sidney_ticket = VIP(sidney_ticket)
    print_ticket('Sidney', sidney_ticket)
```

Multiple drink coupons

The cost results are the same as in the first version of our application, although formatted differently:

```
      base ticket price: $30
  pregame party price: $25
       VIP seating price: $20
     drink coupon price: $ 5
     drink coupon price: $ 5

   John's ticket TOTAL: $85
-----------------------------
      base ticket price: $30
     drink coupon price: $ 5
```

```
     drink coupon price: $ 5
   pregame party price: $25
     drink coupon price: $ 5

   Mary's ticket TOTAL: $70
-------------------------------
     base ticket price: $30

 Leslie's ticket TOTAL: $30
-------------------------------
     base ticket price: $30
     drink coupon price: $ 5
      VIP seating price: $20

 Sidney's ticket TOTAL: $55
-------------------------------
```

As usual, modeling the application after a design pattern added more classes. But these classes appear to be cohesive and loosely coupled.

The Decorator Design Pattern made our application much more flexible. We can add, remove, or modify ticket enhancements without modifying any existing classes.

The benefits of modeling our ticket application after the Decorator Design Pattern include the following:

- *Dynamically enhanced objects*—We can enhance objects during run time by adding responsibilities.

- *No hardcoded enhancements*—It won't be hard to create new ticket enhancements, such as a reserved parking space. We would add another Enhancement subclass, say Parking. It will also be easy to remove any enhancements we no longer want.

- *Loosely coupled and cohesive classes*—The ticket enhancement subclasses are loosely coupled with each other. Each one has the sole responsibility for its enhancement. The Ticket class and the Enhancement classes are loosely coupled with each other. A ticket does not need to know how it is enhanced, if at all.

- *Uniform treatment of base ticket and decorated ticket objects*—We don't have to write special code for each.

14.3.4 *Decorator's generic model*

Figure 14.12 shows the generic model of the Decorator Design Pattern. From a design pattern's generic model, we can create a custom solution to an architecture problem. Table 14.3 shows how the example application applies the pattern.

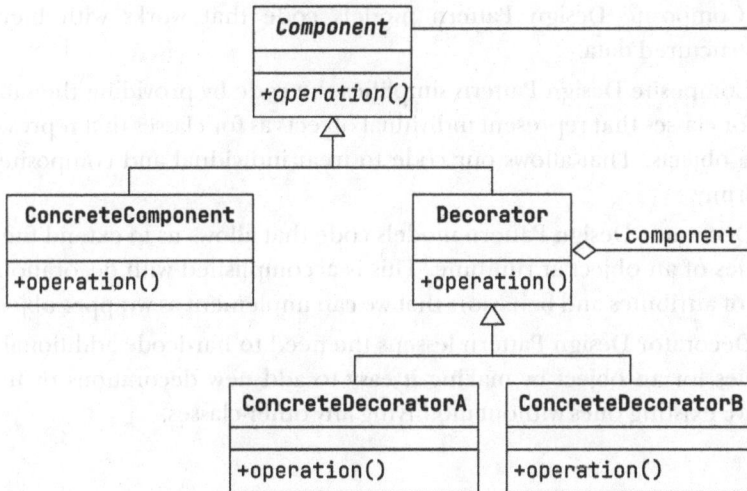

Figure 14.12   The generic model of the Decorator Design Pattern. Compare with figure 14.11.
A ConcreteComponent object by itself is a Component. A ConcreteComponent wrapped by Decorator objects is also a Component. The private component instance variable of superclass Decorator is either a ConcreteComponent object or a Decorator object. This chain implements the nested wrapping of the Decorator objects.

Table 14.3 The Decorator Design Pattern as applied by the example application

Design pattern	Applied by the example application
Superclass Component	Superclass Ticket
Subclass ConcreteComponent	Subclass BaseTicket
Superclass Decorator	Superclass Enhancement
Subclasses ConcreteDecoratorA and ConcreteDecoratorB	Subclasses Party, VIP, and Coupon
Method operation()	Method cost()

Summary

- The Singleton Design Pattern models code that must ensure that at most one object of a given class can exist during the run time of an application. We must control the creation of the object to ensure that there can be at most one instance of the singleton. A static instance variable points to the singleton object at run time.
- The Singleton Design Pattern also requires overriding the singleton class's built-in __copy__() and __deepcopy__() methods. This prevents making copies of the singleton object during run time. We must be cautious that a multithreaded application does not create multiple singleton objects.

- The Composite Design Pattern models code that works with hierarchical tree-structured data.

- The Composite Design Pattern simplifies the code by providing the same interface for classes that represent individual objects as for classes that represent composite objects. That allows our code to treat individual and composite objects uniformly.

- The Decorator Design Pattern models code that allows us to extend the responsibilities of an object at run time. This is accomplished with decorations in the form of attributes and behaviors that we can implement as wrapper objects.

- The Decorator Design Pattern lessens the need to hardcode additional responsibilities for an object by making it easy to add new decorations or modify or remove existing ones without modifying any other classes.

Part 5

Additional design techniques

Recursion is a powerful technique supported by modern programming languages. Well-designed recursive programs can be simpler and more elegantly designed than their iterative counterparts. But recursive thinking is required to know when to use recursion and how to do it appropriately. Recursion combined with backtracking can exploit a computer's ability to try many solution paths rapidly and exhaustively. The example programs in chapter 15 introduce recursive thinking, and they demonstrate recursion and recursion with backtracking.

Multithreading is a technique that enables a program to run multiple execution paths simultaneously. Well-designed multithreaded programs can perform better than their single-threaded versions, especially on multicore machines. Chapter 16 briefly introduces the topic of multithreading through several classic example applications.

15

Designing solutions with recursion and backtracking

This chapter covers

- Recursion for designing solutions to programming problems
- Dynamic backtracking to try different solution paths during run time

Recursion is a software design technique that we can use to create solutions to certain programming problems. It involves a function or method that calls itself, and nearly all modern programming languages support this important technique. If we use recursion properly with certain classes of programming problems, we can design solutions that are simple and elegant—and, some might claim, magical. With recursion, we can design solutions that may be difficult otherwise.

Recursion requires a different way of thinking about how to design a programming solution to a problem. Unfortunately, for some programmers, it is too mysterious and forbidding to use. This chapter clears away the mystery and demonstrates how combining recursion with dynamic backtracking gives us even more powerful design tools. But we'll also see how misusing recursion can cause surprising performance disasters. With experience, we can learn when it is appropriate to design with recursion.

15.1 Recursion compared to the for loop

The key idea behind recursion is to solve a programming problem by reducing it into a smaller but similar problem that we can solve the same way, and that solving the smaller problem leads to the solution of the larger problem. We keep reducing a problem into smaller and smaller similar problems until the problem is so small that its solution is obvious and immediate. That solution becomes part of the solution to the next-to-the-smallest problem, which in turn becomes part of the solution to the next-larger problem. As we "unwind" from the recursion all the way back to the largest problem, the solutions to the smaller problems become part of the solution to the original problem.

When we write a recursive function (or method) to solve a programming problem, the function calls itself to solve a smaller but similar problem. A function makes a *recursive call* when it calls itself. This is often called a *nested* call. The recursive calls repeat and nest deeper and deeper to solve smaller and smaller problems until the problem is small enough for the function to return immediately with its result without making another recursive call, thereby preventing infinite recursion. This smallest problem is called a *base case* of the recursion. The result from a base case enables the second-to-last recursive call to return with a result, and so on, with return results one by one from all the recursive calls back up the chain to the original call. The return from the original call solves the original programming problem. The recursive calls and the results from unwinding the calls are what can make such solutions simple and elegant.

We can remove some of the mystery behind recursion by comparing it to a basic counting for loop, such as

```
for i in range(INITIAL_VALUE, LIMIT_VALUE): ...
```

Table 15.1 shows the comparison.

Table 15.1 Comparing a for loop to recursion

	for loop	Recursion
Initial condition	i = INITIAL_VALUE	The original problem
Repeated updating	Set i to the next value in the range.	Reduce the problem into a smaller but similar problem.
Terminating condition	i >= LIMIT_VALUE	The problem is so small that its solution is immediate and obvious (a base case).

It is vitally important for the for loop to eventually complete. Therefore, each iteration of the loop must update the control variable so that the variable's value approaches the terminating condition. Similarly, for the recursion to eventually end, the problem must become smaller and smaller and approach a base case, where the problem is so small that its solution is immediate and obvious and there are no further recursive calls.

The two example programs in sections 15.2 and 15.3 demonstrate recursion. Neither of the problems that these programs solve ought to be done with recursion—they are much more efficiently solved with conventional iteration, such as for loops or while loops. But we'll use them to show clearly how recursion works.

15.2 Finding the largest value in a list by recursion

Our first example program uses recursion to find the largest value in a nonempty list of integer values. To design the recursive solution, we must determine the entries in the last column of table 15.1:

- *Initial condition*—The original list of values
- *Update*—A smaller but similar problem of finding the largest value in a shorter list
- *Terminating condition*—The base case of a list consisting of a single element

Figure 15.1 shows how the recursion works. We start by passing the original list of values to recursive function largest(). The function records the value of the list's first element in variable first_value, and then it removes the first element, producing a shorter list that consists of the rest of the list. The function compares first_value to the largest value in the rest of the list, and the larger of the two is the solution to the original problem.

But how does function largest() know what the largest value in the rest of the list is? That's the result of a recursive call to the function with the shorter list. Each recursive call receives a list argument that is one element shorter, so the calls approach the base case.

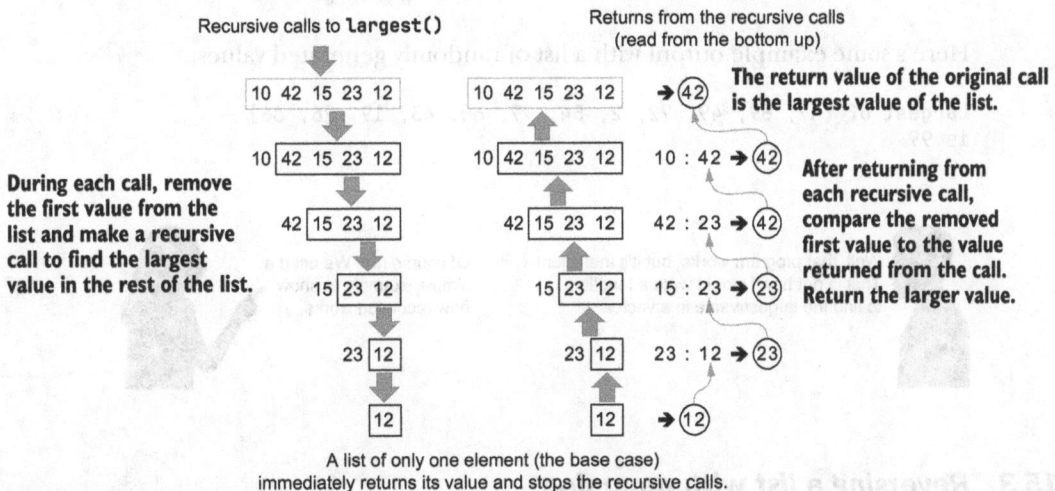

Figure 15.1 How the recursive function largest() finds the largest value in a list. The boxed values are the evershortening list arguments of the calls. The return value of each recursive call enables the caller to return its value.

Each recursive call returns the solution to its problem. The last call receives a list argument that consists of only one element, which is the call's immediate and obvious return value. The last call does not make another recursive call, thereby stopping the chain of recursive calls. The immediate return value enables the caller of the base case to complete its comparison and return a value. As the recursion unwinds, the return value from each recursive call enables the caller to complete its comparison and return a result until the original call returns with the largest value in the entire list.

Recursive function `largest()` works as suggested by figure 15.1.

Listing 15.1   (Program 15.1 Largest) largest.py (recursion demonstration only)

```
from random import randint          Recursive function

SIZE = 12                           Base case: no recursive call
                                    needed for a list of size 1
def largest(v):
    if len(v) == 1:
        return v[0]                 Remembers the value
                                    of the first element
    first_value = v[0]              Shortens the list by
    v.pop(0)                        removing the first element
    largest_of_rest = largest(v)    Recursive call to find the largest
                                    value in the rest of the list
    return first_value if first_value > largest_of_rest \
           else largest_of_rest
                                    Returns the larger of the
if __name__ == '__main__':          value of the first element
    data = [ randint(0, 100) for _ in range(SIZE) ]   to the largest value in the
    print(f'Largest of {data}')                       rest of the list
    print(f'is {largest(data)}')    Initial function call
                                    passing the original list
```

Here's some example output with a list of randomly generated values:

```
Largest of [47, 89, 49, 72, 2, 54, 99, 60, 43, 19, 26, 66]
is 99
```

Well, that program works, but it's inefficient. That is not how I would write a function to find the largest value in a vector.

Of course not. We used a simple example to show *how* recursion works.

15.3   *Reversing a list with recursion*

Here's another example program that shows how recursion works: a recursive function `reverse()` that reverses the contents of a list. As with the previous example, this is not the best way to solve this problem, but it's another good way to show how recursion works.

We first pass the original list containing, for example, integer values 10, 20, 30, 40, and 50 to recursive function reverse(). The function removes the first element of the list, recursively reverses the rest of the list, which is shorter, and then appends the removed first element to the end of the list:

```
10 [ 20, 30, 40, 50 ]
   [ 50, 40, 30, 20 ] 10
```

We reverse the shorter list by passing it to a recursive call to reverse(). Each recursive call gets a shorter list. The recursion ends when the list eventually reaches the base case of only one element. The final result is a list containing 50, 40, 30, 20, and 10. Figure 15.2 shows how to recursively reverse the list contents.

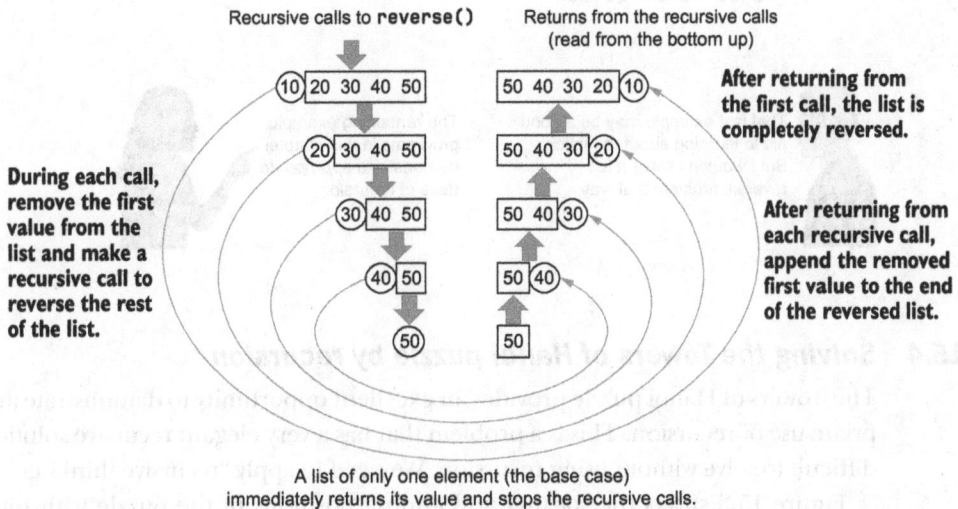

Recursive calls to **reverse()**   Returns from the recursive calls (read from the bottom up)

During each call, remove the first value from the list and make a recursive call to reverse the rest of the list.

After returning from the first call, the list is completely reversed.

After returning from each recursive call, append the removed first value to the end of the reversed list.

A list of only one element (the base case) immediately returns its value and stops the recursive calls.

Figure 15.2 **How the recursive function reverse() reverses the contents of a list. Each call removes the first value, recursively reverses the rest of the list, and then appends the removed first value to the end.**

Recursive function reverse() works as suggested by figure 15.2.

Listing 15.2 (Program 15.2 Reverse) reverse.py (recursion demonstration only)

```
SIZE = 5

def reverse(v):                    ◄──  Recursive function
    if len(v) == 1:
        return v[0]                     Base case: no recursive call
                                        needed for a list of size 1

    first_value = v[0]            ◄──── Remembers the value of the first element
```

```
v.pop(0)                              ◄────  Shortens the list by
                                             removing the first element
reverse(v)          ◄──────────────── Recursive call to reverse the
                                      contents of the rest of the list

return v.append(first_value)    ◄──── Appends the first element to
                                      the end of the reversed list

if __name__ == '__main__':
    data = [ 10*i for i in range(SIZE + 1)]
    print(f'Reverse of {data}')

    reverse(data)       ◄──────────────  Initial function call
    print(f'        is {data}')
```

Here's the example output:

```
Reverse of 10 20 30 40 50
        is 50 40 30 20 10
```

That last example may be a good aid to learning about recursion. But I wouldn't solve a list reversal problem that way.

The remaining example programs in this chapter demonstrate *appropriate* uses of recursion.

15.4   Solving the Towers of Hanoi puzzle by recursion

The Towers of Hanoi puzzle provides an excellent opportunity to demonstrate an appropriate use of recursion. This is a problem that has a very elegant recursive solution but is difficult to solve without using recursion. We need to apply "recursive thinking."

Figure 15.3 shows the starting and ending positions of the puzzle with four disks. Each disk has a hole in its center, and they are stacked in size order on one of three pins with the smallest disk on top. The goal is to move all the disks from the source pin to the destination pin, where they are again stacked in size order. We've labeled the pins L, M, and R (for left, middle, and right, respectively).

The rules for moving the disks from the source pin to the destination pin are as follows:

1 Move only one disk at a time.

2 Never put a larger disk on top of a smaller disk.

3 Use the third pin as a temporary location to move a disk.

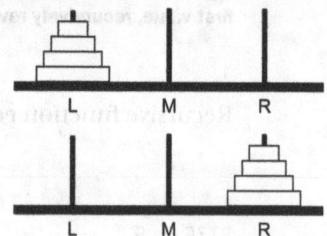

Figure 15.3   The starting and ending positions of four disks in the Towers of Hanoi puzzle. We moved the disks from source pin L to destination pin R.

Figure 15.4 shows conceptually how we could solve the puzzle if rule 1 didn't exist: we move the top three disks to temporary pin M, then we move the largest disk from pin L to pin R, and finally we move the three disks from pin M to pin R, and we're done.

But how do we move three disks without violating the rule about moving only one disk at a time? Moving three disks is a smaller problem than moving four disks. This is a problem that suggests a recursive solution.

To convince ourselves that a recursive solution is possible, let's start with the base case. Figure 15.5 shows that moving a single disk from the source pin L to its destination pin R is an immediate operation—no recursion needed. So indeed, the base case will stop further recursion.

Figure 15.6 shows the sequence of moves to get two disks from source pin L to destination pin R. It requires using pin M as the temporary. There are three single-disk moves: first the small disk from pin L to pin M (L is the source and M is the destination of this move), then the large disk from pin L to pin R (L is the source and R is the destination of this move), and finally the small disk from pin M to pin R (M is the source and R is the destination of this move). Note that the pins can change roles: in step 1, M was the destination, and in step 3, M was the source. We used the base case of only one disk to solve the single-disk moves.

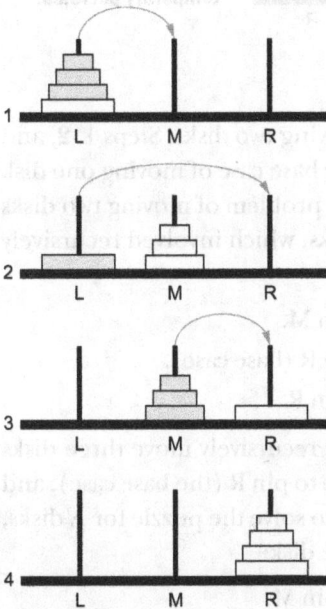

Figure 15.4   A conceptual solution with four disks that uses pin M as the temporary pin

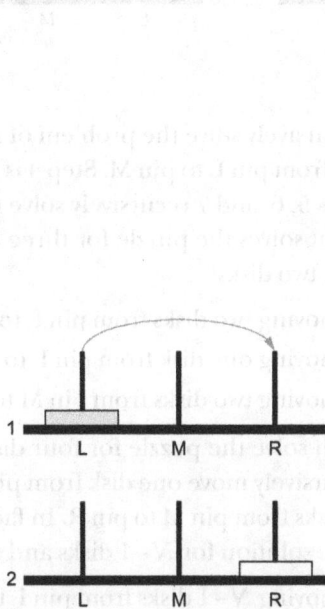

Figure 15.5   The base case of moving a single disk from pin L to pin R. No recursion needed.

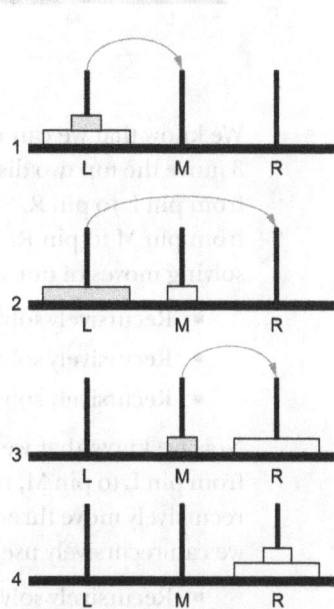

Figure 15.6   The sequence of moves to get two disks from pin L to pin R, using pin M as the temporary pin

Next we can solve the puzzle for three disks. To more clearly demonstrate that we're using recursion, figure 15.7 solves the puzzle, moving the disks from pin L to pin R.

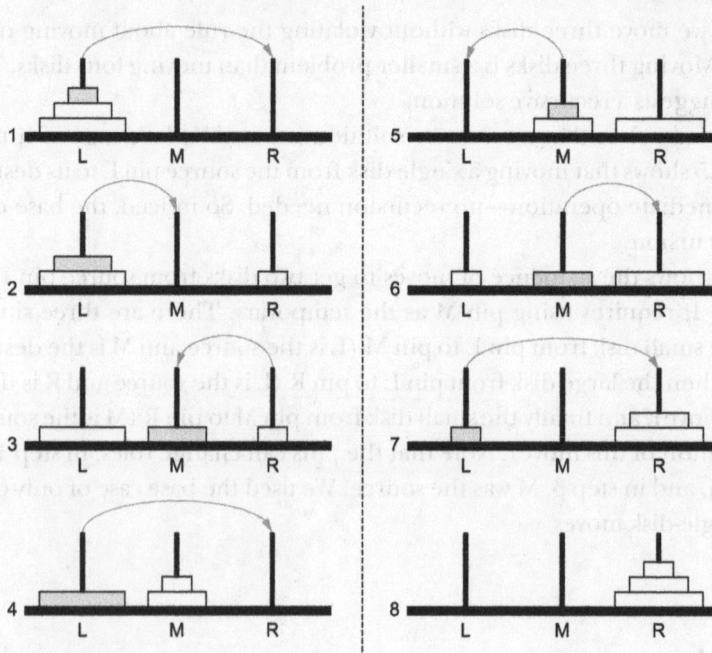

Figure 15.7 The sequence of moves to get three disks from pin L to pin R. During the steps, the pins change source, destination, and temporary pin roles.

We know that we can recursively solve the problem of moving two disks. Steps 1, 2, and 3 move the top two disks from pin L to pin M. Step 4 is the base case of moving one disk from pin L to pin R. Steps 5, 6, and 7 recursively solve the problem of moving two disks from pin M to pin R. That solves the puzzle for three disks, which involved recursively solving moves of one and two disks:

- Recursively solve moving two disks from pin L to pin M.
- Recursively solve moving one disk from pin L to pin R (base case).
- Recursively solve moving two disks from pin M to pin R.

Now we know that we can solve the puzzle for four disks: recursively move three disks from pin L to pin M, recursively move one disk from pin L to pin R (the base case), and recursively move three disks from pin M to pin R. In fact, to solve the puzzle for *N* disks, we can recursively use the solution for *N* − 1 disks and one disk:

- Recursively solve moving *N* − 1 disks from pin L to pin M.
- Recursively solve moving one disk from pin L to pin R (base case).
- Recursively solve moving *N* − 1 disks from pin M to pin R.

Therefore, solving the puzzle with recursion requires only a few lines of code.

Listing 15.3　(Program 15.3 Towers) towers.py

```
N = 4

def solve(n, source, temporary, destination):        ◄──  Recursive function
    if n == 1:
        print(f'Move {source} ==> {destination}')     │  Base case
    else:
        solve (n - 1, source,     destination, temporary)    │  Recursive calls with
        solve (    1, source,     temporary,   destination)  │  fewer disks and
        solve (n - 1, temporary,  source,      destination)  │  different pin roles


if __name__ == '__main__':              │  Initial call with N disks
    solve(N, 'L', 'M', 'R')     ◄──────┘  with pin names and roles
```

Here is the output from the solution for N = 4 disks:

```
Move L ==> M
Move L ==> R
Move M ==> R
Move L ==> M
Move R ==> L
Move R ==> M
Move L ==> M
Move L ==> R
Move M ==> R
Move M ==> L
Move R ==> L
Move M ==> R
Move L ==> M
Move L ==> R
Move M ==> R
```

It's impressive how those three calls to recursive function solve() can solve the puzzle for any number of disks.

It would be very challenging to write a program to solve the Towers of Hanoi puzzle without using recursion.

15.5 Recursive algorithms for a binary search tree

Recursive algorithms can be ideal for data structures that are recursively defined. One such recursive data structure is the binary tree, and we'll see how to design recursive functions to operate on the tree nodes.

A *binary tree* is a tree structure in which each nonempty node has zero, one, or two children. Therefore, the node has two links (references): the left child link and the right child link. Each link either is None or refers to a child node that is the root of a subtree (figure 15.8). Each subtree is itself a binary tree, and therefore, a binary tree is recursively defined. The root represents the entire tree. We can consider a link that's None to be a reference to an empty node, which represents an empty tree. The subtrees get smaller and smaller as we move down until we reach a base case of an empty tree.

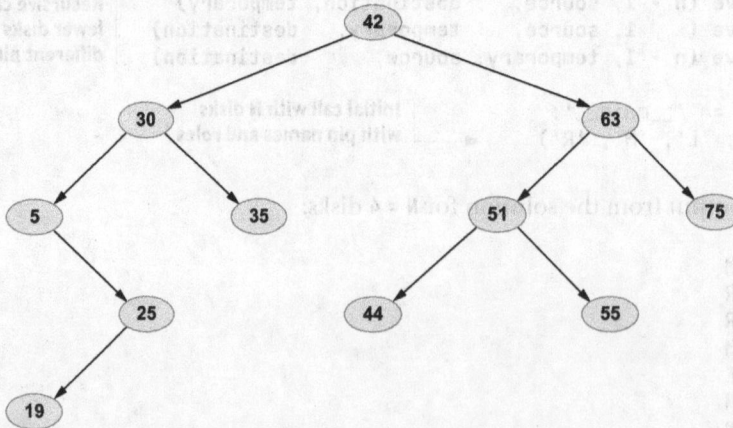

Figure 15.8 A binary tree, where each nonempty node has zero, one, or two child nodes that are roots of subtrees. Each subtree is itself a binary tree, so a binary tree is recursively defined. This binary tree is also a binary search tree (BST), where at each nonempty parent node, values in the left child subtree are less than or equal to the parent node's value, and values in the right subtree are greater. Each subtree is itself a BST, so a BST is recursively defined.

In class Node, each left and right link is a settable property.

Listing 15.4   (Program 15.4-BST) node.py

```python
class Node:
    def __init__(self, value):
        self._value = value
        self._left = None
        self._right = None


    @property
    def value(self):
        return self._value

    @property
    def left(self):
        return self._left

    @left.setter
    def left(self, node):
        self._left = node
```

```
        @property
        def right(self):
            return self._right

        @right.setter
        def right(self, node):
            self._right = node
```

A binary tree is a *binary search tree* (BST) if it further meets these conditions:

- Each nonempty node has a value.
- The left child (if it exists) of any nonempty parent node is a subtree whose node values are all less than or equal to the value of the parent node.
- The right child (if it exists) of any nonempty parent node is a subtree whose node values are all greater than the value of the parent node.

A BST is recursively defined because each node is the root of a subtree that is itself a BST (figure 15.8). Note that a binary tree becomes a BST because of the way we manage it during run time. How we implement class Node is the same for an ordinary binary tree and for a BST.

We'll define two recursive algorithms for a BST: inserting nodes and printing all the nodes.

15.5.1 Inserting into a BST with recursion

To recursively insert a new Node object into a BST, public method insert() starts at the root of the tree by calling the corresponding private method _insert(), which does all the work. The new Node object will be created from the parameter value.

Listing 15.5 (Program 15.4-BST) BST.py (part 1 of 2)

```
from node import Node

class BST:
    def __init__(self):
        self._root = None                                   Public method insert():
                                                            starts at the tree root
    def insert(self, value):
        self._root = self._insert(value, self._root)  ◄──  Recursive private
                                                            method _insert()
    def _insert(self, value, node):  ◄──
        if node is None:                 Base case: creates and
            return Node(value)           returns a new node       Recursive insert into
                                                                  the left subtree
        if value <= node.value:
            node.left = self._insert(value, node.left)  ◄──  Recursive insert
        else:                                                into the right
            node.right = self._insert(value, node.right) ◄── subtree

        return node  ◄──    Each call returns the
    ...                     newly inserted node.
```

Private method _insert() first checks its node parameter. If the node is None, that's the base case to create and return a new Node object. Otherwise, recursive calls to the method proceed down the left or right subtree via link node.left or link node.right, respectively, depending on how the new value compares with each node value along the way. As the method recursively travels down the links, the subtrees become smaller and smaller. It reaches a base case at a link whose value is None—an empty subtree—at which time it creates and returns the new Node object. The method sets the link that was None to refer to the newly created Node object. In particular, when the tree is initially empty, the public insert() method sets the root of the BST to the very first inserted Node object. Figure 15.9 shows inserting a new node with value 60 into a sample BST.

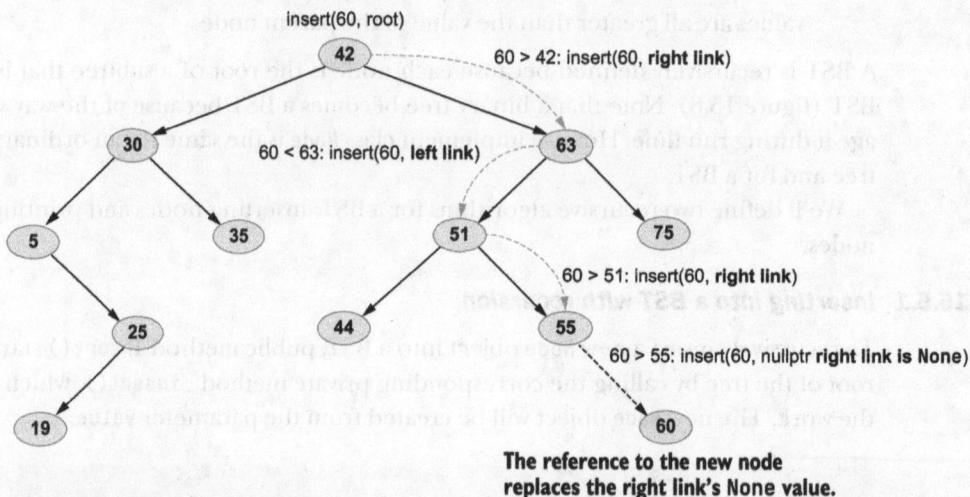

Figure 15.9   The values were inserted into this BST in the order 42, 30, 5, 35, 63, 75, 25, 51, 44, 19, 55. To insert the new value 60 into the tree, private method _insert() is called recursively until it reaches a base case of an empty subtree. The new node replaces the empty subtree, and the value is thereby inserted into the tree at its proper place.

15.5.2 *Printing a BST with recursion*

Figure 15.10 shows how to print the nodes of a BST in sorted order. Public method print() calls private method _print() to recursively print the values of the BST nodes in sorted order, starting at the root.

Listing 15.6   (Program 15.4-BST) BST.py (part 2 of 2)

```
    ...

    def print_tree(self):
        self._print_tree(self._root)
```

Public method print():
starts at the tree root

Recursive private method _print_tree()

Checks for the base
case of an empty node

```
def _print_tree(self, node):
    if node is not None:
        self._print_tree(node.left)
        print(f'{node.value:3d}', end='')
        self._print_tree(node.right)
```

Recursively prints
the left subtree

Recursively prints
the right subtree

Prints the node's value

6 **42**

4 **30**

63 11

1 **5**

35 5

8 **51**

75 12

25 3

7 **44**

55 9

2 **19**

60 10

5 19 25 30 35 42 44 51 55 60 63 75

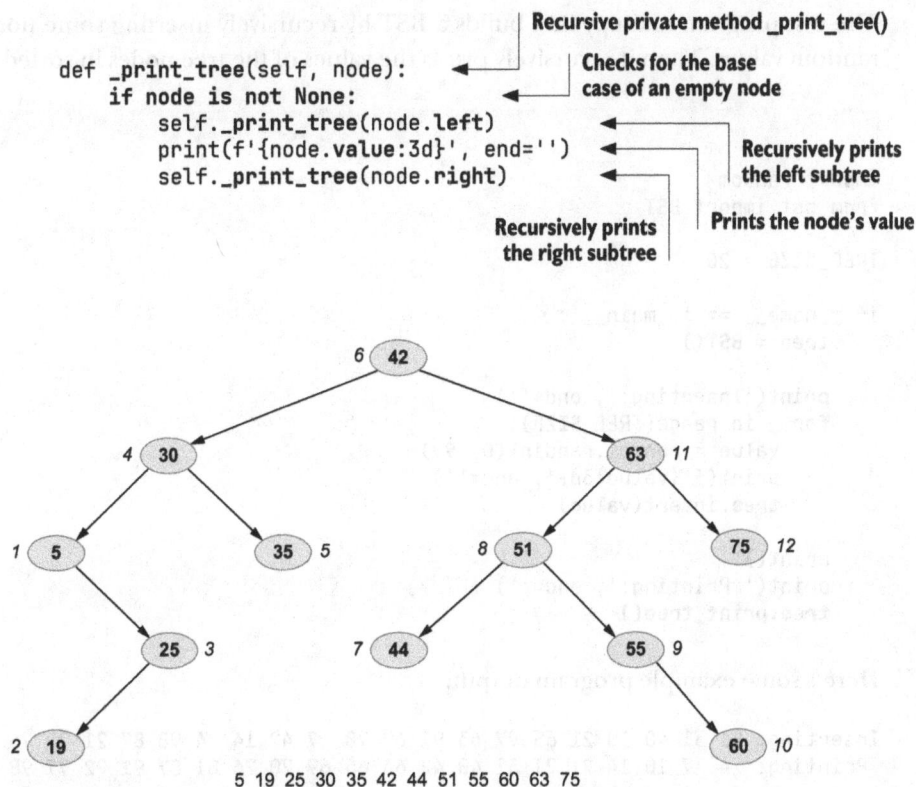

Figure 15.10 Recursively printing the values of a BST in sorted order. At each parent node, we first recursively print the values in its left child subtree if one exists, next print the parent node's value, and then recursively print the values in the parent node's right child subtree if one exists. The small numbers next to each node indicate the order in which the nodes are printed.

Printing a BST starts with a call to public method print_tree(), which passes the tree root to private recursive method _print_tree(). The private method first calls itself recursively on the node's left subtree. Next, it prints the node's value. Then it calls itself recursively on the node's right subtree. The base case is an empty node, where the method returns without doing anything.

Tree traversals

We printed the BST using an *inorder tree traversal*, because we printed a node's value *in between* first "traversing" the node's left subtree and then the right subtree.

A *preorder tree traversal* prints the node's value *before* traversing both the left and right subtrees. A *postorder tree traversal* prints the node's value *after* traversing both the left and right subtrees. Both of these traversals can also be accomplished with recursion.

The test program main.py first builds a BST by recursively inserting some nodes with random values. Then it recursively prints the values of the tree nodes in sorted order.

Listing 15.7   (Program 15.4-BST) main.py

```python
import random
from bst import BST

TREE_SIZE = 20

if __name__ == '__main__':
    tree = BST()

    print('Inserting:', end='')
    for _ in range(TREE_SIZE):
        value = random.randint(0, 99)
        print(f'{value:3d}', end='')
        tree.insert(value)

    print()
    print(' Printing:', end='')
    tree.print_tree()
```

Here's some example program output:

```
Inserting: 81 31 40 10 21 65 97 63 91 69 70  7 42 14  4 98 87 21 92 76
 Printing:  4  7 10 14 21 21 31 40 42 63 65 69 70 76 81 87 91 92 97 98
```

Why is it called a binary *search* tree?

The way the values are stored in a BST makes it easy to write a fast and efficient algorithm to search the tree for a particular value.

15.6   *Quicksorting a list with recursion*

A famous example of the use of recursion is the quicksort algorithm for rapidly sorting a list of values. Sorting is a common and important operation in many applications, such as for printing data records in order or for indexing records in a database. It is usually much more efficient to search for values in a sorted list.

Quicksort relies on a procedure to partition a list into two sublists. For example, to quicksort the list

76   34   61   21   51   (16)   26   61   6   32   15

we first choose an element at or near the center of the list as the *pivot element* 16 (circled). In the partitioning procedure explained in a moment, we rearrange the elements so that all the values less than or equal to the pivot value are to the left of the pivot and all the values greater than the pivot value are to the right of the pivot:

| 6 | 15 | 16 | 21 | 51 | 34 | 26 | 61 | 76 | 32 | 61 |

Now we have two independent sublists (boxed) on both sides of the pivot. Neither sublist is necessarily sorted, and we will recursively quicksort each one.

The quicksort algorithm is as follows:

1 Choose a pivot element. In this example, we'll choose the element at or near the middle of the list.

2 Partition the list to be sorted into two sublists on either side of the pivot.

   – Base case #1: If the sublist size is 0 or 1, do nothing because it is already sorted.

   – Base case #2: If the sublist size is 2, swap the two elements if necessary.

   – Otherwise, recursively quicksort the two sublists.

These are some key facts about the algorithm:

- After we've chosen the pivot element and performed the partitioning, the pivot element is already in its proper place in the final sorted list.

- Elements in sublists that meet either base case (after swapping if necessary in base case #2) are already in their proper places in the final sorted list.

15.6.1 Quicksort in action

Figure 15.11 shows the quicksort algorithm in action as it sorts a list. Line A is the original list, and line L is the sorted list. As the sort progresses line by line, the circled value is the pivot value in each line; values less than or equal to the pivot are moved to the left, and values greater than the pivot are moved to the right. The sublists to be recursively quicksorted are boxed, and the sublist being quicksorted in each line is shaded. After quicksorting a sublist, the bold values are already in their proper places in the final sorted list.

Line A shows the original list. Line B shows that we have started sorting the entire list. We choose 7 to be the pivot element because it's near the middle of the list. Using the pivot element, we partition the list into two sublists (line C). Then we recursively sort the first sublist consisting of the two values 4 and 3, which we swap. This is base case #2.

Next (line D), we recursively sort the other sublist by first picking 71 as the pivot element. This results in two more sublists (line E). We recursively sort the left sublist, choosing 65 as the pivot element (line E). Because the pivot value ends up at the right end of the sublist after partitioning, the resulting sublist to the right of 65 is empty (base case #1).

A:	4	65	72	31	3	7	71	29	99	22	77
B:	4	3	(7)	31	65	77	71	29	99	22	72
C:	3	4	7	31	65	77	71	29	99	22	72	Base case #2
D:	3	4	7	31	65	22	29	(71)	99	77	72
E:	3	4	7	31	29	22	(65)	71	99	77	72	Base case #1
F:	3	4	7	22	(29)	31	65	71	99	77	72
G:	3	4	7	22	29	31	65	71	99	77	72	Base case #1
H:	3	4	7	22	29	31	65	71	99	77	72	Base case #1
I:	3	4	7	22	29	31	65	71	72	(77)	99
J:	3	4	7	22	29	31	65	71	72	77	99	Base case #1
K:	3	4	7	22	29	31	65	71	72	77	99	Base case #1
L:	3	4	7	22	29	31	65	71	72	77	99

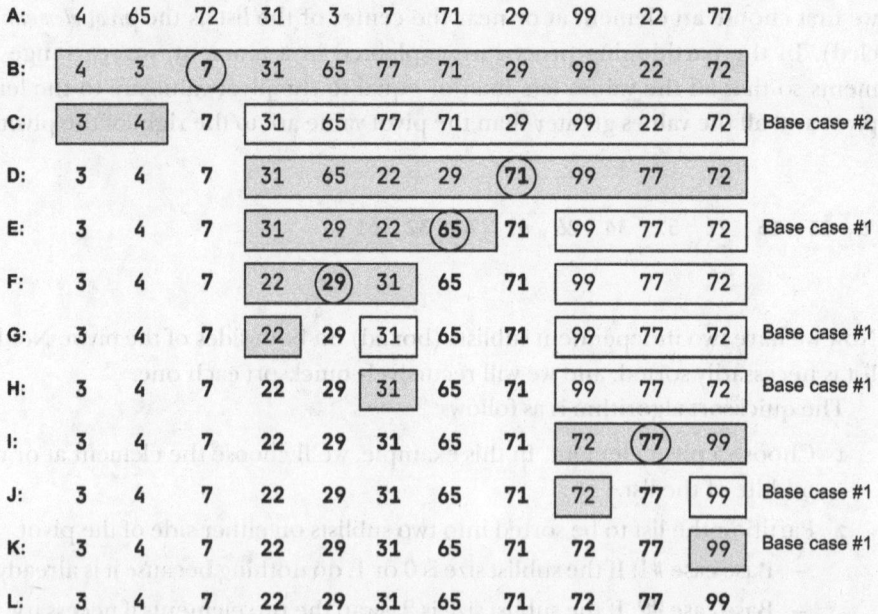

Figure 15.11   The quicksort algorithm in action as it sorts a list. The circled values are the chosen pivot elements that create the sublists on both sides after partitioning. The rectangles enclose the sublists to be quicksorted recursively. In each line, the shaded sublist is the one actively being sorted. The values in bold are already in their correct places in the final sorted list. Note that the chosen pivot elements are already in their correct places after partitioning.

Lines G, H, J, and K show sublists that each contain only one element (base case #1). Their values are already in their proper places.

It's breathtaking watching quicksort in action.

Many regard it as the most elegant algorithm in computer science.

15.6.2 *Partitioning a list into sublists*

The key procedure in the quicksort algorithm is partitioning a list into two sublists. Figure 15.12 shows how to do it line by line with pivot value 52 (circled). Following are the steps to partition a list:

1   Choose one element of the list to be the pivot element. In our examples, we'll choose 52 in the middle (line A).

	1	2	3	4	5	6	7	8	9	10	11	
A:	60	16	49	63	6	(52)	23	31	72	74	1	Pivot 52
B:	60 i	16	49	63	6	1	23	31	72	74 j	(52)	1↔52
C:	60 i	16	49	63	6	1	23	31 j	72	74	(52)	Moved j
D:	31 i	16	49	63	6	1	23	60 j	72	74	(52)	31↔60
E:	31	16	49	63 i	6	1	23	60 j	72	74	(52)	Moved i
F:	31	16	49	63 i	6	1	23 j	60	72	74	(52)	Moved j
G:	31	16	49	23 i	6	1	63 j	60	72	74	(52)	23↔63
H:	31	16	49	23	6	1	63 ij	60	72	74	(52)	Moved i
I:	31	16	49	23	6	1 j	63 i	60	72	74	(52)	Moved j
J:	31	16	49	23	6	1	52	60	72	74	63	52↔63

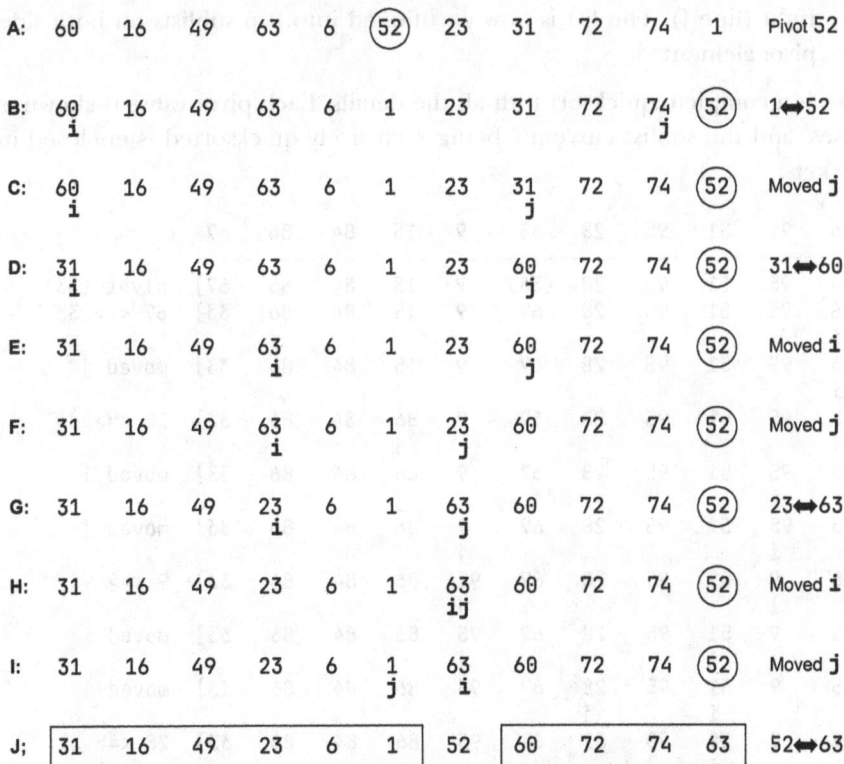

Figure 15.12 Choosing 52 (circled) to be the pivot value and then partitioning the list into two sublists. Variables i and j are list indexes. After partitioning, all values to the left of 52 are less than or equal to it, and all values to the right of 52 are greater. The two boxed sublists on either side of the pivot are now ready to be recursively quicksorted.

2 Park the pivot element out of the way by swapping it with the rightmost element of the list (line B). Set variable i to the element index of the leftmost element and variable j to be the index of the element just to the left of the parked pivot element.

3 Move i to the right (i.e., increment i) while the value of the ith element is less than or equal to the pivot value. It might not move if that condition is already false.

4 Move j to the left (i.e., decrement j) while the value of the jth element is greater than the pivot value (line C). It might not move if that condition is already false.

5 After i and j have both stopped moving, if i < j, swap the ith and jth element values (line D).

6 Repeat steps 3, 4, and 5 (lines E through I) until j crosses i (line I). Swap the value of the ith element with the pivot element that we had parked earlier at the

right (line J). The list is now partitioned into two sublists on both sides of the pivot element.

Here is a complete quicksort with all the details. Each pivot value is shown in parentheses, and the sublist currently being recursively quicksorted is enclosed in square brackets:

```
86    95    51    95    28    33    9     15    84    86    67
-------------------------------------------------------------
[86    95    51    95    28   (33)   9     15    84    86    67]   pivot (33)
[86    95    51    95    28    67    9     15    84    86    33]   67 <=> 33
 i                                              j
[86    95    51    95    28    67    9     15    84    86    33]   moved j
 i                                        j
[15    95    51    95    28    67    9     86    84    86    33]   15 <=> 86
 i                                        j
[15    95    51    95    28    67    9     86    84    86    33]   moved i
       i                                  j
[15    95    51    95    28    67    9     86    84    86    33]   moved j
       i                            j
[15    9     51    95    28    67    95    86    84    86    33]   9 <=> 95
       i                            j
[15    9     51    95    28    67    95    86    84    86    33]   moved i
             i                      j
[15    9     51    95    28    67    95    86    84    86    33]   moved j
             i           j
[15    9     28    95    51    67    95    86    84    86    33]   28 <=> 51
             i           j
[15    9     28    95    51    67    95    86    84    86    33]   moved i
                   i     j
[15    9     28    95    51    67    95    86    84    86    33]   moved j
                   j     i
[15    9     28   (33)   51    67    95    86    84    86    95]   33 <=> 95
-------------------------------------------------------------
[15   ( 9)   28]   33    51    67    95    86    84    86    95    pivot (9)
[15    28    9]    33    51    67    95    86    84    86    95    28 <=> 9
 i     j
[15    28    9]    33    51    67    95    86    84    86    95    moved j
 i
[ 9)   28    15]   33    51    67    95    86    84    86    95    9 <=> 15
-------------------------------------------------------------
 9    [28    15]   33    51    67    95    86    84    86    95
 9    [15    28]   33    51    67    95    86    84    86    95    15 <=> 28
-------------------------------------------------------------
 9     15    28    33   [51    67    95   (86)   84    86    95]   pivot (86)
 9     15    28    33   [51    67    95    95    84    86    86]   95 <=> 86
                              i                       j
 9     15    28    33   [51    67    95    95    84    86    86]   moved i
                                    i                 j
 9     15    28    33   [51    67    86    95    84    95    86]   86 <=> 95
                                    i                 j
 9     15    28    33   [51    67    86    95    84    95    86]   moved i
                                          i           j
 9     15    28    33   [51    67    86    95    84    95    86]   moved j
```

```
                                     i        j
9   15   28   33   [51   67   86   84   95   95   86]   84 <=> 95
                                  i    j
9   15   28   33   [51   67   86   84   95   95   86]   moved i
                                     ji
9   15   28   33   [51   67   86   84   95   95   86]   moved j
                                  j    i
9   15   28   33   [51   67   86   84   (86)  95   95]   86 <=> 95
------------------------------------------------------------------
9   15   28   33   [51   (67)  86   84]  86   95   95    pivot (67)
9   15   28   33   [51   84   86   67]  86   95   95    84 <=> 67
                         i         j
9   15   28   33   [51   84   86   67]  86   95   95    moved i
                              i    j
9   15   28   33   [51   84   86   67]  86   95   95    moved j
                         j    i
9   15   28   33   [51   (67)  86   84]  86   95   95    67 <=> 84
------------------------------------------------------------------
9   15   28   33   [51]   67   86   84   86   95   95
------------------------------------------------------------------
9   15   28   33   51    67   [86   84]   86   95   95
9   15   28   33   51    67   [84   86]   86   95   95    84 <=> 86
------------------------------------------------------------------
9   15   28   33   51    67   84   86   86   [95   95]
```

15.6.3 Quicksort Implementation

Class Quicksort implements the quicksort algorithm. Private method _swap_values_ at() swaps two values in a list at indexes index1 and index2.

```python
class Quicksort:
    def __init__(self, data):
        self._data = data          ◀─────┤  Data list to be sorted

    def _swap_values_at(self, index1, index2):          ◀──────┐  Swaps the data values
        self._data[index1], self._data[index2] = \                │  at the two list indexes
            self._data[index2], self._data[index1]
    ...
```

Private method _partition() partitions a list whose leftmost and rightmost element indexes are left_index and right_index, respectively, into two sublists. It chooses a pivot element and implements the partitioning procedure. It returns the final index of the pivot element.

```python
    ...
    def _partition(self, left_index, right_index):
```

```
        middle_index = (left_index + right_index)//2
        pivot_element = self._data[middle_index]                    ┐  Chooses the
                                                                       pivot element
        self._swap_values_at(middle_index, right_index)  ◄─          at or near the
                                                                       middle of the
                                                                       sublist
        i = left_index - 1
        j = right_index              Loops until indexes            Parks the pivot
                                     i and j cross                  element
        while i < j:
            i += 1
            while (    (i < right_index)                   ◄────┐
                   and (self._data[i] <= pivot_element)):       │ Moves index i
                i += 1                                      ◄───┘ to the right


            j -= 1
            while (    (j >= left_index)                   ◄────┐
                   and (self._data[j] > pivot_element)):        │ Moves index j
                j -= 1                                     ◄────┘ to the left


            if i < j:                               ┐  Swaps the elements
                self._swap_values_at(i, j)  ◄───────┘  at indexes i and j

        self._swap_values_at(i, right_index)  ◄──┐  Swaps the pivot element
        return i                              ◄──┤  into its final position
                                                 │
                             Returns the index of the
                             pivot element's final position
...
```

Public method `sort()` calls private recursive method `_sort()` to start with the entire list. The latter calls `_partition()` to create two sublists on either side of the pivot element, and then it calls itself to sort the left and right sublists.

Listing 15.10   (Program 15.5 Quicksort) quicksort.py (part 3 of 4)

```
    ...
    def sort(self):
        self._sort(0, len(self._data) - 1)  ◄──────┤ Public sort(): sorts the entire list

    def _sort(self, left_index, right_index):   ◄──────┤ Recursive private _sort()
        partition_size = right_index - left_index + 1

        if partition_size < 2:                ◄───┐
            return                                │ Base cases
        elif partition_size == 2:             ◄───┘
            if (  self._data[left_index]
                > self._data[right_index]):
                self._swap_values_at(left_index,
                                     right_index)
        else:                                          ┐ Partitions into
            pivot_index = self._partition(left_index,  ┘ the two sublists
                                          right_index)  ┐
            self._sort(left_index, pivot_index - 1)  ◄──┘ Recursively quicksorts
                                                           the left sublist
```

```
        self._sort(pivot_index + 1, right_index)  ◄────┐ Recursively quicksorts
    ...                                                 │ the right sublist
```

As a simple defensive measure, public method `verify_sorted()` verifies that the list is properly sorted.

Listing 15.11 (Program 15.5 Quicksort) quicksort.py (part 4 of 4)

```
    ...

    def verify_sorted(self):                          Is each element less
        for i in range(len(self._data) - 1):          than or equal to the
            if self._data[i] > self._data[i+1]:  ◄──┐ following element?
                return False

        return True
```

The test program main.py generates a list of random values to demonstrate the quicksort algorithm.

Listing 15.12 (Program 15.5 Quicksort) main.py

```
from random import randint
from quicksort import Quicksort

SIZE = 20

if __name__ == '__main__':
    data = [ randint(0, SIZE - 1) for _ in range(SIZE)]

    qsorter = Quicksort(data)

    print(f'Before: {data}')
    qsorter.sort()
    print(f' After: {data}')

    print()
    if qsorter.verify_sorted():
        print('Successfully sorted!')
    else:
        print('*** FAILED ***')
```

Here's some example output:

```
Before: [6, 1, 16, 6, 3, 17, 12, 15, 16, 10, 0, 1, 2, 3, 6, 8, 2, 3, 17, 8]
 After: [0, 1, 1, 2, 2, 3, 3, 3, 6, 6, 6, 8, 8, 10, 12, 15, 16, 16, 17, 17]

Successfully sorted!
```

How many recursive calls does the quicksort program make to sort *N* values? Each partitioning operation places one pivot value in its correct position. After pivoting, there can be two recursive calls. So, there can be up to $2N$ recursive calls. Fortunately, the base cases, which correctly position values without making recursive calls, significantly reduce the total number of calls.

15.7   *The Fibonacci sequence and a recursion disaster*

Recursion is a very powerful tool, but as with all power tools, we must be very careful using it. A classic example of what can go wrong if we improperly design with recursion is the Fibonacci sequence: 0, 1, 2, 3, 5, 8, 13, 21, ... Starting with 0 and 1, each subsequent term is the sum of the two previous terms. The mathematical definition of the sequence is

$$f_n = \begin{cases} 0 & \text{if } n = 0 \\ 1 & \text{if } n = 1 \\ f_{n-2} + f_{n-1} & \text{if } n > 1 \end{cases}$$

We might be tempted to follow this recursive mathematical definition and write a recursive function f().

Listing 15.13   (Program 15.6 Fibonacci) fibonacci.py (recursion disaster!)

```python
def f(n):
    if n < 2:
        return n
    else:
        return f(n - 2) + f(n - 1)

if __name__ == '__main__':
    print('  n        f[n]')
    print('---------------')

    for n in range(51):
        print(f'{n:3d} {f(n):11d}')
```

The output starts like this:

```
 n        f[n]
---------------
 0         0
 1         1
 2         1
 3         2
 4         3
 5         5
 6         8
 7        13
 8        21
 9        34
10        55
```

11	89
12	144
13	233
14	377
15	610
16	987
17	1597
18	2584
19	4181
20	6765
21	10946
22	17711
23	28657
24	46368
25	75025
26	121393
27	196418
28	317811
29	514229
30	832040
31	1346269
32	2178309
33	3524578
34	5702887
35	9227465
36	14930352
37	24157817
38	39088169
39	63245986
40	102334155

...

But the function becomes increasingly slow. Figure 15.13 shows the reason.

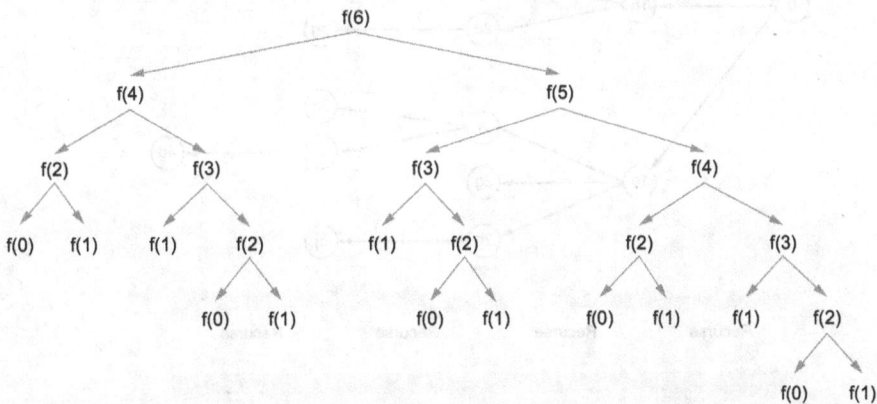

Figure 15.13 The tree of recursive calls to compute f(6). There are already many repeated calls with the same arguments. To compute f(n) as n becomes greater, the tree will grow larger, and the computation will take exponentially longer.

Another danger of recursion is failing to reach a base case, so the recursive calls don't stop. This is the "infinite recursion" error that is analogous to an infinite loop. During run time, Python will raise a `RecursionError` exception after the nonstopping recursive calls reach the recursion limit of around 1,000.

A recursive solution may appear simple and elegant, but if we don't understand how the recursive calls are made, or how many calls there are, we can suffer a very nasty performance surprise. All method and function calls, recursive or otherwise, incur run-time and memory costs.

15.8   *Dynamic backtracking increases the power of recursion*

The combination of recursion and dynamic backtracking is an extremely powerful design tool we can employ to solve a programming problem that involves multiple steps, when each step has several possible solution paths. Figure 15.15 shows a decision

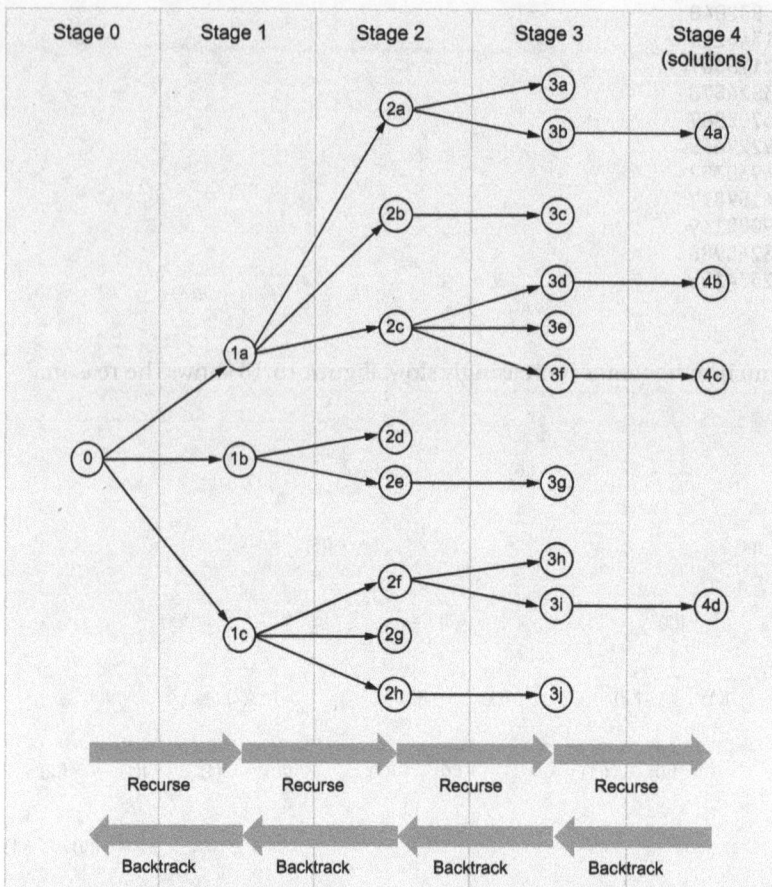

Figure 15.15   A decision tree showing recursion to move from one stage to the next and backtracking to try other paths in earlier stages

tree for an example problem where we search for solutions using recursion and backtracking. Each node represents a step from which there can be several (including no) solution paths. The figure suggests grouping the steps into stages. We start at step 0. The steps in stage 4 represent solutions to the problem.

At each step, we go from one stage to the next by taking a solution path. This operation of taking a solution path from one step to the next is recursive because at the next step, we perform the same operation, but the remaining path is shorter and closer to a base case.

A base case means reaching a step from which there are no solution paths, such as steps 2d and 3c in the figure. Then we backtrack to the previous step and take the next solution path from there. For example, after reaching step 2d, we backtrack to step 1b and try the next path from there, starting at step 2e. After reaching step 3c, we backtrack twice to step 1a, and from there, we try the next path starting at step 2c. Even after reaching a solution in stage 4, we can backtrack to search for more solutions; eventually we go back to starting step 0, where we try all its remaining solution paths. Or we can stop in stage 4 if we only want one solution.

Recursion with dynamic backtracking often constitutes a brute-force solution to a problem. We exploit the speed of the computer to try many solution paths.

Our first example program uses recursion with backtracking to solve the eight queens puzzle. The second example program solves Sudoku puzzles.

15.9　*Solving the eight queens puzzle with recursion and backtracking*

The goal of the puzzle is to place eight chess queens on a chessboard so that no queen can attack another, either horizontally, vertically, or diagonally. Here's an example solution:

```
Q . . . . . . .
. . . . . . Q .
. . . . Q . . .
. . . . . . . Q
Q . . . . . . .
. . . Q . . . .
. . . . . Q . .
. . Q . . . . .
```

Including reflections and rotations, there are 92 solutions.

In class `Queens`, private Boolean matrix `_occupied` records the positions of the queens. An element is `True` if the corresponding position is occupied by a queen and `False` otherwise. Private method `_print_board()` prints a solution.

Listing 15.14　(Program 15.7 Queens) queens.py (part 1 of 2)

```
class Queens(object):
    _SIZE = 8

    def __init__(self):
```

```
        self._count = 0
        self._occupied = [ [False]*Queens._SIZE
                               for _ in range(Queens._SIZE)
                          ]

    def _print_board(self):
        self._count += 1

        print()
        print(f'Solution #{self._count}')
        print()

        for row in range(Queens._SIZE):
            for col in range(Queens._SIZE):
                piece = 'Q ' if self._occupied[row][col] \
                        else '. '
                print(piece, end='')
            print()

    ...
```

We can solve this problem one column of the chessboard at a time, from left to right, using figure 15.15 as a guide:

- Each column is a stage of the solution.
- Each safe placement of a queen in a column is a step of a solution path.
- A safe placement is one where the queen is not attacked by any queens in the previous columns.
- In each column, we try the safe positions from top to bottom.
- Once a queen is placed in a column, the recursive action is to safely place a queen in the next column. This is the equivalent in figure 15.15 of following a solution path from a step in one stage to the next stage. Each recursive action starts with one fewer remaining column.
- A base case is when a queen cannot be placed safely in column $N+1$. Then we must backtrack and look for another safe placement in column N. We backtrack as many times as necessary.
- Another base case is safely placing a queen in the rightmost column. This constitutes a solution to the puzzle, which we print.
- Because there are multiple solutions, we backtrack from the rightmost column to recursively try other paths.

Private recursive method _find_solutions() in listing 15.15 looks for solutions to the puzzle, one column of the chessboard at a time. We pass the method a column number, and it attempts to find solutions starting at that column. Therefore, public method find_solutions() starts the solution searches by calling _find_solutions() with column 0. Private method _is_safe_position() determines whether a position is safe for a queen.

Listing 15.15 (Program 15.7 Queens) queens.py (part 2 of 2)

```
    ...

    def find_solutions(self):
        self._find_solutions(0)          ◄——⎤ Initial call for column 0

    def _find_solutions(self, col):      ◄——⎤ Recursive function
        for row in range(Queens._SIZE):
            if self._is_safe_position(row, col):
                self._occupied[row][col] = True   ◄——⎤ Places the queen
                                                       at a safe position

                if col == Queens._SIZE - 1:      ┐ Prints the solution
                    self._print_board()          ◄ found at the base case
                else:
                    self._find_solutions(col + 1)    ◄——⎤ Recursively continues
                                                          to search, starting at
                                                          the next column
                self._occupied[row][col] = False   ◄——
                                                       Removes the queen to check
                                                       the next safe position
    def _is_safe_position(self, row, col):
        for c in range(0, col):
            if self._occupied[row][c]:
                return False          ┐ Not safe: attacked
                                        from the same row


        r = row - 1
        c = col - 1

        while r >= 0 and c >= 0:
            if self._occupied[r][c]:       ┐ Not safe: attacked along
                return False               ┘ one diagonal
            r -= 1
            c -= 1

        r = row + 1
        c = col - 1

        while r < Queens._SIZE and c >= 0:
            if self._occupied[r][c]:       ┐ Not safe: attacked along
                return False               ┘ the other diagonal
            r += 1
            c -= 1

    return True
```

In each column, `_find_solutions()` looks for a safe position for a queen in that column. Safe positions for a queen are wherever the queen cannot be attacked by any other queens already placed in the columns to the left. If the method finds a safe position, it places a queen there, and then it recursively calls itself to continue searching, starting at the next column. Now the problem is smaller because there is one fewer remaining column to consider.

The recursive search for a solution from the queen's position in a column will ultimately either succeed or fail. If a base case is reached—after safely placing a queen in column *N*, there are no safe positions in column *N* + 1—the program backtracks and attempts to move the queen down to the next safe position in column *N*. If a solution is found at the base case of the rightmost column, the program prints the board. After any base case, the program backtracks to the previous column and attempts to move the queen to the next safe position.

This dynamic backtracking sets up a recursive search for a solution from the new position. If there are no more safe positions in a column, the program backtracks again to the previous column and moves the queen to the next safe position in that column. The program ends when method _find_solutions() has backtracked to the first column and has tried each position of that column.

Recursive method **_find_solutions()** is simple and yet it handles looking for solutions column by column and backtracking.

It would be a very instructive challenge to write the method without using recursion.

Private Boolean method _is_safe_position() checks a board position to see whether it can be attacked by already-placed queens in the previous columns. It checks the queen's row to the left, the diagonal from the queen to the upper left, and the diagonal from the queen to the lower left. Because there is only one queen per column, there can be no attacks from another queen in the same column.

The test program main.py prints the solutions.

Listing 15.16   (Program 15.7 Queens) main.py

```python
from queens import Queens

if __name__ == '__main__':
    q = Queens()
    q.find_solutions()

    print()
    print('Done!')
```

The output includes all 92 solutions:

```
Solution #1

Q . . . . . . .
. . . . . . Q .
. . . . Q . . .
. . . . . . . Q
. Q . . . . . .
. . . Q . . . .
```

```
. . . . . Q . .
. . Q . . . . .
```

Solution #2

```
Q . . . . . . .
. . . . . . Q .
. . . Q . . . .
. . . . . Q . .
. . . . . . . Q
. Q . . . . . .
. . . . Q . . .
. . Q . . . . .
```

Solution #3

```
Q . . . . . . .
. . . . . Q . .
. . . . . . . Q
. . Q . . . . .
. . . . . . Q .
. . . Q . . . .
. Q . . . . . .
. . . . Q . . .
```

...

Solution #92

```
. . Q . . . . .
. . . . . Q . .
. . . Q . . . .
. Q . . . . . .
. . . . . . . Q
. . . . Q . . .
. . . . . . Q .
Q . . . . . . .
```

Done!

15.10 Solving Sudoku puzzles with recursion and backtracking

We can design a program that solves Sudoku puzzles using the same strategy of recursion with backtracking. Each puzzle has some prefilled cells. For example, here is an input file containing the prefilled cell values and zeros elsewhere:

```
4 9 0   6 0 7   0 0 0
0 0 7   0 0 0   0 0 0
5 0 0   1 9 0   0 2 0

0 8 0   0 7 0   0 0 3
0 7 4   0 0 0   6 5 0
2 0 0   0 1 0   0 9 0
```

```
0 4 0   0 5 1   0 0 6
0 0 0   0 0 0   2 0 0
0 0 0   3 0 8   0 1 5
```

The program produces the output

```
Input:

4 9 . | 6 . 7 | . . .
. . 7 | . . . | . . .
5 . . | 1 9 . | . 2 .
------+-------+-------
. 8 . | . 7 . | . . 3
. 7 4 | . . . | 6 5 .
2 . . | . 1 . | . 9 .
------+-------+-------
. 4 . | . 5 1 | . . 6
. . . | . . . | 2 . .
. . . | 3 . 8 | . 1 5

Solution:

4 9 2 | 6 3 7 | 5 8 1
3 1 7 | 8 2 5 | 4 6 9
5 6 8 | 1 9 4 | 3 2 7
------+-------+-------
6 8 9 | 5 7 2 | 1 4 3
1 7 4 | 9 8 3 | 6 5 2
2 3 5 | 4 1 6 | 7 9 8
------+-------+-------
9 4 3 | 2 5 1 | 8 7 6
8 5 1 | 7 6 9 | 2 3 4
7 2 6 | 3 4 8 | 9 1 5
```

We can solve this problem one cell of the grid at a time, starting with the upper-left corner and going from left to right and top to bottom. We use figure 15.15 as a guide:

- Each cell is a stage of the solution.
- Each valid number entered into a cell is a step of the solution path.
- A valid number is in the range 1 through 9, it doesn't appear in the same row or column, and it doesn't appear in the same three-by-three block.
- In each cell, we try the numbers 1 through 9 in order.
- Once a valid number is entered into a cell, the recursive action is to enter a valid number in the next unfilled cell. This is the equivalent in figure 15.15 of following a solution path from a step in one stage to a later stage. Each recursive action starts with at least one fewer remaining cells.
- A base case is when no number is valid in the next unfilled cell. Then we must backtrack to the previous cell and try the next number in that cell. We backtrack as many times as necessary.

- Another base case is when we enter a valid number into the last cell in the lower-right corner. This is the solution to the puzzle, which we print; then we quit.

Class Sudoku has a private instance variable _grid: an eight-by-eight matrix (a list of lists) to hold the grid of numbers and empty cells read in from a text file. The constructor reads the input file and initializes the grid with the prefilled numbers and zeros elsewhere.

Listing 15.17 (Program 15.8 Sudoku) sudoku.py (part 1 of 3)

```python
class Sudoku(object):
    _BLOCK_SIZE = 3
    _GRID_SIZE  = _BLOCK_SIZE*_BLOCK_SIZE

    def __init__(self, file_name):
        self._grid = []                          ◀── Puzzle grid of numbers

        with open(file_name, 'r') as elements:   ◀── Reads the initial grid
            for line in elements:                     from a text file
                if len(line) > 1:
                    row = line.split()
                    for i in range(len(row)):
                        row[i] = int(row[i])
                    self._grid.append(row)

    def print_grid(self):
        for row in range(Sudoku._GRID_SIZE):
            if row > 0 and row%Sudoku._BLOCK_SIZE == 0:
                print('-------+-------+--------')

            for col in range(Sudoku._GRID_SIZE):
                if col > 0 and col%Sudoku._BLOCK_SIZE == 0:
                    print('| ', end='')

                g = self._grid[row][col]
                if g > 0:
                    print(f'{g} ', end='')
                else:
                    print('. ', end='')

            print()
    ...
```

Public method solve() starts at the upper-left corner to search for a solution. After entering a number in a cell, private recursive method _solve() returns either True or False to indicate whether a solution exists starting with that number. The method recursively calls itself to test subsequent cells for the solution. The for loop controls the backtracking. If the number entered into a cell won't yield the solution, the loop tries the next number.

Listing 15.18   (Program 15.8 Sudoku) sudoku.py (part 2 of 3)

```
...
    def solve(self):                          Starts at the upper-left cell
        return self._solve(0, 0)

    def _solve(self, row, col):               Recursive function
        if (    row == Sudoku._GRID_SIZE - 1
            and col == Sudoku._GRID_SIZE):    Base case: solution at
            return True;                      the lower-right cell

        if col == Sudoku._GRID_SIZE:          Wraps to the      Recursively skips
            row += 1                          next row          over a cell with a
            col = 0                                             prefilled number

        if self._grid[row][col] != 0:                          Tries each
            return self._solve(row, col + 1)                   number in a cell

        for number in range(1, Sudoku._GRID_SIZE + 1):         Tests whether this
            if self._is_number_valid(row, col, number):        number is valid
                self._grid[row][col] = number

                if self._solve(row, col + 1):   Recursively solves
                    return True                 starting at the next cell

        self._grid[row][col] = 0      Prepares to backtrack    Returns True if successful
        return False
...
```

There are two recursive calls to method _solve(). The first call recursively tries the next cell if the current cell contains one of the prefilled numbers. In the for loop, after an allowable number is assigned to a cell, the second recursive call checks the next cell to see whether there's a solution starting from there. The call returns True if there's a solution. Otherwise, the loop tries the next number. After unsuccessfully trying all the numbers, the function resets the cell to zero ("empty") and returns False. This causes the previous recursive call to backtrack to the next allowable number for the previous cell.

The base case that stops the recursion is reaching the last cell at the lower-right corner. If _solve() can place an allowable number there, that is the solution to the puzzle. After all the recursive calls unwind back to the first cell, the original call to the method either returns True because it found a solution or returns False because the puzzle is unsolvable.

Private Boolean method _is_number_valid() tests whether a number is allowed in a cell by checking whether that number already appears in the cell's row, column, or block.

Listing 15.19   (Program 15.8 Sudoku) sudoku.py (part 3 of 3)

```
...
    def _is_number_valid(self, row, col, number):
        for c in range(Sudoku._GRID_SIZE):
```

```
        if self._grid[row][c] == number:          The number already
            return False                          exists in the cell's row.

    for r in range(Sudoku._GRID_SIZE):
        if self._grid[r][col] == number:          The number already exists
            return False                          in the cell's column.

    block_row_start = row - row%Sudoku._BLOCK_SIZE;
    block_col_start = col - col%Sudoku._BLOCK_SIZE;
    block_row_end = block_row_start + Sudoku._BLOCK_SIZE;
    block_col_end = block_col_start + Sudoku._BLOCK_SIZE;

    for r in range(block_row_start, block_row_end):
        for c in range(block_col_start, block_col_end):
            if self._grid[r][c] == number:        The number already
                return False                      exists in the cell's block.

    return True          ◀────  The number is valid for the cell.
```

The test program prints the initial grid with the given numbers, calls the solve()
method of class Sudoku, and prints the solution grid if there is a solution.

Listing 15.20   (Program 15.8 Sudoku) main.py

```
import sys
from sudoku import Sudoku

if __name__ == '__main__':
    file_name = sys.argv[1]
    sudoku = Sudoku(file_name)        ◀───  Creates the Sudoku object
                                            from the file input data

    print('Input:')
    print()
    solved = sudoku.print_grid()

    solved = sudoku.solve()           ◀───  Call to solve the puzzle

    if solved:
        print()
        print('Solution:')
        print()
        sudoku.print_grid()
    else:
        print()
        print('No solution')
```

This is a brute-force solution that doesn't use any Sudoku strategies —only recursion and backtracking.

It relies on a computer's speed to work effectively.

Summary

- Recursion is a software design technique that solves a problem by repeatedly reducing it into smaller and smaller but similar subproblems. We recursively solve each subproblem the same way.

- The recursion stops at a base case where the subproblem is so small that it has an obvious and immediate solution. Then the original problem is solved as the recursion unwinds.

- When designed properly, a recursive programming solution can be simple and elegant. But improper use can lead to serious performance problems.

- The combination of recursion and dynamic backtracking is a potent design tool for programs that explore multiple solution paths.

- Each step can have multiple solution paths that are explored using recursion. After trying a path, we backtrack and try the next path.

- When all the solution paths at a step have been tried, we backtrack to the previous step and continue trying the previous step's paths.

- When we've backtracked to the starting step, either we've found all the solutions or we've discovered that the problem is unsolvable.

A good way to develop recursive programs is to print intermediate results.

You'll see how what seems like magic is actually done.

Designing multithreaded programs

This chapter covers

- Designing and creating multiple threads of execution
- Protecting shared resources
- Synchronizing multiple threads of execution

Knowing how to design and develop multithreaded applications allows us to take advantage of a computer's ability to handle multiple threads of execution. A *thread* is a path the computer takes through the code as it executes your program. Multi-threading means the computer is running multiple paths at the same time. Some applications inherently require simultaneous operations, and we can only design them to be multithreaded. We'll look at a few typical examples such as an application where multiple producer threads simultaneously enter data into a queue while multiple consumer threads remove data from that queue.

This chapter introduces designing multithreaded applications where we must properly synchronize the threads' execution to prevent them from stepping on each other. We'll start with a simple printing example that demonstrates using a *mutex*, a software object that enforces *mutual exclusion* to protect a shared resource. It allows only one thread at a time to access the resource. We'll progress to using mutexes and another software object called a *semaphore* to solve an example of the classic reader–writer problem. A semaphore allows multiple reader threads to simultaneously access a shared resource without modifying it, while at the same time it prevents a writer thread from modifying the resource. Then we'll solve an example of the classic producer–consumer problem by using a *condition object* that enables us to more finely synchronize the execution of multiple threads.

16.1 How do things happen simultaneously?

Early computers were single-threaded and could run only one path through a program at a time. Later computers with hardware and operating system support enabled *concurrent execution*, where the single CPU switched rapidly among multiple threads—hence the term *multithreading*. Switching among multiple threads is called *context switching*.

Modern computers are multicore with multiple CPUs on a single chip. Now *parallel execution* is possible, where the different cores (CPUs) are each executing one or more threads at the same time. Therefore, a computer can simultaneously execute more threads than it has CPUs.

Whenever a program starts, it runs in its main thread. Any thread can *spawn* (create and start) child threads.

Concurrency vs. parallelism

A good analogy of the difference between *concurrency* and *parallelism* involves planning a dinner party. You can do all the work yourself, cleaning the house, cooking the meal, setting the table, etc. When you switch among the various tasks (rapidly or otherwise) during the day, you are doing them concurrently. In computer terms, you are *multitasking*. You must plan your work carefully in order to get all the tasks done on time.

But if you have friends come over to help, and each friend takes care of a task, the work can be done simultaneously in parallel. If each friend multitasks, even more work can get done at the same time. You must manage your friends to keep their work synchronized. You can't have them multitasking too much, or they will become less efficient.

Whether you do all the work yourself or have friends help, you must protect shared resources, such as the cleaning supplies, cooking utensils, the food being prepared, and so on. You certainly don't want your friends arguing over who can use the mop or trying to cook different parts of the meal at the same time using the same pan. You enforce mutual exclusion on the frying pan, for example, when you allow only one friend to use the pan at a time while excluding others from using it.

When you design a multithreaded application, your code must manage and synchronize the threads, whether they execute concurrently or in parallel, and your code must protect any shared resources, such as data in memory or external files.

Python's multithreading capabilities are limited by the *global interpreter lock* (GIL) of its runtime system. The GIL allows only one thread to run at any one time. That simplifies runtime thread and memory management and helps to prevent problems such as race conditions (explained in a moment). Therefore, multithreaded Python programs can execute threads concurrently but not in parallel. In general, Python programs should use multithreading only for applications that inherently require multiple threads, as we shall see with the example programs in this chapter.

For most of our applications, we don't worry about multithreading but instead allow the runtime system to manage the threads. For example, when one thread is suspended to wait for an I/O operation to complete, the runtime system automatically performs a context switch to another thread. But we can design programs that explicitly perform multithreading and protect any shared resources. To do so, we'll use objects from Python's threading module.

Figure 16.1 shows that when we design and write a multithreaded application, we must be aware that the application's threads all share the application's internal resources of the code and data in memory and external resources such as printers and files. Therefore, a major design concern is how to properly manage the sharing. The runtime system will give each thread its own runtime stack (a part of memory that a thread uses to maintain the values of its local variables) and the appearance of having its own set of machine registers. Depending on the machine hardware, the latter can be achieved by saving and restoring the register contents during context switching, or by having multiple banks of registers.

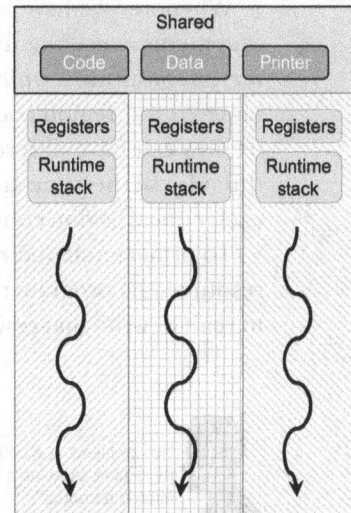

Figure 16.1 A multithreaded application with three threads. The threads share the application's internal resources of code and data in memory and external resources such as printers and files. The runtime system gives each thread its own runtime stack and the appearance of having its own set of machine registers.

Topics not covered in this chapter

This introductory chapter does not cover the following:

- The ability to turn off the GIL starting with Python 3.14
- Multithreading vs. multiprocessing
- Python's asyncio and multiprocessing modules

16.2   *A mutex enforces mutual exclusion*

A multithreaded program must protect shared resources. If multiple threads attempt to access a shared resource (data in memory, a file, a printer, etc.), they must synchronize their actions properly and not step on each other. For example, if multiple threads simultaneously modify the value of a shared variable, what is the final value of that variable? This is known as a *race condition*, where the value of a variable depends on which thread happened to modify it last. Race conditions are a major debugging nightmare of multithreaded applications.

Whenever we have a shared resource in a multithreaded program, there could be statements executing in different threads that access that shared resource. Such statements constitute a *critical region* associated with that resource. The threads can use the same critical region code (remember that a program's code is shared by the threads), or they can have different statements in their own critical regions. Whether multiple threads use the same critical region, or each thread has its own unique critical region, each critical region contains statements that access the shared resource.

To protect a shared resource, if a thread is in its critical region to modify the shared resource, the program must prevent other threads from going into their critical regions to read or write that resource. This is mutual exclusion, enforced by a mutex.

I'm confused. Is a critical region the same as a shared resource?

No. A critical region is the *code* in each thread that *accesses* a particular shared resource. It can be one critical region that all the threads use, or each thread can have its own critical region.

Before a thread can go into its critical region, it must first attempt to lock the mutex guarding the critical region. If the mutex is already locked, the thread *blocks* (suspends execution) until another thread unlocks the mutex. As soon as the mutex becomes unlocked, a thread that was blocked on the mutex can attempt to lock it. There may be other threads blocked on the mutex that are also attempting to lock it. If a thread succeeds in locking the mutex, it can proceed into its critical region. Later, before it leaves the critical region, it must unlock the mutex to give another thread a chance to run.

In figure 16.2, thread A and thread B both can access a variable X, the shared resource. Therefore, each thread has a critical region containing statements that reference X. When thread A goes into its critical region to modify the value of X, we must prevent thread B from going into its critical region to read or modify the value of X. Only after thread A leaves its critical region can we allow thread B to proceed into its critical region. The threads lock and unlock the mutex that guards the critical regions. The mutex protects the shared variable X by controlling when a thread can go into its critical region.

Protected shared resource
Variable X

Thread A enters
its critical region
to modify the value
of shared variable X.

Thread A exits
its critical region.

Thread A is in its critical region
to modify the value of X.

Thread A
timeline

Successfully lock
the mutex.

Unlock
the mutex.

Thread B is in its critical region
to read the value of X.

Thread B blocked

Thread B
timeline

Attempt to lock
the mutex.

Successfully lock
the mutex.

Unlock
the mutex.

Thread B attempts
to enter its critical region
to access the value of
shared variable X,
but the mutex is already locked.

Thread B enters
its critical region.

Thread B exits
its critical region.

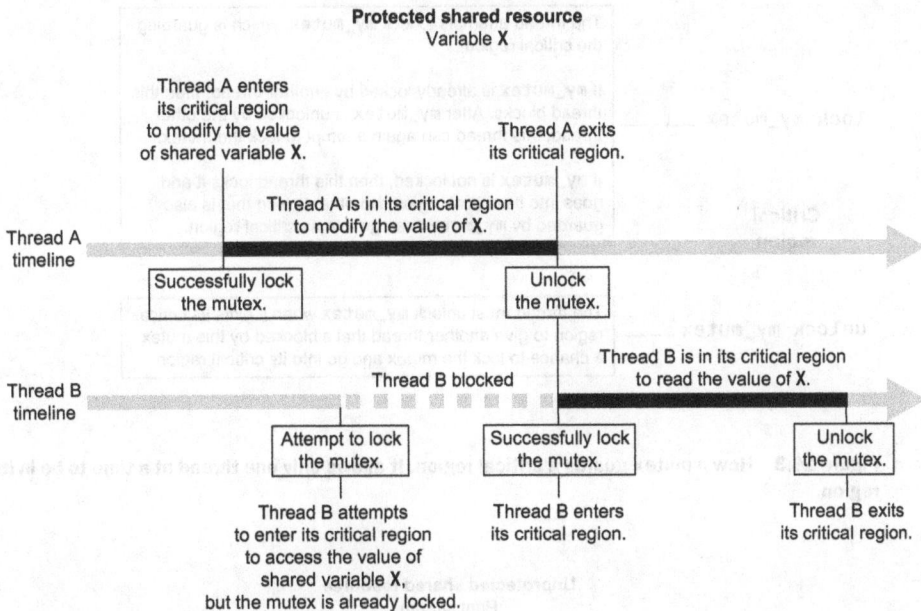

Figure 16.2 The critical regions of thread A and thread B modify variable X, the shared resource. A mutex object guards the critical regions to protect the shared resource. A thread that successfully locks the mutex can proceed into its critical region. Attempting to lock a mutex that's already locked causes the thread to block. The thread that's exiting its critical region must unlock the mutex to allow another thread to lock it.

If several threads are blocked by a locked mutex, then when the mutex is unlocked, the Python runtime system will choose which of the blocked threads can lock the mutex and proceed into its critical region. Because we cannot always predict which thread will successfully lock the mutex, each run of a multithreaded program can behave differently. Unfortunately, this randomness can make multithreaded programs notoriously difficult to debug when things go wrong.

Figure 16.3 illustrates how a mutex works to guard a critical region within a thread. We use the same mutex to guard each critical region associated with a shared resource, whether different threads run the same code and therefore have the same critical region, or the threads run different code and therefore each thread has its own critical region.

16.2.1 *Protect the integrity of a shared printing resource*

With a simple printing example, we can demonstrate multithreading, a shared resource, a critical region, and a mutex that enforces mutual exclusion. The first version of our example printing program creates three threads assigned to variables `hello_thread`, `use_thread`, and `go_thread` (figure 16.4). Each thread executes function `print()`, but each thread passes a different string argument to the function.

Thread execution flow

lock my_mutex ——

> The thread attempts to lock **my_mutex**, which is guarding the critical region.
>
> If **my_mutex** is already locked by another thread, then this thread blocks. After **my_mutex** is unlocked by the other thread, this thread can again attempt to lock the mutex.
>
> If **my_mutex** is not locked, then this thread locks it and goes into its critical region. No other thread that is also guarded by **my_mutex** can go into its critical region.

Critical region

unlock my_mutex ——

> The thread must unlock **my_mutex** when it exits its critical region to give another thread that's blocked by this mutex a chance to lock the mutex and go into its critical region.

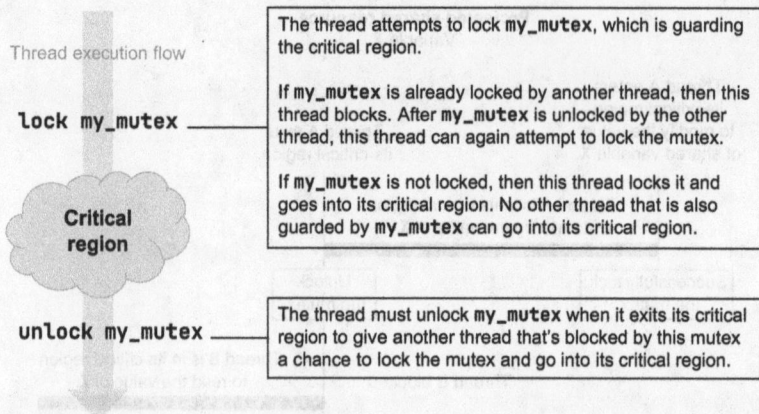

Figure 16.3   How a mutex guards a critical region. It allows only one thread at a time to be in its critical region.

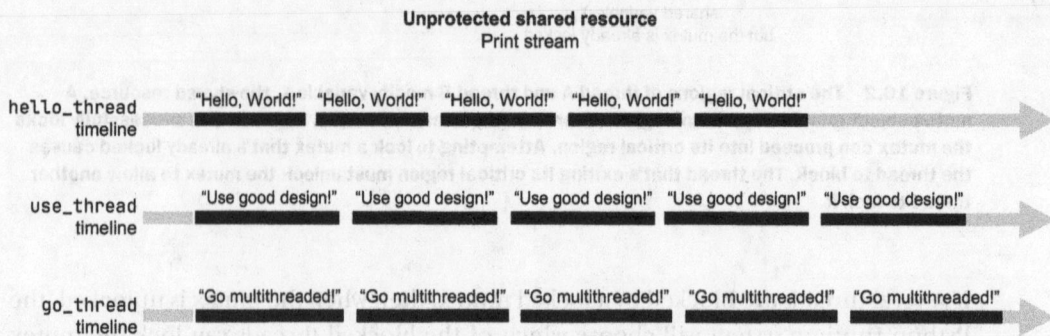

Unprotected shared resource
Print stream

hello_thread timeline   "Hello, World!" "Hello, World!" "Hello, World!" "Hello, World!" "Hello, World!"

use_thread timeline   "Use good design!" "Use good design!" "Use good design!" "Use good design!" "Use good design!"

go_thread timeline   "Go multithreaded!" "Go multithreaded!" "Go multithreaded!" "Go multithreaded!" "Go multithreaded!"

Figure 16.4   Three threads simultaneously print to the shared print stream, the unprotected shared resource.

Function print() writes to the shared print stream one character at a time.

Listing 16.1   (Program 16.1 Printing-Unprotected) main.py (bad design!)

```python
from threading import Thread
COUNT = 5

def print_message(msg):          # The function executed by each thread
    for _ in range(COUNT):
        for ch in msg:           # Critical region: accesses
            print(ch, end='')    # the print stream

def test_mt():
    hello_thread = Thread(target=print_message,
                          args=('Hello, world!\n',))   # Spawns (creates)
    use_thread = Thread(target=print_message,          # each thread
```

```
                      args=('Use good design!\n',))
    go_thread = Thread(target=print_message,
                      args=('Go multithreaded\n',))
```
Spawns (creates) each thread

```
    hello_thread.start()
    use_thread.start()
    go_thread.start()
```
Starts each thread

```
    hello_thread.join()
    use_thread.join()
    go_thread.join()
```
Waits for each thread to complete

```
if __name__ == '__main__':
    test_mt()

    print()
    print('Done!')
```

In the main thread, function `test_mt()` creates and starts each thread, which executes function `print_message()`. The function executes simultaneously in three threads, each with a different string argument to print. Therefore, the print stream is a shared resource among the threads, but it is unprotected in this version of the program. The critical region of each thread is the function's inner `for` loop that prints its string argument one character at a time.

Meanwhile, the main thread of the program that spawned the three threads by calling their `start()` methods waits for each one to complete with calls to `join()`. Only after all three threads are done can the main thread terminate.

Here's some example output:

```
HeUsGllo, world!
Hello moeulti, gthreaded
Go  mwood ouldrldt!ite
hsign!
HUerllso,eadee w gooodrd
dGeos mliultgn!
dith!re
Haelldo, Usew ed
gGooodo r dmeulstitldign!!

HhreeaUslldoee,d
wGo  gmorood dultesld!iit
hgnrea!d
ed
Use good design!

Done!
```

Quite a mess! We did not protect the shared resource. Each of the threads is free to execute in its critical region to print the characters of its string. All three threads run simultaneously, but an I/O operation (such as printing a character) interrupts a thread's execution and allows another thread to print a character. Therefore, we get intermixed output from the threads. We'll get different results each time we run the program because the runtime system controls the order that the threads run.

In the second version of our multithreaded printing program, we can fix its problems by introducing a mutex to guard the critical region and thereby protect the shared print stream resource (see figure 16.5). The mutex starts out unlocked. Each thread attempts to lock the mutex before going into the critical region. If the mutex is already locked by another thread, the thread blocks. When the thread that locked the mutex unlocks it, the blocked threads each again attempt to lock the mutex. One thread will successfully lock the mutex and proceed into the critical region to print its string. That thread must unlock the mutex when it's done printing and is ready to exit the critical region. Therefore, only one thread at a time can be inside the critical region to print its string.

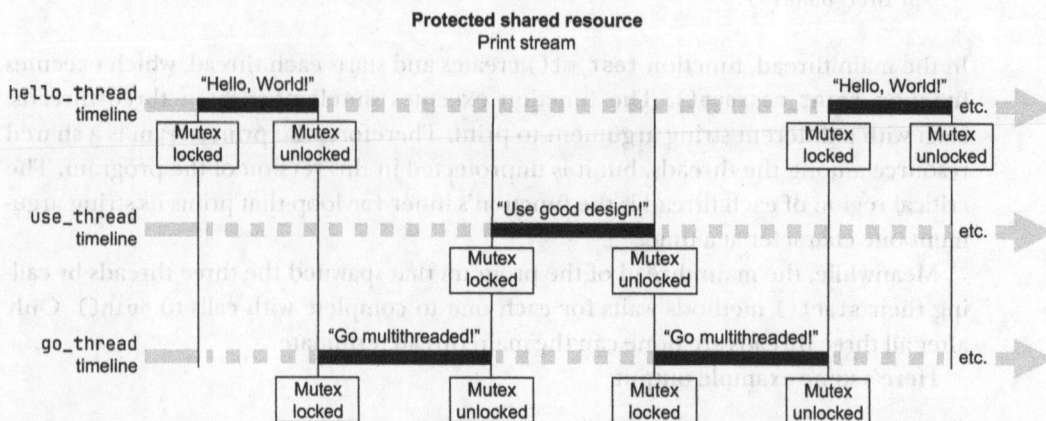

Figure 16.5 With a mutex guarding the critical regions of the threads, only one thread at a time can print to the print stream, which is the shared resource. When a thread wants to go into its critical region, it attempts to lock the mutex. If it succeeds, it can enter its critical region and print. If it doesn't succeed, it blocks until another thread unlocks the mutex. Then the thread can attempt to lock the mutex again. A thread must unlock the mutex before it exits its critical region. Whenever the mutex unlocks, the runtime system determines which blocked thread can lock it.

Python implements a mutex with a `Lock` object from the `threading` module. Our next example program is the same as the first, except that we introduce the mutex named `printing_mutex` in function `print_message()` to guard the critical region. We call method `acquire()` on the mutex to attempt to lock it, and later we call method `release()` on the mutex to unlock it.

Listing 16.2   (Program 16.2 Printing-MT) main.py

```python
from threading import Thread
from threading import Lock

COUNT = 5
```

```
printing_mutex = Lock()          ◄──┐ The printing mutex

def print_message(msg):
    for _ in range(COUNT):              Attempts to acquire (lock)
        printing_mutex.acquire()  ◄──┘ the printing mutex

        for ch in msg:
            print(ch, end='', flush=True)

        printing_mutex.release()  ◄──┐ Releases (unlocks) the
                                       printing mutex
def test_mt():
    ...

if __name__ == '__main__':
    ...
```

Now the output is much more reasonable:

```
Hello, world!
Hello, world!
Hello, world!
Hello, world!
Hello, world!
Use good design!
Use good design!
Use good design!
Use good design!
Use good design!
Go multithreaded
Go multithreaded
Go multithreaded
Go multithreaded
Go multithreaded

Done!
```

As before, the runtime system determines the order in which the threads start and the
order in which they print. But with the mutex, only one thread can be in its critical
region at a time. Therefore, a thread is allowed to write out its entire string argument
each time without another thread "jumping in" with its output.

With only five printed lines each, once a thread starts, it's able to print all its lines
before another thread starts. Therefore, in this version of the program, each thread's
printed lines are together.

In the final version of our multithreaded printing program, we introduce time
.sleep(0.1) to cause a thread to take a quick 0.1-second "nap" before attempting to
lock the mutex. Putting a thread to sleep interrupts its execution and allows another
thread to run. A sleeping thread resumes execution when it awakes. The threads' lines
are now scrambled but still whole.

Listing 16.3 (Program 16.3 Printing-MT-sleep) main.py

```
import time
from threading import Thread
from threading import Lock

COUNT = 5

printing_mutex = Lock()

def print_message(msg):
    for _ in range(COUNT):
        time.sleep(0.1)          ◄─── Interrupts the
                                       thread's execution

        with printing_mutex:     ◄─── The with statement and its mutex
            for ch in msg:
                print(ch, end='', flush=True)

def test_mt():
    ...

if __name__ == '__main__':
    ...
```

It is very important that a thread releases the mutex as it leaves its critical region. Failure to do so can cause a program to *deadlock* and stop running entirely if no other thread can run. Instead of explicitly calling acquire() and release() on printing_matrix, this version of our example uses the with statement

```
with printing_mutex:
```

which precedes the critical region. The with statement attempts to acquire its mutex, and later it automatically releases the mutex when the critical region completes its execution.

The output from this final version of multithreaded printing is as follows:

```
Hello, world!
Use good design!
Go multithreaded
Hello, world!
Use good design!
Go multithreaded
Use good design!
Go multithreaded
Hello, world!
Hello, world!
Go multithreaded
Use good design!
Go multithreaded
Hello, world!
Use good design!

Done!
```

16.3 A semaphore accepts multiple threads

As we've seen, a mutex enforces mutual exclusion by allowing only one thread at a time to be in its critical region, thereby protecting a shared resource. But consider this situation:

- Multiple threads are allowed to read simultaneously from the shared resource without modifying it.
- Only one thread at a time is allowed to write to (modify) the shared resource.
- All writer threads must block while any reader threads are actively reading.
- No reader thread can read while a writer thread is writing.

We can accomplish these four points with a semaphore, another object from the threading module. We initialize a semaphore with the number of simultaneous reader threads we want to allow. Each time a reader thread acquires the semaphore, the semaphore's value decrements by 1. Therefore, a reader thread blocks trying to acquire a semaphore if its value is 0. A writer thread blocks on the semaphore if its value is less than the number of reader threads, meaning a reader thread is currently reading the meter. When a reader thread releases the semaphore, the semaphore's value increases by 1.

16.3.1 The classic reader–writer problem

An inherently multithreaded application is the classic reader–writer problem. Our next example program simulates a meter that can be set to different values. Multiple technicians (the writers) each make several attempts to set the meter's value. Meanwhile, several loggers (the readers) attempt to read and log the meter's current setting. Therefore, the meter is a shared resource (figure 16.6).

We'll use both a mutex object named setting_mutex and a semaphore object named logging_semaphore. The technician threads will use the mutex to allow only one technician thread at a time to set the meter. The mutex will also block any logger threads from reading the meter while a technician thread is setting the meter. The logger threads will use the semaphore to allow up to three logger threads to simultaneously read the meter and log its current setting. The semaphore will also block a technician thread from changing the meter's setting while any logger thread is reading it.

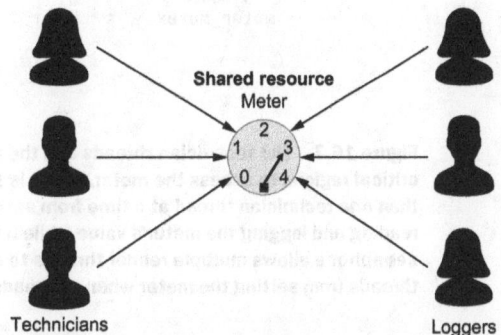

Figure 16.6   Three technicians simultaneously attempt to set the meter's value. Meanwhile, three loggers attempt to read and log the meter's current setting. Therefore, the meter is the shared resource. Only one technician at a time should be setting the meter, and no logger should read the meter while a technician is setting it. However, as long as no technician is setting the meter, multiple loggers can be reading it at the same time.

To enhance the simulation, the technician and logger threads will each sleep for a random brief period before an attempt to set or log the meter, respectively. As described in the previous example, putting a thread to sleep interrupts its execution and allows another thread to take over. Figure 16.7 shows this in a simplified fashion.

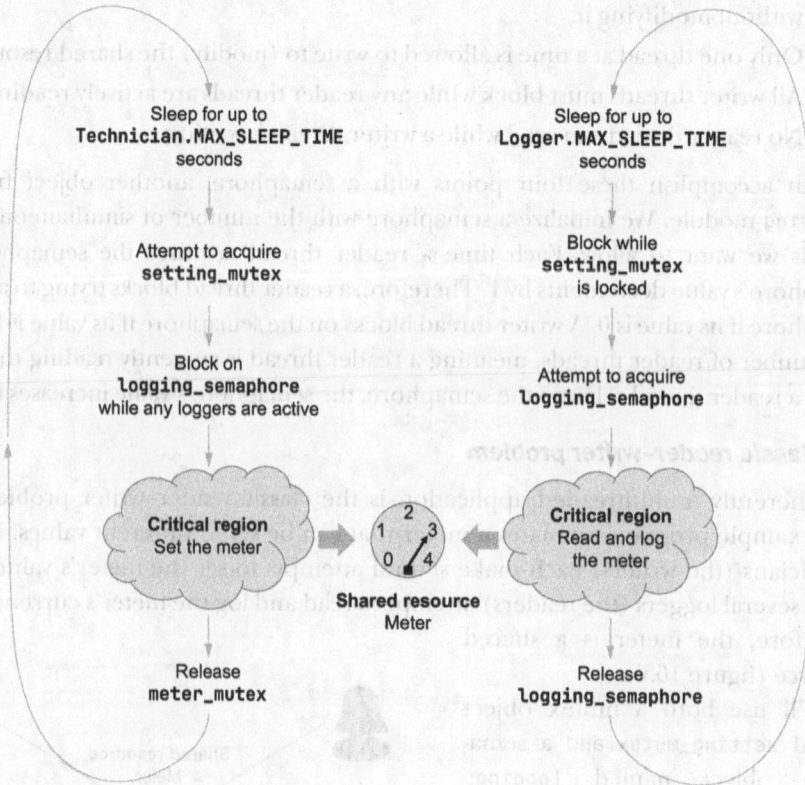

Figure 16.7 The technician threads and the logger threads each loop and attempt to go into their critical regions to access the meter, which is the shared resource. The `setting_mutex` **prevents more than one technician thread at a time from setting the meter. The same mutex prevents a logger from reading and logging the meter's value while a technician thread is setting the meter. The** `logging_semaphore` **allows multiple reader threads to simultaneously read the meter, and it will block technician threads from setting the meter when any reader thread is reading it.**

Our program simulates each technician with a thread, and each thread has a critical region that accesses the meter. Each technician thread can set the meter randomly to level 1, 2, 3, or 4. Setting the meter's setting requires 1 second per level: for example, it takes 3 seconds to set the meter to level 3. The application simulates this by having the thread do a *busy wait* of one second for each level. The difference between sleeping and busy waiting is that the latter does not interrupt a thread and therefore doesn't allow another thread to take over.

The application simulates each logger with a thread, and each thread also has a critical region that accesses the meter. Each logger thread takes 2 seconds to read and log the meter's current setting, which the application simulates by having the thread do a busy wait for 2 seconds after reading and printing the setting.

A timer keeps track of the number of elapsed seconds as the program runs in real time. When a technician thread sets the meter, the output shows the number of elapsed seconds, the thread's ID (such as 21 TECH #2), and a count of the seconds to make the setting (such as 1 2 3 for level 3). When a logger thread reads the meter, the output shows the elapsed time, the thread's ID (such as LOGGER #3), and the current meter setting that it read.

Because of the random sleep times of the threads, each run of the application can generate different output. Here's some example output:

```
06 TECH #1: 1 2
                              08 LOGGER #3: logging 2
                              09 LOGGER #1: logging 2
                              09 LOGGER #2: logging 2

11 TECH #2: 1 2 3 4
15 TECH #3: 1 2 3 4
                              19 LOGGER #3: logging 4
                              19 LOGGER #1: logging 4
21 TECH #1: 1 2 3
                              24 LOGGER #1: logging 3
                              24 LOGGER #2: logging 3
                              24 LOGGER #3: logging 3
26 TECH #2: 1 2 3 4
30 TECH #3: 1 2 3 4
                              34 LOGGER #1: logging 4
                              34 LOGGER #2: logging 4
37 TECH #1: 1 2 3
40 TECH #1: done!
                              40 LOGGER #2: logging 3
                              40 LOGGER #3: logging 3
42 TECH #2: 1 2 3 4
46 TECH #2: done!
                              46 LOGGER #3: logging 4
                              46 LOGGER #1: logging 4
48 TECH #3: 1
49 TECH #3: done!
                              49 LOGGER #2: logging 1
                              49 LOGGER #1: logging 1
                              49 LOGGER #3: logging 1
                              51 LOGGER #1: logging 1

                              53 LOGGER #2: done!
                              53 LOGGER #3: done!
                              53 LOGGER #1: done!

Program done!
```

From examining the output, we can see that while a technician thread is setting the meter, no other thread, neither technician nor logger, can run. However, multiple logger threads can start at the same time, such as at time 19, or have overlapping logging durations, such as at times 08 and 09. Whenever any logger thread is running, no technician thread can run.

What isn't shown in figure 16.7 and may not be immediately obvious from the example output is that no logger thread should start logging until a technician thread has set the meter. Logger threads can start logging only after the meter has been set for the first time.

> I'm confused again. A program can have multiple objects and multiple threads during its run time?

> A single object can spawn multiple threads that share data. The threads contain critical regions that access the shared data. Therefore, the threads use mutexes and semaphores to guard the critical regions and protect the shared data.

Class `Meter` has a settable property, `setting`, which technician threads will set and logger threads will read.

The class provides several public time-related methods. Method `busy_wait()` simulates the time a thread is busy setting or logging the meter. It differs from function `time.sleep()` by not causing the calling thread to relinquish control. Method `elapsed_seconds()` returns the number of seconds since the simulation started.

Listing 16.4   (Program 16.4 Reader-Writer) meter.py

```python
import time

class Meter:
    def __init__(self, max_meter_setting):
        self._max_setting = max_meter_setting

        self._setting = 0
        self._start_time = round(time.time())

    @property
    def setting(self):              # ← Reads the meter's current setting
        return self._setting

    @setting.setter
    def setting(self, setting):     # ← Changes the meter's current setting
        self._setting = setting

    @property
    def max_setting(self):
        return self._max_setting
```

```
    def busy_wait(self, seconds):
        start_busy_wait = time.time()
        while time.time() - start_busy_wait < seconds:
            continue

    def elapsed_seconds(self):
        return round(time.time()) - self._start_time
```

In the test program main.py, function `run_simulation()` runs the simulation. It creates the `Meter` object. It creates the `TechnicianThreads` and `LoggerThreads` objects, which will manage their respective threads. The function creates `setting_mutex` and `logging_semaphore`, and it initializes the semaphore's value to `LOGGERS_COUNT`, the maximum number of logging threads that can simultaneously read the meter. The function also creates the `Event` object `setting_started_event`, which technician threads will use to signal the logging threads that setting the meter has started. Finally, the function starts the threads and waits for them to finish.

Listing 16.5   (Program 16.4 Reader-Writer) main.py

```
from threading import Lock, Semaphore, Event
from meter import Meter
from technician import TechnicianThreads
from logger import LoggerThreads

MAX_METER_SETTING =   4
TECHNICIANS_COUNT =   3
LOGGERS_COUNT     =   3

def run_simulation():
    setting_mutex = Lock()
    logging_semaphore = Semaphore(LOGGERS_COUNT)        Multithreading objects
    setting_started_event = Event()

    meter = Meter(MAX_METER_SETTING)

    technician_threads = TechnicianThreads(
                            meter,
                            TECHNICIANS_COUNT,
                            LOGGERS_COUNT,
                            setting_mutex,
                            logging_semaphore,
                            setting_started_event)

    logger_threads = LoggerThreads(meter,
                            LOGGERS_COUNT,
                            setting_mutex,
                            logging_semaphore,
                            setting_started_event)

    technician_threads.start()          Starts the technician
    logger_threads.start()              and logger threads
```

```
            technician_threads.finish()        Waits for the threads
            logger_threads.finish()            to complete

if __name__ == '__main__':
    run_simulation()

    print()
    print('Program done!')
```

The constructor of class TechnicianThreads creates technicians_count number of threads, and each one will execute private method _set_meter(). Public method start() starts the threads, and public method finish() waits for the threads to complete. When all the technician threads have completed, the method sleeps for 3 seconds to allow any active logger threads to finish logging. Then it sets the meter to 0 as a sentinel to the logger threads that there will be no further meter settings.

Listing 16.6   (Program 16.4 Reader-Writer) technician.py (part 1 of 2)

```
import random
import time
from threading import Thread

class TechnicianThreads:
    _TURNS          = 3
    _SETTING_TIME   = 1
    _MIN_SLEEP_TIME = 6
    _MAX_SLEEP_TIME = 10

    def __init__(self, meter,
                       technicians_count,
                       loggers_count,
                       setting_mutex,
                       logging_semaphore,
                       setting_started_event):
        self._meter = meter
        self._technicians_count = technicians_count
        self._loggers_count = loggers_count
        self._setting_mutex = setting_mutex
        self._logging_semaphore = logging_semaphore
        self._setting_started_event = setting_started_event

        self._threads = []

        for i in range(self._technicians_count):
            self._threads.append(                    Creates a list of
                Thread(target=self._set_meter,       technician threads
                       args=(i + 1,)))

    def start(self):
        for thread in self._threads:
            thread.start()
```

```
def finish(self):
    for thread in self._threads:
        thread.join()

    time.sleep(3)
    self._set(0, 0, 0)
    ...
```

Allows time for any active logger threads to finish logging

Sets the meter to 0 as an end sentinel for the logger threads

Each technician thread executes private method _set_meter() to set the meter _TURNS times. First the thread sleeps for a random number of seconds, and then it randomly generates a new_setting value and calls private method _set() to set the meter to _new_setting.

```
    ...

    def _set_meter(self, thread_id):
        for turn in range(self._TURNS):
            time.sleep(
                random.randint(self._MIN_SLEEP_TIME,
                               self._MAX_SLEEP_TIME)
            )

            new_setting = random.randint(
                1, self._meter.max_setting)
            self._set(thread_id, turn, new_setting)

    def _set(self, thread_id, turn, new_setting):
        with self._setting_mutex:
            while (self._logging_semaphore._value
                            != self._loggers_count):
                continue

            if new_setting > 0:
                time_started = self._meter.elapsed_seconds()
                print(f'{time_started:02d}'
                      f' TECH #{thread_id}:', end='', flush=True)

                for s in range(1, new_setting + 1):
                    self._meter.busy_wait(
                                TechnicianThreads._SETTING_TIME)
                    print(f'{s:2d}', end='', flush=True)

                print(flush=True)

            self._meter.setting = new_setting
            self._setting_started_event.set()

            if turn == TechnicianThreads._TURNS - 1:
                time_started = self._meter.elapsed_seconds()
                print(f'{time_started:02d}'
                      f' TECH #{thread_id}: done!', flush=True)
```

Randomly generates the new meter setting

Attempts to lock the _setting_mutex

Blocks if any logger threads are actively logging

Busy-wait _SETTING_TIME seconds per setting level

Sets the meter to the new setting

Signals the logger threads that a setting occurred

Method _set() first attempts to lock _setting_mutex. If successful, it goes into its critical region, where its first action is to wait on the _logging_semaphore if any logging thread is actively reading the meter. The test program had initialized the semaphore's value to the number of loggers (listing 16.5). Each time a logger thread starts to log, it decrements the semaphore's value by 1, and then it increments the value by 1 when it is done logging. Therefore, if the semaphore's value is _loggers_count, no logger threads are actively reading. Thus, the semaphore enables any active logger thread to block a technician thread from changing the meter's setting.

When none of the logger threads are active, method _set() can finally set the meter to new_setting. Then the technician thread must signal any logger threads that have been waiting for the first meter setting. It signals by calling the set() method on the _setting_started_event object. If an Event object is already set, calling the set() method has no effect. Therefore, it's the very first call to the set() method that unblocks logger threads waiting for the first meter setting.

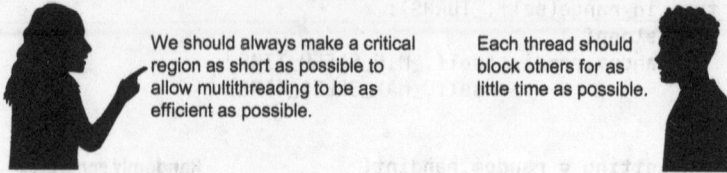

We should always make a critical region as short as possible to allow multithreading to be as efficient as possible.

Each thread should block others for as little time as possible.

The constructor of class LoggerThreads creates a list of _loggers_count number of threads, and each one will execute the private method _log_meter(). Public method start() starts each thread, and public method finish() waits for each thread to complete. Because several logger threads can attempt to print simultaneously, we need to use _printing_mutex to protect the print stream.

```
import random
import time
from threading import Thread, Lock

class LoggerThreads:
    _LOGGING_TIME   = 2
    _PRINT_MARGIN   = 25
    _MIN_SLEEP_TIME = 0
    _MAX_SLEEP_TIME = 1

    def __init__(self, meter,
                 loggers_count,
                 setting_mutex,
                 logging_semaphore,
                 setting_started_event):
```

```
            self._meter = meter
            self._loggers_count = loggers_count
            self._setting_mutex = setting_mutex
            self._logging_semaphore = logging_semaphore
            self._setting_started_event = setting_started_event

            self._printing_mutex = Lock()      ◀─────┐  Mutex for printing
            self._threads = []

            for i in range(self._loggers_count):
                self._threads.append(                      Creates a list of
                    Thread(target=self._log_meter,         logger threads
                           args=(i + 1,)))

        def start(self):
            for thread in self._threads:
                thread.start()

        def finish(self):
            for thread in self._threads:
                thread.join()

    ...
```

Each logger thread runs private method _log_meter(). In a loop, the thread blocks until the _setting_mutex is unlocked by a producer thread. It attempts to acquire _logging_semaphore. When it succeeds, it goes into its critical region to read the current meter setting. Up to loggers_count number of logger threads can acquire the semaphore at once. If the setting is the end sentinel 0, the thread exits the loop.

Listing 16.9   (Program 16.4 Reader-Writer) logger.py (part 2 of 2)

```
    ...

    def _log_meter(self, thread_id):
        self._setting_started_event.wait()   ◀─────┐  Waits for the first meter setting
        keep_logging = True

        while keep_logging:
            time.sleep(
                random.randint(LoggerThreads._MIN_SLEEP_TIME,
                               LoggerThreads._MAX_SLEEP_TIME))

            while self._setting_mutex.locked():   ◀─────┐  Blocks if the meter is being set
                continue
                                                        Attempts to lock the
                                                        _logging_semaphore
            with self._logging_semaphore:   ◀─────┘
                setting = self._meter.setting   ◀─────┐
                time_started = self._meter.elapsed_seconds()   Reads the current
                                                               meter setting

                if setting > 0:   ◀─────┐  A 0 setting means the
                    with self._printing_mutex:   technical threads are done.
                        print(' '*self._PRINT_MARGIN,
```

```
                        f' {time_started:02d}'
                        f' LOGGER #{thread_id}:'
                        f' logging {setting}',
                        flush=True)
                self._meter.busy_wait(
                        LoggerThreads._LOGGING_TIME)
            else:
                keep_logging = False
```

Busy-wait to simulate time logging the setting

```
            with self._printing_mutex:
                print(' '*self._PRINT_MARGIN,
                        f' {time_started:02d}'
                        f' LOGGER #{thread_id}: done!',
                        flush=True)
```

Running this application with its technician (writer) and logger (reader) threads will generate output similar to that shown after figure 16.7.

Why do the logger threads need a critical region for printing, but the technician threads don't?

There can be only one technician thread active at a time, but there can be several logger threads simultaneously active.

16.4 *Condition objects synchronize threads*

Certain multithreaded applications require even greater synchronization among their threads. Mutexes and semaphores alone may not be sufficient.

The classic multithreading producer–consumer application has multiple producer threads and multiple consumer threads that simultaneously access a data container with a fixed capacity, such as a bounded queue. The producer threads enter values into the container, and the consumer threads remove values from the container (figure 16.8). The container is a shared resource.

The critical region of the producer threads is the code that enters values into the queue, and the critical region of the consumer threads is the code that removes values from the queue. This application requires better synchronization among the threads than mutexes or semaphores alone can provide.

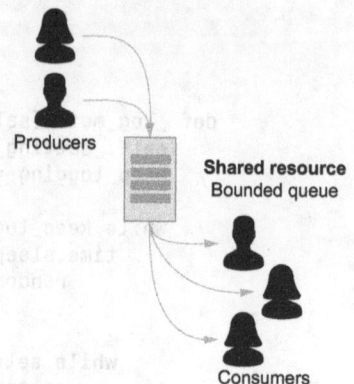

Producers

Shared resource
Bounded queue

Consumers

Figure 16.8   Simultaneously, multiple producers enter values into the bounded queue and multiple consumers remove values from the queue. The queue—the shared resource—has limited capacity.

Assume that method `queue.size()` returns the number of values currently in the shared queue and that constant `CAPACITY` is the limited capacity of the queue:

- `queue.size() == CAPACITY`—If the queue is currently full, the producer threads must wait until the queue is no longer full before entering values.
- `queue.size() == 0`—If the queue is currently empty, the consumer threads must wait until the queue is no longer empty before removing values.
- `queue.size() == 1`—The queue was empty but just became not empty after a producer thread entered a value into the queue. That producer thread must notify all the consumer threads that are waiting for the queue to become not empty.
- `queue.size() == CAPACITY-1`—The queue was full but just became not full after a consumer thread removed a value from the queue. That consumer thread must notify all the producer threads that are waiting for the queue to become not full.

16.4.1 How condition objects synchronize threads

The Python `threading` module provides *condition objects* that we can use to synchronize the producer and consumer threads to a greater degree than we can with only mutexes and semaphores. A condition object combines the functionality of a mutex `Lock` object and an `Event` object to protect a shared resource and to allow threads to signal each other.

Figure 16.9 shows that the producer threads operate in one loop and the consumer threads operate in another loop. At the top of each loop, a thread attempts to acquire the `queue.condition` object as it would a mutex. If a producer thread succeeds, it must next check whether the bounded queue is full. If the queue is full, the thread must then wait on the condition object. On the other hand, if a consumer thread successfully acquires `queue.condition`, it must next check whether the queue is empty. If the queue is empty, the thread must then wait on the condition object.

If the queue just became not empty after a producer thread entered a value, that producer thread must notify (signal) `queue.condition` to allow a consumer thread that may be waiting on the condition object to proceed into its critical region. If the queue becomes not full after a consumer thread removed a value, that thread must notify `queue.condition` to allow a producer thread that may be waiting on the condition object to proceed into its critical region.

When a thread blocks by waiting on a condition object, it releases the object to give another thread a chance to run. Then, when the condition object is notified, the waiting thread unblocks and performs these operations:

1. Acquire the condition object.
2. Check the condition again: is the queue still full or empty? Another thread may have jumped in and reestablished the condition.

Producer thread

```
acquire queue.condition
while the queue is full: wait on queue.condition
```

> **Critical region**
> Enter a value
> into the queue.

```
if the queue just became not empty: notify queue.condition
release queue.condition
```

Consumer thread

```
acquire queue.condition
while the queue is empty: consumer_cv.wait(queue_lock)
```

> **Critical region**
> Remove a value
> from the queue.

```
if the queue just became not full: notify queue.condition
release queue.condition
```

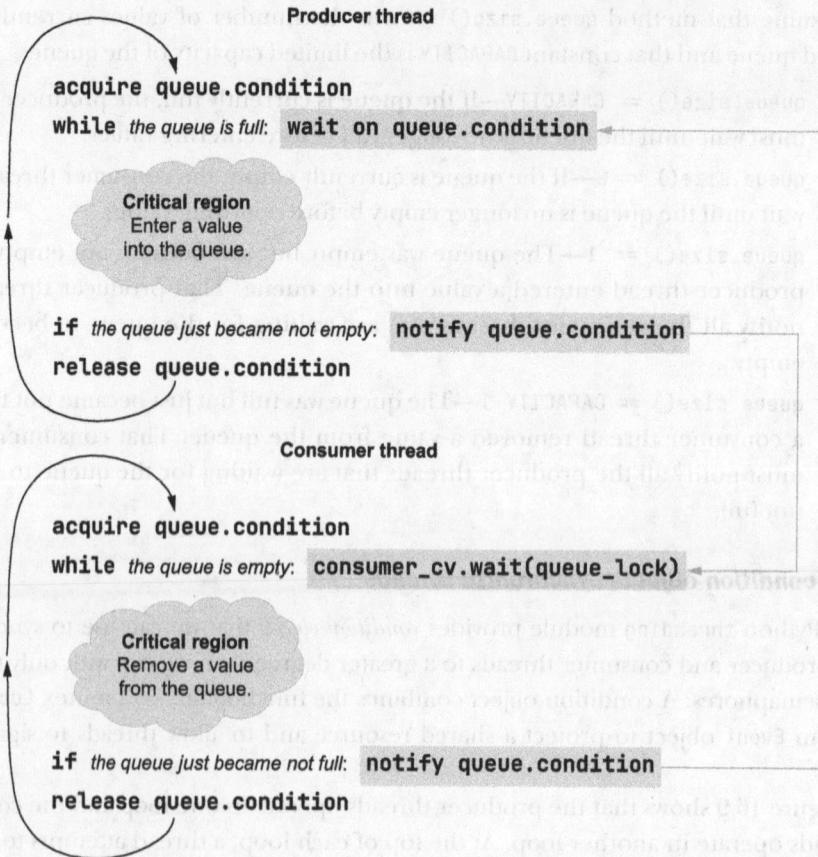

Figure 16.9 The producer and consumer threads each attempt to acquire `queue.condition` at the top of its loop. The condition object synchronizes the producer and consumer threads. The producer threads loop to enter values into the shared bounded queue, and the consumer threads loop to remove values from the queue. A producer thread cannot enter a value into the queue when the queue is full. A consumer thread cannot remove a value from an empty queue.

3 If the condition is still true,
   – Release the condition object.
   – Resume waiting.
4 If the condition is false,
   – Proceed into the critical region with the condition object still acquired.

16.4.2 *The classic producer–consumer problem*

We now have some of the necessary tools to implement the classic multithreaded producer–consumer application. Figure 16.10 shows example output with two producers and three consumers.

```
Producer#1 Producer#2 Consumer#1 Consumer#2 Consumer#3
 ①[1]
              ②[1, 2]
                      ⊖①[2]
                                               ⊖②[]
 ③[3]
              ④[3, 4]
                              ⊖③[4]
 ⑤[4, 5]
              ⑥[4, 5, 6]
                      ⊖④[5, 6]
                                       ⊖⑤[6]
 ⑦[6, 7]
              ⑧[6, 7, 8]
              ⑨[7, 8, 9]
                              ⊖⑥[7, 8]
              Done!
 ⑩[7, 8, 9, 10]
   Done!
                      ⊖⑦[8, 9, 10, 0]
                      ⊖⑧[9, 10, 0]
                              ⊖⑨[10, 0]
              ⊖⑩[0]
                                       ⓪[0]
                                       Done!
                      ⓪[0]
                      Done!
              ⓪[0]
              Done!

Program done!
```

Figure 16.10 In order by time from top to bottom, each line shows the action of one of the producer or consumer threads, depending on which column the line begins in. The circled integer is the value entered into the shared bounded queue by a producer thread or the value (shown as a negative value) removed from the queue by a consumer thread. The list in square brackets after each circled integer is the contents of the queue after the action. A zero value is the end sentinel.

The output lines show the actions of the threads in order by time, from top to bottom. Depending on which column the line begins in, each line shows either the circled value that a producer thread entered into the shared bounded queue or the circled value that a consumer thread removed from the queue. The output shows the values that the consumer threads removed as negative to help emphasize that the values were removed. The list in square brackets after each circled value is the contents of the queue after a thread action. Each producer thread enters five values before terminating. After all the producer threads have terminated, a zero is entered into the queue as an end sentinel. The consumer threads terminate after all the producer threads are done and the end sentinel is all that's left in the queue.

A BoundedQueue object is the shared resource, a queue with a limited capacity. Public method enter() enters a value at the tail of the queue, and public method remove()

removes a value from the head of the queue and returns the removed value. Public method peek() returns the value at the head of the queue but doesn't remove it.

Listing 16.10   (Program 16.4 ProducerConsumer) bounded_queue.py

```python
from threading import Condition

class BoundedQueue(object):
    def __init__(self, capacity):
        self._capacity = capacity          # Bounded queue of values
        self._data = []                    # and its maximum capacity
        self._condition = Condition()      # Queue Condition object

    @property
    def capacity(self):
        return self._capacity
    w
    @property
    def condition(self):
        return self._condition

    @property
    def data(self):
        return self._data

    def size(self):                        # Number of values
        return len(self._data)             # in the queue

    def enter(self, value):
        self._data.append(value)

    def remove(self):
        return self._data.pop(0)

    def peek(self):
        return None if self.is_empty() else self.data[0]

    def is_empty(self):
        return len(self._data) == 0

    def is_full(self):
        return len(self.data) == self._capacity

    def just_became_not_empty(self):
        return len(self._data) == 1

    def just_became_not_full(self):
        return len(self._data) == self._capacity - 1
```

Public Boolean methods is_empty(), is_full(), just_became_not_empty(), and just_became_not_full() test the condition of the queue.

In listing 16.11, the constructor of class Producer creates the producer threads, each of which will execute the private method _produce(). Public method start() starts the threads. The runtime system controls the order in which threads start and when they execute, so each run of the program is different. Method finish() waits for them to complete and then enters a 0 into the bounded queue as the end sentinel for each of the consumer threads. Private method _print_spaces() is used to format the output lines by beginning each line in the proper column.

Listing 16.11 (Program 16.4 ProducerConsumer) producer.py (part 1 of 2)

```python
import time
from threading import Thread
from random import randint

class Producer:
    def __init__(self, producer_count, turns,
                 min_sleep_time, max_sleep_time,
                 queue):
        self._turns = turns
        self._min_sleep_time = min_sleep_time
        self._max_sleep_time = max_sleep_time
        self._queue = queue                         ◄──┐ Shared bounded queue

        self._value = 0
        self._threads = []

        for i in range(producer_count):
            self._threads.append(                   ┐ Creates the
                Thread(target=self._produce,        │ producer threads
                    args=(i + 1,))
        )

    def start(self):
        for th in self._threads:
            th.start()

    def finish(self):
        for th in self._threads:
            th.join()                               ┐ Enters the end sentinel
        self._enter(0, 0, 0)                    ◄──┘ for the consumer threads

    def _print_spaces(self, thread_id):
        for _ in range(1, thread_id):
            print('                ', end='')

    ...
```

In each producer thread, private methods _produce() and _enter() work together in a loop to enter values into the bounded queue. Method _enter() first attempts to acquire _queue.condition. If it succeeds, it waits on the condition that the queue is full. After successfully going into its critical region and entering a value, it notifies the condition object if the queue is no longer empty to wake up any consumer threads that were waiting because the queue was empty.

Listing 16.12   (Program 16.4 ProducerConsumer) producer.py (part 2 of 2)

```
...
    def _produce(self, thread_id):                    ◀──┐ Executed by each
        for turn in range(self._turns):                   │ producer thread
            time.sleep(
                    randint(self._min_sleep_time,
                            self._max_sleep_time))

            self._value += 1
            self._enter(thread_id, turn, self._value)
                                                          ┌── Attempts to acquire
    def _enter(self, thread_id, turn, value):             │   the condition object
        with self._queue.condition:               ◀──────┘
            while self._queue.is_full():
                self._queue.condition.wait()              ┐── Waits on the
                                                          │   condition object
            self._queue.enter(value)       ◀── Enters a value │ while the queue is full
                                               into the queue
            if thread_id > 0:
                self._print_spaces(thread_id)
                print(f'{value:3d} {self._queue.data}   ')

            if turn == self._turns - 1:
                self._print_spaces(thread_id)
                print('   Done!')

            if self._queue.just_became_not_empty():    │ Notifies consumer threads
                self._queue.condition.notify()         │ that were waiting
```

Likewise, the constructor of class Consumer in listing 16.13 creates the consumer threads, each of which will execute the private method _consume(). The public methods start() and finish() start the threads and wait for them to complete, respectively, and the private method _print_spaces() is for print formatting. The runtime system controls the order in which the threads start and when they execute.

Listing 16.13   (Program 16.4 ProducerConsumer) consumer.py (part 1 of 2)

```
import time
from threading import Thread
from random import randint

class Consumer:
    def __init__(self, producer_count, consumer_count,
                 min_sleep_time, max_sleep_time,
                 queue):
        self._producer_count = producer_count
        self._min_sleep_time = min_sleep_time
        self._max_sleep_time = max_sleep_time
        self._queue = queue                    ◀── Shared bounded queue
```

```
        self._threads = []

        for i in range(consumer_count):
            self._threads.append(
                Thread(target=self._consume,
                    args=(i + 1,))
        )
```

Creates the producer threads

```
    def start(self):
        for th in self._threads:
            th.start()

    def finish(self):
        for th in self._threads:
            th.join()

    def _print_spaces(self, thread_id):
        k = self._producer_count + thread_id
        for _ in range(1, k):
            print('             ', end='')

    ...
```

In each consumer thread, private method `_consume()` removes values from the bounded queue (listing 16.14). The method first attempts to acquire `_queue.condition`. If it succeeds, then it waits on the condition while the queue is empty. After successfully going into its critical region and removing a value, it notifies the condition object if the queue is no longer full to wake up any producer threads that were waiting because the queue was full.

The consumer thread leaves the loop if it sees ("peeks") a 0 at the head of the queue, the end sentinel that method `finish()` of class `Producer` entered into the queue upon finishing (listing 16.11). The consumer thread leaves the 0 in the queue for other consumer threads.

Listing 16.14 (Program 16.4 ProducerConsumer) consumer.py (part 2 of 2)

```
    ...

    def _consume(self, thread_id):
        keep_consuming = True

        while keep_consuming:
            time.sleep(
                randint(self._min_sleep_time,
                    self._max_sleep_time))

            with self._queue.condition:
                while self._queue.is_empty():
                    self._queue.condition.wait()

                value = self._queue.peek()
```

Executed by each consumer thread

Attempts to acquire the condition object

Waits on the condition object while the queue is empty

What's at the head of the queue?

```
            if value > 0:
                self._queue.remove()          ◄─── Removes a nonzero
                                                    value from the queue
            self._print_spaces(thread_id)
            print(f'{-value:4d} {self._queue.data} ')

            if self._queue.just_became_not_full():     Notifies producer threads
                self._queue.condition.notify()         that were waiting

            if value == 0:          ◄─── Done if it's the end sentinel
                keep_consuming = False
                self._print_spaces(thread_id)
                print('    Done!')
```

The test program main.py creates the BoundedQueue object and the Producer and Consumer objects. It starts and finishes the simulation and produces output similar to that shown in figure 16.10.

Listing 16.15 (Program 16.4 ProducerConsumer) main.py

```python
from bounded_queue import BoundedQueue
from producer import Producer
from consumer import Consumer

QUEUE_CAPACITY = 8;

PRODUCER_COUNT = 2;
PRODUCER_TURNS = 5;
MIN_PRODUCER_SLEEP_TIME = 2;
MAX_PRODUCER_SLEEP_TIME = 4;

CONSUMER_COUNT = 3;
MIN_CONSUMER_SLEEP_TIME = 3;
MAX_CONSUMER_SLEEP_TIME = 5;

if __name__ == '__main__':
    for i in range(PRODUCER_COUNT):
        print(f'Producer#{i + 1} ', end='')
    for i in range(CONSUMER_COUNT):
        print(f'Consumer#{i + 1} ', end='')
    print()

    queue = BoundedQueue(QUEUE_CAPACITY)

    producer = Producer(PRODUCER_COUNT,
                        PRODUCER_TURNS,
                        MIN_PRODUCER_SLEEP_TIME,
                        MIN_PRODUCER_SLEEP_TIME,
                        queue)

    consumer = Consumer(PRODUCER_COUNT,
                        CONSUMER_COUNT,
                        MIN_CONSUMER_SLEEP_TIME,
```

```
                        MAX_CONSUMER_SLEEP_TIME,
                        queue)

    producer.start()
    consumer.start()

    producer.finish()
    consumer.finish()

    print()
    print('Program done!')
```

The producer threads logically do not need to know how many consumer threads there are. Similarly, the consumer threads logically do not need to know how many producer threads there are. In our example, we pass PRODUCER_COUNT to the constructor of class Consumer only for its private method _print_spaces() to use.

16.5   A final note on multithreading

This chapter presented only a very brief introduction to an important software design topic. Python supports more features for handling simultaneous operations than this chapter covered.

Python's asyncio module supports I/O-bound applications that work with multiple simultaneous input streams, such as networks, web servers, and databases. Python supports multiprocessing with its multiprocessing module. Multiprocessing sidesteps the limitations of the global interpreter lock by spawning multiple Python runtime systems that run in parallel.

Designing and developing a multithreaded application correctly is a major challenge. Because the Python runtime system usually determines the order in which threads are created and executed, timing issues can cause random and irreproducible behaviors from one run of the application to another. Debugging then becomes a nightmare. Another debugging headache is deadlocks: a deadlock occurs when all the threads are blocked and the entire application hangs.

Even when multithreading is designed properly, increasing the number of threads does not mean that an application's execution time approaches zero! Mutexes, semaphores, and condition objects have runtime performance costs. The costs of context switching from one thread to another can overwhelm the benefit of having more threads. Designing a multithreaded application can be a delicate balancing act if the goal is to increase performance without increasing complexity.

Summary

- Knowing how to design multithreaded programs is important for applications that inherently have concurrent operations. Designing, developing, and debugging multithreaded applications are major challenges.
- Each thread is an execution path through the program.

- Python's global interpreter lock (GIL) limits a program's multiple threads to execute concurrently and not in parallel. The runtime engine switches rapidly among the threads.

- Multiple threads may attempt to access shared resources of the application simultaneously. We must protect the shared resources.

- The code in each thread that accesses the shared resource is the thread's critical region associated with that resource.

- Use a mutex to guard each critical region with mutual exclusion.

- Python implements a mutex with a `Lock` object.

- A thread attempts to acquire (lock) a mutex. A mutex that's already locked blocks the thread from proceeding into a critical region. Once the mutex is released (unlocked), the thread can try again to acquire the mutex.

- A thread that successfully acquires a mutex does not allow any other thread to acquire that mutex. Therefore, only the thread that acquires the mutex can be in the critical region.

- A `Semaphore` object allows multiple reader threads to simultaneously acquire the semaphore to read a shared resource without modifying it. But it also blocks writer threads from modifying the resource while reader threads are reading it.

- To allow another thread to run, a thread must release a mutex or a semaphore before it exits its critical region. Otherwise, a deadlock may occur.

- Deadlocks, race conditions, and random effects are major debugging challenges.

- An `Event` object enables a thread to signal another thread.

- A `Condition` object combines the functionalities of a mutex and an `Event` object to synchronize the simultaneous operation of multiple threads.

- A thread waits on a `Condition` object as long as an associated condition remains true. When the condition object is notified by another thread, a thread that's waiting on the condition variable unblocks and checks if the condition is still true. If the condition is false, the thread can proceed into its critical region. Otherwise, it resumes its wait.

index

Symbols

@abstractmethod decorator 81
@multimethod 155, 232, 352
@multimethod decorator 155, 232, 352
@price.setter decorator 97
@property decorator 22, 97, 352
@staticmethod 24

A

Abstract Factory design pattern 20, 220–225
   after using 220
   before using 220
   choosing between Factory Method and Abstract
     Factory 227
   generic model 225
actors, defined 60
Adapter Design Pattern 228, 229–241
   after using 234–237
   alternative model of 238
   before using 231
   choosing between Adapter and Façade 248
   desired design features 229
   generic model of 238
aggregation relationships 78
AI-generated code 14
alternate action sequences 60

application design, functional specification and
     software validation 62
architecture problems 12
arithmetic, date arithmetic with loops 101
arrays, performance of 132–136
asyncio module 427
attributes of objects 13
avoiding surprises 126–131
   misnamed functions 129–31
   off-by-one errors 126–129

B

backtracking
   solving eight queens puzzle with 389–392
   Sudoku puzzles 393–397
base case 366
birthdate property 119
Birthday object 119
black-box testing 63
BST (binary search tree) 374, 375
   inserting into with recursion 375
   printing with recursion 376
   recursive algorithms for 373

C

case patterns 214
circular buffer, programming by contract 138–140

www.ingramcontent.com/pod-product-compliance
Lightning Source LLC
Chambersburg PA
CBHW012333310126
38948CB00008B/27